SA & College Dictionary

• 2000 Power Words •

**THREE STEPS TO INCREASE VOCABULARY
USING THE HI-LITE SERIES CFR® METHOD**

1. **CONFRONT WORDS** in this book that you don't know.
2. **FAMILIARIZE** yourself with definition and context usage.
3. **REINFORCE** definitions of newly-acquired words by READING.

CONFRONT

FAMILIARIZE

**REINFORCE
(BY READING)**

** VERBAL PROFICIENCY IS THE KEY TO BETTER
WRITING AND CLEARER COMMUNICATION **

Hi-Lite Publishing Company
P.O. Box 6071
Kaneohe, Hawaii 96744
www.test-prepHi.com

"...we take pride in all our books"

Copyright 2004, 2016   Raymond Karelitz

All rights reserved. No part of this book may be reproduced or transmitted in any form or by any means without permission in writing from the publisher, except brief excerpts for newspaper/magazine or radio review.

SAT® is a registered trademark of the College Board, Princeton, New Jersey 08541

Computer-Processing & Layout: Barbara Bower

Cartoon : James Makashima

Cover Design: Doug Behrens
Back-Cover Photo by: Rick Peralta

Karelitz, Raymond, 1952-

SAT & College Dictionary

1. **Dictionary**   I. Title

ISBN 978-1534738256

PRINTED IN THE U.S.A.

A Revolutionary Vocabulary-Building Reference Book

Vocabulary is a key that can unlock doors of opportunity for a lifetime to come, and with the proper command of these "power words" you will discover new horizons you once only dreamed of!

This innovative vocabulary-building dictionary contains 2000 of the most critical words in the English language, those more often encountered in academic settings (via literary essays, erudite lectures, provocative novels and stimulating conversation). Culled from over 40,000 possible entries, these special "power words" represent the difference between mundane conversation and electrifying elocution, between witless writing and perspicacious philosophizing, between self-defeating limitations and unbounded aspirations. The vocabulary one masters can indeed shape one's own destiny!

PRONUNCIATION KEY FOR VARIOUS LETTERS

a:	hAt	e:	pEn	ou:	OUt	u:	bUnch	th	THin
ah:	cAUght/ hOt	ee:	hEAt	oi:	nOIse	ur:	wORd	th:	THis
uh:	sodA	i:	dIg	oo:	mOOn	yoo:	mUsic	zh:	leiSure
ay:	Ate	ie:	hIGH	oo:	bOOk				
				oh:	Old				

pronunciation divided into syllables; accented syllable is CAPITALIZED

NOTE: Pronunciation may vary from region to region, but those included are the generally-favored ones. Occasionally, two pronunciations are given; either is commonly acceptable, though the first is more prevalent.

Also worth noting: Pronunciation-syllables do not necessarily follow grammar syllable-separation rules. For example, DISTORT is pronounced **di STOHRT** but is separated (via grammar syllabification) **dis TORT**. Another example is BELLICOSE, pronounced **BEL uh kohs** but separated (via grammar syllabification) **BEL li cose**. Our concern in this text is pronunciation and definition, but the grammar syllable-distinction is nevertheless worth mentioning.

Building vocabulary is a lifetime effort, as is all communication. But once you begin to gain the upper hand through these concisely-defined "power words," you'll soon find yourself "in the driver's seat"!

"It's never too late to begin a new future..."

ABASE [uh BAYS]
- humble/degrade
(The parishioner **ABASED** himself by removing his hat when entering the house of worship.)

ABATE [uh BAYT]
- subside/decrease
(After several stormy hours, the heavy winds **ABATED**.)

ABDICATE [AB duh kayt]
- formally give up
(Upon hearing of a plot to murder the royal family, the king **ABDICATED** the throne and fled the country.)

ABERRANT [AB uh runt; a BAYR unt]
- abnormal
(A psychologist was called in to determine the root of the young man's **ABERRANT** sexual behavior.)

ABEYANCE [uh BAY uns]
- temporary inactivity
(Construction of the office building was held in **ABEYANCE** until the weather improved.)

ABHOR [ab HOHR]
- hate/find repulsive
(Residents of the peaceful village **ABHORRED** the violent acts perpetrated by their belligerent neighboring tribes.)

ABJECT [AB jekt]
- hopelessly miserable/humiliating
(People in third-world countries often live in **ABJECT** poverty.)

ABJURE [ab JUR]
- renounce
(After fleeing the war-ravaged country, the former insurgent **ABJURED** all allegiance to the rebel faction.)

ABNEGATE [AB nuh gayt]
- deny/forgo
(Henry David Thoreau **ABNEGATED** modern conveniences and instead chose to live simply in his cottage by Walden Pond.)

ABOMINABLE [uh BAHM uh nuh bul]
- awful
(The Abominable Snowman has earned its name due to the reportedly **ABOMINABLE** odor it emits.)

ABORT [uh BOHRT]
- terminate
(The plot to kidnap the queen was abruptly **ABORTED** when it was learned that the king had prepared defensively for such an eventuality.)

ABRIDGE [uh BRIJ]
- condense
*(To accommodate the newspaper's space restrictions, the reporter was asked to **ABRIDGE** his lengthy account of the events.)*

ABROGATE [AB ruh gayt]
- abolish
*(Furious at the unwarranted forays by the neighboring country, the leader **ABROGATED** the previously-established peace settlement.)*

ABRUPT [uh BRUPT]
- sudden
*(Cars came to an **ABRUPT** stop as the family of ducks slowly crossed the road.)*

ABSOLUTION [ab suh LOO shun]
- forgiveness
*(The penitent sinner sought **ABSOLUTION** from the Church for his blasphemous and profane past.)*

ABSOLVE [ab ZAHLV; ab SAHLV]
- free from blame
*(A confession by the bankteller **ABSOLVED** the clerk of the crime of embezzlement.)*

ABSTAIN [ab STAYN]
- refrain
*(Rather than risk the dangers associated with cigarettes, many choose to **ABSTAIN** from smoking altogether.)*

ABSTEMIOUS [ab STEE mee us]
- eating/drinking in moderation
*(Throughout his long life, the **ABSTEMIOUS** octogenarian refrained from excessive imbibing or carousing.)*

ABSTINENT [AB stuh nunt]
- abstaining
*(True to his pledge of religious adherence, the man remained sexually **ABSTINENT** until after he was wed.)*

ABSTRUSE [ab STROOS]
- difficult to comprehend
*(In her discussion, the noted physicist delved into an **ABSTRUSE** analysis of quantum mechanics.)*

ABYSMAL [uh BIZ mul]
- bottomless/endless
*(The wretched inhabitants of the barren wasteland lived in **ABYSMAL** poverty and despair.)*

ACCEDE [ak SEED]
- consent/yield
*(Rather than prolong the argument, the husband **ACCEDED** to the wishes of his distaff mate.)*

ACCLIMATE [AK luh mayt; uh KLIE mit]
- accustom ("get used to")
(Seasoned travelers can quickly ACCLIMATE themselves to new surroundings.)

ACCOLADE [AK uh layd]
- award of praise
(It often takes many hard-fought and laborious years of touring before an artist receives his due recognition and ACCOLADES from the music world.)

ACCORD [uh KOHRD]
- agreement
(After lengthy negotiations, the two rival parties reached a mutual peace ACCORD.)

ACCOUTER [uh KOO tur]
- outfit/equip
(In preparation for battle, the soldiers were ACCOUTERED with protective gear.)

ACCRUE [uh KROO]
- accumulate
(The investment ACCRUED interest at the rate of 5% per annum.)

ACERBIC [uh SUR bik]
- scathingly sarcastic
(His ACERBIC wit added piquant flavor to his caustic movie reviews.)

ACME [AK mee]
- top
(The unparalleled success of her latest novel placed the author at the ACME of her acclaimed literary career.)

ACQUIESCE [ak wee ES]
- consent/submit
(To settle the seemingly interminable strike, management ACQUIESCED to the implacable union's demands.)

ACQUISITIVE [uh KWIZ i tiv]
- desirous
(In the movie Citizen Kane, the ACQUISITIVE mogul sought to run his own daily newspaper.)

ACRID [AK rid]
- harsh and stinging
(An ACRID odor emitted by the geyser burned the tourists' eyes.)

ACRIMONIOUS [ak ruh MOH nee us]
- bitter and spiteful
(As the meeting degenerated into chaos, hostilities turned to ACRIMONIOUS name-calling.)

ACTUATE [AK choo ayt]
- activate
(The boys' cross-country jaunt was ACTUATED by their desire for adventure.)

ACUMEN [uh KYOO mun; AK yuh mun]
- keenness/shrewdness
*(Her business **ACUMEN** was greatly responsible for her financial success.)*

ACUTE [uh KYOOT]
- sharp/intense
*(The patient experienced an **ACUTE** pain in his side.)*

ACUTE [uh KYOOT]
- perceptive
*(Beagles possess an **ACUTE** sense of smell.)*

ADAMANT [AD uh munt]
- insistent
*(In his own defense, the lad was **ADAMANT** that he did not leave his sister unattended.)*

ADDLED [AD ld]
- confused
*(**ADDLED** by the complex problem, the youngster refused to work on it any longer.)*

ADDUCE [uh DOOS; uh DYOOS]
- cite/offer as evidence
*(Relevant facts were **ADDUCED** to further bolster the thesis of the argument.)*

ADEPT [uh DEPT]
- skillful/expert
*(The **ADEPT** juggler mesmerized the audience with his gravity-defying act.)*

ADHERENT [ad HEER unt]
- follower/supporter
*(The cult leader's **ADHERENTS** were a fanatic bunch.)*

ADJURE [uh JOOR]
- beg earnestly
*(Desperate, the lost sailors **ADJURED** the gods to show them the way to safety from the storm.)*

ADMONISH [ad MAHN ish]
- scold
*(The policeman **ADMONISHED** the heedless pedestrian for jaywalking.)*

ADO [uh DOO]
- commotion
*(There was much **ADO** about which child would sit in the front seat during the weekend excursion.)*

ADROIT [uh DROIT]
- skillful and proficient
*(The candidate was an **ADROIT** and eloquent speaker.)*

ADULATION [aj uh LAY shun]
- lavish praise and admiration
(Rock stars are often the objects of teenage ADULATION.)

ADUMBRATE [AD um brayt; uh DUM brayt]
- foreshadow
(Low initial customer turnout ADUMBRATED a shaky future for the retail store.)

ADVENT [AD vent]
- arrival
(Personal computers marked the ADVENT of a new age of mobile technology.)

ADVENTITIOUS [ad ven TISH us]
- abnormally appearing
(Neighbors marveled at the ADVENTITIOUS growth of an apple tree in the middle of the otherwise barren plot of land.)

ADVERSARY [AD vur ser ee]
- rival/enemy
(Prosecuting and defense attorneys are ADVERSARIES in the courtroom.)

ADVERSE [ad VURS]
- unfavorable
(Unwilling to accept defeat, search rescuers persevered through ADVERSE weather conditions.)

ADVERSITY [ad VUR si tee]
- hardship/misfortune
(Many famous and successful people have had to overcome their share of ADVERSITY in their earlier years.)

ADVOCATE [AD vuh kayt]
- support
(In her speech, the pacifist candidate ADVOCATED military restraint.)

AEGIS [EE jis]
- sponsorship
(The young artist worked under the AEGIS of a movie magnate.)

AESTHETIC [es THET ik] (also, **ESTHETIC**)
- artistically beautiful
(Lakes offer visitors a pleasingly AESTHETIC vista.)

AFFABLE [AF uh bul]
- pleasantly friendly
(The AFFABLE youngster made friends with everyone he met.)

AFFECTATION [af ek TAY shun]
- façade/pretense
*(The kindness displayed by the veteran actress was just an **AFFECTATION**; she was actually bitterly envious of the young upstart.)*

AFFECTED [uh FEK tid]
- artificial/pretended
*(The young actress's **AFFECTED** smile reflected her uneasiness at the awards ceremony.)*

AFFINITY [uh FIN i tee]
- natural liking/attraction
*(Some people have an **AFFINITY** for taking risks while behind the wheel of a car.)*

AFFLUENT [AF loo unt]
- wealthy
*(Beverly Hills is an **AFFLUENT** neighborhood.)*

AGGRANDIZE [uh GRAN diez; AG run diez]
- exalt/enhance socially
*(By **AGGRANDIZING** his own accomplishments, he gained a reputation both for his expertise and his immodesty.)*

AGGREGATE [AG ruh git]
- composite/collection
*(The unusual compound was an **AGGREGATE** of rare gemstones.)*

AGHAST [uh GAST]
- shocked
*(Visitors stood **AGHAST** at the sight of the devastation.)*

AGILE [AJ ul]
- quick and well-coordinated
*(The **AGILE** mountain goat pranced from ledge to ledge with apparent ease.)*

AGITATE [AJ i tayt]
- excite and upset
*(Approaching fire trucks **AGITATED** the skittish zoo animals.)*

AGRARIAN [uh GRAYR ee un]
- agricultural
*(Although they occasionally traded with neighboring villages, the **AGRARIAN** community was basically self-sufficient.)*

ALACRITY [uh LAK ri tee]
- eager willingness/promptness
*(The ambitious lad completed his chores with **ALACRITY**.)*

ALIENABLE [AY lee uh nuh bul; AYL yuh nuh bul]
- saleable/transferable
(The will granted ALIENABLE property rights to the heirs.)

ALIENATE [AYL yuh nayt; AY lee uh nayt]
- make hostile
(Years of quarreling ALIENATED the Hatfields and the McCoys.)

ALLAY [uh LAY]
- ease/calm
(Soothing words by the scoutmaster ALLAYED the children's fear of spending the night outdoors.)

ALLEGE [uh LEJ]
- claim
(The irate gambler ALLEGED that the dealer was cheating.)

ALLEVIATE [uh LEE vee ayt]
- ease/relieve
(An additional lane was added to help ALLEVIATE the rush-hour traffic.)

ALLIANCE [uh LIE uns]
- association
(To defend against the school bully, the group of younger boys formed a protective ALLIANCE.)

ALLUDE [uh LOOD]
- refer indirectly
(The folk singer's poetically lyrical tunes ALLUDED to a bygone era.)

ALOOF [uh LOOF]
- distant and detached
(As a result of his ALOOF manner when around strangers, he acquired the reputation of a snob)

ALTERCATION [ahl tur KAY shun]
- heated argument
(The couple's verbal ALTERCATION intensified as the evening progressed.)

AMBIDEXTROUS [am bi DEK strus]
- skillful with both hands
(A good juggler must be AMBIDEXTROUS.)

AMBIENCE [AM bee uns]
- environment/atmosphere
(Visitors enjoyed the restful AMBIENCE of the serene neighborhood park.)

AMBIGUOUS [am BIG yoo us]
- unclear
(The meaning of the cryptic cave writing was AMBIGUOUS and subject to interpretation.)

AMBIVALENT [am BIV uh lunt]
- waveringly undecided
(When asked whether she wanted to go to the mall or the movies, the young girl gave an AMBIVALENT shrug.)

AMBROSIAL [am BROH zhul]
- delicious
(The AMBROSIAL feast was fit for a king.)

AMBULATORY [AM byuh luh tohr ee]
- capable of (or adapted for) walking
(In the hospital, AMBULATORY patients conversed with bedridden ones.)

AMELIORATE [uh MEEL yuh rayt]
- improve/rectify
(To AMELIORATE the tragic shortage of food in the war-torn village, canned goods and bags of rice were donated.)

AMENABLE [uh MEE nuh bul; uh MEN uh bul]
- responsive and agreeable
(Both nations were AMENABLE to compromise over the contested land.)

AMEND [uh MEND]
- change/revise
(Due to a sudden upsurge in sales, the company AMENDED its estimated quarterly profits.)

AMIABLE [AY mee uh bul]
- friendly
(All the guests at the party were charmed by the host's AMIABLE young daughter.)

AMICABLE [AM uh kuh bul]
- peacefully friendly
(An AMICABLE resolution brought closure to the month-long divorce proceedings.)

AMISS [uh MIS]
- wrong
(When the prisoners greeted him warmly, the warden sensed intuitively that something was AMISS.)

AMITY [AM i tee]
- friendship
(Common goals fostered an AMITY between the former rivals.)

AMOROUS [AM ur us]
- loving
(The movie star's AMOROUS glance caught the admiring fan off guard.)

AMORPHOUS [uh MOHR fus]
- lacking specific shape
(Jellyfish are AMORPHOUS sea creatures.)

ANATHEMA [uh NATH uh muh]
- taboo/outlawed
(During the long-standing feud between the Hatfields and McCoys, uttering the other family's name was ANATHEMA.)

ANATHEMA [uh NATH uh muh]
- a person/thing cursed and condemned
(Drug dealers are ANATHEMA to all who value the welfare of children.)

ANCILLIARY [AN suh ler ee]
- auxiliary
(An ANCILLARY clause was added to the author's contract, giving him full television rights.)

ANGST [ahngkst]
- feeling of fear/uneasiness
(The haunted house produced an ANGST in those who ventured within.)

ANGUISH [ANG gwish]
- suffer pain/distress
(The distraught parents ANGUISHED over the disappearance of their daughter.)

ANIMADVERSION [an uh mad VUR zhun]
- harsh criticism
(Modern teaching methods were subjected to unrelenting ANIMADVERSION from the conservative educator.)

ANIMOSITY [an uh MAHS i tee]
- hatred and bitterness
(Once happily married, the estranged couple found their relationship degrading into virulent ANIMOSITY.)

ANIMUS [AN uh mus]
- bitter hostility
(Years of feuding festered an ANIMUS between the two families.)

ANNEX [uh NEKS]
- add on
(To expand his already vast empire, the king ANNEXED the territory that lay to the south.)

ANOMALY [uh NAHM uh lee]
- abnormality
(Although frequent in mice, pink-colored eyes are an ANOMALY in humans.)

ANTHROPOMORPHIC [an thruh puh MOHR fik]
- characterizing as human
(Madame Pele is an ANTHROPOMORPHIC representation of the Hawaiian volcano goddess.)

ANTIPATHY [an TIP uh thee]
- strong dislike
(Residents of the isolated village held a deep-seated ANTIPATHY toward strangers.)

ANTIPODES [an TIP uh deez]
- exact opposites
*(The two countries were geographical **ANTIPODES**.)*

ANXIETY [ang ZIE uh tee]
- great uneasiness
*(On the eve of the play's debut, the cast members felt a high level of **ANXIETY**.)*

APATHETIC [ap uh THET ik]
- uninterested/unconcerned
*(Even after witnessing firsthand the maltreatment of street children, government officials remained **APATHETIC** toward helping them.)*

APERTURE [AP ur chur]
- opening
*(Sunlight passed through the tiny **APERTURE** in the wall.)*

APEX [AY peks]
- peak
*(Winning the coveted world championship title marked the **APEX** of the chess master's brilliant career.)*

APLOMB [uh PLAHM]
- poise/self-assurance
*(The young diplomat handled the delicate negotiation with the **APLOMB** of a veteran.)*

APOCALYPSE [uh PAHK uh lips]
- prophetic/revealing vision
*(Guided by the prophet's **APOCALYPSE**, the voyagers braved the seas in search of the New World.)*

APOCRYPHAL [uh PAHK ruh ful]
- of questionable authenticity
*(Experts considered the unsigned painting an **APOCRYPHAL** work uncannily resembling the art of Edouard Manet.)*

APOGEE [AP uh jee]
- zenith
*(Wholesale annihilation reached its **APOGEE** during World War II when two atomic bombs were dropped on unsuspecting cities.)*

APOLOGIST [uh PAHL uh jist]
- defender
*(Throughout his political and personal life, Jimmy Carter was known as an **APOLOGIST** for human rights.)*

APOSTATE [uh PAHS tayt]
- renegade
*(His former Republican constituents branded the senator an **APOSTATE** for switching political parties.)*

APOTHEOSIS [uh PAHTH ee oh sis]
- epitome
*(To the Greeks, Aphrodite was the **APOTHEOSIS** of beauty.)*

APPALL [uh PAHL]
- horrify
*(The brutality of the unprovoked attack **APPALLED** the citizens of the tiny community.)*

APPEASE [uh PEEZ]
- pacify
*(To **APPEASE** his critics, the songwriter altered the tune's offensive lyrics.)*

APPEND [uh PEND]
- attach
*(For added clarity, a glossary was **APPENDED** to the textbook.)*

APPOSITE [AP uh zit]
- appropriate
*(An **APPOSITE** witty aphorism leavened the tension of the precarious predicament.)*

APPREHENSIVE [ap ri HEN siv]
- fearful
*(The diminutive lad was **APPREHENSIVE** when it came to jumping off the highest diving board.)*

APPRISE [uh PRIEZ]
- inform
*(A scout **APPRISED** the commander of the nature of terrain that lay ahead.)*

APPROBATION [ap ruh BAY shun]
- approval/praise
*(For his money-saving idea, the clerk received **APPROBATION** from upper-level management.)*

APPROPRIATE [uh PROH pree ayt]
- allocate/authorize
*(To build the neighborhood playground, the City Council first needed to **APPROPRIATE** necessary funds.)*

APPROPRIATE [uh PROH pree ayt]
- seize
*(Native groups accused the government of **APPROPRIATING** their rightful lands.)*

APROPOS [ap ruh POH]
- appropriate and opportune
*(Announcing his wedding plans during a gala family reunion proved most **APROPOS**.)*

ARABLE [AYR uh bul]
- suitable for farming
*(Land in mountainous regions is usually not **ARABLE**.)*

ARBITER [AHR bi tur]
- qualified judge/authority
*(Emily Post has long been regarded an **ARBITER** of social etiquette.)*

ARBITRARY [AHR bi trer ee]
- subjective/personal
*(An **ARBITRARY** decision was made as to which supplies to throw out of the imperiled airplane.)*

ARBITRARY [AHR bi trer ee]
- dictatorial
*(Julius Caesar was an **ARBITRARY** and much-feared Roman emperor.)*

ARBOREAL [ahr BOHR ee ul]
- living in trees
*(Sloths are **ARBOREAL** mammals.)*

ARCANE [ahr KAYN]
- secret and mysterious
*(Featured in the tribal ceremony was an **ARCANE** voodoo ritual.)*

ARCHAIC [ahr KAY ik]
- ancient
*(Researchers unearthed an **ARCHAIC** language when they discovered the cave drawings.)*

ARCHETYPE [AHR ki tiep]
- original model
*(A noisy, bulky contraption was the **ARCHETYPE** of today's modern computer.)*

ARDENT [AHR dnt]
- intensely devoted
*(The musicians' benefit concert reflected an **ARDENT** desire to raise money to assist the world's impoverished children.)*

ARDUOUS [AHR joo us; AHRJ wus]
- difficult/strenuous
*(Having climbed the first thousand feet, the hikers readied themselves for the **ARDUOUS** ascent of the steepest part of the mountain.)*

ARGUABLY [AHR gyoo uh blee]
- convincingly
*(Many feel that Tiger Woods is **ARGUABLY** the most exciting golfer on the professional circuit today.)*

ARID [AYR id]
- extremely dry
*(The Sahara Desert is an **ARID** region in North Africa.)*

ARRANT [AYR unt]
- outright/thorough
*(The renegade was branded an **ARRANT** coward.)*

ARRAY [uh RAY]
- arrange
*(At the wedding banquet, the coordinator **ARRAYED** the lights in a colorful, eye-catching sequence.)*

ARROGANT [AYR uh gunt]
- snobby
*(The lad's **ARROGANT** behavior was not appreciated by his peers in school.)*

ARROGATE [AYR uh gayt]
- seize
*(By proclaiming himself its president, the bold upstart **ARROGATED** to himself control of the newly-formed club.)*

ARTFUL [AHRT ful]
- clever/cunning
*(An **ARTFUL** plan was conceived to capture the escaped convicts.)*

ARTFUL [AHRT ful]
- skillful/masterful
*(Yo Yo Ma's **ARTFUL** solo cello performance drew a standing ovation.)*

ARTIFICE [AHR tuh fis]
- cleverness/trickery
*(The elusive mouse employed an effective **ARTIFICE** to confuse the attacking hawk.)*

ARTLESS [AHRT lis]
- unsophisticated
*(The **ARTLESS** boor could not relate with his worldly associates.)*

ARTLESS [AHRT lis]
- sincere and natural
*(Anticipating the bravado typical of her former suitors, the woman was pleasantly surprised by the young man's **ARTLESS** humility.)*

ASCERTAIN [as ur TAYN]
- determine with certainty
*(Investigators were unable to immediately **ASCERTAIN** the cause of the fire.)*

ASCETIC [uh SET ik]
- self-disciplined and abstinent
*(Hindu monks lead an **ASCETIC** life.)*

ASCRIBE [uh SKRIEB]
- attribute/credit
*(Although unsigned, the poignant circus painting was **ASCRIBED** to early Pablo Picasso.)*

ASKANCE [uh SKANS]
- with a side glance
*(The student looked **ASKANCE** to see what answers the person seated next to him had selected.)*

ASKANCE [uh SKANS]
- suspiciously
*(The weary woman looked **ASKANCE** at the hooded man sitting on the other side of the bus.)*

ASPERITY [uh SPER i tee]
- harshness of temper
*(The defendant responded to the prosecutor's accusations with **ASPERITY**.)*

ASPERSION [uh SPUR zhun]
- slanderous insult
*(It is not polite to cast **ASPERSIONS** on another's character.)*

ASPIRE [uh SPIER]
- eagerly desire
*(The young girl **ASPIRED** to one day become a famous doctor.)*

ASSAIL [uh SAYL]
- attack
*(The controversial talk-show host was **ASSAILED** with boos and hisses during his appearance at the political rally.)*

ASSAY [AS ay; a SAY]
- evaluate
*(A panel was commissioned to **ASSAY** the budget's practicability.)*

ASSAY [AS ay; a SAY]
- attempt
*(The doughty hiker **ASSAYED** to surmount the sheer cliff.)*

ASSENT [uh SENT]
- agree
*(Reluctantly, the lone holdout **ASSENTED** to the majority opinion.)*

ASSERT [uh SURT]
- declare/claim
*(It is natural for teenagers to **ASSERT** their independence from parental controls.)*

ASSESS [uh SES]
- evaluate
*(The city council **ASSESSED** the likelihood of balancing the budget without having to raise local taxes.)*

ASSEVERATE [uh SEV uh rayt]
- declare firmly/sincerely
*(The defendant vocally **ASSEVERATED** his noninvolvement in the crime.)*

ASSIDUOUS [uh SIJ oo us; uh SIJ wus]
- hardworking and determined
*(An **ASSIDUOUS** student of Japanese language and culture, the young man hoped to one day return to the faraway land of the rising sun.)*

ASSIMILATE [uh SIM uh layt]
- absorb/incorporate
*(After spending a leisurely week on the exotic island, visitors often sought to **ASSIMILATE** the relaxed and carefree lifestyle into their own.)*

ASSUAGE [uh SWAYJ]
- soothe/appease
*(The mother's reassuring words helped **ASSUAGE** her young daughter's fears of riding the roller coaster.)*

ASTUTE [uh STOOT; uh STYOOT]
- perceptive
*(An **ASTUTE** judge of character, the captain knew to whom to delegate crucial responsibilities.)*

ASYLUM [uh SIE lum]
- refuge
*(During the violent civil uprising, fleeing families sought **ASYLUM** in neighboring villages.)*

ATONE [uh TOHN]
- make amends
*(To **ATONE** for a lifetime of sexual promiscuity, the contrite man vowed to embark upon a life of marital fidelity.)*

ATTENUATE [uh TEN yoo ayt]
- make thin/slender
*(Before being shaped into necklaces, the gold was **ATTENUATED** into one long strand.)*

ATTENUATE [uh TEN yoo ayt]
- weaken in force/intensity
*(Time **ATTENUATES** old grudges.)*

ATTEST [uh TEST]
- testify/give proof
*(Corroborating evidence **ATTESTED** to the veracity of the witness's account.)*

ATTRITION [uh TRISH un]
- wearing down (from a constant source)
*(Through **ATTRITION** from an endless barrage of pointed questions, the suspect eventually confessed.)*

ATYPICAL [ay TIP i kul]
- unusual
*(In most areas, snow in spring is highly **ATYPICAL**.)*

AUDACIOUS [ah DAY shus]
- daringly fearless
*(The **AUDACIOUS** lad defied the school bully.)*

AUGMENT [ahg MENT]
- increase
*(A second job is always a viable option to **AUGMENT** the family's income.)*

AUGUR [AH gur]
- signal in advance
*(Latest economic signs **AUGURED** well for continued business growth in the retail sector.)*

AUGUST [ah GUST]
- awe-inspiring
*(Abraham Lincoln was a person of **AUGUST** countenance.)*

AUREATE [OHR ee it; OHR ee ayt]
- ornately splendid
*(Mark Antony delivered an **AUREATE** speech to the Roman masses.)*

AUSPICIOUS [ah SPISH us]
- favorable
*(Sales for the first month reflected an **AUSPICIOUS** beginning for the fledgling business.)*

AUSTERE [ah STEER]
- stern/strict
*(The **AUSTERE** professor did not invite student discussion.)*

AUSTERE [au STEER]
- simple/unadorned
*(Amish people live an **AUSTERE** life, forgoing many modern conveniences.)*

AUTHORITARIAN [uh thohr i TAYR ee un]
- strict and unyielding
*(The family was under the matriarch's **AUTHORITARIAN** rule.)*

AUTHORITATIVE [uh THOHR i tay tiv]
- commanding/dominating
*(Napoleon led his troops with an **AUTHORITATIVE** certainty few dared challenge.)*

AUTHORITATIVE [uh THOHR i tay tiv]
- expert/reliable
*(To better inform the council of their various options, an **AUTHORITATIVE** historian was brought in to illustrate similar instances in the past.)*

AUTOCHTHONOUS [ah TAHK thuh nus]
- indigenous
*(Medical personnel were flown in to the remote jungle to attempt to eradicate the **AUTOCHTHONOUS** strain of malaria.)*

AUTOCRATIC [ah tuh KRAT ik]
- dictatorial
*(Adolph Hilter ruled Germany in an **AUTOCRATIC** manner.)*

AUTONOMOUS [ah TAHN uh mus]
- self-governing/independent
*(The alternative learning center was established as an **AUTONOMOUS** extension of the local high school.)*

AUXILIARY [ahg ZIL yuh ree; ahg ZIL uh ree]
- supplemental ("backup")
(AUXILIARY troops were brought in to reinforce those soldiers already on the front lines.)

AVARICE [AV uh ris]
- greed
(In his AVARICE, the business mogul was not satisfied until he had driven his competitor to bankruptcy.)

AVENGE [un VENDJ]
- seek revenge for
(At the battle of Little Bighorn, the Sioux Indians AVENGED the broken promises by the white man by brutally defeating General Custer and the men of the 7th Cavalry.)

AVER [uh VUR]
- assert
(Residents vehemently AVERRED that the reported midnight celestial sightings were no hoax.)

AVERSION [uh VUR zhun]
- strong dislike
(Many people have an AVERSION to cockroaches.)

AVERT [uh VERT]
- prevent
(Last-minute negotiations helped AVERT a crippling strike.)

AVID [AV id]
- enthusiastic
(From her earliest childhood, she was an AVID and devoted tennis fan.)

AVOW [uh VOU]
- declare openly
(Sir Lancelot AVOWED his love for Guinevere.)

AWRY [uh RIE]
- wrong
(When communication with the airliner was lost, ground personnel feared that something serious might have gone AWRY.)

BACCHANALIAN [bak uh NAY lee un]
- drunken
(Visitors to the island resort participated in a week of BACCHANALIAN revelry.)

BALEFUL [BAYL ful]
- sinister and malicious
(The vengeful wizard levied a BALEFUL curse on the entire town.)

BALK [bahk]
- hesitate and resist
(When asked to contribute fifty dollars to the holiday fund, the secretary initially BALKED but then reluctantly consented.)

BANAL [buh NAL]
- pointlessly dull and unoriginal
(Few were moved or impressed by the candidate's simplistically BANAL remedies to the city's complex traffic problems.)

BANEFUL [BAYN ful]
- harmful
(Close friends cautioned the young man that his allegiance to the subversive organization would prove a BANEFUL influence on his political career.)

BANTER [BAN tur]
- tease jokingly
(The awkward lad was BANTERED by his friends for his performance on the dance floor.)

BATHOS [BAY thahs]
- overdone sentimentalism
(The drama ran the gamut from gripping realism to near-comical BATHOS.)

BEATIFIC [bee uh TIF ik]
- blissful
(The birth of a child is a BEATIFIC event.)

BECOMING [bi KUM ing]
- attractive
(The young man wore a most BECOMING suit and tie to church.)

BECOMING [bi KUM ing]
- suitable
(When visited by her grandmother, the lass exhibited behavior BECOMING of a young princess.)

BEDLAM [BED lum]
- pandemonium/chaos
(When the football team won the championship game, there was BEDLAM that evening in the streets.)

BEDRAGGLED [bi DRAG uld]
- messy and dirty/grimy
(The BEDRAGGLED beggar had not taken a shower in months.)

BEFRIEND [bi FREND]
- make friends with
(The generous benefactor BEFRIENDED the homeless lad.)

BEGUILE [bi GIEL]
- lure astray
(BEGUILED by the sweet promise of Hollywood fame and fortune, the young woman packed her suitcase and left her family behind.)

BEHOOVE [bi HOOV]
 - be proper/necessary
*(When taking a vacation, it **BEHOOVES** a person to confirm hotel lodgings one final time to avoid unexpected problems.)*

BELATED [bi LAY tid]
 - late/overdue
*(Discovering that he had forgotten his friend's birthday, the chagrined colleague immediately sent an apologetic **BELATED** birthday card.)*

BELIE [bi LIE]
 - disguise/camouflage
*(The villain's smile **BELIED** his evil intent.)*

BELIE [bi LIE]
 - expose as false
*(Eyewitness testimony **BELIED** the defendant's account of the incident.)*

BELLICOSE [BEL uh kohs]
 - hostile/quarrelsome
*(Villagers avoided inflaming the ever-present temper of their **BELLICOSE** adversaries to the north.)*

BELLIGERENT [buh LIJ uh runt]
 - warlike/hostile
*(The **BELLIGERENT** nation aggressively threatened its peaceful neighbors.)*

BEMUSED [bi MYOOZD]
 - puzzled/confused
*(Eating an artichoke for the first time, the little tyke had a **BEMUSED** look on his face.)*

BENEFICIAL [ben uh FISH ul]
 - helpful/advantageous
*(A regimen of daily exercise is highly **BENEFICIAL** for young and old alike.)*

BENEVOLENT [buh NEV uh lunt]
 - kindhearted
*(The **BENEVOLENT** man treated the lowly beggar to a hearty meal.)*

BERATE [bi RAYT]
 - scold severely
*(The new employee was **BERATED** for his constant tardiness.)*

BEREFT [bi REFT]
 - deprived
*(Failing the bar examination left the young man **BEREFT** of all hope of ever becoming a lawyer.)*

BESEECH [bi SEECH]
 - beg
*(The ambassador **BESEECHED** the king to reconsider his decision to declare war.)*

BESMIRCH [bi SMURCH]
- tarnish ("smear")
*(In the lawsuit, the litigant accused the reporter of **BESMIRCHING** his good name by calling him a crooked politician.)*

BESTOW [bi STOH]
- grant
*(The Medal of Honor was **BESTOWED** upon the valiant soldier.)*

BICKER [BIK ur]
- quarrel
*(Teenage siblings often **BICKER** over use of the telephone.)*

BILIOUS [BIL yus]
- ill-natured and irritable
*(The **BILIOUS** old curmudgeon chased the group of friendly youngsters out of his front yard.)*

BLANCH [blanch; blahnch]
- turn white/pale
*(Upon seeing the spectral vision, Scrooge **BLANCHED** with fright.)*

BLAND [bland]
- not spicy
*(His weak stomach condition necessitated a **BLAND** diet.)*

BLAND [bland]
- unexciting
*(Although his older sister enjoyed the poignant love story, he found the slow-paced movie too **BLAND** for his taste.)*

BLANDISH [BLAN dish]
- coax (with flattery)
*(Christopher Columbus **BLANDISHED** the queen into giving him additional sailors for his voyage in search of a new world.)*

BLASPHEMOUS [BLAS fuh mus]
- religiously disrespectful
*(The **BLASPHEMOUS** speech attacked both the divine sanctity of the family and the Scriptures which espouse it.)*

BLATANT [BLAYT nt]
- glaringly obvious
*(Drunk drivers exhibit a **BLATANT** disregard for human life.)*

BLEAK [bleek]
- gloomy/hopeless
*(Faced with mounting debts and economic uncertainty, the company's future looked **BLEAK**.)*

BLISS [blis]
- extreme happiness
*(The joyous parents experienced the **BLISS** of watching their child take her first steps.)*

BLITHE [blie<u>th</u>; blieth]
- merry and carefree
*(The **BLITHE** lass skipped gleefully home.)*

BLITHE [blie<u>th</u>; blieth]
- careless/thoughtless
*(People who litter show a **BLITHE** disrespect for the land upon which they live.)*

BOLSTER [BOHL stur]
- support/reinforce
*(Diversifying their selection helped the candy company **BOLSTER** its sagging sales.)*

BOMBASTIC [bahm BAS tik]
- pompous and exaggerated
*(Few believed the old coot's **BOMBASTIC** claims of heroism during the war.)*

BON MOT [bahn MOH]
- clever remark
*(At the testimonial dinner, the guest of honor amused his well-wishers with a litany of **BON MOTS**.)*

BOON [boon]
- blessing
*(The unexpectedly cold weather proved a **BOON** to businesses specializing in sales of winter clothes.)*

BOORISH [B<u>OO</u>R ish]
- crude/unmannerly
*(Few cared to socialize with the **BOORISH**, vulgar lout.)*

BOOTLESS [BOOT lis]
- fruitless/futile
*(The lad's **BOOTLESS** attempts to persuade his folks to let him attend the carnival left him angry and frustrated.)*

BOUNTIFUL [BOUN ti ful]
- abundant
*(Farmers were grateful for the **BOUNTIFUL** spring harvest.)*

BRAGGADOCIO [brag uh DOH shee oh]
- empty boasting
*(The old sailor was known for his vain **BRAGGADOCIO**.)*

BRASH [brash]
- boldly rude
*(The **BRASH** youngster talked back to the principal.)*

BRAVADO [bruh VAH doh]
- pretentious show of courage
*(Once the threat had passed, the pusillanimous poseur demonstrated his **BRAVADO** by claiming he could have stood up to the bully at any time.)*

BRAWNY [BRAH nee]
- muscular
*(The **BRAWNY** bodybuilder was the envy of all the girls at the beach.)*

BRAZEN [BRAY zun]
- shamelessly bold
*(When the truth became known, the boy's **BRAZEN** lies did not go unpunished.)*

BROUHAHA [BROO hah hah]
- uproar
*(The arguable call by the referee caused a **BROUHAHA** throughout the soccer stadium.)*

BROWBEAT [BROU beet]
- bully and intimidate
*(The drill instructor was known for **BROWBEATING** the young cadets to the brink of tears.)*

BRUSQUE [brusk]
- rudely abrupt
*(His **BRUSQUE** refusal to help his wife clean the dishes incurred her wrath.)*

BUCOLIC [byoo KAHL ik]
- pastoral
*(The **BUCOLIC** setting was ideal for the naturalist painter.)*

BUMPTIOUS [BUMP shus]
- offensively presumptuous
*(The **BUMPTIOUS** neighbor couldn't keep his nose out of other people's affairs.)*

BURGEON [BUR jun]
- sprout and flourish
*(In the spring, the island **BURGEONED** with lush vegetation.)*

BURNISH [BUR nish]
- polish
*(The coppersmith **BURNISHED** the coins to a bright luster.)*

BUTTRESS [BUH tris]
- support
*(Thick wooden beams helped **BUTTRESS** the sagging ceiling.)*

CACHE [kash]
- stow secretly/safely away
*(For safety, supernumerary military supplies were **CACHED** in a nearby cave.)*

CACOPHONOUS [kuh KAHF uh nus]
- harsh and discordant
(CACOPHONOUS sounds filled the auditorium as the orchestral instruments were tuned.)

CAJOLE [kuh JOHL]
- coax by flattery/promises
(The buxom blonde CAJOLED the love-stricken guard into abandoning his sentry post.)

CALAMITOUS [kuh LAM i tus]
- catastrophic
(The 1963 assassination of President John F. Kennedy was a globally CALAMITOUS event.)

CALLOW [KAL oh]
- immature and inexperienced
(The CALLOW youngster didn't realize it was impolite to call the teacher by her first name.)

CALUMNIATE [kuh LUM nee ayt]
- slander maliciously
(The underhanded politician CALUMNIATED his rival by spreading groundless rumors.)

CANARD [kuh NAHRD]
- false/unfounded story
(Benjamin Franklin was himself the victim of an unusual newspaper CANARD: an article, which, in short, claimed that he was dead.)

CANDID [KAN did]
- honest
(When asked by his wife for his CANDID opinion, he admitted that the dress did not look good on her.)

CANTANKEROUS [kan TANG kur us]
- cross and quarrelsome
(The CANTANKEROUS old man did not endear himself to children.)

CAPACIOUS [kuh PAY shus]
- spacious (in capacity)
(The latest computer models feature CAPACIOUS data storage coupled with easy access to immediate retrieval.)

CAPITULATE [kuh PICH uh layt]
- surrender
(After the smaller army CAPITULATED, a meeting was held to officially turn over the contested land.)

CAPRICIOUS [kuh PRISH us; kuh PREE shus]
- unpredictably changeable
(The CAPRICIOUS lad could not be depended upon to complete any serious task.)

CAPTIOUS [KAP shus]
- faultfinding/nitpicky
(His CAPTIOUS boss was constantly nagging him over the most trivial of details.)

CARICATURE [KAYR uh kuh chur]
- comical exaggeration
(A magazine CARICATURE of Bob Hope featured the television icon with a Pinocchio-sized nose.)

CARTE BLANCHE [kahrt BLAHNCH]
- absolute discretionary power ("a free hand")
(The first mate was given CARTE BLANCHE on all decisions concerning the upcoming transoceanic race.)

CASTIGATE [KAS tuh gayt]
- criticize severely
(As a result of their rudeness to the guest speaker, the class of fifth graders was publicly CASTIGATED by their teacher.)

CATALYST [KAT uh list]
- accelerator ("spark plug")
(In the 1960s, protest marches served as a CATALYST for social change.)

CATEGORICAL [kat uh GOHR i kul]
- absolute
(The suspect issued a CATEGORICAL denial of any involvement in the crime.)

CATHARTIC [kuh THAHR tik]
- purging
(Crying can be a CATHARTIC way to relieve the stress of grief.)

CAUSERIE [koh zuh REE]
- chat
(The two friends engaged in a pleasant telephone CAUSERIE.)

CAUSTIC [KAH stik]
- corrosive
(The CAUSTIC chemical had to be stored in a cool, dry location.)

CAUSTIC [KAH stik]
- harshly sarcastic
(In his anger, the motorist lashed out with a CAUSTIC barrage of insults.)

CAVEAT [KA vee at]
- warning
(One should always heed the CAVEAT "buyer beware" when purchasing a used car "as is.")

CAVIL [KAV ul]
- quibble and complain
(The persistent defense attorney CAVILED at every point raised by the prosecutor during the trial.)

CEDE [seed]
- relinquish
(The government CEDED a portion of the contested land back to the native inhabitants.)

CELEBRATED [SEL uh bray tid]
- famous
*(Landing on the moon was one of man's most **CELEBRATED** achievements.)*

CELERITY [suh LER i tee]
- swiftness/speed
*(The youngster completed the challenging task with amazing **CELERITY**.)*

CELESTIAL [suh LES chul]
- heavenly
*(A **CELESTIAL** light shone down upon the tiny village.)*

CENSOR [SEN sur]
- screen (to delete)
*(Movies are reviewed and objectionable scenes **CENSORED** before they are allowed to be shown during family programming.)*

CENSURE [SEN shur]
- criticize harshly
*(The committee **CENSURED** the treasurer for having squandered much of their investment capital on worthless stocks.)*

CERTIFY [SUR tuh fie]
- confirm
*(An expert was brought in to **CERTIFY** the authenticity of the dubious painting.)*

CHAGRIN [shuh GRIN]
- shame/humiliation
*(Much to his **CHAGRIN**, the aspiring basketball player was cut from the varsity squad.)*

CHARISMA [kuh RIZ muh]
- powerful/influencing charm
*(The demagogue's **CHARISMA** so affected his followers that he had them tightly at his beck and call.)*

CHARLATAN [SHAHR luh tun]
- fake
*(Many so-called psychics and fortune-tellers are mere **CHARLATANS**.)*

CHARY [CHAYR ee]
- guardedly cautious
*(The lowly subject was **CHARY** about what he uttered while in the presence of the king.)*

CHASTE [chayst]
- morally pure
*(Chivalrous knights from near and far sought the hand of the beautiful and **CHASTE** princess.)*

CHASTISE [chas TIEZ; CHAS tiez]
- scold severely
*(The distraught parent **CHASTISED** his son for coming home after midnight.)*

CHIC [sheek]
- cleverly stylish
*(The **CHIC** fashion outfit sported buttons on the side to allow an undisturbed full frontal figure.)*

CHICANERY [shi KAY nuh ree]
- trickery/deception
*(Through cunning **CHICANERY**, Huckleberry Finn persuaded his friends to paint his fence while he sat back and observed.)*

CHIDE [chied]
- scold mildly
*(The mother **CHIDED** the young girl for not paying attention.)*

CHIMERICAL [ki MER i kul]
- wildly fanciful
*(The religious cleric had a **CHIMERICAL** notion that in his lifetime he would witness a world devoid of human conflict.)*

CHOLERIC [KAHL uh rik; kuh LER ik]
- easily angered
*(The **CHOLERIC** baseball coach often became embroiled in verbal fisticuffs.)*

CHRONIC [KRAHN ik]
- recurring frequently
*(Those who are heavy smokers sooner or later often find themselves suffering from **CHRONIC** breathing difficulties.)*

CHRONIC [KRAHN ik]
- habitual
*(Had the boy who cried "wolf" not been a **CHRONIC** liar, he may have been saved when the wolf finally did appear.)*

CHRONOLOGICAL [krahn uh LAHJ i kul]
- arranged by time
*(In the historical maritime account, the events preceding the collision of the Titanic with the iceberg were detailed in **CHRONOLOGICAL** order.)*

CHTHONIAN [THOH nee un]
- infernal
*(In Paradise Lost, John Milton described the **CHTHONIAN** world of Satan.)*

CHURLISH [CHUR lish]
- rude and ill-tempered
*(Prior to having his breakfast, her husband was particularly **CHURLISH**.)*

CIRCUITOUS [sur KYOO i tus]
- roundabout/indirect
*(Unable to ascend the mountain's face, the hikers reached the summit via a **CIRCUITOUS** route.)*

CIRCUMSCRIBE [sur kum SCRIEB; SUR kum scrieb]
- limit
(His debilitating illness CIRCUMSCRIBED his daily activities.)

CIRCUMSCRIBE [sur kum SCRIEB; SUR kum scrieb]
- encircle
(The ranch was CIRCUMSCRIBED by a wooden picket fence.)

CIRCUMSPECT [SUR kum spekt]
- cautiously prudent
(The committee examined in a CIRCUMSPECT manner alternatives to raising money other than by increasing local taxes.)

CIRCUMVENT [sur kum VENT; SUR kum vent]
- evade
(The homeowner attempted to CIRCUMVENT state law by building the extension without proper permits.)

CLANDESTINE [klan DES tin]
- secret
(A CLANDESTINE meeting was arranged between the two young lovers.)

CLARION [KLAYR ee un]
- loud and clear
(Unexpectedly heavy turnout at the polls signaled a CLARION call for political change.)

CLICHÉD [klee SHAYD]
- unoriginal and overused
("To kill two birds with one stone" is a CLICHÉD expression that offends nature-loving conservationists.)

CLOY [kloi]
- glut/stuff to excess
(Children who CLOY themselves of chocolates soon realize that too much of a good thing is not always healthy or pleasant.)

COALESCE [koh uh LES]
- unite
(The various lobbyist groups COALESCED to form a more potent unit.)

COALITION [koh uh LISH un]
- union
(A COALITION of labor leaders met to determine whether a strike was necessary.)

COERCE [koh URS]
- pressure
(Junior employees were COERCED by senior staff into participating in the financially risky investment.)

COGENT [KOH junt]
- soundly convincing
(The panelist's COGENT argument could not be readily refuted.)

COGITATE [KAHJ i tayt]
- ponder
(The captain COGITATED the dilemma before formulating a plan of escape from the sinking ship.)

COGNIZANT [KAHG ni zunt]
- aware
(The defendant was fully COGNIZANT of the seriousness of the crime he was charged with.)

COHERENT [koh HEER unt]
- logical/intelligible
(Under the influence of alcohol, the motorist's words and thoughts were not COHERENT.)

COHESIVE [koh HEE siv]
- unified
(The backbone of American society is the COHESIVE family unit.)

COLLABORATE [kuh LAB uh rayt]
- work together
(Three authors COLLABORATED on a book chronicling the events leading up to the Civil War.)

COLLUDE [kuh LOOD]
- scheme together
(The trio COLLUDED to smuggle diamonds through customs.)

COMBUSTIBLE [kum BUS tuh bul]
- flammable
(Paint is a highly COMBUSTIBLE material that should not be stored in containers exposed to extreme heat.)

COMELY [KUM lee]
- pleasingly attractive
(A magic spell transformed the disheveled Cinderella into a COMELY young woman.)

COMITY [KAHM i tee]
- social harmony
(A COMITY developed among the ambassadors at the international conference.)

COMMEND [kuh MEND]
- praise
(The valorous sailor was COMMENDED for his bravery.)

COMMENSURATE [kuh MEN sur it; kuh MEN shur it]
- comparable/proportionate
(The judge sentenced the man to a punishment COMMENSURATE with the heinous crime.)

COMMODIOUS [kuh MOH dee us]
- spacious/roomy
(Four large bedrooms and a COMMODIOUS living area helped the house sell quickly when placed on the real estate market.)

COMPACT [KAHM pakt]
- compressed
(To maximize space conservation, mobile homes have COMPACT kitchens.)

COMPEL [kum PEL]
- force
(Fatigue COMPELLED the hiker to rest awhile.)

COMPENSATE [KAHM pen sayt]
- offset
(The shortstop's outstanding defensive capabilities COMPENSATED for his mediocre batting average.)

COMPENSATE [KAHM pen sayt]
- pay back
(The delivery person was COMPENSATED handsomely for his expeditious service.)

COMPLACENT [kum PLAY sunt]
- self-satisfied
(Two prisoners escaped as a result of overly COMPLACENT guards who erroneously felt they had the cells well secured.)

COMPLAISANT [kum PLAY sunt; kum PLAY zunt]
- obliging and congenial
(Passengers always appreciate a COMPLAISANT flight attendant.)

COMPLEMENT [KAHM pluh ment]
- make complete
(Ham COMPLEMENTS a breakfast with eggs.)

COMPLY [kum PLIE]
- conform/obey
(The headstrong lad refused to COMPLY with the school's strict dress code.)

COMPORT [kum POHRT]
- conduct/behave
(The elderly gentleman COMPORTED himself with poise and dignity.)

COMPREHENSIBLE [kahm pri HEN suh bul]
- understandable
(Technical legal jargon is hardly COMPREHENSIBLE to the lay person.)

COMPREHENSIVE [kahm pri HEN siv]
- broad and inclusive
(A suggestion was made to take a more COMPREHENSIVE look at the traffic problem before instituting any stopgap measures.)

COMPRISE [kum PRIEZ]
- consist (of)
(The alphabet is COMPRISED of twenty-six letters.)

COMPULSIVE [kum PUL siv]
- obsessive
*(Kleptomaniacs have a **COMPULSIVE** desire to steal things.)*

COMPULSORY [kum PUL suh ree]
- mandatory
*(Serving in the military is **COMPULSORY** in many countries.)*

COMPUNCTION [kum PUNGK shun]
- feeling of regret/guilt
*(The misdirected lad had no **COMPUNCTIONS** about taking money out of the store's cash register for his personal use.)*

CONCATENATE [kahn KAT uh nayt]
- link
*(An assortment of recollections was **CONCATENATED** to produce a moving tribute during the eulogy.)*

CONCEDE [kun SEED]
- acknowledge as true
*(After realizing that he was driving down a dead end street, the shamefaced man **CONCEDED** that he should have followed his wife's directions.)*

CONCERTED [kun SUR tid]
- united
*(A **CONCERTED** effort was made by the guests to find the missing ring.)*

CONCILIATE [kun SIL ee ayt]
- appease
*(Having offended his sister with his callous comment, the youngster sought to **CONCILIATE** her with a sincere apology.)*

CONCISE [kun SIES]
- brief and to the point
*(The report was both clear and **CONCISE**.)*

CONCOCT [kahn KOKT; kun KOKT]
- create/devise
*(An ingenious scheme was **CONCOCTED** to trick the enemy soldiers into believing they were outnumbered.)*

CONCOMITANT [kun KAHM i tunt]
- additional (though secondary)
*(The platoon's request for supplies was **CONCOMITANT** to their greater need for more manpower.)*

CONCUPISCENT [kahn KYOO pi sunt]
- lustful
*(Television censors refused to air the **CONCUPISCENT** scene.)*

CONCUR [kun KUR]
- agree/correspond
(Results of the experiment CONCURRED with recent research findings.)

CONCURRENT [kun KUR unt]
- simultaneous
(The two CONCURRENT comedy acts played in different parts of the arena.)

CONDESCEND [kahn di SEND]
- lower oneself/stoop down
(The wealthy businessman CONDESCENDED to speak a few moments to the group of youngsters.)

CONDIGN [kun DIEN]
- appropriate/deserved
(Twenty years in prison seemed CONDIGN punishment for the scoundrel's treacherous deeds.)

CONDONE [kun DOHN]
- excuse
(His parents would not CONDONE any foul language spoken in the house.)

CONFIRM [kun FURM]
- verify
(Eyewitness accounts CONFIRMED the existence of a large alligator in the nearby lake.)

CONFISCATE [KAHN fi skayt]
- seize
(Border guards CONFISCATED the smuggled diamonds.)

CONFLAGRATION [kahn fluh GRAY shun]
- large/destructive fire
(Three city blocks were devastated by the awesome CONFLAGRATION.)

CONFOUND [kahn FOUND; kun FOUND]
- baffle
(The kissing bandit CONFOUNDED the authorities by leaving behind no clues.)

CONFRONT [kun FRUNT]
- face/encounter
(It is better to CONFRONT one's problems than try to run from them.)

CONFUTE [kun FYOOT]
- disprove/invalidate
(Victory was close at hand when she CONFUTED the opposing debater's primary premise.)

CONGENIAL [kun JEEN yul]
- pleasant and agreeable
(The happy-go-lucky lad was a most CONGENIAL traveling partner.)

CONGLOMERATE [kun GLAHM ur it]
- cluster/diversified group
(A powerful business CONGLOMERATE was formed from several smaller companies.)

CONGREGATE [KAHN gruh gayt]
- gather/assemble
(Animals from far and wide CONGREGATED at the watering hole.)

CONJECTURE [kun JEK cher]
- theorize
(Based on past experience, the business analyst CONJECTURED that interest rates were bound to rise in the coming months.)

CONJOIN [kun JOIN]
- unite
(At birth, the twins were CONJOINED at the hip.)

CONJUGAL [KAHN juh gul]
- marital
(In some prisons, inmates are granted occasional CONJUGAL visits.)

CONNIVE [kuh NIEV]
- scheme/plot together secretly
(An opposing faction CONNIVED to oust the senator from his leadership position.)

CONNOTE [kuh NOHT]
- suggest
(The American flag often CONNOTES patriotism and freedom.)

CONNUBIAL [kuh NOO bee ul; kuh NYOO bee ul]
- marital
(Everyone wished the newlyweds a long life of CONNUBIAL bliss.)

CONSCIENTIOUS [kahn shee EN shus]
- honest and responsible
(Because she was a CONSCIENTIOUS worker, her services were in particularly high demand.)

CONSCIENTIOUS [kahn shee EN shus]
- painstaking
(A CONSCIENTIOUS effort was made to correct all spelling errors in his report.)

CONSECRATE [KAHN suh krayt]
- bless
(A holy man was summoned to CONSECRATE the parcel of land where the ancient bones were unearthed.)

CONSENSUS [kun SEN sus]
- general agreement
(Once a CONSENSUS of the committee was achieved regarding the date for their next meeting, a motion was made to adjourn the session for the afternoon.)

CONSEQUENTIAL [kahn suh KWEN shul]
- important
(The decision to enter World War II was, for all Americans, a grave and highly CONSEQUENTIAL action.)

CONSOLE [kun SOHL]
- comfort
(Close friends CONSOLED the couple in their hour of grief.)

CONSOLIDATE [kun SAHL i dayt]
- combine
(To help streamline costs, business operations were CONSOLIDATED into one main headquarters.)

CONSORT [kun SOHRT]
- associate
(The traitor was accused of CONSORTING with the enemy.)

CONSPICUOUS [kun SPIK yoo us]
- easily noticed
(To be more easily spotted in the crowd, the girl wore CONSPICUOUS colors.)

CONSTERNATION [kahn stur NAY shun]
- shock and alarm
(Much to the CONSTERNATION of coastline residents, the national meteorological center reported that their towns would likely soon be hit by a powerful tsunami generated by a sizable seismic disturbance.)

CONSTRAINT [kun STRAYNT]
- restraint
(Despite his anger toward the clumsy waiter, he maintained his composure and handled the matter with CONSTRAINT.)

CONSUMMATE [KAHN suh mit; kun SUM it]
- superb/perfect
(Applause erupted at the completion of the gymnast's CONSUMMATE performance.)

CONTAGION [kun TAY jun]
- contagious disease
(The village's population was decimated by the virulent CONTAGION.)

CONTEMPORARY [kun TEM puh rer ee]
- modern
(The newly refurbished hotel boasted a CONTEMPORARY decor.)

CONTEMPTIBLE [kun TEMP tuh bul]
- shamefully detestable
(The CONTEMPTIBLE cur would even rob his own family to support his drug habit.)

CONTEMPTUOUS [kun TEMP choo us]
- scornful/disrespectful
*(The veteran writer was **CONTEMPTUOUS** of the young upstart, regarding him as merely a talentless opportunist.)*

CONTENTIOUS [kun TEN shus]
- quarrelsome/combative
*(The **CONTENTIOUS** couple bickered over every little issue.)*

CONTIGUOUS [kun TIG yoo us]
- adjacent
*(California and Oregon are **CONTIGUOUS** states.)*

CONTINGENT [kun TIN junt]
- dependent
*(Implementation of the back-up plan was **CONTINGENT** upon the failure of the explosives to detonate as expected.)*

CONTRAVENE [kahn truh VEEN]
- oppose/contradict
*(Because the new city ordinance **CONTRAVENED** existing state law, it was reviewed for possible amending.)*

CONTRAVENE [kahn truh VEEN]
- violate
*(The captain **CONTRAVENED** maritime authority by sailing his ship into the restricted harbor.)*

CONTRITE [kun TRIET]
- sincerely remorseful
*(The **CONTRITE** man vowed never again to drive after having consumed alcohol.)*

CONTRIVE [kun TRIEV]
- scheme
*(The stowaway **CONTRIVED** to board and exit the ship without being detected.)*

CONTROVERT [KAHN truh vurt; kahn truh VURT]
- dispute/deny
*(Many scientists have **CONTROVERTED** the existence of higher life forms on other planets.)*

CONTUMACIOUS [kahn too MAY shus]
- stubbornly disobedient/rebellious
*(The **CONTUMACIOUS** whelp defied the teacher's demands by continuing to play his radio in class.)*

CONTUMELIOUS [kahn too MEE lee us]
- vulgar and abusive
*(Hostile fans levied a barrage of **CONTUMELIOUS** insults against the referee for his questionable call.)*

CONTUMELY [kahn TOO muh lee]
- insulting contempt
*(The heated argument was replete with derisive taunts and unabashed **CONTUMELY**.)*

CONUNDRUM [kuh NUN drum]
- complex/puzzling problem
*(The "meaning of life" is a philosophical **CONUNDRUM** that has haunted mankind for millennia.)*

CONVENE [kun VEEN]
- assemble
*(The local chapter of the Chamber of Commerce **CONVENED** to address the latest downturn in business sales.)*

CONVENE [kun VEEN]
- come/call together
*(A special council meeting was **CONVENED** to address the sudden increase in neighborhood crime.)*

CONVERGE [kun VURJ]
- come together
*(As they neared the end of the search, the treasure hunters **CONVERGED** at the same location.)*

CONVERSANT [kun VUR sunt]
- familiar/knowledgeable
*(The young scholar was **CONVERSANT** with Shakespeare's earliest writings.)*

CONVIVIAL [kun VIV ee ul]
- festive and jovial
*(Neighbors enjoyed the **CONVIVIAL** block-party.)*

CONVOLUTED [KAHN vuh loo tid]
- complicated/intricate
*(The **CONVOLUTED** mathematical word problem challenged even the brightest of students.)*

CONVOLUTED [KAHN vuh loo tid]
- twisted
*(Because the essay contained such muddled and **CONVOLUTED** ideas, the instructor could not give it a passing grade.)*

COPIOUS [KOH pee us]
- plentiful/abundant
*(During the annual meeting of stockholders, corporate executives were deluged by **COPIOUS** complaints from disgruntled investors.)*

CORDIAL [KOHR jul]
- friendly and gracious
*(Hotel staff always greeted the guests in a most **CORDIAL** manner.)*

CORNUCOPIA [kohr nuh KOH pee uh; kohr nyuh KOH pee uh]
- abundant supply
*(The tropical island featured a veritable **CORNUCOPIA** of fruits and vegetables.)*

CORPOREAL [kohr POHR ee ul]
- physical/material
*(Flesh and bones comprise our **CORPOREAL** being.)*

CORPULENT [KOHR pyuh lunt]
  - fat/overweight
  (The CORPULENT man had difficult purchasing well-fitting clothes.)

CORRELATE [KOHR uh layt]
  - relate together
  (Jurors had difficulty CORRELATING the witnesses' vastly differing accounts of the incident.)

CORROBORATE [kuh RAHB uh rayt]
  - confirm
  (Patrons of the bar CORROBORATED the man's alibi regarding his whereabouts during the period of the crime.)

CORRUPT [kuh RUPT]
  - dishonest/immoral
  (The socialist government was accused of being run by CORRUPT officials.)

COTERIE [KOH tuh ree]
  - close/intimate association
  (A COTERIE of stock analysts gathered every Friday to discuss the week's business events.)

COUNTENANCE [KOUN tuh nuns]
  - expression/look
  (The bearded man projected a kindly COUNTENANCE.)

COUNTENANCE [KOUN tuh nuns]
  - tolerate/approve
  (The movie director would not COUNTENANCE tardiness by any member of his crew.)

COUNTERMAND [koun tur MAND]
  - revoke/cancel
  (An executive directive to retreat COUNTERMANDED all previous orders.)

COVENANT [KUV uh nunt]
  - solemn agreement/pact
  (Members of the cabal agreed under COVENANT not to disclose the identity of the faction's headquarters even if threatened by death.)

COVERT [KOH vurt; koh VURT]
  - secret
  (Espionage is often conducted under COVERT, cloak-and-dagger conditions.)

COVET [KUV it]
  - jealously desire
  (The malcontent COVETED his brother's executive position.)

COY [koi]
  - artfully shy
  (With her COY wiles, the vixen had the sailors baying at her every whim.)

CRASS [kras]
- crude and insensitive
*(The boorish man's **CRASS** behavior offended the aristocratic couple.)*

CRAVEN [KRAY vun]
- cowardly
*(The **CRAVEN** man deserted his battalion while in the midst of combat.)*

CREDENCE [KREED ins]
- belief
*(Most scientists lend no **CREDENCE** to tales of alien abduction.)*

CREDIBLE [KRED uh bul]
- believable
*(The newspaper article endeavored to present a **CREDIBLE** explanation for the unusual disappearance of ships in the Bermuda Triangle.)*

CREDULOUS [KREJ uh lus]
- gullible
*(**CREDULOUS** followers truly believed that alchemists could turn lead into gold.)*

CRYPTIC [KRIP tik]
- mysteriously baffling
*(Only those closest to the case could decode the **CRYPTIC** message left behind.)*

CULINARY [KYOO luh ner ee; KUL uh ner ee]
- cooking
*(Chefs prepared a **CULINARY** feast for the visiting dignitaries.)*

CULL [kul]
- gather and select
*(Tabloid reporters often **CULL** from a speech only those words that can be construed in a controversial manner.)*

CULMINATE [KUL muh nayt]
- climax/conclude
*(Scoring his final touchdown at age forty **CULMINATED** an already stellar football career.)*

CULPABLE [KUL puh bul]
- guilty
*(The court's ruling found the captain **CULPABLE** of negligence in the devastating oil spill.)*

CULPRIT [KUL prit]
- lawbreaker
*(Witnesses identified the bearded man as the **CULPRIT** who committed the robbery.)*

CUMBERSOME [KUM bur sum]
- heavy and bulky
*(Moving the **CUMBERSOME** old cabinet proved quite a challenge.)*

CUMULATIVE [KYOO myuh luh tiv]
- collective/accumulating
(Emphysema can result from the CUMULATIVE effects of smoking over the period of a lifetime.)

CUPIDITY [kyoo PID i tee]
- greed
(To satiate his CUPIDITY, the king levied an additional tax on his already-overburdened subjects.)

CURSORY [KUR suh ree]
- hasty and superficial
(Once the letter was typed up, the secretary gave it a CURSORY review for any obvious errors.)

CURTAIL [kur TAYL]
- shorten
(Rain showers CURTAILED the outdoor festivities.)

DAUNTLESS [DAHNT lis]
- fearless
(During the Civil War, the DAUNTLESS Confederates fought against an unending stream of opposition.)

DEARTH [durth]
- scarcity
(Over the years, the DEARTH of rainfall turned the once-thriving savanna into a barren wasteland.)

DEBACLE [di BAH kul; day BAH kul]
- catastrophe/collapse
(Thousands of people lost their life's savings during the 1929 stock market DEBACLE.)

DEBASE [di BAYS]
- cheapen/degrade
(Impurities in gold DEBASE its value.)

DEBAUCH [di BAHCH]
- corrupt
(DEBAUCHED by the tempting island lifestyle, the vacationer found it difficult to return to his mundane routine as husband and father.)

DEBILITATE [di BIL i tayt]
- weaken
(The lengthy illness greatly DEBILITATED the elderly patient.)

DEBONAIR [deb uh NAYR]
- gracefully charming
(All the women at the ball were enchanted by the DEBONAIR gentleman.)

DEBUNK [di BUNGK]
- expose as false
(The television exposé sought to DEBUNK magicians' claims that a table can be made to magically rise off the floor.)

DECAMP [di KAMP]
- leave suddenly ("split")
*(The suspect **DECAMPED** through the back door just as the authorities arrived at his house.)*

DECIMATE [DES uh mayt]
- destroy a large portion of
*(As a result of human incursion, the population of the Tasmanian wolf was **DECIMATED** to the point of extinction.)*

DECOROUS [DEK ur us; di KOHR us]
- proper
*(Guests displayed **DECOROUS** conduct during the formal celebrity dinner.)*

DECREPIT [di KREP it]
- aged and run-down
*(A bulldozer was brought in to raze the **DECREPIT** building.)*

DECRY [di KRIE]
- criticize/denounce
*(Many environmentalists **DECRY** man's insensitivity toward protection of the rain forest.)*

DEFAMATORY [di FAM uh tohr ee]
- slanderous
*(The candidate inveighed against the **DEFAMATORY** comments levied upon him by his opponent.)*

DEFAME [di FAYM]
- belittle the reputation of
*(The war veteran asserted that he was **DEFAMED** when unjustly called a Nazi sympathizer.)*

DEFER [di FUR]
- postpone
*(The committee voted to **DEFER** its final decision until after both sides had presented their cases.)*

DEFERENCE [DEF uh runs]
- respect
*(Out of **DEFERENCE** to the elder statesman's senior position, the junior senator allowed the more experienced one to present his views first.)*

DEFILE [di FIEL]
- dishonor
*(In the lawsuit, the actor claimed that malicious reporting had **DEFILED** his good name.)*

DEFINITIVE [di FIN i tiv]
- reliable and complete
*(In the library display window lay the **DEFINITIVE** book on the Roman Empire.)*

DEFT [deft]
- skillfully capable
*(The young girl embroidered the dress with the **DEFT** precision of a master seamstress.)*

DEFUNCT [di FUNGKT]
- dead/no longer functioning
*(Many companies that are now **DEFUNCT** were, in their time, industry leaders.)*

DEFY [di FIE]
- challenge/resist
*(The insubordinate sailor **DEFIED** the captain's orders.)*

DEIFY [DEE uh fie]
- adore/worship
*(A devoted legion of fans **DEIFIED** the rock star.)*

DEIGN [dayn]
- stoop
*(The aloof supervisor would not **DEIGN** to converse casually with her underlings.)*

DÉJÀ VU [day zhah VOO; day zhah VYOO]
- something familiar
*(The confrontation on the gridiron with his old nemesis seemed like a case of **DÉJÀ VU**.)*

DELECTABLE [di LEK tuh bul]
- delicious
*(The **DELECTABLE** Hawaiian feast was fit for a king.)*

DELEGATE [DEL uh gayt]
- assign
*(To more quickly finish cleaning the house, a specific task was **DELEGATED** to each of the children.)*

DELETERIOUS [del i TEER ee us]
- harmful
*(Alcohol can be **DELETERIOUS** to one's memory as well as one's health.)*

DELIBERATE [di LIB ur it]
- intentional
*(The little rascal's misbehavior was a **DELIBERATE** attempt to anger and frustrate his babysitter.)*

DELIBERATE [di LIB ur it]
- slow and careful
*(Visitors proceeded in a **DELIBERATE** manner down the rickety staircase.)*

DELINEATE [di LIN ee ayt]
- portray/depict
*(In most cowboy movies, the good and bad guys are clearly **DELINEATED**.)*

DELIVERANCE [di LIV uh runs]
- liberation
*(The desperate farmers prayed for **DELIVERANCE** from the year-long drought.)*

DELUGE [DEL yooj]
- flood
*(The week-long **DELUGE** caused total ruination of the region's harvest.)*

DELUSION [di LOO zhun]
- false belief
*(Many schizophrenics suffer from **DELUSIONS** of grandeur.)*

DEMAGOGUE [DEM uh gahg]
- power-seeking leader
*(Speeches by the political **DEMAGOGUE** stirred up the passion of revolt in his young and malleable audience.)*

DEMEAN [di MEEN]
- degrade/disgrace
*(The proud lady refused to **DEMEAN** herself by scrubbing the kitchen floor.)*

DEMEANOR [di MEE nur]
- manner/behavior
*(The man's humble and unobtrusive **DEMEANOR** endeared him to strangers.)*

DEMISE [di MIEZ]
- death
*(Fans were shocked at the young singer's untimely **DEMISE**.)*

DEMISE [di MIEZ]
- termination/end
*(Social and political corruption led to the ancient Roman civilization's **DEMISE**.)*

DEMOTE [di MOHT]
- lower in rank
*(As a result of spotty attendance, the club member was **DEMOTED** from secretary to assistant treasurer.)*

DEMUR [di MUR]
- object
*(Poolside bathers **DEMURRED** at the children's boisterous horseplay.)*

DEMURE [di MYOOR]
- shy and modest
*(The **DEMURE** young lass caught the fancy of the older boys.)*

DENIGRATE [DEN uh grayt]
- defame/belittle
*(In an interview prior to the arrival of the home team, the visiting coach callously **DENIGRATED** their talent and leadership.)*

DENIZEN [DEN i zun]
- inhabitant
*(The Loch Ness monster has long been reported to be an actual surviving **DENIZEN** of the deep.)*

DENOUNCE [di NOUNS]
- publicly condemn
*(In the 1960s, draft dodgers were often **DENOUNCED** as traitors.)*

DENSE [dens]
- thick/crowded
*(A **DENSE** fog slowed the flow of traffic on the freeway.)*

DEPLETE [di PLEET]
- use up
*(After a week on the island, the castaways had **DEPLETED** their food supplies.)*

DEPLORE [di PLOHR]
- disapprove of
*(Pacifists **DEPLORE** the use of violence to settle disputes.)*

DEPLORE [di PLOHR]
- regret deeply
*(Firing his trustworthy servant to conserve money was a decision he both dreaded and **DEPLORED**.)*

DEPRAVED [di PRAYVD]
- morally corrupt
*(The **DEPRAVED** man derived pleasure from showing the neighborhood children lewd and suggestive films.)*

DEPRECATORY [DEP ruh kuh tohr ee]
- disapproving
*(The mayor's unfavorable decision to support a ban on fireworks prompted hundreds of **DEPRECATORY** telephone calls to his office.)*

DEPRECATORY [DEP ruh kuh tohr ee]
- apologetic
*(Having missed the scheduled appointment due to car trouble, the college applicant felt obliged to write a **DEPRECATORY** letter to the admissions counselor.)*

DERELICT [DAYR uh likt]
- negligent
*(Several guards were found to have been **DERELICT** in their duties on the evening the prisoner escaped.)*

DERELICT [DAYR uh likt]
- abandoned
*(A tow truck was brought in to remove the **DERELICT** vehicles parked on the street.)*

DERIDE [di RIED]
- ridicule scornfully
*(Critics **DERIDED** the negotiator's halfhearted efforts to resolve the bitter dispute.)*

DERISIVE [di RIE siv]
- scornfully ridiculing
*(For dropping the potentially game-winning touchdown pass, the player was the target of **DERISIVE** commentary by the press.)*

DEROGATORY [di RAHG uh tohr ee]
- insulting and belittling
*(In a show of poor sportsmanship, the losing team captain interjected a **DEROGATORY** remark regarding his counterpart's integrity.)*

DESCRY [di SKRIE]
- notice
*(After a lengthy survey of the picnic area, the young man finally **DESCRIED** his girlfriend sitting on a park bench.)*

DESECRATE [DES uh krayt]
- dishonor
*(Vandals **DESCRATED** the war memorial plaque by painting a swastika on it.)*

DESICCATE [DES uh kayt]
- dry up
*(**DESICCATED** apricots are a delicious snack food.)*

DESOLATE [DES uh lit]
- lonely
*(In her later years, the opera star led a reclusive and **DESOLATE** existence far from the spotlight of adulation.)*

DESOLATE [DES uh lit]
- deserted
*(Campers came upon a **DESOLATE** ghost town once heavily populated by gold miners and their families.)*

DESPICABLE [DES pi kuh bul; di SPIK uh bul]
- disgraceful/abominable
*(Deserting one's friend in his hour of need is a **DESPICABLE** and selfish act of insensitivity and cowardice.)*

DESPISE [di SPIEZ]
- dislike scornfully
*(The two veteran rivals **DESPISED** one another on and off the football field.)*

DESPOIL [di SPOIL]
- plunder/rob
*(The invading army **DESPOILED** the captured city, driving off in fancy cars filled with gold and silver.)*

DESPOT [DES put; DES paht]
- tyrant
*(The cruel **DESPOT** summarily executed those who defied his authority.)*

DESTITUTE [DES ti toot; DES ti tyoot]
- penniless
(The widespread apartment blaze left several families homeless and DESTITUTE.)

DESUETUDE [DES wi tood; DES wi tyood]
- disuse
(Many popular expressions soon fall into DESUETUDE and are quickly replaced by more-contemporary ones.)

DESULTORY [DES ul tohr ee]
- random/aimless
(The teenager's DESULTORY telephone conversation lasted for two hours.)

DETER [di TUR]
- prevent/discourage
(Not even the earthquake's aftershocks could DETER the rescuers' efforts to locate survivors.)

DETERIORATE [di TEER ee uh rayt]
- worsen
(Through years of neglect, the condition of the house DETERIORATED to such an extent that it was condemned by the State.)

DETEST [di TEST]
- hate
(Many students DETEST final exams week.)

DETRIMENT [DEH truh munt]
- danger
(Having committed several serious crimes, the man was deemed a DETRIMENT to society and sentenced to prison.)

DEVASTATE [DEV uh stayt]
- destroy ("lay waste to")
(Vast tracts of forest were DEVASTATED by the extensive fire.)

DEVIOUS [DEE vee us]
- deceitful
(While the customer was not looking, the DEVIOUS salesman raised the price on the sale item.)

DEVOID [di VOID]
- totally lacking
(The threadbare plot was DEVOID of novelty or originality.)

DEVOUT [di VOUT]
- deeply devoted
(The entire family, including in-laws, were DEVOUT Christians.)

DEXTERITY [dek STER i tee]
- manual skillfulness
(A juggler must possess coordination and DEXTERITY.)

DIABOLIC [die uh BAHL ik] (also, **DIABOLICAL**)
- devilish/evil
*(In the spy novel, the mad scientist hatched a **DIABOLIC** scheme to rule the world.)*

DIAPHONOUS [die AF uh nus]
- sheer/transparent
*(The **DIAPHANOUS** gown was made from silk and lace.)*

DIATRIBE [DIE uh trieb]
- bitter/angry denunciation
*(A spokesman for the embittered opposition launched a lengthy **DIATRIBE** against the government for increasing taxes to purportedly whitewash years of rampant spending.)*

DICHOTOMY [die KAHT uh mee]
- division
*(A distinct **DICHOTOMY** separates vertebrates from invertebrates.)*

DICTATORIAL [dik tuh TOHR ee ul]
- domineering/authoritative
*(Fidel Castro enjoyed **DICTATORIAL** control over Cuba during his long reign as President.)*

DIDACTIC [die DAK tik]
- informational
*(Both **DIDACTIC** and entertaining, the lesson inspired students to become more politically involved.)*

DIFFIDENT [DIF i dunt]
- lacking confidence
*(Unable to muster enough courage to ask her boyfriend to the dance, the **DIFFIDENT** adolescent anxiously awaited a phone call from him instead.)*

DIFFUSE [di FYOOS]
- scattered
*(Rather than densely concentrated, the atom's molecules were uncharacteristically **DIFFUSE**.)*

DIFFUSE [di FYOOS]
- wordy
*(The young writer's agent recommended that her characterizations be less **DIFFUSE** and instead more succinctly delineated.)*

DIGRESS [di GRES; die GRES]
- stray
*(**DIGRESSING** from his speech, the guest of honor recalled an amusing incident that had occurred earlier in the day.)*

DILATE [die LAYT]
- expand/widen
*(Lungs **DILATE** during inhalation.)*

DILATORY [DIL uh tohr ee]
- delaying/stalling
*(She was habitually **DILATORY** in sending out her Christmas cards.)*

DILEMMA [di LEM uh]
- difficult situation
*(Faced with mounting medical bills, the couple was faced with the **DILEMMA** of either selling their stocks at a loss or taking out a third mortgage.)*

DILIGENT [DIL i junt]
- persistently hardworking
*(The **DILIGENT** student always submitted his homework on time.)*

DIMINUTIVE [di MIN yuh tiv]
- tiny
*(Children and adults alike were fascinated by the **DIMINUTIVE** horses featured at the carnival.)*

DIN [din]
- loud/confused noise
*(In the cafeteria's dishwashing room, one could hear the **DIN** of pots, pans and dishes clattering.)*

DIRE [dier]
- desperately urgent
*(After three days stranded on the deserted island, the shipwreck survivors found themselves in **DIRE** need of food and water.)*

DIRE [dier]
- disastrous
*(Stealing the sacred talisman led to **DIRE** consequences for the avaricious explorer.)*

DIRECTIVE [di REK tiv; die REK tiv]
- authoritative order
*(The captain issued a **DIRECTIVE** for all crewmen to return immediately to the ship.)*

DISABUSE [dis uh BYOOZ]
- enlighten ("set straight")
*(It is important that young athletes be **DISABUSED** of the notion that all professional sports figures are millionaires.)*

DISAFFECTED [dis uh FEK tid]
- rebelliously discontent
*(The **DISAFFECTED** workers sought union representation.)*

DISAVOW [dis uh VOU]
- disclaim knowledge of/deny responsibility for
*(When asked if he had authorized the break-in of the Watergate offices, President Nixon initially **DISAVOWED** any involvement in the crime.)*

DISCERN [di SURN]
- distinguish/perceive
*(Without his glasses, he could not **DISCERN** whether the flight number was 65 or 85.)*

DISCIPLE [di SIE pul]
- pupil/follower
*(Preaching to his **DISCIPLES**, the priest cautioned against succumbing to the temptations of evil.)*

DISCLOSE [di SKLOHZ]
- reveal
*(Two days after the winning lottery number was announced, the local newspaper **DISCLOSED** the names of the winners.)*

DISCOMFIT [dis KUM fit]
- disconcert and unnerve ("rattle")
*(Constant hostile outbursts from the audience **DISCOMFITED** the comedian.)*

DISCONCERT [dis kun SURT]
- disturb and fluster
*(When the sound system unexpectedly failed, the band was noticeably **DISCONCERTED**.)*

DISCONSOLATE [dis KAHN suh lit]
- depressed/dejected
*(After being turned down for a promotion he had counted on for months, the man became **DISCONSOLATE**.)*

DISCORD [DIS kohrd]
- disagreement/friction
*(Constant bickering fostered **DISCORD** amongst the committee members.)*

DISCOURSE [DIS kohrs]
- conversation/discussion
*(While playing cards, the women engaged in pleasant **DISCOURSE**.)*

DISCREET [di SKREET]
- sensitively/thoughtfully careful
*(To avoid embarrassment to her close friend, she alluded to the outstanding debt in a tactful and **DISCREET** manner.)*

DISCRETE [di SKREET]
- distinct/separate
*(The chemical compound consisted of three **DISCRETE** elements.)*

DISCRETION [di SKRESH un]
- individual choice
*(The decision regarding which cereal to buy was left to the **DISCRETION** of her two children.)*

DISCURSIVE [di SKUR siv]
- rambling
*(The actor's **DISCURSIVE** speech at the awards ceremony was agonizingly painful to endure.)*

DISDAIN [dis DAYN]
- look down scornfully upon
(The highly successful businesswoman DISDAINED those who were too lazy to work for a living.)

DISGRUNTLED [dis GRUN tuld]
- discontented
(Police charged a DISGRUNTLED former employee with two counts of arson.)

DISHEVELED [di SHEV ld]
- messy/disorderly
(It is unwise to come to work appearing slovenly and DISHEVELED.)

DISINGENUOUS [dis in JEN yoo us]
- dishonest and insincere/calculating
(It seemed obvious to all that the DISINGENUOUS beggar's request for a financial handout was a mere ruse to support his dependency on alcohol.)

DISINTERESTED [dis IN tuh res tid]
- impartial
(A DISINTERESTED party was brought in to help negotiate a fair and equitable compromise.)

DISMAY [dis MAY]
- alarm
(The captain's urgent announcement to securely fasten seat belts DISMAYED the nervous passengers.)

DISPARAGE [di SPAYR ij]
- belittle
(After the team's loss in the playoffs, the press DISPARAGED the manager and his staff, calling them "amateurs.")

DISPARATE [DIS pur it; di SPAYR it]
- different/distinct
(In the two reports, the committee discovered DISPARATE findings regarding areas in need of improvement.)

DISPASSIONATE [dis PASH uh nit]
- impartial and unemotional
(The radio news reporter provided a DISPASSIONATE minute-by-minute account of the highly-publicized execution.)

DISPEL [di SPEL]
- scatter/drive away
(Words of motherly comfort helped DISPEL the child's fear of getting a haircut.)

DISPENSE [di SPENS]
- distribute
(Upon their arrival, the medical supplies were DISPENSED to eagerly-awaiting doctors.)

DISPERSE [di SPURS]
 - scatter and spread
 *(The spilled chemicals quickly **DISPERSED** throughout the lake.)*

DISPORT [di SPOHRT]
 - entertain with amusement
 *(The group of youths **DISPORTED** themselves with a game of miniature golf.)*

DISPUTATIOUS [dis pyoo TAY shus]
 - argumentative
 *(The **DISPUTATIOUS** couple could not even reach a consensus as to where to eat out.)*

DISQUIETUDE [dis KWIE i tood; dis KWIE i tyood]
 - nervous restlessness
 *(Informed that a bear had been spotted in the vicinity, the campers spent the evening in mute **DISQUIETUDE**.)*

DISREPUTABLE [dis REP yuh tuh bul]
 - shameful/dishonorable
 *(The **DISREPUTABLE** gang of hooligans were derided for their acts of thievery and drug-dealing.)*

DISSECT [di SEKT; die SEKT]
 - analyze (piece by piece)
 *(To pinpoint possible contradictions, analysts **DISSECTED** the President's speech on foreign affairs.)*

DISSEMBLE [di SEM bul]
 - mask
 *(The thunderstruck father **DISSEMBLED** his anger and disappointment when told that his daughter had eloped by offering a toast to the couple's happiness.)*

DISSEMINATE [di SEM uh nayt]
 - circulate
 *(Information regarding the dangers of nuclear waste was **DISSEMINATED** throughout the community.)*

DISSENT [di SENT]
 - disagree
 *(Although four councilmen favored the proposal, a majority **DISSENTED**.)*

DISSIMULATE [di SIM yuh layt]
 - mask
 *(Praising the current leader in a show of loyalty **DISSIMULATED** the corporal's true desire to become the next commander.)*

DISSIPATE [DIS uh payt]
 - break up and scatter
 *(The clouds **DISSIPATED** as the day turned sunny.)*

DISSOLUTE [DIS uh loot]
 - morally unrestrained/corrupt
 *(The oil magnate's wayward son led a **DISSOLUTE** life as playboy and debaucher.)*

DISSONANT [DIS uh nunt]
- clashing
*(The television show's panelists were renowned for their **DISSONANT** viewpoints on most political issues.)*

DISSUADE [di SWAYD]
- persuade against
*(Despite his best effort, he could not **DISSUADE** his friend from entering the dark and forbidding cave.)*

DISTEND [di STEND]
- swell
*(Recent television ads seeking contributions to help the poor in Third World countries have shown children with stomachs **DISTENDED** as a result of severe malnutrition.)*

DISTORT [di STOHRT]
- misrepresent
*(It is not good policy for a reporter to **DISTORT** the truth to make his article more sensational.)*

DISTORT [di STOHRT]
- twist out of shape
*(Facial features were **DISTORTED** in the surrealistic painting, producing a macabre effect.)*

DISTRAIT [di STRAYT]
- absent-mindedly preoccupied
*(At work, the **DISTRAIT** dentist could not keep his mind off his pregnant wife, whom he knew might give birth at any moment.)*

DISTRAUGHT [di STRAHT]
- frantically confused/distressed
*(**DISTRAUGHT** over the disappearance of her child, the woman had to be sedated by medical personnel.)*

DIURNAL [die UR nul]
- daytime
*(Bats are nocturnal creatures; humans are generally **DIURNAL** ones.)*

DIVERGE [di VURJ; die VURJ]
- branch
*(The stream **DIVERGED** into two rivulets, each heading in a distinctly different direction.)*

DIVERSE [di VURS; die VURS]
- varied
*(A **DIVERSE** crowd attended the gala celebration.)*

DIVERSION [di VUR zhun; die VUR zhun]
- pastime/recreation
*(Fishing had long been the doctor's weekend **DIVERSION**.)*

DIVERSITY [di VUR suh tee; die VUR suh tee]
- variety
*(Most universities offer students a **DIVERSITY** of undergraduate courses from which to choose.)*

DIVERT [di VURT; die VURT]
- sidetrack
*(A loud noise outside momentarily **DIVERTED** the housekeeper's attention from her activities.)*

DIVERT [di VURT; die VURT]
- amuse/entertain
*(At the birthday party, a professional clown **DIVERTED** the young children.)*

DIVISIVE [di VIE siv]
- creating discord/disunity
*(A **DIVISIVE** quarrel led to the band's breakup.)*

DIVULGE [di VULJ; die VULJ]
- disclose
*(Despite pressure from the police, the reporter refused to **DIVULGE** the source of his confidential information.)*

DOCILE [DAHS ul]
- manageably obedient
*(Children could pet the **DOCILE** horse without fear of being bitten or attacked.)*

DOCTRINAIRE [dahk truh NAYR]
- inflexibly dogmatic
*(Rather than seek to resolve the problem with a pragmatic approach, the school administrator adhered to his ineffectual **DOCTRINAIRE** ideologies.)*

DOGGED [DAH gid]
- stubbornly persistent
*(With **DOGGED** determination, she completed the arduous task in only one day.)*

DOGMATIC [dahg MAT ik]
- opinionated
*(Copernicus met with much resistance from the **DOGMATIC** society of his day when he proposed that the Earth revolved around the Sun.)*

DOLE [dohl]
- distribute ("hand out")
*(At the shopping mall, Santa Claus **DOLED** out candy to each visiting child.)*

DOLEFUL [DOHL ful]
- mournfully sad
*(A funeral is a **DOLEFUL** affair.)*

DOLOROUS [DOH lur us; DAHL ur us]
- sorrowful/mournful
*(The untimely death of the President marked a truly **DOLOROUS** day for the nation.)*

DOMINEERING [dahm uh NEE ring]
- oppressively controlling
*(Her **DOMINEERING** husband restricted her from seeing old friends.)*

DORMANT [DOHR munt]
- inactive
*(Prior to the sudden and violent eruption, the volcano had been **DORMANT** for many years.)*

DOUBLE ENTENDRE [DUB ul ahn TAHN druh; DUB ul ah TAHND]
- word/expression with two interpretations
*(In comedies, the expression "going to bed" is often intended as a **DOUBLE ENTENDRE**.)*

DOUGHTY [DOU tee]
- fearless and determined
*(The **DOUGHTY** diminutive David challenged the mighty Goliath.)*

DOUR [DOU ur]
- gloomy and ill-humored
*(After his favorite hockey team was eliminated in the playoffs, the man was in a particularly **DOUR** mood.)*

DOUR [DOU ur]
- stern and uninviting
*(The professor's **DOUR** expression left little doubt that he was not the sociable type.)*

DRACONIAN [druh KOH nee un; dray KOH nee un]
- harsh and cruel
*(The **DRACONIAN** leader brooked no dissension, dispatching offenders with a swift and merciless public execution.)*

DREAD [dred]
- fear
*(Everyone on the team **DREADED** the day the list of those cut from the squad would be posted.)*

DROLL [drohl]
- oddly amusing
*(Comedian Steven Wright's offbeat perspective adds to his **DROLL** sense of humor.)*

DUBIOUS [DOO bee us]
- skeptical
*(Schoolmates were **DUBIOUS** about the lad's claim to having appeared in a nationally-televised commercial.)*

DUBIOUS [DOO bee us]
- doubtful/questionable
*(The authenticity of the newly-discovered Rembrandt painting was highly **DUBIOUS**.)*

DUCTILE [DUK tul]
- flexible/shapeable
*(Aluminum is a **DUCTILE** metallic element often used as an electrical or thermal conductor.)*

DUCTILE [DUK tul]
- easily influenced
*(The demagogue sought to sway the **DUCTILE** masses to violence and revolt.)*

DUDGEON [DUJ un]
- resentful anger
*(Being overruled by his aide in front of the other national leaders left the President in high **DUDGEON**.)*

DULCET [DUL sit]
- melodious/sweet-sounding
*(The auditorium was filled with the harp's **DULCET** mellifluence.)*

DUMBFOUND [dum FOUND]
- stun/astonish
*(David Blaine's seemingly magical powers **DUMBFOUNDED** bystanders.)*

DUPE [doop]
- trick/deceive
*(Several unsuspecting victims were **DUPED** into purchasing outdated lottery tickets.)*

DUPLICITY [doo PLIS i tee; dyoo PLIS i tee]
- deceitfulness
*(Although he thought the bar hostess really loved him, the young romantic was in fact merely another victim of the temptress's **DUPLICITY**.)*

DURABLE [DOOR uh bul]
- sturdy and resistant
*(The **DURABLE** building material was both fireproof and water-resistant.)*

DURESS [doo RES]
- threatening pressure
*(His attorney claimed he had confessed under **DURESS** and not of his own volition.)*

DURESS [doo RES]
- forced restraint
*(The suspect was held under **DURESS** until the police arrived.)*

DYNAMIC [die NAM ik]
- forceful and energetic
*(The **DYNAMIC** and financially-successful speaker motivated audiences wherever he traveled.)*

EARNEST [UR nist]
- sincere and heartfelt
*(The defendant's **EARNEST** appeal for clemency drew compassion from the judge.)*

EARNEST [UR nist]
- serious and intense
*(The science fair participants were **EARNEST** and industrious students.)*

EBB [eb]
- decline/recede
*(Once the soccer star turned forty, his future prospects quickly began to **EBB**.)*

EBULLIENT [i BUL yunt]
- lively and enthusiastic
*(Pollyanna was an **EBULLIENT** lass with irrepressible optimism.)*

ECCENTRIC [ik SEN trik; ek SEN trik]
- odd
*(Only his closest friends knew the real reason for the man's **ECCENTRIC** behavior.)*

ÉCLAT [ay KLAH]
- brilliance of display
*(The acrobat performed the daring feat with dazzling **ÉCLAT** and amazing ease.)*

ECLECTIC [i KLEK tik]
- diverse
*(An **ECLECTIC** array of musical pieces was played during the evening concert.)*

ECSTATIC [ek STAT ik]
- extremely joyful
*(When told by the doctor that she had given birth to healthy twins, the new mother was **ECSTATIC**.)*

ECUMENICAL [ek yoo MEN i kul]
- universal
*(The **ECUMENICAL** society, with members in over forty different countries worldwide, strived to promote international religious harmony.)*

EDIFY [ED uh fie]
- instruct/enlighten
*(A selected parable helped **EDIFY** the class to the moral righteousness of being true to oneself.)*

EDUCE [i DOOS]
- elicit
*(The provocative presentation **EDUCED** a surprising number of questions from the young audience.)*

EFFACE [i FAYS]
- erase/rub out
*(The rising tide **EFFACED** all the footprints on the shoreline.)*

EFFECTUATE [i FEK choo ayt]
- accomplish
*(Marathon negotiations **EFFECTUATED** a new and lasting peace agreement between the neighboring countries.)*

EFFERVESCENT [e fur VES unt]
- bubbly
(Champagne is an EFFERVESCENT beverage.)

EFFERVESCENT [e fur VES unt]
- lively/exhilarated
(Nothing could dampen the enthusiasm of the EFFERVESCENT tot.)

EFFETE [i FEET; e FEET]
- weak and decaying
(In its final century, the Roman civilization had grown EFFETE through political malfeasance and corruption.)

EFFETE [i FEET; e FEET]
- sterile and unproductive
(Years of constant grazing and trampling had turned the topsoil EFFETE.)

EFFICACIOUS [ef uh KAY shus]
- effective
(Penicillin has proven an EFFICACIOUS antidote for bee stings.)

EFFIGY [EF i jee]
- representation (of a usually-hated person)
(The unpopular ruler was hanged in EFFIGY, but the police removed the dummy before the leader arrived.)

EFFRONTERY [i FRUN tuh ree]
- shameless boldness
(The wayward lad had the EFFRONTERY to blame his parents for his own misdeeds.)

EFFULGENCE [i FUL juns]
- brilliance
(To the lovestruck teenage boy, the blonde-haired beauty was the embodiment of an angel as she passed by in her radiant EFFULGENCE.)

EFFUSIVE [i FYOO siv]
- emotionally unrestrained
(Many in the courtroom were taken aback by the defendant's EFFUSIVE apology to his victim.)

EGREGIOUS [i GREE jus; i GREE jee us]
- flagrant
(Desecrating a tomb is an EGREGIOUS act of disrespect.)

ELAN [ay LAHN]
- vigorous enthusiasm
(The actor portrayed Romeo with such passion and ÉLAN that all the women in the audience wished they were his Juliet.)

ELATED [ee LAY tid]
- joyful
*(Her parents were **ELATED** over the news that the youngster had won the state spelling bee.)*

ELEEMOSYNARY [el uh MAHS uh ner ee; el ee uh MAHS uh ner ee]
- charitable
*(The **ELEEMOSYNARY** trust was renowned for its support of academic arts through scholarships and grants.)*

ELEGIAC [el uh JIE uk; el uh JIE ak] (also, **ELEGIACAL**)
- expressing sorrow
*(An **ELEGIAC** poem was read to commemorate the anniversary of the tragic event.)*

ELICIT [i LIS it]
- bring forth/draw out
*(Rumors of a sales tax increase **ELICITED** an angry outcry from the community.)*

ELITE [i LEET; ay LEET]
- superior
*(The Navy Seals are an **ELITE** military group.)*

ELOQUENT [EL uh kwunt]
- forceful/persuasive in speech
*(Mark Antony was an **ELOQUENT** Roman statesman who lived during the reign of Julius Caesar.)*

ELUCIDATE [i LOO si dayt]
- clarify
*(To avoid any erosion of investor confidence, the chairman **ELUCIDATED** the company's growth-oriented goals for the coming year with a series of carefully-constructed charts.)*

ELUDE [i LOOD]
- evade cleverly
*(Hiding in a drainage ditch, the crafty fox **ELUDED** the hungry dogs.)*

ELUSIVE [i LOO siv]
- hard to grasp/catch
*(The only clue the **ELUSIVE** kissing bandit left behind was a purple rose.)*

ELYSIAN [i LIZH un]
- heavenly
*(Adam and Eve resided in an **ELYSIAN** world of purity and innocence.)*

EMACIATED [i MAY shee ay tid]
- very thin and haggard ("physically wasted")
*(After months in concentration camps, many of the **EMACIATED** prisoners were at the brink of starvation.)*

EMANCIPATE [i MAN suh payt]
- free
*(In 1863, Abraham Lincoln issued a decree **EMANCIPATING** all slaves.)*

EMBELLISH [em BEL ish]
- enhance/adorn
(An entire string section was added to EMBELLISH the dramatic musical piece.)

EMBLEMATIC [em bluh MAT ik]
- symbolic
(The Purple Heart is EMBLEMATIC of wartime injury through valor.)

EMBRYONIC [em bree AHN ik]
- early developing
(Plans to visit faraway planets are still in their EMBRYONIC stages.)

EMINENT [EM uh nunt]
- well-known and respected
(Over a dozen EMINENT scientists attended the international symposium.)

EMOLLIENT [i MAHL yunt]
- soothing/softening
(Salve can be applied as an EMOLLIENT cream for sunburns.)

EMPATHY [EM puh thee]
- compassion
(The governor felt EMPATHY for those whose homes had been destroyed in the hurricane.)

EMPHATIC [em FAT ik]
- forceful and definite
(His girlfriend's EMPHATIC refusal to go to the dance with him left him no other alternative but to go alone.)

EMPIRICAL [em PIR i kul]
- experienced/observed firsthand
(Based on EMPIRICAL data, surveyors felt the road needed to be expanded to accommodate the increased traffic flow.)

EMPYREAL [em PUR ee ul] (also, **EMPYREAN**)
- heavenly
(Twentieth century flight has afforded man the opportunity to share the EMPYREAL realm once exclusively the domain of winged creatures.)

EMULATE [EM yuh layt]
- model oneself after
(Many young fans EMULATE their favorite rock stars by dressing and talking in similar fashion.)

ENCAPSULATE [en KAP suh layt]
- condense
(Yearbooks often ENCAPSULATE the past twelve months' most memorable moments.)

ENCOMIUM [en KOH mee um]
- formal praise
(Friends and fellow associates poured forth ENCOMIUMS at the beloved foreman's retirement party.)

ENCROACH [en KROHCH]
- intrude
(Fences were constructed to prevent outsiders from ENCROACHING on the farmer's land.)

ENCUMBER [en KUM bur]
- burden
(During the recession, the retail store found itself ENCUMBERED with mounting debts.)

ENDEAVOR [en DEV ur]
- attempt
(Meteorologists ENDEAVORED to explain the unusual atmospheric conditions.)

ENDEMIC [en DEM ik]
- native (and exclusive to the region)
(The exotic plant was ENDEMIC to the small chain of tropical islands.)

ENDORSE [en DOHRS]
- support actively
(Committee members unanimously ENDORSED the proposal to build a new skateboard park.)

ENERVATE [EN ur vayt]
- exhaust/weaken
(The grueling hike up the steep hill ENERVATED the cadets.)

ENGENDER [en JEN dur]
- create/generate
(Mutual interest in hip-hop music ENGENDERED a camaraderie between the two former rivals.)

ENIGMA [uh NIG muh]
- mystery
(The life of the reclusive actress was a paradoxical ENIGMA that baffled even her most ardent fans.)

ENMITY [EN mi tee]
- hostility
(Over the years, a deep ENMITY had developed between the two rival football coaches.)

ENNUI [ahn WEE; AHN wee]
- listless boredom
(The interminable summer vacation had produced in the children a state of lingering ENNUI.)

ENSUE [en SOO]
- follow
(After the suspects jumped into the getaway car, a high-speed chase ENSUED.)

ENTERPRISING [EN tur prie zing]
- ambitious and energetic
(Early promotions are usually reserved for only the most ENTERPRISING of employees.)

ENTHRALL [en THRAHL]
- captivate and delight
*(The prestidigitator **ENTHRALLED** the audience with his stunning feats of sleight-of-hand magic.)*

ENTICE [en TIES]
- tempt
*(With the video camera focused directly on him, the emboldened lad was **ENTICED** to stick his hand into the lion's cage.)*

ENTREAT [en TREET]
- beg
*(The defense attorney **ENTREATED** the judge to allow her more time to prepare for trial.)*

EPHEMERAL [i FEM ur ul]
- brief/short-lived
*(Youth is an **EPHEMERAL** yet unforgettable period in one's life.)*

EPIPHANY [i PIF uh nee]
- sudden revelation
*(In his hour of deep despair brought on by a life of desultory purposelessness, the lost soul experienced a personally earthshaking **EPIPHANY** that enlightened him to direct his energies toward helping the nation's homeless children.)*

EPITOME [i PIT uh mee]
- ideal embodiment
*(Audie Murphy, the most decorated soldier of World War II, was the **EPITOME** of bravery.)*

EQUABLE [EK wuh bul]
- stable/uniform
*(The tiny nation's **EQUABLE** climate made it a year-round haven for tourists.)*

EQUANIMITY [ee kwuh NIM i tee; ek wuh NIM i tee]
- composure
*(The stewardess maintained her **EQUANIMITY** even as the plane tossed and turned in the storm.)*

EQUILIBRIUM [ee kwuh LIB ree um]
- balance
*(When supply equals demand, there is economic **EQUILIBRIUM**.)*

EQUIPOISE [EK wuh poiz; EE kwuh poiz]
- state of equilibrium
*(It is ecologically unsound to disturb the **EQUIPOISE** in the food chain by causing the extinction of any living species.)*

EQUITABLE [EK wi tuh bul]
- fair
*(All parties felt that the court settlement was both **EQUITABLE** and feasible.)*

EQUIVOCAL [i KWIV uh kul]
- ambiguous
*(When asked by news reporters if war with the neighboring country was inevitable, the diplomat's **EQUIVOCAL** response was that only peace is inevitable.)*

EQUIVOCATE [i KWIV uh kayt]
- evade/hedge ("beat around the bush")
*(Rather than answer to the charges, the suspect **EQUIVOCATED** as he awaited the arrival of his attorney.)*

ERADICATE [i RAD uh kayt]
- eliminate ("wipe out")
*(Medical research has led us closer to **ERADICATING** dreaded diseases such as polio and small pox.)*

ERODE [i ROHD]
- wear away
*(Giant waves generated by the storm severely **ERODED** the island's shoreline.)*

ERRATIC [i RAT ik]
- unusual and unpredictable
*(A local veterinarian was summoned when the zoo's lions began exhibiting **ERRATIC** behavior.)*

ERUDITE [AYR yoo diet]
- extensively knowledgeable
*(The **ERUDITE** political analyst helped explain the historical significance of the referendum.)*

ESCALATE [ES kuh layt]
- increase
*(When oil supplies became abnormally low, wholesale prices quickly **ESCALATED**.)*

ESCHEW [es CHOO]
- avoid
*(While on his diet, he made it a point to **ESCHEW** dairy products.)*

ESCULENT [ES kyuh lunt]
- edible
*(Escargot is a popular **ESCULENT** delicacy.)*

ESOTERIC [es uh TER ik]
- very difficult to comprehend (except by experts in the field)
*(Nietzsche's **ESOTERIC** philosophy questioned contemporary religion and morality.)*

ESOTERIC [es uh TER ik]
- secret/private
*(Only members of the tribe were privy to their **ESOTERIC** rituals.)*

ESPOUSE [e SPOUZ]
- advocate
*(In her lectures, the renowned community leader **ESPOUSED** school and national pride.)*

ESPRIT DE CORPS [e spree duh KOHR]
- solidarity
*(Over time, an **ESPRIT DE CORPS** developed among the recruits.)*

ESPY [e SPIE; i SPIE]
- notice
*(The detective **ESPIED** the suspect lurking in the bushes.)*

ESSAY [e SAY]
- attempt
*(After a tentative pause, the boy **ESSAYED** climbing the rope.)*

ESTRANGE [e STRAYNJ]
- alienate
*(Years of bickering **ESTRANGED** the once-happy couple.)*

ESTRANGE [e STRAYNJ]
- distance
*(The passing of years living abroad **ESTRANGED** him from his hometown companions.)*

ETERNAL [i TUR nul]
- endless/lasting forever
*(Romeo pledged his **ETERNAL** love for Juliet.)*

ETHEREAL [i THEER ee ul]
- heavenly
*(The graceful ballerina radiated an **ETHEREAL** beauty that both enchanted and mesmerized.)*

EULOGIZE [YOO luh jiez]
- praise
*(Former players **EULOGIZED** their coach at a testimonial dinner.)*

EUPHEMISTIC [yoo fuh MIS tik]
- politely restrained
*("Downsizing staff" is a **EUPHEMISTIC** equivalent to "firing employees.")*

EUPHONIOUS [yoo FOH nee us]
- melodious
*(Listeners were enraptured by the **EUPHONIOUS** sounds produced by the trio of harps.)*

EUPHORIA [yoo FOHR ee uh]
- ecstasy
*(Winning the million-dollar lottery left the housewife in a state of shock and **EUPHORIA**.)*

EUPHUISTIC [yoo fyuh WIS tik]
- ornately rhetorical
*(The sonnets of William Shakespeare were the epitome of **EUPHUISTIC** Elizabethan verse.)*

EVADE [i VAYD]
- cleverly avoid
(Hiding inside a garbage can, the refugee managed to EVADE capture by his pursuers.)

EVANESCENT [ev uh NES unt]
- vanishing/fading away
(The shooting star produced an EVANESCENT vaporous trail that resembled a brilliant but fleeting tail.)

EVENTUATE [i VEN choo ayt]
- result
(Weeks of diligent negotiation EVENTUATED in a lasting peace treaty.)

EVINCE [i VINS]
- clearly demonstrate
(After the presentation, one enthusiastic lad EVINCED his deep interest in the subject by heading directly for the library to undertake additional research.)

EVOKE [i VOHK]
- bring out/draw forth
(The anarchist's highly charged rhetoric EVOKED an angry response from the conservative crowd.)

EXACERBATE [ig ZAS ur bayt]
- aggravate
(Bringing up her colleague's frequent tardiness EXACERBATED an already-strained working relationship.)

EXALT [ig ZAHLT]
- glorify
(The sensational young quarterback was EXALTED by fans and fellow players alike.)

EXCORIATE [ek SKOHR ee ayt]
- scold/denounce severely
(The judge EXCORIATED the juror for having discussed the case with a newspaper reporter.)

EXCORIATE [ek SKOHR ee ayt]
- abrade/wear away
(Sliding down the twisted rope EXCORIATED his hand.)

EXCRUCIATING [ik SKROO shee ay ting]
- agonizing
(A migraine headache can cause EXCRUCIATING pain.)

EXCULPATE [EK skul payt; ik SKUL payt]
- clear from blame
(The court EXCULPATED the janitor from the charge of petty theft when another man confessed to the crime.)

EXECRABLE [EK suh kruh bul]
- abominable
(The team was lambasted by the press for their EXECRABLE performance on the field.)

EXEMPLARY [ig ZEM pluh ree]
- worthy of praise
*(The well-behaved lad was given an award for his **EXEMPLARY** class conduct.)*

EXHAUSTIVE [ig ZAHS tiv]
- thorough
*(Rescuers conducted an **EXHAUSTIVE** all-night search for survivors.)*

EXHILARATING [ig ZIL uh ray ting]
- exciting and refreshing
*(Riding on a roller coaster can be an **EXHILARATING** and memorable experience.)*

EXHORT [ig ZOHRT]
- encourage/urge strongly
*(As enemy troops approached, the battalion commander **EXHORTED** his men to hold their ground.)*

EXHORT [ig ZOHRT]
- warn advisingly
*(The preacher **EXHORTED** the congregation to cease their evil and blasphemous ways and begin a new life of righteousness.)*

EXHUME [ig ZOOM]
- dig up
*(To confirm the disputed cause of death, the coroner ordered that the body be **EXHUMED** and an autopsy performed.)*

EXIGENCY [EK si jun see]
- basic/immediate need
*(Lifeboat survivors had to cope with the **EXIGENCIES** of being stranded in the open ocean.)*

EXIGENCY [EK si jun see]
- emergency/crisis
*(Due to mismanagement, the state found itself enmeshed in an inextricable financial **EXIGENCY**.)*

EXIGUOUS [ig ZIG yoo us]
- meager
*(With the threat of war looming near, the tiny nation urgently needed to expand its **EXIGUOUS** army.)*

EXODUS [EK suh dus]
- mass departure
*(The invasion of hostile troops resulted in a sudden **EXODUS** of the native villagers to safer outlying territories.)*

EXONERATE [ig ZAHN uh rayt]
- clear from blame
*(When the true culprit of the crime confessed, the innocent suspect was at last **EXONERATED**.)*

EXORBITANT [ig ZOHR bi tunt]
- excessive
*(Prices in the fancy store were unaffordably **EXORBITANT**.)*

EXORCISE [EK sohr siez]
- expel
*(A priest was summoned to **EXORCISE** the demonic spirits that lived in the haunted house.)*

EXOTIC [ig ZAHT ik; ik ZAHT ik]
- excitingly unusual
*(Botanists were baffled as to the classification of the **EXOTIC** species of plant newly discovered on the remote island.)*

EXPEDIENT [ik SPEE dee unt]
- helpful and advantageous
*(Visual aids proved an **EXPEDIENT** supplement to the lecturer's discussion.)*

EXPEDIENT [ik SPEE dee unt]
- opportunistically self-serving
*(Exploiting children to perform adult tasks is an **EXPEDIENT** way to save money.)*

EXPEDITE [EK spi diet]
- hasten
*(During Christmastime, delivery of packages is **EXPEDITED** to ensure customer satisfaction.)*

EXPEDITIOUS [ek spi DISH us]
- speedy and efficient
*(A crew of workers repaired the downed telephone cable in an **EXPEDITIOUS** manner.)*

EXPEND [ik SPEND]
- use up
*(Having **EXPENDED** their food supplies, the stranded hikers were forced to subsist on insects and berries.)*

EXPENDABLE [ik SPEN duh bul]
- usable/replaceable
*(Money is **EXPENDABLE**; human life is not.)*

EXPIATE [EK spee ayt]
- make amends for
*(The repentant man **EXPIATED** his transgressions through volunteer service to the community.)*

EXPLICIT [ik SPLIS it]
- clear and precise
*(Before the family left on their vacation, the house-sitter was given **EXPLICIT** instructions for the care of the plants and goldfish.)*

EXPONENT [ik SPOH nunt]
- advocate
*(Susan B. Anthony was an early **EXPONENT** of social change.)*

EXPOSTULATE [ik SPAHS chuh layt]
- protest
(Although the committee seemed resolute in their decision, one concerned citizen nevertheless addressed the panel and vehemently EXPOSTULATED against removal of the old banyan tree.)

EXPOUND [ik SPOUND]
- state/explain in detail
(At the symposium, the eminent scientist EXPOUNDED his views regarding the origin of the universe.)

EXPROPRIATE [eks PROH pree ayt]
- confiscate
(The government EXPROPRIATED all property purchased from the proceeds of the felon's illegal activities.)

EXPUNGE [ik SPUNJ]
- delete
(Once the miscreant had successfully completed the rehabilitation program, the charge of vandalism was EXPUNGED from his criminal record.)

EXPURGATE [EK spur gayt]
- remove/delete
(To make the novel suitable for younger audiences, all objectionable language was EXPURGATED and all violent scenes toned down.)

EXQUISITE [ek SKWI zit]
- superb
(The antique watch reflected EXQUISITE detail and workmanship.)

EXTANT [EK stunt]
- still in existence
(The earliest EXTANT tools date as far back as the Paleolithic period.)

EXTENSIVE [ik STEN siv]
- broad/lengthy
(The marine biologist possessed EXTENSIVE knowledge of whales and dolphins.)

EXTENUATING [ik STEN yoo ay ting]
- partially justifiable/excusable
(EXTENUATING circumstances moved the jury to find the defendant guilty of the lesser charge.)

EXTIRPATE [EK stur payt; ik STUR payt]
- uproot and destroy
(When the dictator seized power, his first mission was to EXTIRPATE all opposing political factions.)

EXTOL [ik STOHL]
- praise
(The evangelist EXTOLLED the virtues of chastity and abstinence.)

EXTRANEOUS [ik STRAY nee us]
- irrelevant
*(To keep the news article brief but succinct, **EXTRANEOUS** comments were omitted.)*

EXTRAVAGANT [ik STRAV uh gunt]
- excessive
*(After receiving her payout, the lottery winner immediately began to spend money in an unwise and **EXTRAVAGANT** manner.)*

EXTRICATE [EK struh kayt]
- liberate
*(Firemen were called to **EXTRICATE** trapped passengers from the wreckage.)*

EXTROVERTED [EK stroh vur tid]
- outgoing
*(The popular new student was **EXTROVERTED** and highly personable.)*

EXUBERANT [ig ZOO bur unt]
- joyfully enthusiastic
*(The **EXUBERANT** lad shouted wildly when he saw his visiting uncle descending the airplane.)*

EXUDE [ig ZOOD]
- display/give off
*(His vibrant personality **EXUDED** warmth and charm.)*

EXULT [ig ZULT]
- rejoice
*(Fans **EXULTED** in their team's thrilling come-from-behind victory.)*

FABRICATE [FAB ruh kayt]
- construct
*(The makeshift hut was **FABRICATED** from palm leaves and bamboo.)*

FABRICATE [FAB ruh kayt]
- invent
*(To cover up his misdeed, the boy **FABRICATED** an alibi that he had gone to the movies that afternoon.)*

FAÇADE [fuh SAHD]
- face/front
*(Their new house sported a red brick **FAÇADE** with blue and white trim.)*

FAÇADE [fuh SAHD]
- mask
*(As a show of respect, the runner-up contained her disappointment behind a **FAÇADE** of happiness and joy for the contest winner.)*

FACETIOUS [fuh SEE shus]
- humorous but silly
*(The waggish lad annoyed the substitute teacher with his **FACETIOUS** remarks.)*

FACILITATE [fuh SIL i tayt]
- simplify
(Wheelchair ramps help FACILITATE access into and out of buildings.)

FACTIOUS [FAK shus]
- quarrelsome and divisive
(An arbitrator was called upon to resolve the FACTIOUS dispute between management and the employees' union.)

FACTITIOUS [fak TISH us]
- artificial
(Avaricious salesmen in the fancy boutique rushed to greet each customer with a FACTITIOUS display of unctuous servility.)

FAIL-SAFE [FAYL sayf]
- reliable/foolproof
(To prevent child-tampering, many medicines are housed in FAIL-SAFE unbreakable bottles.)

FALLACIOUS [fuh LAY shus]
- misleading and erroneous
(Rumors often stem from FALLACIOUS speculation.)

FALLOW [FAL oh]
- inactive/uncultivated
(FALLOW land lay adjacent to the active croplands.)

FAMISHED [FAM isht]
- extremely hungry
(After spending two days in the cave without food, the boys were FAMISHED.)

FANCIFUL [FAN si ful]
- creatively imaginary
(Lord of the Rings is a FANCIFUL tale of wizards and dragons.)

FASTIDIOUS [fa STID ee us]
- fussy and demanding
(The FASTIDIOUS headwaiter insisted that utensils be set in a specific arrangement.)

FATHOM [FATH um]
- comprehend
(Few in the audience could FATHOM the philosopher's explanation regarding existential morality.)

FATUOUS [FACH oo us]
- silly and mindless
(The law student's FATUOUS remark exposed his ignorance regarding the workings of the judicial system.)

FAUX PAS [foh PAH]
- social blunder
*(The guest committed a most embarrassing **FAUX PAS** when he addressed the short-haired hostess as "Mr. Smith.")*

FAWN [fahn]
- show servile affection
*(The powerful movie director's toadies **FAWNED** over him in hope that they might be in his next movie.)*

FEARSOME [FEER sum]
- frightening
*(Hydra was a **FEARSOME** beast in Greek legend.)*

FEARSOME [FEER sum]
- fearfully timid
*(The helpless and **FEARSOME** fawn clung to its mother.)*

FEASIBLE [FEE zuh bul]
- possible/conceivable
*(Though obviously embellished, the fisherman's tale was nevertheless somewhat **FEASIBLE**.)*

FEASIBLE [FEE zuh bul]
- reasonable and workable
*(The plan to build a corridor across the two buildings was both **FEASIBLE** and affordable.)*

FECKLESS [FEK lis]
- carelessly irresponsible
*(The **FECKLESS** employee caused more problems than he was worth.)*

FECKLESS [FEK lis]
- hopelessly ineffectual
*(Relations between the two neighboring countries began to deteriorate after two months of **FECKLESS** peace negotiations.)*

FECUND [FEE kund; FEK und]
- fertile
*(From his irrepressibly **FECUND** imagination, Ray Bradbury wrote extensively in the science fiction genre.)*

FEEBLE [FEE bul]
- weak
*(The toll of age had left the once-virile athlete frail and **FEEBLE**.)*

FEEBLE [FEE bul]
- ineffective
*(The court jester made a **FEEBLE** attempt to soothe the emperor's wrath.)*

FEIGN [fayn]
- simulate/pretend
*(An animal may **FEIGN** death to ward off an attack from a belligerent adversary.)*

FELICITOUS [fi LIS i tus]
- joyful/delightful
*(New Year's Eve is a convivial and **FELICITOUS** occasion.)*

FELICITOUS [fi LIS i tus]
- appropriate
*(A few **FELICITOUS** words from the wealthy baron expressed his heartfelt gratitude for the retiring butler's many years of devoted service.)*

FERAL [FEER ul; FER ul]
- wild
*(Wolves are **FERAL** creatures.)*

FERAL [FEER ul; FER ul]
- no longer domesticated
*(Once house pets, many dogs in poor neighborhoods have become **FERAL** and dangerous.)*

FERVENT [FUR vunt]
- passionate
*(The callous judge dismissed the attorney's **FERVENT** plea for leniency for her client.)*

FESTIVE [FES tiv]
- joyous/merry
*(Family reunions are usually **FESTIVE** and memorable events.)*

FETID [FET id]
- smelly/stinking
*(During the month-long garbage strike, a **FETID** odor permeated the city streets.)*

FEY [fay]
- supernaturally magical
*(Elves were known to be **FEY** creatures.)*

FIASCO [fee AS koh]
- disastrous failure
*(The athlete's first acting role turned out to be a **FIASCO** and a box-office bomb.)*

FICKLE [FIK ul]
- inconstant/changeable
*(Fame plays to a **FICKLE** crowd, as many a forgotten star will attest.)*

FIDELITY [fi DEL i tee]
- loyalty
*(Even during times of political instability, the military leader's army maintained unwavering **FIDELITY** to the regime.)*

FINESSE [fi NES]
- delicate skillfulness
*(The stone sculpture reflected the **FINESSE** of a master craftsman.)*

FLACCID [FLAK sid; FLAS id]
- limp and powerless
(Lack of daily exercise had left him with FLACCID muscles.)

FLAG [flag]
- droop
(The once-turgid plant FLAGGED in the intense summer sun.)

FLAG [flag]
- weaken
(After an hour of constant marching in the parade, the drummer's energy began to FLAG.)

FLAGITIOUS [fluh JI shus]
- shamefully wicked
(In some societies, FLAGITIOUS acts of adultery are punishable by death.)

FLAGRANT [FLAY grunt]
- conspicuously bad
(FLAGRANT disregard of the rules was grounds for immediate expulsion from the club.)

FLAMBOYANT [flam BOI unt]
- strikingly flashy/showy
(Liberace was a FLAMBOYANT pianist who entertained the audience with his comic wit and musical genius.)

FLATULENT [FLACH uh lunt]
- pompous and pretentious
(Few believed the weightlifter's FLATULENT claim that he was being considered for the upcoming Olympic games.)

FLAUNT [flahnt]
- show off/parade
(The vain socialite FLAUNTED her gold rings and fancy jewelry at the gala event.)

FLEET [fleet]
- swift
(Mountain goats are FLEET animals that can leap from ledge to ledge with the greatest of ease.)

FLEETING [FLEE ting]
- passing swiftly
(The crowd caught a FLEETING glimpse of the glamorous singer as she drove by in her motorcade.)

FLIPPANT [FLIP unt]
- disrespectfully silly
(The principal did not appreciate the lad's FLIPPANT commentary.)

FLORID [FLOHR id]
- excessively decorative/embellished
(In his poetry, William Wordsworth provided us with a FLORID description of the English countryside.)

FLOURISH [FLUR ish]
- blossom and prosper
*(Vegetation **FLOURISHES** in the rain forest.)*

FLOUT [flout]
- scoff at and disregard
*(The headstrong child **FLOUTED** his parents' wishes to be home by eight o'clock.)*

FOE [foh]
- opponent/enemy
*(The top two teams' star quarterbacks were friends during the off-season but **FOES** on the gridiron.)*

FOIBLE [FOI bul]
- shortcoming/weakness
*(Vanity is one of man's many **FOIBLES**.)*

FOIL [foil]
- prevent from succeeding
*(A newly-installed alarm system **FOILED** the attempted break-in.)*

FOLIAGE [FOH lee ij]
- leaves
*(In the spring, the orchard was alive with the trees' ripe fruit and lush **FOLIAGE**.)*

FOMENT [foh MENT]
- provoke
*(Unhappy with university policy, the disgruntled professor sought to **FOMENT** insurgence within the academic ranks.)*

FORAY [FOHR ay]
- quick/sudden raid
*(To enhance its own wealth, the truculent tribe conducted periodic **FORAYS** on its weaker neighbors.)*

FORBEARANCE [fohr BAYR uns]
- patience/self-control
*(**FORBEARANCE** is a must when caring for little tykes.)*

FORBIDDING [fur BID ing; fohr BID ing]
- hostile/threatening
*(The powerful watchdog flashed its **FORBIDDING** teeth at the would-be trespasser.)*

FORESIGHT [FOHR siet]
- careful planning/preparedness
*(A person of shrewd business **FORESIGHT**, the woman knew not to sell her share in the fledgling but promising company.)*

FORESTALL [fohr STAHL]
- prevent
*(Selling its unprofitable subsidiary allowed the firm to **FORESTALL** bankruptcy.)*

FORGO [fohr GOH]
- do without
*(In some religions, followers must **FORGO** eating meat on occasion.)*

FORLORN [fohr LOHRN]
- lonely and abandoned
*(Relegated to obscurity following the decline of her movie career, the **FORLORN** woman lived a reclusive existence bereft of her once-adoring fans.)*

FORMIDABLE [FOHR mi duh bul]
- fearfully impressive
*(Lions are **FORMIDABLE** creatures who predominate on the savanna.)*

FORMIDABLE [FOHR mi duh bul]
- extremely difficult
*(Many consider filling out tax forms a **FORMIDABLE** task.)*

FORSAKE [fohr SAYK]
- abandon/desert
*(It is an ignominious act to **FORSAKE** one's friends in their hour of need.)*

FORSAKE [fohr SAYK]
- renounce
*(In his sermon, the preacher admonished the licentious sinner, urging him to **FORSAKE** his wanton lifestyle.)*

FORSWEAR [fohr SWAYR]
- promise to give up
*(For his health, he made a New Year's resolution to **FORSWEAR** his alcoholic ways.)*

FORSWEAR [fohr SWAYR]
- renounce under oath
*(As a newly-inducted American citizen, he was asked to **FORSWEAR** allegiance to any hostile government or regime.)*

FORTE [fohrt; FOHR tay]
- strong point
*(Courses in mathematics were the student's **FORTE** throughout high school.)*

FORTIFY [FOHR tuh fie]
- strengthen
*(To gird for battle, the village **FORTIFIED** its military might.)*

FORTITUDE [FOHR ti tood; FOHR ti tyood]
- courage and endurance
*(Traveling through uncharted wilderness tested the gold miners' **FORTITUDE**.)*

FORTUITOUS [fohr TOO i tus; fohr TYOO i tus]
- accidental/fortunate
(Amazingly, the two childhood friends met twenty years later in a FORTUITOUS meeting at Waikiki Beach.)

FOUNDER [FOUN dur]
- sink
(The helpless ship FOUNDERED amid the jagged rocks.)

FOUNDER [FOUN dur]
- fail completely
(Hostage negotiations FOUNDERED as a result of mutual distrust.)

FRACAS [FRAY kus; FRAK us]
- noisy quarrel
(The two drinking buddies were asked to leave the establishment after they initiated a barroom FRACAS.)

FRACTIOUS [FRAK shus]
- irritably quarrelsome
(The FRACTIOUS couple complained about everything the waiter did.)

FRACTIOUS [FRAK shus]
- unruly
(The FRACTIOUS horse could not be successfully domesticated.)

FRAIL [frayl]
- physically weak and fragile
(People in their nineties are usually rather FRAIL.)

FRANCHISE [FRAN chiez]
- right to vote
(Only recently have citizens in lesser-developed nations been extended the FRANCHISE.)

FRANGIBLE [FRAN juh bul]
- fragile/easily broken
(The FRANGIBLE china was packed in padded boxes for shipping.)

FRANK [frangk]
- honest and straightforward
(When asked if he liked the hat his wife had chosen for the occasion, he replied in a FRANK manner that offended her.)

FRANTIC [FRAN tik]
- wildly excited
(When fire broke out in the theater, the audience became FRANTIC.)

FRENETIC [fruh NET ik]
- hectic/wildly enthusiastic
(The FRENETIC pace of the championship basketball game kept the audience on its feet.)

FRETFUL [FRET ful]
- irritably uneasy
*(The **FRETFUL** duck scurried about, frantically searching for her two missing ducklings.)*

FRIVOLOUS [FRIV uh lus]
- lacking in seriousness
*(Rather than take her job seriously, the **FRIVOLOUS** receptionist polished her nails while chatting on the phone to her equally flighty friends.)*

FRIVOLOUS [FRIV uh lus]
- trivial/silly and pointless
*(**FRIVOLOUS** lawsuits waste taxpayer money.)*

FROWARD [FROH wurd]
- stubbornly contrary
*(The **FROWARD** youngster refused to conform to school rules.)*

FRUGAL [FROO gul]
- thrifty/stingy
*(True to his **FRUGAL** nature, the elderly man left only a meager tip.)*

FRUITION [froo ISH un]
- fulfillment/realization
*(After years of hard work and resolute frugality, the couple's dream of buying their own home came to **FRUITION**.)*

FULMINATE [FUL muh nayt]
- denounce violently
*(As he was being transferred to another location, the unruly prisoner **FULMINATED** against his handlers.)*

FULSOME [FOOL sum; FUL sum]
- excessive/overdone
*(The **FULSOME** praise bestowed upon the despotic ruler by his lowly subjects did not sway him to compassion or mercy.)*

FUNDAMENTAL [fun duh MEN tul]
- basic/essential
*(Air is a **FUNDAMENTAL** component for the survival of all living matter.)*

FUNEREAL [fyoo NEER ee ul]
- mournful/gloomy
*(After the disheartening loss, the bus ride home assumed a **FUNEREAL** atmosphere for the entire soccer team.)*

FUROR [FYOOR ohr]
- commotion/rage
*(A proposal to raise taxes caused widespread **FUROR** throughout the community.)*

FURTIVE [FUR tiv]
- sneaky/sly
*(The lad's **FURTIVE** glances at his neighbor's test did not go unnoticed by the teacher.)*

FUTILE [FYOOT l; FYOO tiel]
- useless/ineffective
*(It soon became clear that any attempt to persuade her parents to let her borrow the car would be **FUTILE**.)*

GAINFUL [GAYN ful]
- profitable
*(After graduating from college, it is time to seek **GAINFUL** employment in the workplace.)*

GAINSAY [GAYN say]
- deny/dispute
*(Although a few physicists questioned the methods employed in the kinetic experiment, none could **GAINSAY** the accuracy of the report's findings.)*

GALVANIZE [GAL vuh niez]
- stimulate suddenly
*(Visible signs of an impending hurricane **GALVANIZED** the tiny community into preparedness.)*

GAMBOL [GAM bul]
- romp/skip about playfully
*(The young deer **GAMBOLED** in the open field.)*

GAMELY [GAYM lee]
- fearlessly courageous
*(The tribal youths were **GAMELY** warriors.)*

GAMUT [GAM ut]
- full extent
*(The introductory math course ran the **GAMUT** from basic arithmetic to advanced algebra.)*

GARISH [GAYR ish]
- tastelessly showy
*(Television viewers were repulsed by the immodest sheik's **GARISH** display of his wealth.)*

GARNER [GAHR nur]
- accumulate
*(Spencer Tracy **GARNERED** many awards over his illustrious acting career.)*

GARRULOUS [GAR uh lus]
- talkative
*(Sociably **GARRULOUS**, the affable starlet soon became the center of attraction at the ball.)*

GAUCHE [gohsh]
- crude and awkward
*(The country boy's **GAUCHE** manners were somewhat embarrassing to his sophisticated friends.)*

GAUDY [GAH dee]
- tastelessly showy
*(Large imitation pearls adorned the **GAUDY** dress.)*

GAUNT [gahnt]
- haggard
*(Weeks of overwork and stress had left the newspaper editor appearing pale and **GAUNT**.)*

GENESIS [JEN i sis]
- origin/beginning
*(The issue regarding man's evolution has often been the **GENESIS** of heated and protracted debate.)*

GENIAL [JEEN yul]
- cheerful and friendly
*(The junior executive had a most ingratiatingly **GENIAL** personality.)*

GENIAL [JEEN yul]
- pleasant
*(The remote island enjoyed a **GENIAL** year-round climate.)*

GENTEEL [jen TEEL]
- elegant/polite
*(The **GENTEEL** woman comported herself with an aristocratic air.)*

GERMANE [jur MAYN]
- pertinent
*(New evidence **GERMANE** to the case was introduced prior to closing summation.)*

GHASTLY [GAST lee]
- shockingly hideous
*(Residents of the sleepy town were stunned by the string of **GHASTLY** murders.)*

GIBE [jieb]
- taunt teasingly
*(Hecklers **GIBED** at and harassed the unwelcome speaker.)*

GINGERLY [JIN jur lee]
- very carefully
*(After spraining her ankle, the salesperson walked **GINGERLY** on it for the remainder of her work shift.)*

GIRTH [gurth]
- distance around/perimeter
*(The **GIRTH** of the bulky package was forty-eight inches.)*

GIST [jist]
- main point
*(The youngster could not grasp the **GIST** of the adult conversation.)*

GLACIAL [GLAY shul]
- freezingly cold
*(Only the hardiest of explorers could endure the arctic region's **GLACIAL** climate.)*

GLEAN [gleen]
- gather gradually
*(Over the years, the basketball announcer **GLEANED** valuable tidbits of information from interviews with the sport's top players.)*

GLIB [glib]
- smooth-talking (though often insincere)
*(During the televised interview, the **GLIB** politician pledged sweeping changes in administrative policy, though few seriously expected him to deliver on any of his promises.)*

GLOAMING [GLOH ming]
- twilight
*(The verdant fields seemed so majestically serene in the **GLOAMING**.)*

GLOWER [GLOU ur]
- stare angrily
*(After repeated warnings to be quiet, the teacher **GLOWERED** at the student in a baleful look that promised detention if he didn't cease his chatter that very instant.)*

GLUM [glum]
- silently gloomy
*(While everyone else at the party was having fun, the snubbed lad sat alone **GLUM** and dejected.)*

GLUTTONY [GLUT uh nee]
- excessive eating/drinking
*(As a result of his **GLUTTONY**, the young boy soon found himself noticeably overweight.)*

GOAD [gohd]
- urge into action
*(His anxious wife **GOADED** him into asking his boss for a long-overdue raise.)*

GOSSAMER [GAHS uh mur]
- light and delicate
*(The young girl marveled at the **GOSSAMER** threads of the spider's web.)*

GRANDIOSE [GRAN dee ohs]
- grand and showy
*(The Arab leader's mansion boasted **GRANDIOSE** halls lined with precious objects d'art.)*

GRAPHIC [GRAF ik]
- vividly clear/realistic
*(In its true form, cinema verité does not exercise restraint when depicting **GRAPHIC** sex or violence.)*

GRATUITOUS [gruh TOO i tus; gruh TYOO i tus]
- free/without charge
*(The community came together to offer **GRATUITOUS** assistance in rebuilding those homes that had been destroyed in the fire.)*

GRATUITOUS [gruh TOO i tus; gruh TYOO i tus]
- unprovoked/unjustified
*(The **GRATUITOUS** insult provoked a row that required the intervention of the police to quell.)*

GRAVE [grayv]
- serious
*(War is a matter of **GRAVE** concern to all involved.)*

GREGARIOUS [gri GAYR ee us]
- sociable
*(The **GREGARIOUS** woman enjoyed hosting informal parties.)*

GROTESQUE [groh TESK]
- absurdly bizarre
*(In his latest attempt at twisted humor, the satirist featured **GROTESQUE** cartoon characters with multiple eyes and no feet.)*

GRUELING [GROO ling; GROO uh ling]
- difficult and tiring
*(Army cadets are subjected to a **GRUELING** and rigorous training program.)*

GRUFF [gruff]
- discourteously/crudely abrupt
*(The rustic cowboy responded to the urban sophisticate's question in a **GRUFF** and terse manner.)*

GUILEFUL [GIEL ful]
- clever and deceitful
*(The scoundrel's **GUILEFUL** attempt to convince the old woman to sign over the deed to her house failed when her husband showed up.)*

GUISE [giez]
- appearance
*(In the children's fairy tale, the wolf appeared in the **GUISE** of a sheep.)*

GULLIBLE [GUL uh bul]
- easily fooled
*(The **GULLIBLE** boy believed even the most outlandish of stories.)*

HABITUATE [huh BICH oo ayt]
- accustom (through habit)
*(Living beneath the train tracks **HABITUATED** the dwellers to noise.)*

HACKNEYED [HAK need]
- overused and unimaginative
*(Critics decried the novel as a **HACKNEYED** reconstitution of situational schlock.)*

HAGGARD [HAG urd]
- thin and weary
*(After spending a week adrift on the ocean, the rescued survivors appeared **HAGGARD** and emotionally drained.)*

HALCYON [HAL see un]
- peaceful and untroubled
*(In his waning years, the wealthy and powerful ruler yearned for those **HALCYON** days of youth.)*

HALE [hayl]
- healthy and energetic
*(Even into her nineties, she remained a **HALE** and hearty woman.)*

HALLOWED [HAL ohd]
- sacred
*(Residents protested the construction of a shopping mall on what was regarded as **HALLOWED** ground.)*

HAMPER [HAM pur]
- hinder/disrupt
*(Continuous rain **HAMPERED** the workers' efforts to complete the roof repairs.)*

HAPLESS [HAP lis]
- unlucky
*(Although in a rush to get to the airport, the **HAPLESS** man could do no better than encounter red lights at every traffic intersection he reached.)*

HARANGUE [huh RANG]
- lengthy and passionate speech
*(In her half-time **HARANGUE**, the basketball coach emphasized the need for total personal commitment to achieve success both in sports and in life.)*

HARASS [huh RAS; HAR us]
- bother repeatedly
*(After being continually **HARASSED** by his wife to buy her the expensive dress in the showroom window, he relented and presented it to her as an anniversary gift.)*

HARBINGER [HAHR bin jur]
- first indication/precursor
*(The groundhog is an early **HARBINGER** of the coming of spring.)*

HARDSHIP [HAHRD ship]
- suffering/misfortune
*(The powerful storm inflicted great **HARDSHIP** upon residents of neighboring coastal towns and villages.)*

HARDY [HAHR dee]
- rugged
*(Early pioneers were a **HARDY** and determined group.)*

HARDY [HAHR dee]
- courageous
*(The **HARDY** David slew the giant Goliath.)*

HARROWING [HAR oh ing]
- distressful
*(The plane's rough landing was a **HARROWING** experience for all aboard.)*

HARRY [HAR ee]
- plague/trouble
*(Many members of the jury would be forever **HARRIED** by the guilty verdict they hastily handed down.)*

HAUGHTY [HAH tee]
- arrogant
*(In the company of her minions, the beauty queen displayed a **HAUGHTY** air of superiority.)*

HAUTEUR [hoh TOOR; hoh TUR]
- arrogance
*(The overbearing upstart exhibited an egotistical **HAUTEUR** that rankled his peers.)*

HAVEN [HAY vun]
- refuge
*(In underdeveloped countries, sewers are often the **HAVEN** for homeless children.)*

HAVOC [HAV uk]
- chaos and destruction
*(The Southern California earthquake wreaked **HAVOC** for millions of residents in 1994.)*

HAZARDOUS [HAZ ur dus]
- dangerous/unsafe
*(Signs cautioned against proceeding further along the **HAZARDOUS** trail.)*

HEADSTRONG [HED strahng]
- stubbornly defiant
*(The **HEADSTRONG** lad would not admit he was wrong even in the face of irrefutable evidence.)*

HEDONISTIC [heed n IS tik]
- pleasure-seeking
*(Playboys enjoy a **HEDONISTIC**, carefree lifestyle.)*

HEED [heed]
- pay close attention to
*(When swimming at an unfamiliar beach, it is wise to always **HEED** the lifeguard's advice.)*

HEINOUS [HAY nus]
- shockingly horrible and despicable
*(During World War II, **HEINOUS** crimes were perpetrated against unsuspecting Jews.)*

HERCULEAN [hur kyoo LEE un; hur KYOO lee un]
- physically powerful
*(Andre the Giant was a **HERCULEAN** wrestler.)*

HERCULEAN [hur kyoo LEE un; hur KYOO lee un]
- extremely difficult
*(While the guards were asleep, the prisoners embarked upon the **HERCULEAN** task of burrowing an underground escape tunnel by hand.)*

HERETICAL [huh RET i kul]
- unorthodox
*(Many religious leaders have been ostracized for their **HERETICAL** ideologies.)*

HIATUS [hie AY tus]
- interval/break
*(There was a **HIATUS** of three days between contract-negotiations sessions.)*

HIDEBOUND [HIED bound]
- stubbornly narrow-minded
*(People in religiously-sensitive small towns tend to be **HIDEBOUND** in their beliefs.)*

HINDER [HIN dur]
- stop/hold back
*(Severe rainstorms **HINDERED** the rescuers' efforts to reach the stranded hikers.)*

HIRSUTE [HUR soot; hur SOOT]
- hairy
*(Cavemen were **HIRSUTE** creatures.)*

HISTRIONIC [his tree AHN ik]
- overly theatrical
*(In his melodramatic way, the movie star expressed his heartfelt sympathy with **HISTRIONIC** hyperbole.)*

HOMAGE [AHM ij; HAHM ij]
- dutiful respect
*(At the baseball Hall of Fame, fans pay **HOMAGE** to the best in the sport, past and present.)*

HOMOLOGOUS [huh MAHL uh gus]
- comparatively similar
*(A bird's wings are **HOMOLOGOUS** to a human's arms.)*

HONE [hohn]
- sharpen
*(Practicing daily helped the young prodigy **HONE** his piano skills.)*

HORTATORY [HOHR tuh tohr ee]
- strongly urging
*(The **HORTATORY** speech sought to raise community involvement in crime prevention.)*

HOSPITABLE [HAHS pi tuh bul; hah SPIT uh bul]
- warm and friendly
*(**HOSPITABLE** to strangers in need, the kindly woman offered them free meals and overnight lodging.)*

HOSTILE [HAHS tul]
- unfriendly
*(As they entered the dense jungle, the explorers encountered a band of **HOSTILE** natives.)*

HUBRIS [HYOO bris]
- excessive pride
*(In an impulsive and imprudent display of **HUBRIS**, the warrior soldier slapped the captive general in front of his own men.)*

HULKING [HUL king]
- bulky/massive
*(The champion wrestler was a **HULKING** and imposing figure.)*

HUMANE [hyoo MAYN]
- kind/compassionate
*(It is only fitting and proper to treat animals in a **HUMANE** manner.)*

HUMILITY [hyoo MIL i tee]
- humbleness
*(The recipient of the actor-of-the-year award accepted the honor with grace and **HUMILITY**.)*

HYGIENIC [hie jee EN ik]
- clean and healthful
*(Restaurant food is prepared under strictly **HYGIENIC** conditions.)*

HYPERBOLE [hie PUR buh lee]
- obvious exaggeration
*(To create a more vivid picture of the loveliness of the tropical island, the author wrote in poetic **HYPERBOLE**.)*

HYPOCRITICAL [hip uh KRIT i kul]
- phony ("two-faced")
*(It is **HYPOCRITICAL** for a smoker to tell others that smoking is bad for one's health.)*

ICONOCLASTIC [ie kahn uh KLAS tik]
- rebelliously anti-establishment
*(His **ICONOCLASTIC** religious and political views alienated him from mainstream society.)*

IDIOSYNCRASY [id ee uh SING kruh see]
- individual peculiarity
*(Among the eccentric millionaire's **IDIOSYNCRASIES** was a fascination to wear matching green socks and shoes.)*

IDYLLIC [ie DIL ik]
- peaceful and serenely rural
*(In the midst of his busy workweek in the city, the executive longed for those **IDYLLIC** weekends spent at his country estate.)*

IGNOBLE [ig NOH bul]
- shameful
*(Stealing from his own parents was a most **IGNOBLE** act.)*

IGNOMINIOUS [ig nuh MIN ee us]
- disgraceful
*(The powerful nation suffered an **IGNOMINIOUS** defeat at the hands of their tiny neighbor to the south.)*

ILLICIT [i LIS it]
- unlawful
*(For conducting allegedly **ILLICIT** activities, the organization was constantly under police surveillance.)*

ILLUSORY [i LOO suh ree; i LOO zuh ree]
- misleading/unrealistic
*(People buy lottery tickets with **ILLUSORY** hopes of becoming millionaires overnight.)*

ILLUSTRIOUS [i LUS tree us]
- brilliantly outstanding
*(Vince Lombardi had an **ILLUSTRIOUS** career as head football coach for the Green Bay Packers.)*

IMBROGLIO [im BROHL yoh]
- confused entanglement/embarrassing situation
*(The man found himself in a most peculiar and upsetting **IMBROGLIO** when he realized he had taken home one child that was not his own.)*

IMBROGLIO [im BROHL yoh]
- bitter/complicated dispute
*(The two rival city-states became enmeshed in an **IMBROGLIO** over border rights.)*

IMBUE [im BYOO]
- saturate
*(In his grand murals, artist Wyland **IMBUED** his underwater scenes with deeply penetrating blues and greens.)*

IMBUE [im BYOO]
- inspire
*(Winning the class spelling bee **IMBUED** the youngster with renewed self-confidence.)*

IMMACULATE [i MAK yuh lit]
- spotlessly clean
*(A true perfectionist, the man kept his car in **IMMACULATE** condition.)*

IMMEMORIAL [im uh MOHR ee ul]
- ancient/beyond memory
*(The tribal rain dance has been performed since time **IMMEMORIAL**.)*

IMMINENT [IM uh nunt]
- soon to happen/close at hand
*(Those within close political circles realized that the old leader's death was **IMMINENT**.)*

IMMOLATE [IM uh layt]
- sacrifice
*(The lamb was **IMMOLATED** in the holy fire.)*

IMMURE [i MYOOR]
- imprison
*(In the horrific short story, the victim was **IMMURED** within the cement walls of the dark dungeon.)*

IMMUTABLE [i MYOO tuh bul]
- unchanging
*(Truth is **IMMUTABLE**.)*

IMPARTIAL [im PAHR shul]
- unbiased
*(Judges pride themselves on their **IMPARTIAL** analysis of disputes presented before them.)*

IMPASSIONED [im PASH und]
- passionate
*(The condemned prisoner issued an **IMPASSIONED** plea for mercy.)*

IMPASSIVE [im PAS iv]
- emotionless
*(Throughout the heated debate, the moderator maintained an **IMPASSIVE** and objective countenance.)*

IMPECCABLE [im PEK uh bul]
- flawless/faultless
*(The strikingly attractive baroness was a woman of **IMPECCABLE** taste in fashion.)*

IMPECUNIOUS [im puh KYOO nee us]
- penniless (often, habitually)
*(He refused to lend any additional money to his **IMPECUNIOUS** brother, knowing that the money would likely be gambled away at the racetrack.)*

IMPEDE [im PEED]
- hinder
*(Bad weather **IMPEDED** construction of the bridge.)*

IMPENDING [im PEN ding]
- threateningly near
*(Dark clouds signaled an **IMPENDING** storm.)*

IMPERATIVE [im PER uh tiv]
- absolutely necessary
*(Before an airplane ascends, it is **IMPERATIVE** that all doors and latches be fully secured.)*

IMPERMEABLE [im PUR mee uh bul]
- not allowing penetration
(Glass is IMPERMEABLE to water.)

IMPERTINENT [im PUR tuh nunt]
- rude
(The IMPERTINENT child constantly interrupted his mother.)

IMPERVIOUS [im PUR vee us]
- unaffected by/insensitive (to)
(Through the power of concentration, some people can walk barefoot over glass and remain IMPERVIOUS to the pain.)

IMPETUOUS [im PECH oo us]
- impulsive
(A romantically IMPETUOUS man, the mariner fell in love with every beautiful woman he met.)

IMPETUS [IM pi tus]
- stimulus
(Success was the IMPETUS that impelled the ambitious entrepreneur to work both day and night.)

IMPLACABLE [im PLAK uh bul; im PLAY kuh bul]
- unable to be appeased
(Despite the mediator's best efforts to arrange a compromise, both opposing factions remained IMPLACABLE and vowed to escalate the conflict.)

IMPLAUSIBLE [im PLAH zuh bul]
- not credible
(His account of how he landed the huge marlin was vividly exciting though equally IMPLAUSIBLE.)

IMPLEMENT [IM pluh ment]
- activate
(An amended budget policy was IMPLEMENTED shortly after the new governor assumed office.)

IMPLICIT [im PLIS it]
- understood (though not expressly spoken)
(Though no word was uttered, there was an IMPLICIT agreement between the leaders of the rival gangs to ease hostilities and seek a peaceful coexistence.)

IMPLICIT [im PLIS it]
- unquestioning/absolute
(In times of trouble at sea, the crew had IMPLICIT faith in their captain's judgment and decisions.)

IMPLORE [im PLOHR]
- plead with
(His attorney IMPLORED the judge to consider the mitigating circumstances surrounding the case.)

IMPORTUNE [im pohr TOON; im pohr TYOON]
- beg urgently/persistently
(The determined teen IMPORTUNED her mother to let her drive home.)

IMPOVERISHED [im PAHV ur isht]
- poor
*(Many citizens of third-world nations live under **IMPOVERISHED** and life-threatening conditions.)*

IMPRECATE [IM pruh kayt]
- curse/damn
*(Rather than seek absolution for his crime, the prisoner **IMPRECATED** those responsible for his capture.)*

IMPREGNABLE [im PREG nuh bul]
- resistant to attack
*(Before the successful raid by Sana Anna's men, the Alamo was considered an **IMPREGNABLE** fortress.)*

IMPROMPTU [im PRAHMP too]
- offhand
*(The nightclub entertainer's **IMPROMPTU** quips were well received by the audience.)*

IMPUDENT [IM pyuh dunt]
- boldly disrespectful
*(When scolded by his teacher, the **IMPUDENT** lad defended his misguided behavior.)*

IMPUGN [im PYOON]
- attack verbally
*(The gubernatorial candidate threatened to sue the newspaper for **IMPUGNING** his character in a disparaging editorial.)*

IMPUNITY [im PYOO ni tee]
- freedom from punishment
*(Dictators have been known to loot their nations' treasuries with **IMPUNITY**.)*

IMPUTE [im PYOOT]
- blame
*(Business failures are often **IMPUTED** to poor management.)*

INADVERTENT [in ud VUR tunt]
- unintentional
*(Through an **INADVERTENT** error, the esteemed professor was excluded from the list of invited guests.)*

INALIENABLE [in AYL yuh nuh bul; in AY lee un uh bul]
- inseparable and untransferable
*(Life, liberty and the pursuit of happiness are every American's **INALIENABLE** rights.)*

INANE [i NAYN]
- silly and pointless
*(No one else on the panel concurred with the **INANE** comment that politics is responsible for all the ills in the world today.)*

INANIMATE [in AN uh mit]
- not alive
*(A rock is an **INANIMATE** object.)*

INAUGURAL [in AH gyur ul; in AH gur ul]
- initial
(There was extensive press coverage when the Concorde made its INAUGURAL flight.)

INCAPACITATE [in kuh PAS i tayt]
- disable
(During battle, the beetle sought to INCAPACITATE the rival by turning it on its back.)

INCARNATE [in KAHR nit; in KAHR nayt]
- personified in flesh and body
(The evil ruler was regarded by many of his subjects as the devil INCARNATE.)

INCENDIARY [in SEN dee ayr ee]
- explosive
(The massive explosion was traced to a single INCENDIARY device.)

INCENDIARY [in SEN dee ayr ee]
- inflammatory
(INCENDIARY remarks oftentimes trigger heated confrontations.)

INCENSE [in SENS]
- anger
(Veiled intimidation by the police INCENSED the rock concert fans.)

INCEPTION [in SEP shun]
- beginning
(The dutiful clerk had been with the small private company since its INCEPTION.)

INCESSANT [in SES unt]
- continual
(The child's INCESSANT chatter nearly drove the babysitter to madness.)

INCHOATE [in KOH it]
- rudimentary
(Prior to working out the details, the prisoners drafted an INCHOATE plan of escape.)

INCIPIENT [in SIP ee unt]
- beginning to appear
(Spring is heralded by the INCIPIENT sprouting of flowers.)

INCISIVE [in SIE siv]
- mentally sharp
(An INCISIVE analysis of the problem clarified many of the reporters' lingering questions.)

INCITE [in SIET]
- provoke
(The arrest of a prominent political protester INCITED a civil riot.)

INCLEMENT [in KLEM unt]
- stormy
(INCLEMENT weather forced the cancellation of the annual employee picnic.)

INCLINATION [in kluh NAY shun]
- tendency
(Children of doctors often have a strong INCLINATION to also enter the medical profession.)

INCLINATION [in kluh NAY shun]
- preference/fondness
(Independent individuals generally have a stronger INCLINATION toward cats than dogs.)

INCLUSIVE [in KLOO siv]
- everything included
(The sum of the integers from 1 to 5, INCLUSIVE, equals 15.)

INCOGNITO [in kahg NEE toh; in KAHG nit oh]
- in disguise
(Movie stars often travel INCOGNITO to avoid being hounded by fans.)

INCONGRUOUS [in KAHNG groo us]
- inconsistent
(The girl's poor test scores were INCONGRUOUS with her brilliant academic potential.)

INCONSEQUENTIAL [in kahn suh KWEN shul]
- insignificant
(The company's rosy earnings outlook proved somewhat INCONSEQUENTIAL to investors; the stock had already risen in anticipation of the favorable news.)

INCONSIDERABLE [in kun SID ur uh bul]
- insignificant
(The proposed two percent raise was deemed an INCONSIDERABLE amount by the employees' union.)

INCONSIDERATE [in kun SID ur it]
- thoughtless/insensitive
(The INCONSIDERATE lad ate the last piece of cake and left his younger sister with nothing but leftover crumbs.)

INCONTROVERTIBLE [in kahn truh VUR tuh bul]
- indisputable
(Faced with such INCONTROVERTIBLE evidence against him, the suspect had no other choice but to plead guilty and place himself at the mercy of the court.)

INCORRIGIBLE [in KOHR i juh bul]
- hopelessly chronic/habitual ("hard-core")
(Having earned the dubious reputation as an INCORRIGIBLE gambler, the man found it nearly impossible to secure a loan from anyone.)

INCREDULOUS [in KREJ uh lus]
- skeptical/disbelieving
(His friends were INCREDULOUS when told he had braved forty-foot seas in his tiny sailboat.)

INCREMENT [IN kruh munt; ING kruh munt]
- quantity/increased quantity
(Unless they want to receive a single lump-sum payment, lottery winners are paid in annual INCREMENTS over a period of a lifetime.)

INCRIMINATE [in KRIM uh nayt]
- charge with/involve in a crime
(New and irrefutable evidence in the case clearly INCRIMINATED the two lead suspects.)

INCULCATE [in KUL kayt; IN kul kayt]
- teach/instill (through repetition)
(Through her own refined actions and behavior, the dutiful mother hoped to INCULCATE in her children a sense of social propriety.)

INCULPATE [in KUL payt; IN kul payt]
- incriminate
(Several students were INCULPATED in the graffiti incident.)

INCUMBENT [in KUM bunt]
- obligatory
(In Japan, it is INCUMBENT upon a visitor to remove his shoes before entering the house.)

INCURSION [in KUR zhun]
- hostile/sudden invasion
(Neighboring kingdoms feared the powerful emperor, whose armies staged periodic INCURSIONS in search of new slaves.)

INDEFATIGABLE [in di FAT uh guh bul]
- tireless
(The INDEFATIGABLE defense attorney ferreted out and interviewed every witness to the crime.)

INDEFEASIBLE [in di FEE zuh bul]
- absolute and irrevocable
(In a free society, liberty is an INDEFEASIBLE human right.)

INDELIBLE [in DEL uh bul]
- permanent/not erasable
(Juliet's charm left an INDELIBLE impression in Romeo's heart.)

INDICT [in DIET]
- charge/accuse
(The grand jury INDICTED six men in connection with the string of recent bank robberies.)

INDIFFERENT [in DIF uh runt]
- not caring
*(When asked whether she wanted to go to the movies or stay home, the girl shrugged her shoulders in an **INDIFFERENT** manner.)*

INDIFFERENT [in DIF uh runt]
- not concerned
*(Despite numerous pleas from his advisers, the wealthy and powerful king remained **INDIFFERENT** to the plight of his impoverished subjects.)*

INDIGENOUS [in DIJ uh nus]
- native
*(Wallabies are **INDIGENOUS** to Australia.)*

INDIGENT [IN di junt]
- poor
*(The 1929 stock market crash left a large segment of the nation's population **INDIGENT** and placed the country's economy on the brink of collapse.)*

INDIGNANT [in DIG nunt]
- angrily offended
*(The man's wife became **INDIGNANT** at the inference that she alone was responsible for the family's financial woes.)*

INDIGNATION [in dig NAY shun]
- righteous and warranted anger
*(Animal lovers expressed their **INDIGNATION** over the barbaric means employed to rid the community of the unwanted stray dogs.)*

INDISPOSED [in di SPOHZD]
- ill
*(**INDISPOSED** and bedridden with the flu, the young secretary was unable to go to work as scheduled.)*

INDISPOSED [in di SPOHZD]
- unwilling
*(Already on a tight budget, the father was **INDISPOSED** to raising his son's weekly allowance.)*

INDOCTRINATE [in DAHK truh nayt]
- instruct
*(New members of the fraternity were **INDOCTRINATED** in the club's codes and practices.)*

INDOLENT [IN duh lunt]
- lazy
*(The **INDOLENT** boy had no intention of working during the summer vacation months, choosing instead to idle away the time in restful repose.)*

INDOMITABLE [in DAHM it uh bul]
- unconquerable
*(The gifted young performer possessed an **INDOMITABLE** spirit that destined him to eventual stardom.)*

INDUCE [in DOOS]
 - persuade
(The promise of riches beyond their wildest dreams INDUCED the exhausted prospectors to continue in their search for gold.)

INDUCE [in DOOS]
 - cause
(Her nervous breakdown was INDUCED by job-related stress.)

INDULGENT [in DUL junt]
 - lenient and obliging
(The INDULGENT parent set few restrictions on her children.)

INDURATE [IN door it; IN dyoo rit]
 - hardened and callous
(Few ever penetrated the INDURATE sea captain's crusty shell.)

INDUSTRIOUS [in DUS tree us]
 - hardworking and devoted
(Employers are always eager to hire INDUSTRIOUS individuals.)

INEBRIATED [in EE bree ay tid]
 - intoxicated/drunk
(Some people become embarrassingly INEBRIATED after imbibing only one or two beers.)

INEFFABLE [in EF uh bul]
 - indescribable
(In the celestial light, her face radiated an INEFFABLE loveliness.)

INEFFECTUAL [in i FEK choo ul]
 - ineffective
(His scheme to get a promotion was, for the most part, INEFFECTUAL.)

INELUCTABLE [in i LUK tuh bul]
 - inescapable
(Man is but a pawn of the INELUCTABLE hand of fate.)

INEPT [in EPT]
 - incompetent
(The INEPT young warrior could not shoot his arrow straight.)

INEVITABLE [in EV i tuh bul]
 - unavoidable
(Despite a valiant effort to remain solvent, it soon became clear to all that the company's demise was INEVITABLE.)

INEXORABLE [in EK sur uh bul]
 - unrelenting/unalterable
(Nothing could be done to stop the lava flow from its INEXORABLE path headed directly towards the center of town.)

INEXPLICABLE [in ik SPLIK uh bul; in EKS pluh kuh bul]
- unexplainable
(For some INEXPLICABLE reason, the lights in the auditorium suddenly started flickering.)

INEXTRICABLE [in ek STRIK uh bul]
- hopelessly entangled
(The philanderer found himself caught in an INEXTRICABLE web of lies.)

INFALLIBLE [in FAL uh bul]
- totally reliable ("foolproof")
(Though it hadn't been tested, the escape plan appeared to be INFALLIBLE.)

INFAMOUS [IN fuh mus]
- disgracefully bad
(The INFAMOUS pirate was decried for his dastardly deeds.)

INFAMOUS [IN fuh mus]
- associated with a disgraceful act
(The INFAMOUS trial of the international spies brought worldwide attention.)

INFATUATED [in FACH oo ay tid]
- blindly/passionately excited
(The starry-eyed schoolgirl became INFATUATED with the new boy in school.)

INFER [in FUR]
- conclude
(From his wife's gruff tone of voice, he INFERRED that she was not in a pleasant mood.)

INFERNAL [in FUR nul]
- hellish
(Coal miners must endure INFERNAL working conditions deep underground.)

INFIDEL [IN fi dul]
- religious nonbeliever
(During the Crusades, INFIDELS were often condemned to die on the gallows.)

INFINITE [IN fuh nit]
- endless
(There are an INFINITE number of stars in the universe.)

INFINITESIMAL [in fin i TES uh mul]
- extremely tiny
(An autopsy revealed only an INFINITESIMAL amount of arsenic in the blood stream, hardly a lethal dose.)

INFLAMMABLE [in FLAM uh bul]
- able to catch fire
(INFLAMMABLE liquids should be stored in a cool, dry place.)

INFLAMMATORY [in FLAM uh tohr ee]
- arousing anger
*(The senator's **INFLAMMATORY** remarks were met with swift retaliation from his detractors.)*

INFLUX [IN fluks]
- inflow/arrival
*(Summer on the lush island was always greeted with an **INFLUX** of vacationers.)*

INFRACTION [in FRAK shun]
- violation
*(Automatic suspension from school was meted out for any **INFRACTION** involving cheating.)*

INFRINGE [in FRINJ]
- trespass
*(It is impolite and disrespectful to **INFRINGE** on another's chosen privacy.)*

INFURIATE [in FYOOR ee ayt]
- enrage
*(Misplacing the important company report **INFURIATED** her boss.)*

INGENUOUS [in JEN yoo us]
- simple/naïve and honest
*(After years of stress dealing with city slickers, the doctor relocated to a more idyllic location where he found solace amongst the **INGENUOUS** country folk.)*

INGRATIATING [in GRAY shee ay ting]
- charmingly likeable
*(Shirley Temple's **INGRATIATING** dimpled smile made her everyone's favorite child actress.)*

INHERENT [in HER unt]
- basic and essential/intrinsic
*(Due to an **INHERENT** flaw in the escape plan, the entire venture was not practicable.)*

INHIBIT [in HIB it]
- restrain
*(Lack of rainfall may **INHIBIT** the growth of plants.)*

INIMICAL [i NIM i kul]
- threateningly hostile
*(On the bus, the stranger's **INIMICAL** stare left the young woman feeling fearfully uneasy.)*

INIMICAL [i NIM i kul]
- harmful
*(A poor diet can prove **INIMICAL** to one's health and welfare.)*

INIQUITOUS [i NIK wuh tis]
- unjust
*(In many countries, **INIQUITOUS** treatment of the poor is evidenced by a general lack of government-supported welfare programs.)*

INITIAL [i NISH ul]
- first
*An **INITIAL** investment is prerequisite for any business startup.)*

INITIATIVE [i NISH uh tiv; i NISH ee uh tiv]
- drive
*(Success in business demands **INITIATIVE** and follow-through.)*

INKLING [INGK ling]
- hint/vague idea
*(At many stores, shoppers are monitored by cameras, though most don't have the slightest **INKLING** that they are being observed.)*

INNATE [i NAYT; IN ayt]
- inborn
*(Mules are known for their **INNATE** stubbornness.)*

INNOCUOUS [i NAHK yoo us]
- harmless
*(The boys good-naturedly engaged one another in a round of **INNOCUOUS** banter.)*

INNOCUOUS [i NAHK yoo us]
- dull and pointless
*(Critics disparaged the comedic play as an **INNOCUOUS** descent into mediocrity.)*

INNOVATIVE [in uh VAY tiv]
- new and creative
*(City planners came up with an **INNOVATIVE** and economical way to reduce downtown traffic congestion.)*

INNUENDO [in yoo EN doh]
- subtle suggestion/hint
*(Unfounded rumors and **INNUENDOS** can besmirch a person's good name.)*

INNUMERABLE [i NOO mur uh bul]
- countless
*(In life, every new challenge carries with it **INNUMERABLE** opportunities and possibilities.)*

INORDINATE [in OHR duh nit]
- excessive
*(The librarian was visibly disturbed by the **INORDINATE** amount of chatter around her.)*

INQUIETUDE [in KWIE i tood; in KWIE i tyood]
- uneasiness
*(With tornadoes in the vicinity, residents spent the evening in restless **INQUIETUDE**.)*

INSATIABLE [in SAY shuh bul]
- unquenchable
*(The child prodigy had an **INSATIABLE** desire to read.)*

INSCRUTABLE [in SKROO tuh bul]
- mysterious
(Man has long been in awe of Mother Nature's INSCRUTABLE powers.)

INSIDIOUS [in SID ee us]
- devious and sly
(Iago conceived an INSIDIOUS plot to make Othello believe his wife was cheating on him.)

INSIGHTFUL [in SIET ful]
- penetratingly perceptive
(The documentary on mental illness afforded viewers an INSIGHTFUL glimpse into the world of schizophrenia.)

INSINUATE [in SIN yoo ayt]
- imply subtly
(Although not coming right out and saying it, the newspaper article nevertheless INSINUATED that the judges of the beauty contest had been bribed.)

INSIPID [in SIP id]
- dull and uninteresting
(Critics had little good to say about the INSIPID and shopworn boy-meets-girl situation comedy.)

INSIPID [in SIP id]
- tasteless
(Adding grandmother's piquant sauce to the INSIPID stew gave it a zesty flavor.)

INSOLENT [IN suh lunt]
- insultingly rude
(The INSOLENT boy refused to take off his cap during dinner.)

INSOUCIANT [in SOO see unt]
- carefree and untroubled
(As he cruised in his Corvette playing his radio at full volume, the INSOUCIANT playboy scoured the streets for attractive single girls.)

INSTIGATE [IN stuh gayt]
- initiate and provoke
(At an international soccer game, one questionable call by a referee can INSTIGATE a serious row in the stands.)

INSTILL [in STIL]
- teach/inspire gradually
(By taking care of homeless animals, the mother INSTILLED in her children a healthy love and respect for all living things.)

INSTRUMENTAL [in struh MEN tul]
- useful/helpful
(The Salk vaccine has proven INSTRUMENTAL in helping reduce the incidence of paralytic poliomyelitis.)

INSUFFERABLE [in SUF ur uh bul]
- unbearable
*(Her blind date turned out to be an **INSUFFERABLE** bore.)*

INSUPERABLE [in SOO pur uh bul]
- insurmountable
*(Unexpected and **INSUPERABLE** problems hindered timely completion of the massive construction project.)*

INSURGENT [in SUR junt]
- rebellious/revolutionary
*(The new military leader had to contend with a cabal of **INSURGENT** soldiers.)*

INTACT [in TAKT]
- whole and undamaged
*(During the violent earthquake, only the most well-constructed buildings remained **INTACT**.)*

INTEGRAL [IN tuh grul]
- essential
*(Brushing one's teeth is an **INTEGRAL** part of oral hygiene.)*

INTEGRITY [in TEG ruh tee]
- honesty
*(The beloved senator was a man of utmost moral **INTEGRITY**.)*

INTEMPERATE [in TEM pur it; in TEM prit]
- excessive
*(Even though he considered himself only a social drinker, his **INTEMPERATE** ways eventually led him to seeking help from Alcoholics Anonymous.)*

INTENSE [in TENS]
- powerful/extreme
*(A backache often produces **INTENSE** pain in the lumbar region.)*

INTER [in TUR]
- bury
*(Upon his death, the king was **INTERRED** in an elaborate crypt.)*

INTERLOPER [IN tur loh pur]
- intruder
*(With rifle in hand, the cattle rancher confronted the **INTERLOPER**.)*

INTERMINABLE [in TUR muh nuh bul]
- endless
*(Due to enhanced security at the airport, passengers were forced to endure frustratingly **INTERMINABLE** delays.)*

INTERMITTENT [in tur MIT unt]
- periodic and recurring
*(**INTERMITTENT** rain showers were forecast for the weekend.)*

INTERVENE [in tur VEEN]
- step in (to resolve)
*(Several teachers had to **INTERVENE** to break up the playground melee.)*

INTIMIDATE [in TIM i dayt]
- frighten
*(The neighborhood gang of ruffians endeavored to **INTIMIDATE** the citizens with veiled threats of retaliation should their illicit activities be reported to the authorities.)*

INTOLERABLE [in TAHL ur uh bul]
- unbearable
*(The constant noise of the jackhammers soon became **INTOLERABLE** to nearby tenants.)*

INTOLERANT [in TAHL uh runt]
- not open-minded
*(A bigot is **INTOLERANT** of those expressing conflicting opinions or beliefs.)*

INTRACTABLE [in TRAK tuh bul]
- stubborn and unmanageable
*(Constant reminders from his mother had little effect in persuading the **INTRACTABLE** tyke to remain in his playpen.)*

INTRANSIGENT [in TRAN si junt]
- stubbornly uncompromising
*(Despite a court order to return to work, the **INTRANSIGENT** strikers refused to yield an inch until all their demands were met.)*

INTREPID [in TREP id]
- fearless
*(Despite the other boy's physical superiority, the **INTREPID** lightweight stood his ground and refused to let the mighty Goliath push him around.)*

INTRICATE [IN truh kit]
- elaborate and complicated
*(An **INTRICATE** interlaced network of cables and wires connected the communication system.)*

INTRINSIC [in TRIN sik; in TRIN zik]
- basic and innate
*(Gold has a high **INTRINSIC** value and fetches hundreds of dollars per ounce.)*

INTROVERTED [IN truh vur tid]
- withdrawn
*(Uninterested in socializing with peers, the **INTROVERTED** lad preferred instead the desolate comfort of staying home and recording his thoughts in poetry.)*

INTRUSIVE [in TROO siv]
- meddlesome
*(His **INTRUSIVE** mother-in-law was always giving him unasked-for advice.)*

INUNDATE [IN un dayt]
- flood
(Two constant days of torrential rain INUNDATED the low-lying village.)

INURE [in YOOR]
- habituate/accustom
(Years of living in the Alaskan wilderness INURED the explorer to the biting cold.)

INVALUABLE [in VAL yoo uh bul]
- priceless
(Witnessing the effects of alcoholic abuse by his older sibling taught the young man an INVALUABLE lesson.)

INVECTIVE [in VEK tiv]
- insulting denunciation
(As the press eagerly looked on, the two wrestlers attacked one another with scathing INVECTIVE.)

INVEIGH [in VAY]
- complain bitterly
(Representing those living in the family shelter, the spokesman INVEIGHED against the state government for turning a deaf ear on the homeless.)

INVEIGLE [in VAY gul; in VEE gul]
- entice schemingly
(The buxom blonde INVEIGLED the rich old romantic into buying her a diamond ring.)

INVETERATE [in VET ur it]
- habitual
(It is nearly impossible for an INVETERATE gambler to change his risk-taking ways.)

INVIDIOUS [in VID ee us]
- offensively malicious
(Bitterly envious that his classmate was chosen to lead the band, the rancorous lad spawned an INVIDIOUS rumor to derail the selection.)

INVIGORATE [in VIG uh rayt]
- energize and refresh
(A cold shower INVIGORATED the fatigued jogger.)

INVINCIBLE [in VIN suh bul]
- unbeatable
(In the dominant years of ancient Rome, the INVINCIBLE Roman army conquered Italy and the entire Mediterranean world.)

INVIOLABLE [in VIE uh luh bul]
- sacred and not to be violated
(As teens, the group developed an INVIOLABLE bond of trust that never waned through the passing of time.)

INVIOLATE [in VIE uh lit]
- pure/unspoiled
*(Eden was an **INVIOLATE** paradise.)*

IRASCIBLE [i RAS uh bul]
- snappishly hot-tempered
*(Before having had his morning cup of coffee, the man was particularly **IRASCIBLE**.)*

IRATE [ie RAYT]
- furious
*(The customer became **IRATE** when told the sale item could not be exchanged.)*

IRE [ier]
- anger
*(Staying out later than permitted kindled her parents' **IRE**.)*

IRIDESCENT [ir i DES unt]
- rainbow-like
*(In the light, a soap bubble displays an **IRIDESCENT** glow.)*

IRK [urk]
- annoy/irritate
*(The baby's incessant crying **IRKED** the babysitter.)*

IRONIC [ie RAHN ik]
- unexpectedly odd and contrary
*(It was **IRONIC** that the millionaire was stricken with a common cold.)*

IRONIC [ie RAHN ik]
- sarcastic
*(In his reply to constituents, the beleaguered councilman laced his comments with **IRONIC** praise for the integrity of his accuser, who herself was the target of similar allegations.)*

IRRECONCILABLE [i rek un SIEL uh bul]
- incompatible/irremediable
*(Divorces often stem from a couple's **IRRECONCILABLE** differences.)*

IRREFUTABLE [i REF yuh tuh bul; ir i FYOO tuh bul]
- indisputable
*(Faced with **IRREFUTABLE** evidence, the defendant changed his plea to "guilty.")*

IRREPROACHABLE [ir i PROH chuh bul]
- faultless/blameless
*(The senator's moral integrity was **IRREPROACHABLE**.)*

IRREVOCABLE [i REV uh kuh bul]
- unchangeable
*(Once made, he knew his decision to resign as head basketball coach would be **IRREVOCABLE**.)*

ITINERANT [ie TIN uh runt]
- traveling
*(His occupation was that of an **ITINERANT** salesman.)*

JADED [JAY did]
- dulled (from experience/overexposure)
*(The television audience has become so **JADED** from all the violence shown that, when an actual murder is reported on the news, few are shocked.)*

JADED [JAY did]
- overused ("tired")
*(The weekly series' increasingly **JADED** plots presaged the show's imminent cancellation.)*

JAUNDICED [JAHN dist]
- envious and resentful
*(The other players watched with **JAUNDICED** eyes as the freshman was promoted to team captain.)*

JAUNDICED [JAHN dist]
- skeptical
*(The general community takes a **JAUNDICED** view of so-called psychics.)*

JAUNTY [JAHN tee]
- lively and spirited
*(The **JAUNTY** teenager enlivened any party.)*

JEER [jeer]
- mock and ridicule
*(The unpopular candidate was booed and **JEERED** throughout his speech.)*

JEJUNE [ji JOON]
- dull and pointless
*(Because of the instructor's reputation for giving **JEJUNE** lectures, students avoided registering for his class.)*

JEJUNE [ji JOON]
- juvenile/immature
*(His **JEJUNE** remarks regarding political ethics surprised his worldly associates.)*

JEOPARDY [JEP ur dee]
- danger
*(Behind on his car payments, the man was in **JEOPARDY** of having the vehicle repossessed.)*

JEREMIAD [jer uh MIE ad]
- lengthy mournful complaint
*(The social critic's essay was a **JEREMIAD** against the poor treatment of mentally ill patients in the early twentieth century.)*

JOCOSE [joh KOHS]
- joking
*(The teacher laughingly pondered the **JOCOSE** suggestion that she let her students exchange clothes as part of their foreign "exchange" program.)*

JOCULAR [JAHK yuh lur]
- humorous
*(To leaven the tense atmosphere, the diplomat interjected a **JOCULAR** anecdote.)*

JOCUND [JAHK und; JOH kund]
- cheerful and pleasant
*(A school reunion affords adults the opportunity to be once again in the **JOCUND** company of childhood friends.)*

JOVIAL [JOH vee ul]
- cheerful and hearty
*(The eminent world traveler was a **JOVIAL** and enlightening conversationalist.)*

JUBILANT [JOO buh lunt]
- joyful
*(The entire town was **JUBILANT** over the home team's glorious championship victory.)*

JUDICIOUS [joo DISH us]
- wise and sensible
*(The legal dispute was resolved in a **JUDICIOUS** and impartial manner.)*

JUGGERNAUT [JUG ur naht]
- large/overpowering force
*(The pirate ships were humbled into submission by the queen's naval **JUGGERNAUT**.)*

JUVENILE [JOO vuh nul; JOO vuh niel]
- childish
*(The boy's **JUVENILE** behavior at the opera embarrassed his mother.)*

JUXTAPOSE [juk stuh POHZ]
- place side by side
*(The unusual painting **JUXTAPOSED** cheerful reds with lugubrious shades of blue.)*

KEN [ken]
- range of knowledge/understanding
*(Because the poetic allusions of John Milton are beyond the **KEN** of most students, only a handful are truly able to appreciate the metaphorical and allegorical richness of works such as Paradise Lost.)*

KIN [kin]
- relatives
*(While in Minnesota, the family visited their **KIN**.)*

KITH [kith]
- friends/acquaintances
*(**KITH** and kin were invited to the reunion celebration.)*

KUDOS [KOO dohz; KYOO dohz]
- praise and glory
*(His international success earned the musician **KUDOS** in his home town.)*

LABYRINTHINE [lab uh RIN thin; lab uh RIN theen]
- intricate
*(The mouse was unable to find its way through the **LABYRINTHINE** maze.)*

LACHRYMOSE [LAK ruh mohs]
- tearful
*(The **LACHRYMOSE** tale of tragedy left not a dry eye in the audience.)*

LACONIC [luh KAHN ik]
- terse and abrupt
*(The actor's **LACONIC** responses reflected his disinterest in being interviewed.)*

LAMBASTE [lam BAYST]
- scold severely
*(In a scathing newspaper article, the politician was **LAMBASTED** for having accepted bribes and then denying the veracity of the filmed evidence.)*

LAMBENT [LAM bunt]
- softly bright
*(The **LAMBENT** moonglow shone in the window.)*

LAMBENT [LAM bunt]
- brilliantly clever
*(Jonathan Swift was a writer known for his **LAMBENT** wit and irony.)*

LAMENT [luh MENT]
- mourn
*(The nation **LAMENTED** the passing of the former leader.)*

LANGUID [LANG gwid]
- listless
*(The heat of the tropics contributed to the predominately **LANGUID** local lifestyle.)*

LANGUISH [LANG gwish]
- lose energy/strength/spirit
*(Jewish prisoners **LANGUISHED** hopelessly in concentration camps during World War II.)*

LARGESS [lahr JES; lahr ZHES] (also, **LARGESSE**)
- generosity
*(The wealthy family was greatly respected for their **LARGESS** to those less fortunate.)*

LASSITUDE [LAS i tood; LAS i tyood]
- listlessness and fatigue
*(The constant strain of deadlines took its toll on the overworked reporter, who suffered in later years from chronic **LASSITUDE**.)*

LATENT [LAYT nt]
- present (though not visibly active)
*(The psychiatrist determined that the youngster's violent nightmares manifested the child's **LATENT** hostility toward his stepfather.)*

LATITUDE [LAT i tood; LAT i tyood]
- freedom of action/choice
*(Students were offered a wide **LATITUDE** of topics for their science projects.)*

LAUD [lahd]
- praise
*(Townsfolk **LAUDED** the efforts of the new police commissioner to reduce crime in the city.)*

LAVISH [LAV ish]
- abundant
*(The proud community heaped **LAVISH** praise on their local hero.)*

LEAVEN [LEV un]
- lighten
*(The lugubrious ambience was **LEAVENED** somewhat with a humorous though inspiring anecdote.)*

LEGERDEMAIN [lej ur duh MAYN]
- magic
*(The veteran prestidigitator was a master of **LEGERDEMAIN**.)*

LETHAL [LEE thul]
- deadly
*(Drugs and alcohol can be a **LETHAL** combination.)*

LETHARGIC [luh THAHR jik]
- sluggish
*(After taking the medicine, she felt **LETHARGIC** and was unable to continue her brisk daily activities.)*

LEVIATHAN [li VIE uh thun]
- giant
*(The blue whale is the **LEVIATHAN** of the seas.)*

LEVITY [LEV i tee]
- lighthearted merriment
*(A funeral is not an appropriate setting for **LEVITY**.)*

LEXICON [LEK suh kahn]
- dictionary
*(This text endeavors to provide a **LEXICON** of words most vital in the college experience.)*

LEXICON [LEK suh kahn]
- vocabulary
*(The **LEXICON** of the legal community includes extensive use of Latin.)*

LIBERATE [LIB uh rayt]
- set free
*(After the war, the tiny nation was **LIBERATED** from totalitarian rule.)*

LICENTIOUS [lie SEN shus]
- morally unrestrained
*(Several bars in the area were shut down for promoting illegal and **LICENTIOUS** activities within their premises.)*

LIMBER [LIM bur]
- flexible
*(Spectators marveled at the **LIMBER** athletes performing in the acrobatics competition.)*

LIMN [lim]
- depict
*(Within the decorative mural, horses were **LIMNED** as winged warriors.)*

LIMPID [LIM pid]
- clear
*(Trout could be seen traveling in schools across the **LIMPID** stream.)*

LIONIZE [LIE uh niez]
- praise and glorify
*(After she had appeared in the national television commercial, all her classmates **LIONIZED** her.)*

LISSOME [LIS um]
- graceful/flexible
*(The beauty queen traversed the catwalk with the **LISSOME** elegance of a seraphic sylph.)*

LISTLESS [LIST lis]
- sluggishly inactive
*(The intense heat made everyone in the classroom rather **LISTLESS**.)*

LITHE [lieth)
- graceful
*(The **LITHE** ballerina dazzled the audience with her physical dexterity.)*

LITHE [lieth]
- flexible
*(The **LITHE** branch swayed resiliently in the breeze.)*

LITIGATE [LIT uh gayt]
- contest (through a lawsuit)
*(Unable to reach an amenable compromise, both parties chose to **LITIGATE** the civil matter.)*

LIVID [LIV id]
- furious
*(When told she could not park in the reserved stall, the shopper became **LIVID**.)*

LIVID [LIV id]
- bruised
*(As a result of falling from the ladder, the librarian's forearm was **LIVID**.)*

LOATH [lohth; loh<u>th</u>]
- reluctant/unwilling
*(The congresswoman was **LOATH** to support a cost-cutting proposal that would adversely affect employment in her home state.)*

LOATHE [loh<u>th</u>]
- hate
*(Many children **LOATHE** taking a bath.)*

LONGEVITY [lahn JEV i tee]
- lifespan
*(Crocodiles have a **LONGEVITY** that can exceed one hundred years.)*

LOQUACIOUS [loh KWAY shus]
- talkative
*(The **LOQUACIOUS** lad wouldn't stop talking long enough to let anyone else speak.)*

LOWER [LOU ur]
- frown angrily
*(The teacher **LOWERED** in a threateningly implicit manner when the class would not settle down.)*

LUCID [LOO sid]
- clear/clearly understood
*(Scientists offered a **LUCID** and credible explanation for the unusual celestial sightings.)*

LUCRATIVE [LOO kruh tiv]
- profitable
*(Selling his patent to the toy manufacturer was, as it turned out, a fortuitous and highly **LUCRATIVE** decision.)*

LUDICROUS [LOO duh krus]
- absurdly laughable
*(Staging Macbeth as a comedy is a **LUDICROUS** notion.)*

LUGUBRIOUS [loo GOO bree us]
- gloomy/mournful
*(The **LUGUBRIOUS** pallbearers carried the casket of their beloved friend to the waiting hearse.)*

LUMINOUS [LOO muh nus]
- glowing/shining
*(The grandfather clock featured **LUMINOUS** hands.)*

MACABRE [muh KAH bruh; muh KAHB]
- gruesome
*(The **MACABRE** tale involved voodoo dolls and ritual human sacrifice.)*

MACHIAVELLIAN [mak ee uh VEL ee un]
- unscrupulously scheming
(The military junta hatched a MACHIAVELLIAN scheme to seize government power.)

MACHINATION [mak uh NAY shun]
- scheming
(The scurrilously sinister scoundrel employed devilish MACHINATIONS to assume complete control of the wealthy woman's vast fortune.)

MAELSTROM [MAYL strum]
- powerful whirlpool
(The helpless boat was sucked into the merciless MAELSTROM.)

MAGNANIMOUS [mag NAN uh mus]
- noble and generously forgiving
(In a MAGNANIMOUS display of absolution, Pope John Paul blessed the very person who had earlier attempted to assassinate him.)

MAGNILOQUENT [mag NIL uh kwunt]
- boastfully eloquent
(The victorious councilman highlighted the evening with a MAGNILOQUENT acceptance speech.)

MAKESHIFT [MAYK shift]
- temporary/substitute
(A MAKESHIFT hut made from bamboo and straw served as battalion headquarters.)

MALADROIT [mal uh DROIT]
- awkward/bungling
(The MALADROIT waiter spilled the wine as he poured it into the glass.)

MALAISE [ma LAYZ; muh LAYZ]
- mental/physical discomfort
(From the lengthy bout of depression lingered a chronically enervating MALAISE.)

MALEDICTION [mal i DIK shun]
- defamatory curse
(At his sentencing, the condemned man bellowed forth a series of MALEDICTIONS against those who indirectly contributed to his life of crime.)

MALEVOLENT [muh LEV uh lunt]
- spitefully vicious
(The MALEVOLENT remark sought to cast aspersions on the winning candidate's probity.)

MALICIOUS [muh LISH us]
- spiteful
(Rumors are often the result of MALICIOUS gossip.)

MALIGN [muh LIEN]
- slander
(The upstanding citizen was MALIGNED by unfounded rumors that he was actually a former Nazi.)

MALINGER [muh LING gur]
- shirk duties (by feigning illness)
(Accused of MALINGERING, the slacker was warned to take his job more seriously if he wanted to keep it.)

MALLEABLE [MAL ee uh bul]
- capable of being stretched/shaped
(Gold is a MALLEABLE metal highly desirable as jewelry.)

MALLEABLE [MAL ee uh bul]
- easily influenced
(Because children are particularly MALLEABLE, it is essential to instill in them moral ethics and positive self-esteem.)

MAMMOTH [MAM uth]
- huge
(Completion of the MAMMOTH construction project was not expected for at least two more years.)

MANDATORY [MAN duh tohr ee]
- required
(In many high schools, successful completion of an algebra and geometry course is MANDATORY for graduation.)

MANIFEST [MAN uh fest]
- reveal
(The castle ghost was said to MANIFEST itself in the guise of a restless knight.)

MANIFEST [MAN uh fest]
- clearly evident
(When informed that she had passed the entrance examination, her relief was MANIFEST.)

MANUMIT [man yuh MIT]
- release from slavery
(The 1863 Emancipation Proclamation MANUMITTED those enslaved in the rebellious southern United States.)

MAR [mahr]
- spoil/blemish
(The sharp-edged ceramic dish MARRED the surface of the new desk.)

MARGINAL [MAHR juh nul]
- barely satisfactory or useful
(Critics viewed the star's lackluster Shakespearean performance as MARGINAL at best.)

MARTINET [mahr tuh NET]
- strict disciplinarian
(The platoon commander was a no-nonsense MARTINET.)

MAUDLIN [MAHD lin]
- overly tearful/excessively emotional
(Patrons chuckled at the drunkard's MAUDLIN display of grief over the spilled drink.)

MAWKISH [MAH kish]
- excessively sentimental
(Whenever she recounted the birth of her child, she would become MAWKISH and melancholy.)

MEAGER [MEE gur]
- inadequately minimal
(The lowly servant earned a MEAGER salary.)

MEANDER [mee AN dur]
- wander randomly
(Cows and other animals drank from the river that MEANDERED through the panoramic countryside.)

MEDDLE [MED ul]
- interfere
(It is rude to MEDDLE in other people's private affairs.)

MEEK [meek]
- humble
(The farmer was a MEEK and God-fearing Christian.)

MEEK [meek]
- submissive
(The MEEK man could not muster enough courage to ask his boss for a raise.)

MELANCHOLY [MEL un kahl ee]
- gloomy
(Dark clouds added to the MELANCHOLY mood of the day.)

MÉLANGE [may LAHNZH]
- confused mixture
(A MÉLANGE of fabrics and metal objects comprised the unusual artwork.)

MELEE [MAY lay; may LAY]
- brawl
(A MELEE erupted among the agitated spectators during the soccer finals.)

MELLIFLUOUS [muh LIF loo us]
- smoothly flowing/sweet-sounding
(Listening to the MELLIFLUOUS words of a Shakespearean sonnet is an ethereal delight.)

MENACE [MEN is]
- nuisance
(Mosquitoes proved to be a major MENACE during the outdoor event.)

MENACE [MEN is]
- threat
(Criminals are seen by many as a MENACE to society.)

MENDACIOUS [men DAY shus]
- lying
(The MENDACIOUS lad could not be trusted.)

MENDICANT [MEN duh kunt]
- beggar
(Tourists are likely to encounter MENDICANTS on the streets of India.)

MENIAL [MEE nee ul]
- lowly/degrading
(To pay his monthly rent, the laid-off pilot was forced to perform MENIAL tasks for minimum wage.)

MEPHITIC [muh FIT ik]
- putrid/stinking
(A MEPHITIC vapor arose from the sewer.)

MERCENARY [MUR suh ner ee]
- selfishly money-motivated
(The politician's corrupt lifestyle developed from MERCENARY ambitions, far from his initial dream of serving the public in a professional and scrupulous manner.)

MERCURIAL [mur KYOOR ee ul]
- impulsively changing
(The queen's MERCURIAL temperament left her subjects uncertain as to what she might demand next.)

MERETRICIOUS [mer i TRISH us]
- flashy but phony
(In a MERETRICIOUS display of wealth, the poseur flaunted her diamond ring with the hope no one would recognize it as merely inferior zirconium.)

MERITORIOUS [mer i TOHR ee us]
- praiseworthy
(Becoming an Eagle Scout is a MERITORIOUS achievement.)

METAMORPHOSIS [met uh MOHR fuh sis]
- striking transformation
(Through an unexpected METAMORPHOSIS, the once-mischievous child became a socially responsible and highly respected teenager.)

METAPHORICAL [met uh FOHR i kul]
- figurative/poetically equivalent
(In METAPHORICAL metonymy, the poet referred to the sun as "a beacon of the holy cross.")

METE [meet]
- dispense
*(The punishment **METED** out befit the gravity of the crime.)*

METEORIC [mee tee OHR ik]
- sudden and brilliant
*(The young singing sensation experienced a **METEORIC** rise to stardom.)*

METICULOUS [muh TIK yuh lus]
- carefully exact
*(Diamond-cutters ply their craft with **METICULOUS** precision.)*

MIEN [meen]
- demeanor
*(The elderly lady had a kindly **MIEN**.)*

MIGATORY [MIE gruh tohr ee]
- journeying/wandering
*(Lemmings are **MIGRATORY** rodents.)*

MILIEU [mil YOO]
- environment/setting
*(The precocious lad took personal pride in being part of the university's academic **MILIEU**.)*

MIMETIC [mi MET ik]
- imitative
*(A model is a **MIMETIC** representation of an actual or idealized object.)*

MINCE [mins]
- moderate/soften
*(The irate husband **MINCED** his words of anger so as to not regret them later.)*

MINUSCULE [MIN uh skyool]
- tiny
*(The **MINUSCULE** portion of cheese was sufficient to feed the scrawny mouse.)*

MINUTIAE [mi NOO shee ee]
- trivial details
*(Rather than attempt to deal with and resolve the more serious matter, the committee seemed resolved to dwell on **MINUTIAE**.)*

MIRTH [murth]
- joy and laughter
*(Summer vacation is a time of **MIRTH** for youngsters.)*

MISCONSTRUE [mis kun STROO]
- misinterpret
*(The randy sailor **MISCONSTRUED** what the hostess meant when told that it was getting late.)*

MISCREANT [MIS kree unt]
- villainous scoundrel
*(The **MISCREANT** gained notoriety for his dastardly acts of desecration.)*

MISERLY [MIE zur lee]
- very stingy
*(Silas Marner was a **MISERLY** person who loved to count his gold.)*

MISGIVINGS [mis GIV ingz]
- worrisome doubts
*(The young author had **MISGIVINGS** about signing the exclusive contract without the presence of his literary agent.)*

MITIGATE [MIT uh gayt]
- lessen (in severity)
*(Self-defense was offered as a motive in the hope of **MITIGATING** the seriousness of the defendant's crime.)*

MNEMONIC [nee MAHN ik]
- relating to/assisting memory
*(There are many **MNEMONIC** devices which aid in recalling people's names.)*

MOBILE [MOH bul]
- easily movable
*(The **MOBILE** stage could be set up within an hour.)*

MOBILIZE [MOH buh liez]
- assemble and activate
*(To protect the town from approaching floodwaters, the National Guard was **MOBILIZED**.)*

MODEST [MAHD ist]
- humble/not flashy
*(Old and young alike enjoyed being in the company of the **MODEST** and pleasant young man.)*

MOLLIFY [MAHL uh fie]
- appease
*(To **MOLLIFY** the angry crowd that had waited an extra hour for the carnival to open, the manager doled out free passes to ride the Ferris wheel.)*

MOLTEN [MOHL tun]
- hot and liquefied
*(After the eruption, **MOLTEN** lava flowed down the side of the volcano.)*

MOMENTOUS [moh MEN tus]
- influentially significant
*(After the infamous attack upon Pearl Harbor took place, President Franklin Roosevelt made a **MOMENTOUS** decision to declare war on Japan.)*

MONOLITHIC [mahn uh LITH ik]
- one-piece and massive
*(A **MONOLITHIC** concrete slab covered the fallout shelter.)*

MOOT [moot]
- open to debate
*(Whether man can survive on planets in distant galaxies is **MOOT** because it may be impossible to ever travel that far.)*

MORBID [MOHR bid]
- gruesome
*(The website displayed **MORBID** pictures of the fatal car crash.)*

MORBID [MOHR bid]
- abnormal and unhealthy
*(The youngster had a **MORBID** fascination for the macabre.)*

MORDANT [MOHR dunt]
- keenly sarcastic
*(Calling the sensationalized farce a "self-fulfilling prophecy" epitomized the critic's **MORDANT** wit.)*

MORIBUND [MOHR uh bund]
- dying
*(Residents fled the town and its **MORIBUND** economy for greener pastures and brighter employment opportunities.)*

MOROSE [muh ROHS]
- gloomy and depressed
*(Unlike his cheerful younger brother, the older sibling was **MOROSE** and ill-tempered.)*

MORTIFY [MOHR tuh fie]
- humiliate
*(The teenager's outrageous behavior at the banquet **MORTIFIED** his parents.)*

MOTIF [moh TEEF]
- dominant theme
*(A recurring **MOTIF** in the novel was man's search for self-identity.)*

MOTLEY [MAHT lee]
- diverse
*(Hitchhiking across the country, the **MOTLEY** group ranged in ages from fourteen to forty-five.)*

MOTLEY [MAHT lee]
- multicolored
*(The clown entered the children's party wearing a **MOTLEY** robe.)*

MOUNTEBANK [MOUN tuh bangk]
- fraud
*(Although the medicine was purported to be a cure for all ailments, the elixir was merely soda water and the seller nothing but a **MOUNTEBANK**.)*

MULCT [mulkt]
- swindle
(By exacting strict penalties for tiny infractions, the king found yet more ways to MULCT his subjects of their gold.)

MULTIFACETED [mul ti FAS i tid]
- many-sided
(International commerce carries with it complex and MULTIFACETED problems.)

MULTIFARIOUS [mul tuh FAHR ee us]
- numerous and diverse
(Life on the moon is fraught with MULTIFARIOUS difficulties and complexities.)

MULTIPLICITY [mul tuh PLIS i tee]
- diverse abundance
(The conference inspired a MULTIPLICITY of ideas and suggestions.)

MUNDANE [mun DAYN; MUN dayn]
- everyday
(Driving home from work in the rush-hour traffic is one of those MUNDANE problems almost everyone must deal with.)

MUNIFICENT [myoo NIF i sunt]
- very generous
(A plaque honored the MUNIFICENT contribution made to help build the neighborhood child-care center.)

MYRIAD [MIR ee ad]
- innumerable/countless
(Sigmund Freud sought to find logical consistencies within the MYRIAD intricacies of the human psyche.)

NADIR [NAY dur]
- lowest point/bottom
(The coach's career reached its NADIR as the team found itself without a single victory.)

NAÏVE [nah EEV]
- unsuspectingly innocent
(The young lady was so NAÏVE that when asked to stay overnight, she thought it was to help tidy up the house.)

NAMESAKE [NAYM sayk]
- thing named after another
(The Galapagos tortoise is the island's NAMESAKE.)

NASCENT [NAS unt; NAY sunt]
- beginning to develop
(Only in their NASCENT stage, the contract talks had much remaining to be resolved.)

NAUSEOUS [NAH shus; NAH zee us]
 - sick/sickening
(After the long and bumpy boat ride, many passengers felt NAUSEOUS.)

NEBULOUS [NEB yuh lus]
 - vague/hazy
(Man's understanding of life after death remains as NEBULOUS today as it was a thousand years ago.)

NEFARIOUS [ni FAHR ee us; ni FAR ee us]
 - wicked
(When caught, the villain paid dearly for his NEFARIOUS deeds.)

NEMESIS [NEM i sis]
 - formidable rival
(The Joker was Batman's NEMESIS.)

NEOPHYTE [NEE uh fiet]
 - novice
(The newly-elected councilman was a NEOPHYTE to the world of politics.)

NEXUS [NEK sus]
 - link
(Satellites provide a global NEXUS in the communication and transmission of ideas.)

NICETY [NIE si tee]
 - careful detail/attention
(The NICETY of the craftsman's work often determines the value of the end product.)

NICHE [nich]
 - suitable place
(She found her NICHE in life as a doctor.)

NIMBLE [NIM bul]
 - swift and light-footed
(The NIMBLE dancer graced the stage with her ballerina-like steps.)

NIMBLE [NIM bul]
 - clever and alert
(Even into his nineties, George Bernard Shaw possessed a NIMBLE mind and trenchant wit.)

NOISOME [NOI sum]
 - offensive/disgusting
(Residents complained bitterly about the NOISOME odor coming from the nearby sewage-treatment plant.)

NOMADIC [noh MA dik]
 - wandering
(The Sahara Desert is home to numerous NOMADIC tribes.)

NONCHALANT [nahn shuh LAHNT]
- casually unconcerned
*(The man's **NONCHALANT** demeanor when recounting the events leading up to his employer's mysterious disappearance raised police suspicions of possible complicity.)*

NONDESCRIPT [nahn di SKRIPT]
- not readily identifiable
*(The hairy animal was **NONDESCRIPT**, though it did resemble a bear in its gait.)*

NONPAREIL [nahn puh REL]
- one without equal
*(Of all the actresses appearing, she was the **NONPAREIL** in terms of movie experience and career success.)*

NONPLUS [nahn PLUS; NAHN plus]
- perplex totally
*(The sound of reporters banging on her front door at midnight **NONPLUSSED** the poor woman.)*

NOSTALGIC [nah STAL jik]
- sentimentally yearning for the past
*(When thinking of one's high school days, it is easy to become **NOSTALGIC**.)*

NOTORIOUS [noh TOHR ee us]
- infamous
*(Local newspapers feasted over the **NOTORIOUS** love affair between the movie star and his younger cousin.)*

NOVEL [NAHV ul]
- excitingly new and original
*(**NOVEL** ideas often precede notable inventions.)*

NOVICE [NAHV is]
- beginner/newcomer
*(Although the ski resort offered a challenging slope for experienced skiers, it also had a more modest one for **NOVICES**.)*

NOXIOUS [NAHK shus]
- harmful
*(**NOXIOUS** fumes emanating from the geyser caused breathing difficulties for several of the visiting tourists.)*

NUGATORY [NOO guh tohr ee]
- worthless/insignificant
*(To the scientific community, uncorroborated assertions are regarded as having **NUGATORY** value.)*

OBDURATE [AHB duh rit; AHB dyoo rit]
- stubborn/unyielding
*(The boy was **OBDURATE** in his refusal to dance with his sister.)*

OBEISANCE [oh BAY suns; oh BEE suns]
- bow of respect
(Upon entering the king's court, the knight made an OBEISANCE to the mighty leader.)

OBFUSCATE [ahb FUS kayt; AHB fuh skayt]
- confuse/obscure
(Through highly-charged accusations, the belligerent protester attempted to OBFUSCATE the peaceful tenor of the senator's speech.)

OBJECTIONABLE [ub JEK shuh nuh bul]
- offensive
(The movie's dialogue included many instances of OBJECTIONABLE language.)

OBJECTIVE [ub JEK tiv]
- unbiased
(The television documentary provided OBJECTIVE coverage of the historic political rally.)

OBJURGATE [AHB jur gayt; ub JUR gayt]
- denounce harshly
(Outraged community activists OBJURGATED the council committee for arbitrarily spending money without first consulting the voters.)

OBLIGATORY [uh BLIG uh tohr ee]
- mandatory
(In the United States, schooling is OBLIGATORY for all minors.)

OBLIVIOUS [uh BLIV ee us]
- unaware
(Beachgoers frolicked in the pounding surf, OBLIVIOUS to the dangers of the accompanying rip current.)

OBLOQUY [AHB luh kwee]
- censure of disgrace
(The accused spy endured the unremitting OBLOQUY from those who had earlier trusted him.)

OBNOXIOUS [ub NAHK shus]
- personally offensive
(The feisty lad was reprimanded for his OBNOXIOUS behavior at the dinner table.)

OBSCURE [ahb SKYOOR]
- unclear
(Lettering on the street signs was OBSCURE due to the dense fog.)

OBSEQUIOUS [ub SEE kwee us]
- servile
(The powerful movie mogul was surrounded by his OBSEQUIOUS toadies.)

OBSESSIVE [ahb SES iv]
- excessive/hauntingly controlling
(A chronic kleptomaniac, he had an OBSESSIVE compulsion to steal.)

OBSOLESCENT [abh suh LES unt]
- becoming obsolete
*(**OBSOLESCENT** bulky computers are rapidly being replaced by more efficient compact models.)*

OBSTINATE [AHB stuh nit]
- stubborn
*(The **OBSTINATE** man would not admit to his obvious error in judgment.)*

OBSTREPEROUS [ub STREP ur us]
- unruly
*(The **OBSTREPEROUS** bottle-throwing crowd bore the onus for the umpires' decision to halt the little-league baseball game.)*

OBTRUSIVE [ub TROO siv]
- meddlesome ("pushy")
*(The **OBTRUSIVE** neighbor constantly stuck her nose into the newlyweds' affairs.)*

OBVIATE [AHB vee ayt]
- make unnecessary
*(Saving money in advance **OBVIATES** the need to later on assume a high-interest loan to pay for college.)*

OCCLUDE [uh KLOOD]
- obstruct
*(Rags **OCCLUDED** the drainage pipe, causing the basement to flood.)*

OCCULT [uh KULT]
- supernatural
*(The tribal shaman was believed powerful enough to communicate directly with **OCCULT** forces.)*

ODIOUS [OH dee us]
- shamefully bad/disgusting
*(Setting his neighbors' house ablaze while they slept was an **ODIOUS** act of cowardly revenge.)*

ODORIFEROUS [oh duh RIF ur us]
- emitting an odor/aroma
*(The pikake plant emits a pleasantly **ODORIFEROUS** perfume.)*

ODYSSEY [AHD i see]
- long/exciting journey
*(The adventurous collegians shared a bicycle **ODYSSEY** through South America.)*

OFFICIOUS [uh FISH us]
- intrusive
*(The **OFFICIOUS** mother-in-law constantly meddled in the young couple's affairs.)*

OLEAGINOUS [oh lee AJ uh nus]
- oily
*(The aloe vera plant contains an **OLEAGINOUS** medicinal substance.)*

OMINOUS [AHM uh nus]
 - foretelling disaster
 *(Nostradamus made several **OMINOUS** predictions in the sixteenth century that have come eerily true four hundred years later.)*

OMNIPOTENT [ahm NIP uh tunt]
 - all-powerful
 *(Julius Caesar was a greatly revered and feared **OMNIPOTENT** ruler.)*

OMNISCIENT [ahm NISH unt]
 - all-seeing/all-knowing
 *(Spiritual leaders of the agrarian tribe performed a ritual dance in honor of their **OMNISCIENT** deity in hope they would receive deliverance from the interminable drought.)*

ONEROUS [AHN ur us; OH nur us]
 - oppressive/burdensome
 *(Caring for the elderly is oftentimes an **ONEROUS** task.)*

ONSET [AHN set]
 - beginning
 *(Chills and a fever often signal the **ONSET** of the flu.)*

ONSET [AHN set]
 - attack
 *(Military reinforcements were brought in to repel the anticipated **ONSET** of rebel forces.)*

ONUS [OH nus]
 - burden/responsibility
 *(Bar owners must also bear the **ONUS** when an intoxicated customer is later involved in an automobile accident.)*

OPPORTUNE [ahp ur TOON; ahp ur TYOON]
 - well-timed
 *(The movie intermission offered an **OPPORTUNE** moment to purchase popcorn and a soft drink.)*

OPPRESSIVE [uh PRES iv]
 - burdensome/depressing
 *(Many feel that the current tax structure is unfairly **OPPRESSIVE** to those most in need of tax relief.)*

OPPRESSIVE [uh PRES iv]
 - harsh and cruel
 *(The **OPPRESSIVE** taskmaster demanded that his crew work nonstop until the cargo was unloaded.)*

OPPROBRIOUS [uh PROH bree us]
 - disgraceful
 *(Sports reporters reviled the coach for his **OPPROBRIOUS** verbal assault upon his own young players.)*

OPTIMISTIC [ahp tuh MIS tik]
- hopeful
(Despite troubling economic signs, the chairman remained OPTIMISTIC about the future.)

OPULENT [AHP yuh lunt]
- lavishly wealthy
(The actor's OPULENT estate included a professional tennis court and two Olympic-sized swimming pools.)

ORDURE [OHR jur]
- filth
(The peasants were destined to forever tread upon the ORDURE of the animals they followed.)

ORNATE [ohr NAYT]
- elaborately decorated
(Rococo furniture is characterized by its highly ORNATE style.)

OROTUND [OHR uh tund]
- rich/full in sound
(The senator's OROTUND voice obviated the need for a microphone.)

OROTUND [OHR uh tund]
- bombastic
(The demagogue's OROTUND oratory ignited the prejudices of his misguided flock.)

ORTHODOX [OHR thuh dahks]
- conventional and accepted
(The young Republican subscribed to generally ORTHODOX political ideology.)

OSTENSIBLE [ah STEN suh bul]
- outwardly appearing
(The teenager's OSTENSIBLE display of bravado was intended to impress his girlfriend.)

OSTENTATIOUS [ahs ten TAY shus]
- showy
(The new-car owner proudly paraded his vehicle in an OSTENTATIOUS display of vanity and self-delight.)

OSTRACIZE [AHS truh siez]
- exclude socially
(In past centuries, those afflicted with leprosy were shunned and OSTRACIZED.)

OTIOSE [OH shee ohs; OH tee ohs]
- valueless/useless
(His OTIOSE commentary had no relevance to the discussion and merely made an already-protracted meeting even lengthier.)

OUST [oust]
- expel
(The majority voted to OUST the current club president.)

OUTLANDISH [out LAN dish]
- strikingly unusual
(The lad's OUTLANDISH hair style attracted stares from other students.)

OUTMODED [out MOH did]
- outdated
(In today's age of technology, even the most advanced computers will soon become OUTMODED.)

OUTSET [OUT set]
- beginning
(There were many problems from the OUTSET of the space mission.)

OVERT [OH vurt; oh VURT]
- apparent/observable
(The brouhaha after the football game was an OVERT display of poor sportsmanship.)

PACIFY [PAS uh fie]
- calm
(Soft music is often used to PACIFY a restless infant.)

PAEAN [PEE un]
- song of praise
(The national anthem of the United States is a PAEAN celebrating the country's independence.)

PAINSTAKING [PAYN stay king]
- careful and thorough
(Renoir's impressionist artworks reflect PAINSTAKING detail.)

PALATABLE [PAL uh tuh bul]
- tasty
(At the lavish buffet, guests were treated to a highly PALATABLE and ambrosial feast.)

PALATABLE [PAL uh tuh bul]
- acceptable
(The tardy lad hoped the school principal would find his excuse to be PALATABLE.)

PALL [pahl]
- cover of darkness
(For many days after the volcano erupted, a PALL of soot hung over the town, blocking out the sun.)

PALL [pahl]
- gloom
(The collapse of the major firm cast a PALL on the entire industry.)

PALLIATE [PAL ee ayt]
- soothe
(Even though they do not offer ultimate curative value, some medicines are beneficial in helping PALLIATE the painful effects of various diseases.)

PALLID [PAL id]
- pale
*(A bout of the flu left the news reporter appearing **PALLID** and sickly.)*

PALPABLE [PAL puh bul]
- clearly noticeable/comprehensible
*(During the daring aerial acrobatics act, the feeling of suspense in the audience was **PALPABLE**.)*

PALTRY [PAHL tree]
- small/worthless
*(For all his efforts, the waiter was rewarded with only a **PALTRY** tip.)*

PANACEA [pan uh SEE uh]
- instant remedy
*(Discovering a **PANACEA** for all the world's ills is a fanciful though highly unlikely prospect.)*

PANACHE [puh NASH]
- flair
*(Throughout his illustrious career, Rudolf Nureyev performed ballet with unparalleled artistry and **PANACHE**.)*

PANDEMIC [pan DEM ik]
- widespread
*(The island chain suffered a **PANDEMIC** outbreak of malaria.)*

PANDEMONIUM [pan duh MOH nee um]
- chaos
*(When the firecracker exploded, the movie theater erupted into **PANDEMONIUM**.)*

PANEGYRIC [pan i JIR ik; pan i JIE rik]
- formal/elaborate praise
*(The governor delivered a **PANEGYRIC** in behalf of the elderly woman's many years of dedicated service to the community.)*

PANORAMIC [pan uh RAM ik]
- scenic
*(The movie star's penthouse afforded her a **PANORAMIC** view of the city below.)*

PANTHEON [PAN thee ahn]
- temple
*(The Hall of Fame is baseball's **PANTHEON**, an homage to the sport's best.)*

PARADIGM [PAR uh diem; PAR uh dim]
- ideal/model example
*(Sports figures are often mistakenly revered as **PARADIGMS** of society.)*

PARADOX [PAYR uh dahks]
- apparent contradiction
*(It is a **PARADOX** that banks are least willing to lend money to those who need it the most.)*

PARAGON [PAYR uh gahn]
- model of excellence
*(Princess Diana was regarded as a **PARAGON** of grace and beauty.)*

PARAMETER [puh RAM i tur]
- characteristic element
*(Many people acknowledge crime as an unwelcome **PARAMETER** of society's emphasis on financial success.)*

PARAMETER [puh RAM i tur]
- guideline
*(Emily Post outlined the **PARAMETERS** within which one must behave to be socially proper.)*

PARAMOUNT [PAYR uh mount]
- foremost/utmost
*(In any classroom, the safety of the students should be of **PARAMOUNT** concern to the teacher.)*

PARCH [pahrch]
- dry completely
*(The desert heat **PARCHED** the land and forced its inhabitants underground.)*

PARIAH [puh RIE uh]
- social outcast
*(Unfortunately, many Viet Nam veterans found themselves treated as **PARIAHS** upon their return to civilian life.)*

PARITY [PAYR i tee]
- equality
*(In an effort to achieve **PARITY**, many businesses have raised women's salaries faster than those of their male counterparts.)*

PAROCHIAL [puh ROH kee ul]
- narrow-minded
*(The insulated curmudgeon obstinately maintained his **PAROCHIAL** dismissal of technological advances.)*

PARSIMONIOUS [pahr suh MOH nee us]
- thrifty/stingy
*(Bonuses were rare when working for the **PARSIMONIOUS** shop owner.)*

PASSE [pa SAY]
- obsolete
*(Many popular hair styles of the past quickly become **PASSÉ**.)*

PASTORAL [PAS tur ul]
- rural and peaceful
*(Fed up with his frenetic and unfulfilling lifestyle, the stockbroker resigned his executive position to pursue a more personally pleasing **PASTORAL** existence.)*

PATENT [PAT unt]
- obvious
*(The mendacious lad's mother knew that his claim of never having filched cookies from the cookie jar was a **PATENT** falsehood.)*

PATHOS [PAY thahs]
- power/ability to arouse sympathy
*(Shakespeare's great tragedies exude a universal **PATHOS**.)*

PATRONIZE [PAY truh niez; PA truh niez]
- support
*(Through generous donations, the philanthropic family **PATRONIZED** the performing arts in their community.)*

PATRONIZE [PAY truh niez; PA truh niez]
- act superior to
*(The young actor resented being **PATRONIZED** by the more seasoned veterans.)*

PAUCITY [PAH si tee]
- scarcity/lack
*(A **PAUCITY** of state funds forced a cutback of transportation services.)*

PECULATE [PEK yuh layt]
- embezzle
*(An audit revealed that funds had been **PECULATED** from the drama club's treasury.)*

PECUNIARY [pi KYOO nee er ee]
- monetary
*(In order to meet his monthly rent obligations, the man sought **PECUNIARY** assistance from his local church.)*

PEDAGOGIC [ped uh GAHJ ik]
- (relating to) teaching
*(Rather than employ a more **PEDAGOGIC** approach, the vocational school preferred on-the-job training.)*

PEDANTIC [puh DAN tik]
- overly bookish
*(The English teacher's **PEDANTIC** proclivity for grammatical correctness stifled student creativity in their fictional writing.)*

PEERLESS [PEER lis]
- incomparable/unequaled
*(Audie Murphy was decorated for his **PEERLESS** valor on the battlefield.)*

PEEVISH [PEE vish]
- cross and irritable
*(Having slept poorly the night before, the man was unusually **PEEVISH** throughout the day.)*

PELAGIC [puh LAJ ik]
- relating to/living in the ocean
*(The plesiosaur was a **PELAGIC** creature of the Mesozoic era that grew as long as forty feet.)*

PELL-MELL [PEL mel]
- hastily and disorderly
*(During the earthquake, students dashed **PELL-MELL** into the hallways.)*

PELLUCID [puh LOO sid]
- clear
*(The instructor's **PELLUCID** analysis made the complex scientific theory pleasantly palpable.)*

PENCHANT [PEN shunt]
- strong liking
*(Many people have a **PENCHANT** for chocolates.)*

PENDING [PEN ding]
- undecided
*(The date of the championship game remained **PENDING** until transportation could be secured.)*

PENITENT [PEN i tunt]
- repentant/remorseful
*(In his later years, the petty thief became **PENITENT** for his misguided life of crime.)*

PENSIVE [PEN siv]
- meditative
*(In his **PENSIVE** moments alone, the young businessman contemplated whether he was truly happy with his career.)*

PENURIOUS [puh NOOR ee us; puh NYOOR ee us]
- stingy
*(The **PENURIOUS** passenger ordered the least expensive entrée on the ship's restaurant menu.)*

PENURIOUS [puh NOOR ee us; puh NYOOR ee us]
- extremely poor
*(The elderly woman lived a **PENURIOUS** life subsisting on her paltry retirement allowance.)*

PENURY [PEN yuh ree]
- extreme poverty
*(Inner-city slums are a magnet for those whose lives are enslaved in **PENURY**.)*

PERAMBULATE [pur AM byuh layt]
- stroll
*(In his leisure moments, the cruise-line passenger **PERAMBULATED** around the deck.)*

PERCEPTIVE [pur SEP tiv]
- aware/intelligent
*(Jane Goodall's research on the habits of primates is a **PERCEPTIVE** and caring glimpse into the behavior of man's closest relatives.)*

PERCIPIENT [pur SIP ee unt]
- keenly perceptive
*(The admissions counselor was a **PERCIPIENT** judge of an applicant's personal commitment.)*

PERDITION [pur DISH un]
- hell
*(A life spiraling out of control was leading the lost soul on a path doomed to **PERDITION**.)*

PEREGRINATION [per uh gruh NAY shun]
- journey
*(The young writer's **PEREGRINATION** to foreign lands inspired his later novels.)*

PEREMPTORY [puh REMP tuh ree; PUR emp tohr ee]
- absolute and irreversible
*(A subpoena is a **PEREMPTORY** legal writ to appear in court.)*

PEREMPTORY [puh REMP tuh ree; PUR emp tohr ee]
- domineering/dictatorial
*(The **PEREMPTORY** supervisor alienated his staff with his intolerance of and callous disregard for their input.)*

PERFIDIOUS [pur FID ee us]
- disloyally deceitful
*(The soldiers suggested that a **PERFIDIOUS** traitor from within their ranks may have led to their capture.)*

PERFUNCTORY [pur FUNGK tuh ree]
- mechanical and unenthusiastic
*(Upon conclusion of the unproductive meeting, the ambassador gave the customary **PERFUNCTORY** bow and then exited the room.)*

PERILOUS [PER uh lus]
- hazardous
*(Mountain climbing can be a **PERILOUS** venture.)*

PERIPATETIC [per uh puh TET ik]
- traveling
*(The **PERIPATETIC** preacher took his message far and wide throughout the land.)*

PERIPHERAL [puh RIF ur ul]
- auxiliary/secondary
*(In the children's television program, adult characters played **PERIPHERAL** roles.)*

PERISH [PER ish]
- die
*(Without water, all plants and animals soon **PERISH**.)*

PERMEABLE [PUR mee uh bul]
- able to be penetrated
*(Because sponges are **PERMEABLE** to water, they are an excellent means to clean up liquid spills quickly and efficiently.)*

PERNICIOUS [pur NISH us]
- highly destructive/dangerous
*(The Ebola is a **PERNICIOUS** strain of virus.)*

PERPETRATE [PUR pi trayt]
- commit
*(Jack the Ripper is thought to have **PERPETRATED** numerous gruesome murders in the 1880's.)*

PERPLEX [pur PLEKS]
- puzzle
*(The cause of the mysterious illness **PERPLEXED** the medical community.)*

PERSEVERE [pur suh VEER]
- not give up
*(Despite the difficulty in lifting the heavy suitcase, the youngster **PERSEVERED** until he managed to get it into the car.)*

PERSONIFY [pur SAHN uh fie]
- represent ideally
*(The Statue of Liberty **PERSONIFIES** individual liberty and freedom.)*

PERSPICACIOUS [pur spuh KAY shus]
- astute
*(Henry Kissinger was revered for his **PERSPICACIOUS** political and diplomatic insight.)*

PERSPICUOUS [pur SPIK yoo us]
- lucid
*(The eminent scientist was able to provide a **PERSPICUOUS** explanation for the highly extraordinary phenomenon.)*

PERTINACIOUS [pur tuh NAY shus]
- stubbornly persistent
*(The **PERTINACIOUS** news reporter would not leave the movie star's dressing room without first getting an interview.)*

PERUSE [puh ROOZ]
- read/examine carefully
*(Before signing on the dotted line, the actor **PERUSED** the contract for possible errors or omissions.)*

PERVERSE [pur VURS]
- rebellious and contrary
*(The lad's stubbornly **PERVERSE** nature manifested itself in his proclivity to do what his parents asked him not to do.)*

PESSIMISTIC [pes uh MIS tik]
- gloomy
*(The economic analyst presented a **PESSIMISTIC** outlook for summer retail sales.)*

PESTILENT [PES tuh lunt]
- destructive
*(The Bubonic Plague was a **PESTILENT** disease that ravaged Europe in the fourteenth century.)*

PESTILENT [PES tuh lunt]
- evil/socially harmful
*(Envy and jealousy perpetrate **PESTILENT** rumors.)*

PETTY [PET ee]
- trivial/insignificant
*(The divisive family feud began as merely a **PETTY** argument.)*

PETULANT [PECH uh lunt]
- impatiently irritable
*(Whenever he did not get things his way, the **PETULANT** lad would throw a temper tantrum.)*

PHILANTHROPIC [fil un THRAHP ik]
- charitable
*(The Rockefeller family have long been renowned for their **PHILANTHROPIC** deeds.)*

PHILIPPIC [fi LIP ik]
- harsh verbal denunciation
*(The nation's leader delivered a violent **PHILIPPIC** against those foreign powers who had profited from the exportation of drugs to his country.)*

PHILISTINE [FIL i steen]
- uncultured
*(Her **PHILISTINE** boyfriend declined the offer to attend an opera.)*

PHLEGMATIC [fleg MAT ik]
- not easily excited
*(The **PHLEGMATIC** passenger remained unruffled even when the airplane encountered severe turbulence.)*

PHYSIOGNOMY [fiz ee AHG nuh mee; fiz ee AHN uh mee]
- facial profile/countenance
*(Abraham Lincoln possessed a strikingly august **PHYSIOGNOMY**.)*

PICARESQUE [PIK uh resk; PEE kuh resk]
- mischievously adventuresome
*(The Adventures of Huckleberry Finn is a **PICARESQUE** novel chronicling a young man's escapades as he travels down the Mississippi River.)*

PICAYUNE [pik ee YOON]
- small and unimportant
(Realizing that his PICAYUNE contributions would benefit few, if any, the senator left the political arena to pursue a more personally satisfying career in education.)

PIED [pied]
- multicolored
(The van had a PIED coloration, blotches of white and grey contrasting with the original black paint.)

PINNACLE [PIN uh kul]
- peak
(J. K. Rowling reached the PINNACLE of success with her Harry Potter novels.)

PIOUS [PIE us]
- religiously devoted
(The peaceful villagers were PIOUS churchgoers.)

PIQUE [peek]
- arouse
(The whisper of gossip PIQUED his curiosity.)

PIQUE [peek]
- offend
(When she discovered that the controversial issue had been debated and voted upon in her absence, the board member was visibly PIQUED.)

PISCATORIAL [pis kuh TOHR ee ul]
- (relating to) fishing
(The sailor's PISCATORIAL adventure involved an enormous man-eating shark.)

PITHY [PITH ee]
- concise and meaningful
("Haste makes waste" is a PITHY epigram.)

PLACATE [PLAY kayt; PLAK ayt]
- appease
(Offering to pay for the broken window helped PLACATE the irate shop owner.)

PLACID [PLAS id]
- peaceful/calm
(On weekends, the PLACID lake attracted scores of tourists and picnickers alike.)

PLAINTIVE [PLAYN tiv]
- woeful/mournful
(In the dead of night, the PLAINTIVE howl of a lone wolf could be heard.)

PLAUDITS [PLAH dits]
- praise and approval
(After years of obscurity, the innovative producer won the PLAUDITS of the movie world with her award-winning documentary.)

PLAUSIBLE [PLAH zuh bul]
- believable
*(Despite its action and suspense, the movie lacked a **PLAUSIBLE** story-line.)*

PLEASANTRY [PLEZ un tree]
- courteous social remark
*(When introduced, the guests exchanged **PLEASANTRIES**.)*

PLEBEIAN [pluh BEE un]
- unrefined/low-class
*(The rustic couple's **PLEBEIAN** manners met with glacial stares from the elite restaurant patrons.)*

PLENARY [PLEE nuh ree; PLEN uh ree]
- absolute
*(The young king was vested with **PLENARY** powers.)*

PLENIPOTENTIARY [plen ee puh TEN shee er ee; plen ee puh TEN shuh ree]
- having full authority
*(At the international convention, the foreign ambassador was granted **PLENIPOTENTIARY** discretion.)*

PLENITUDE [PLEN i tood; PLEN i tyood]
- abundance
*(The Garden of Eden boasted a **PLENITUDE** of vegetation.)*

PLETHORA [PLETH ur uh]
- overabundance/excess
*(Paleontologists have posited a **PLETHORA** of possible explanations for the extinction of dinosaurs during the Cretaceous period.)*

PLIABLE [PLIE uh bul]
- flexible/bendable
*(The **PLIABLE** metal could be bent to fit wherever an electrical conductor was needed.)*

PLIABLE [PLIE uh bul]
- easily influenced
*(Because children are very **PLIABLE**, they are oftentimes the target of unscrupulous adults seeking to enlist their services.)*

PLIANT [PLIE unt]
- flexible/resilient
*(The **PLIANT** twig could not be easily snapped.)*

PLIGHT [pliet]
- troublesome situation
*(The movie documented the **PLIGHT** of the hapless nineteenth century coal miners.)*

PLOY [ploi]
- clever/calculated tactic
*(The scoundrel's flattery was merely a **PLOY** to gain the gullible woman's confidence and the keys to her house.)*

POGROM [POH grum; puh GRUM]
- organized massacre
*(German **POGROMS** during World War II forced Jews to flee en masse.)*

POIGNANT [POIN ynt]
- deeply/painfully emotionally moving
*(No Shakespearean tragedy is more **POIGNANT** than that of Romeo and Juliet.)*

POLARIZE [POH luh riez]
- divide into two opposite extremes
*(The highly controversial issue **POLARIZED** the community.)*

POLEMIC [puh LEM ik; poh LEM ik] (also, **POLEMICAL**)
- controversial
*(Darwin's Theory of Evolution has long been fodder for **POLEMIC** debate.)*

POLTROON [pohl TROON]
- coward
*(For fleeing the battlefield as soon as the fighting began, the young warrior was branded a **POLTROON**.)*

POLYCHROMATIC [pahl ee kruh MAT ik]
- multicolored
*(The rainbow is a **POLYCHROMATIC** arc.)*

POMPOUS [PAHM pus]
- arrogantly self-important
*(The **POMPOUS** man treated his underlings as servants and his peers as rabble.)*

PONDEROUS [PAHN dur us]
- bulky and heavy
*(It took three people to carry the **PONDEROUS** package.)*

PONDEROUS [PAHN dur us]
- tediously boring
*(The esoterically **PONDEROUS** dissertation was a struggle to follow.)*

POPULACE [PAHP yuh lus]
- general population
*(The President addressed the **POPULACE** in his annual nationwide speech.)*

POPULOUS [PAHP yuh lus]
- densely populated
*(China is a **POPULOUS** nation.)*

POROUS [POHR us]
- absorbent
*(A sponge is an elastic and **POROUS** skeletal mass.)*

PORTENTOUS [pohr TEN tus]
- ominous
*(The emperor's **PORTENTOUS** words alerted the citizens to the possibility of war.)*

PORTLY [POHRT lee]
- heavy and bulky
*(In his later years, Orson Wells was a **PORTLY** and imposing figure.)*

POSEUR [POH zur; poh ZUR]
- showoff
*(To impress the girls at school, the self-absorbed **POSEUR** drove up in his father's fancy sports car.)*

POSTHUMOUS [PAHS chuh mus]
- occurring after a person's death
*(The war hero was awarded a **POSTHUMOUS** medal of honor.)*

POSTULATE [PAHS chuh layt]
- assume theoretically
*(Scientists have **POSTULATED** that life beings from distant worlds may well share some resemblance to earthlings.)*

POTABLE [POH tuh bul]
- suitable for drinking
*(Contaminants in the lake rendered the water no longer **POTABLE**.)*

POTENT [POHT nt]
- powerful
*(A **POTENT** and caustic vapor emanated from the geyser.)*

POTPOURRI [poh poo REE]
- mixture
*(The stew was a **POTPOURRI** of savory meats and vegetables.)*

PRACTICABLE [PRAK tuh kuh bul]
- practical/workable
*(Though untested, the concept seemed both **PRACTICABLE** and economically viable.)*

PRAGMATIC [prag MAT ik]
- practical
*(After debating the issue for weeks without resolution, it was agreed upon that a more **PRAGMATIC** approach was needed to help end the strike.)*

PRECARIOUS [pri KAR ee us]
- hazardous
*(Surrounded by wolves, the campers found themselves in a **PRECARIOUS** predicament.)*

PRECIOSITY [presh ee AHS i tee]
- exaggerated refinement
*(To sound more educated, the young woman spoke with an air of **PRECIOSITY**.)*

PRECIPITATION [pri sip i TAY shun]
- rainfall/snowfall
*(Six inches of **PRECIPITATION** fell over a twelve-hour period.)*

PRECIPITOUS [pri SIP i tus]
- very steep
*(From the promontory, the hikers viewed the **PRECIPITOUS** drop to the ocean below.)*

PRECIPITOUS [pri SIP i tus]
- sudden and rash
*(A **PRECIPITOUS** rush into the stock market can prove a financially costly mistake.)*

PRÉCIS [pray SEE; PRAY see]
- concise summary
*(The book report included a **PRÉCIS** of the novel.)*

PRECLUDE [pri KLOOD]
- prevent/stop
*(Turning professional **PRECLUDES** a golfer from participating in amateur tournaments.)*

PRECOCIOUS [pri KOH shus]
- mentally advanced
*(The **PRECOCIOUS** child graduated from high school at age fourteen.)*

PRECURSOR [pri KUR sur; PREE kur sur]
- forerunner/predecessor
*(The Salk Vaccine was a **PRECURSOR** of significant twentieth century medical advancements against dreaded diseases.)*

PRECURSOR [pri KUR sur; PREE kur sur]
- early sign
*(The firm's accounting problems were merely a **PRECURSOR** to more serious financial concerns.)*

PREDICAMENT [pri DIK uh munt]
- dilemma
*(Having lost their luggage, the travelers found themselves in a most uncomfortable and troubling **PREDICAMENT**.)*

PREDICATE [PRED uh kayt]
- base
*(The controversial scientific theory was **PREDICATED** upon the belief that life may exist in other dimensions.)*

PREDILECTION [pred uh LEK shun; preed uh LEK shun]
- preference
*(The avid young reader had a **PREDILECTION** for mystery novels.)*

PREEMINENT [pree EM uh nunt]
- outstanding
*(Albert Einstein was a **PREEMINENT** twentieth century physicist.)*

PREFATORY [PREF uh tohr ee]
- introductory
*(Before the public screening of the movie, a few **PREFATORY** comments were made praising the efforts of the film crew.)*

PRELIMINARY [pri LIM uh ner ee]
- introductory
*(A **PRELIMINARY** investigation into the cause of the fire pointed to electrical failure.)*

PREMONITION [PREE muh nish un; PREM uh nish un]
- forewarning
*(In her dreams she had a **PREMONITION** of an airplane crash.)*

PREOCCUPIED [pree AHK yuh pied]
- lost in thought
*(As the special event neared, the bride became unusually **PREOCCUPIED** with the guests' seating arrangements.)*

PREPOSSESSING [pree puh ZES ing]
- appealing
*(The vivacious emcee had an ingratiatingly **PREPOSSESSING** personality.)*

PREPOSTEROUS [pri PAHS tur us; pri PAHS trus]
- absurd
*(Many believe that Anna Anderson's claim in 1920 to be the long-lost Princess Anastasia was simply **PREPOSTEROUS**.)*

PREREQUISITE [pri REK wi zit]
- required beforehand
*(Two years of high school mathematics are usually **PREREQUISITE** for enrolling in a chemistry class.)*

PREROGATIVE [pri RAHG uh tiv]
- right/privilege
*(It is a person's **PREROGATIVE** to say what he or she believes.)*

PRESAGE [PRES ij; pri SAYJ]
- foreshadow/forecast
*(An early and violent storm **PRESAGED** an unusually hostile winter.)*

PRESENTIMENT [pri ZEN tuh munt]
- premonition
*(Before stepping aboard the bus, the lady had a **PRESENTIMENT** that she would soon meet a long-lost friend.)*

PRESUMPTUOUS [pri ZUMP choo us]
- boldly/excessively intrusive
*(The **PRESUMPTUOUS** neighbor invited himself over for dinner.)*

PRETENSE [PREE tens]
- false display
(The love Judas Iscariot initially showed for Jesus was just a PRETENSE.)

PRETENSE [PREE tens]
- excuse
(Disenchanted by the slow progress of the meeting, the board member excused himself under the PRETENSE of suddenly having a headache.)

PRETENTIOUS [pri TEN shus]
- showy/showing off
(Her PRETENTIOUS display of the borrowed mink stole afforded her little satisfaction, for no one noticed it on her.)

PRETERNATURAL [pree tur NACH ur ul; pree tur NACH rul]
- supernatural
(The sea captain possessed a PRETERNATURAL perspicacity of Mother Nature's inscrutable ways.)

PREVALENT [PREV uh lunt]
- common and widespread
(Automobiles are PREVALENT today even in many of the most remote regions of the world.)

PREVARICATE [pri VAYR uh kayt]
- lie
(When asked by his wife where he had been all afternoon, the beach-going shirker PREVARICATED by claiming he was helping a friend repair a lawnmower.)

PRIMORDIAL [prie MOHR dee ul]
- first created/earliest formed
(Archaeologists continue to find remnants indicating an earlier nascence of PRIMORDIAL man.)

PRISTINE [PRIS teen]
- pure/unspoiled
(William Wordsworth extolled the PRISTINE loveliness of the countryside.)

PRIVATION [prie VAY shun]
- neediness and hardship
(After she was laid off from her job, the mother and her nine children suffered profound and abysmal PRIVATION.)

PROBITY [PROH bi tee; PRAHB i tee]
- virtue and integrity
(Other business executives welcomed association with such an august man of moral PROBITY and social rectitude.)

PROBLEMATIC [prahb luh MAT ik] (also, **PROBLEMATICAL**)
- difficult and uncertain
(Given the precarious location of the trapped miners, reaching them safely became highly PROBLEMATIC.)

PROCLIVITY [proh KLIV i tee]
- natural inclination
*(The stolid lad had a **PROCLIVITY** toward laziness.)*

PROCRASTINATE [proh KRAS tuh nayt]
- delay
*(When it comes time to study, many tend to **PROCRASTINATE** and eventually find themselves cramming the night before.)*

PROCURE [proh KYOOR]
- obtain/acquire
*(At the auction, the art collector **PROCURED** several rare Renaissance paintings.)*

PRODIGAL [PRAHD uh gul]
- wastefully extravagant
*(His lavish and **PRODIGAL** spending habits quickly depleted the family's savings.)*

PRODIGIOUS [pruh DIJ us]
- amazingly enormous
*(Whales have a **PRODIGIOUS** appetite.)*

PRODIGY [PRAHD i jee]
- (young) genius
*(Wolfgang Amadeus Mozart was a musical **PRODIGY**.)*

PROFFER [PRAHF ur]
- offer courteously
*(A passerby **PROFFERED** his assistance to help the elderly lady cross the street.)*

PROFICIENT [pruh FISH unt]
- skillful/expert
*(**PROFICIENT** in several languages, the ambassador was able to negotiate a meeting between the two foreign dignitaries.)*

PROFLIGATE [PRAHF luh git]
- recklessly wasteful
*(His **PROFLIGATE** ways led him from fortune to financial ruin.)*

PROFOUND [pruh FOUND]
- intense
*(The passing of the legendary icon left the musical world with a **PROFOUND** sense of loss.)*

PROFOUND [pruh FOUND]
- thoughtfully insightful
*(The young man's **PROFOUND** remark impressed his teacher.)*

PROFUSE [pruh FYOOS]
- plentiful/abundant
*(After accidentally knocking the bowl off the table, the guest offered his **PROFUSE** apologies.)*

PROGENITOR [proh JEN i tur]
- ancestor
*(According to Old Testament belief, Adam and Eve were our earliest **PROGENITORS**.)*

PROGNOSIS [prahg NOH sis]
- forecast
*(The doctor issued a favorable **PROGNOSIS** regarding the patient's recovery.)*

PROGNOSTICATE [prahg NAHS tuh kayt]
- forecast
*(Based on recent sales results, the company was able to **PROGNOSTICATE** a profitable third quarter.)*

PROLIFERATE [proh LIF uh rayt]
- multiply/increase rapidly
*(Left unchecked, rabbits will **PROLIFERATE** at a remarkable rate.)*

PROLIFIC [proh LIF ik]
- highly productive
*(Louise L'Amour was a **PROLIFIC** writer of the Old West novels.)*

PROLIX [proh LIKS; PROH liks]
- tediously long-winded and wordy
*(The lecturer's **PROLIX** and digressive explanation led many to forget what his original point was.)*

PROMINENT [PRAHM uh nunt]
- easily noticeable
*(The feared mobster wore a **PROMINENT** scar on his face.)*

PROMULGATE [PRAHM ul gayt; proh MUL gayt]
- proclaim and promote
*(The preacher's radical and heretical doctrine **PROMULGATED** tenets that rejected traditional values and orthodox beliefs.)*

PROPAGATE [PRAHP uh gayt]
- reproduce
*(All plants and animals must **PROPAGATE** to ensure survival.)*

PROPAGATE [PRAHP uh gayt]
- circulate
*(The revolutionary organization was accused of **PROPAGATING** terroristic ideology.)*

PROPENSITY [pruh PEN si tee]
- natural inclination
*(The imaginative lad had a **PROPENSITY** for exaggeration.)*

PROPHESY [PRAHF i sie]
- predict
*(Nostradamus **PROPHESIED** turbulent times during the latter part of the first millennium.)*

PROPINQUITY [proh PING kwi tee]
- nearness
*(Class reunions usually lend themselves to much festive conversation, owing largely to the shared **PROPINQUITY** of experiences of those who make up the guest list.)*

PROPITIATE [proh PISH ee ayt]
- appease
*(To **PROPITIATE** the powerful ruler, neighboring villages sent gifts and other offerings of peace and subservience.)*

PROPITIOUS [pruh PISH us]
- favorable
*(Unexpectedly strong sales in their first week presaged a **PROPITIOUS** future for the young business.)*

PROPONENT [pruh POH nunt]
- advocate
*(Ralph Nader has long been a vocal **PROPONENT** for environmental responsibility.)*

PROPOUND [pruh POUND]
- propose
*(For their daily discussion, the professor **PROPOUNDED** to the class the possibility that life may exist in other dimensions.)*

PROPRIETY [pruh PRIE i tee]
- appropriate etiquette
*(While addressing the Vice President, the senator conducted himself with the utmost of **PROPRIETY**.)*

PROSAIC [proh ZAY ik]
- boring
*(It required an effort not to doze off during the lecturer's **PROSAIC** discourse on evolution.)*

PROSCRIBE [proh SKRIEB]
- outlaw and denounce
*(The heretic was **PROSCRIBED** for his inflammatory criticism of the Church.)*

PROTEAN [PROH tee un; proh TEE un]
- changeable
*(Psychologists have long been intrigued by the **PROTEAN** personality of those afflicted by schizophrenia.)*

PROTEGÉ [PROH tuh zhay; proh tuh ZHAY]
- personally-cared-for pupil
*(The young **PROTEGÉ** accompanied the elder opera star to stage performances and social engagements.)*

PROTOTYPE [PROH tuh tiep]
- original model
*(The **PROTOTYPE** of modern computers was a noisy, bulky contraption.)*

PROTRACT [proh TRAKT]
- prolong
*(As the political conversation grew more heated, the initially casual discussion turned into a **PROTRACTED** debate.)*

PROTRUDE [proh TROOD]
- jut out
*(A large nail **PROTRUDED** from the wall where the painting once hung.)*

PROVIDENT [PRAHV i dunt]
- prudently thrifty
*(The couple adhered to a carefully planned budget as a **PROVIDENT** safeguard against future financial uncertainties.)*

PROVINCIAL [pruh VIN shul]
- limited and narrow-minded
*(The **PROVINCIAL** attitude of the townspeople made modernization of the neighborhood an impossibility.)*

PROVISIONAL [pruh VIZH uh nul]
- temporary
*(After the military coup, a **PROVISIONAL** government was established.)*

PROVOKE [pruh VOHK]
- stir up/cause
*(The professor's ill-chosen words **PROVOKED** an argument.)*

PROWESS [PROU is]
- bravery
*(The gallant knight demonstrated his **PROWESS** in battle.)*

PROWESS [PROU is]
- superior skill
*(Few animals can match the tiger's **PROWESS** as a hunter.)*

PROXIMITY [prahk SIM i tee]
- nearness
*(The two brothers' offices were in close **PROXIMITY** to one another.)*

PRUDENT [PROOD nt]
- wise and sensible
*(In retrospect, it was a **PRUDENT** decision not to have invested in the fledgling company.)*

PRURIENT [PROOR ee unt]
- lustful
*(Adult movies oftentimes cater to **PRURIENT** interests.)*

PSEUDONYM [SOOD uh nim]
- pen name
*(Samuel Clemens wrote under the **PSEUDONYM** "Mark Twain.")*

PUERILE [PYOOR il; PYOO ur il]
- childish/immature
*(The waggish lad's **PUERILE** behavior on the bus was met with a swift rebuke by the driver.)*

PUGNACIOUS [pug NAY shus]
- belligerent
*(Tasmanian devils are **PUGNACIOUS** and highly territorial marsupials.)*

PUISSANT [PWIS nt; PYOO i sunt]
- mighty/powerful
*(Julius Caesar was a **PUISSANT** Roman general and statesman.)*

PULCHRITUDE [PUL kri tood; PUL kri tyood]
- physical beauty
*(The impressionable adolescent was bedazzled by the **PULCHRITUDE** of the bikini-clad babes on the beach.)*

PUNCTILIOUS [pungk TIL ee us]
- painstakingly precise (in following convention)
*(The headwaiter was **PUNCTILIOUS** when it came to setting the dinner table; every fork and spoon had to be correctly positioned.)*

PUNGENT [PUN junt]
- sharp/harsh and stinging
*(Geysers exude a **PUNGENT** odor.)*

PUNITIVE [PYOO ni tiv]
- serving as punishment
*(Besides being fined for having committed the crime, the culprit was also ordered to pay **PUNITIVE** damages.)*

PUNY [PYOO nee]
- small and weak
*(A **PUNY** animal often has little chance of survival in the wild.)*

PURGATORY [PUR guh tohr ee]
- temporary hell
*(The inmate viewed the time spent behind bars as his personal **PURGATORY**.)*

PURGE [purj]
- cleanse
*(By confessing, he hoped to **PURGE** himself of the guilt that had haunted him for months.)*

PURITANICAL [pyoor i TAN i kul]
- strict and straitlaced
*(Although she experienced a **PURITANICAL** upbringing, in later years she distanced herself from its intolerance and narrow-mindedness.)*

PURLOIN [pur LOIN; PUR loin]
- steal
(The petty thief PURLOINED the purse that had been left on the table.)

PURVEY [pur VAY]
- supply (as a service)
(Local inns PURVEY food and lodging at reasonable overnight rates to weary travelers.)

PURVIEW [PUR vyoo]
- range of authority/understanding
(Declaring war lies within the PURVIEW of the President.)

PUSILLANIMOUS [pyoo suh LAN uh mus]
- cowardly
(The lion in The Wizard of Oz regarded himself a PUSILLANIMOUS though pretentiously pompous poltroon.)

PUTATIVE [PYOO tuh tiv]
- supposed
(Much debate has taken place regarding the PUTATIVE differences between the sexes.)

PUTREFY [PYOO truh fie]
- decay/rot
(The leftover meal PUTREFIED in the garbage can.)

PUTRID [PYOO trid]
- rotten
(Reporters on the scene were repulsed by the PUTRID smell of decaying flesh.)

QUAGMIRE [KWAG mier]
- bog
(The car's back tires became stuck in a QUAGMIRE.)

QUAGMIRE [KWAG mier]
- predicament
(At the service station, the financially strapped travelers were in a QUAGMIRE over how to pay for groceries and still have money left for gas.)

QUALMS [kwahms]
- misgivings
(The thief had no QUALMS about stealing the lady's purse.)

QUANDARY [KWAHN duh ree]
- dilemma
(She was in a QUANDARY as to whom to ask to the senior prom.)

QUASH [kwahsh]
- suppress completely
(Military reinforcements were brought in to QUASH the peasant uprising.)

QUELL [kwel]
 - quiet/pacify
 (Mother's reassuring words QUELLED her child's fears.)

QUERULOUS [KWER uh lus; KWER yuh lus]
 - constantly complaining
 (The picnic turned unpleasant after her QUERULOUS husband arrived.)

QUIBBLE [KWIB ul]
 - argue trivially
 (The couple QUIBBLED over where to dine.)

QUID PRO QUO [kwid proh KWOH]
 - something offered as a return of favor ("tit for tat")
 (Many people charge that government contracts are often awarded QUID PRO QUO rather than through a fair merit-based system.)

QUIESCENT [kwee ES unt]
 - inactive
 (Although a hurricane appears QUIESCENT when the eye passes overhead, it is only a matter of minutes before the violent winds resume.)

QUIRK [kwurk]
 - peculiarity/abnormality
 (Riding his skateboard in the office was one of the eccentric executive's many QUIRKS.)

QUISLING [KWIZ ling]
 - traitor
 (For aiding the enemy government in time of war, the mercenary was branded a QUISLING.)

QUIXOTIC [kwik SAHT ik]
 - impractically idealistic
 (The pubescent lad devised a QUIXOTIC but sophomoric scheme to win the heart of the homecoming queen.)

QUIZZICAL [KWIZ i kul]
 - puzzled
 (When she turned the gun on her attacker, he gave her a QUIZZICAL look of disbelief.)

QUIZZICAL [KWIZ i kul]
 - teasing/mocking
 (The lad's QUIZZICAL antics made his younger sister cry.)

QUOTIDIAN [kwoh TID ee un]
 - ordinary/everyday
 (Far from the extravagance and variety of her sister's Hollywood lifestyle, the schoolteacher led an uneventful and QUOTIDIAN existence.)

RAMBUNCTIOUS [ram BUNGK shus]
- wild and unruly
*(During Mardi Gras, police are needed to monitor the **RAMBUNCTIOUS** crowds.)*

RAMIFICATION [ram uh fuh KAY shun]
- consequence
*(Any oil embargo usually carries with it serious worldwide **RAMIFICATIONS**.)*

RAMPANT [RAM punt]
- widespread and uncontrolled
*(Anarchy and lawlessness have run **RAMPANT** in some inner-city neighborhoods.)*

RAMSHACKLE [RAM shak ul]
- poorly constructed
*(The hikers unexpectedly came across a **RAMSHACKLE** hut in the middle of nowhere.)*

RANCID [RAN sid]
- stale and smelly
*(After a week out of the refrigerator, the butter had turned **RANCID**.)*

RANCOR [RANG kur]
- hatred and resentment
*(The alienated boy was filled with a deep-rooted **RANCOR** toward his stepfather.)*

RANKLE [RANG kul]
- irritate deeply
*(The teacher's scathing rebuke **RANKLED** the innocent boy.)*

RAPACIOUS [ruh PAY shus]
- thievishly greedy
*(Pirates were known as a **RAPACIOUS** lot who sought one ship after another to plunder.)*

RAPACIOUS [ruh PAY shus]
- predatory
*(The **RAPACIOUS** hawk swooped down and seized the fleeing mouse.)*

RAPPORT [ra POHR]
- harmonious relationship
*(Comedian Danny Kaye had a pleasant **RAPPORT** with children of all ages.)*

RAREFIED [RAYR uh fied]
- thin/less dense
*(Sherpas are acclimated to the **RAREFIED** mountain air of Tibet.)*

RASH [rash]
- hasty and reckless
*(In a regrettably **RASH** moment of despair, the gambler bet the remainder of his money on the long-shot.)*

RATIOCINATION [rash ee ohs uh NAY shun; rat ee ohs n AY shun]
- logical reasoning
*(In the problem-solving approach, one must first establish through **RATIOCINATION** the most appropriate steps to take to achieve the desired result.)*

RAUCOUS [RAH kus]
- rowdy/disorderly
*(Unhappy with the game's outcome, the **RAUCOUS** crowd threw bottles onto the field.)*

RAUCOUS [RAH kus]
- unpleasantly loud/harsh
*(When the apartment window was opened, the **RAUCOUS** sounds of the bustling city below suffused the room.)*

RAVENOUS [RAV uh nus]
- extremely hungry
*(**RAVENOUS** wolves attacked the injured animal.)*

RAZE [rayz]
- demolish
*(Before laying the foundation for the new hospital complex, several old and abandoned buildings on the lot had to be **RAZED**.)*

REBUFF [ri BUF]
- snub/bluntly refuse
*(The lioness **REBUFFED** the male's sexual advances.)*

REBUKE [ri BYOOK]
- criticize sharply
*(The inexperienced teller was publicly **REBUKED** for leaving the bank safe open.)*

REBUT [ri BUT]
- contradict/disprove
*(The prosecuting attorney **REBUTTED** the defense's claim that it was too dark to have identified the attacker.)*

RECALCITRANT [ri KAL si trunt]
- stubbornly defiant
*(The **RECALCITRANT** crew was on the verge of mutiny.)*

RECAPITULATE [ree kuh PICH uh layt]
- review briefly/summarize ("recap")
*(At the conclusion of the news broadcast, the day's top stories were **RECAPITULATED**.)*

RECHERCHÉ [ruh shayr SHAY; ruh SHAYR shay]
- rare and superior
*(The antique store specialized in **RECHERCHÉ** objets d'art.)*

RECHERCHÉ [ruh shayr SHAY; ruh SHAYR shay]
- elegantly refined
*(Gregory Peck comported himself with a noble and **RECHERCHÉ** dignity.)*

RECIPROCATE [ri SIP ruh kayt]
- return (in exchange)
*(She smiled at the new boy in the class who, in turn, **RECIPROCATED** shyly.)*

RECLUSIVE [ri KLOO siv]
- solitary
*(The curmudgeon lived a **RECLUSIVE** life in his cabin in the woods.)*

RECOLLECT [rek uh LEKT]
- remember
*(Locked out of his car, the puzzled man was unable to **RECOLLECT** where he had last placed his keys.)*

RECOMPENSE [REK um pens]
- compensate/pay back
*(The merchant was **RECOMPENSED** for the broken vase.)*

RECONDITE [REK un diet; ri KAHN diet]
- academically profound
*(At the literary seminar, the doctoral candidate presented a **RECONDITE** analysis of the psychological workings of the Renaissance man.)*

RECREANT [REK ree unt]
- coward/deserter
*(For siding with the enemy when the opposition had temporarily gained the upper hand, the **RECREANT** was shunned by his fellow countrymen.)*

RECTIFY [REK tuh fie]
- correct/remedy
*(To **RECTIFY** the embarrassing mishap, the airline management offered a free round trip for each passenger whose luggage had been stolen at the unattended baggage claim station.)*

RECTITUDE [REK ti tood; REK ti tyood]
- moral integrity/righteousness
*(One who serves in the public interest ought to be a person of irreproachable honor and **RECTITUDE**.)*

RECUMBENT [ri KUM bunt]
- lying down
*(The couple lay **RECUMBENT** upon the grass, enjoying their precious moments together.)*

REDOLENT [RED l unt]
- fragrant
*(The **REDOLENT** waft of chocolate chip cookies attracted passersby to enter the store.)*

REDOLENT [RED l unt]
- reminiscent/suggestive
*(The rustic countryside was a scene **REDOLENT** of the poet's early childhood.)*

REDOUBLE [ree DUB ul]
- intensify (by doubling)
*(Upon hearing cries from miners down below, rescuers **REDOUBLED** their efforts to clear the debris and pull the men to safety.)*

REDOUBTABLE [ri DOU tuh bul]
- formidable and fearsome
*(In the famous Al Capp cartoon, Brutus was Popeye's **REDOUBTABLE** foe.)*

REDOUBTABLE [ri DOU tuh bul]
- awesomely inspiring
*(The Dalai Lama is a **REDOUBTABLE** and august religious figure.)*

REFRACTORY [ri FRAK tuh ree]
- stubbornly disobedient
*(The **REFRACTORY** child would not do his homework.)*

REFUGE [REF yooj]
- shelter
*(When the storm descended with full fury, the campers sought **REFUGE** in a nearby cave.)*

REFUGEE [ref yoo JEE]
- fugitive/runaway
*(Many immigrants to America were **REFUGEES** fleeing intolerable conditions in their homeland.)*

REFULGENT [ri FUL junt]
- brilliant/radiant
*(Beachgoers flocked to bask in the noonday sun's **REFULGENT** rays.)*

REFURBISH [ree FUR bish]
- renovate/restore
*(To help the house sell more quickly, the bedrooms were **REFURBISHED** with new carpeting and drapes.)*

REFUTE [ri FYOOT]
- disprove
*(New evidence **REFUTED** previously held theories regarding the whereabouts of the lost civilization.)*

REFUTE [ri FYOOT]
- deny
*(The suspect adamantly **REFUTED** the allegations levied against him.)*

REGAL [REE gul]
- royal
*(The king's palace retained a **REGAL** splendor reminiscent of the Renaissance.)*

REGALE [ri GAYL]
- entertain/amuse
*(The court jester **REGALED** the king with his zany antics.)*

REGIMEN [REJ uh mun]
- structured program
*(To help strengthen one's cardiovascular system, a **REGIMEN** of rigorous daily exercise is often recommended.)*

REGRESS [ri GRESS]
- move backwards/go back
*(In her moments of deep reflection, the aging cinematic star **REGRESSED** to those glorious days when legions of fans followed her every move.)*

REHABILITATE [ree huh BIL i tayt]
- restore
*(Funds were allocated to **REHABILITATE** the decrepit war memorial.)*

REIGN [rayn]
- rule
*(The lion **REIGNS** supreme in the jungle.)*

REITERATE [ree IT uh rayt]
- repeat
*(At the bargaining table, the union representative **REITERATED** the employees' demands.)*

REJUVENATE [ri JOO vuh nayt]
- restore energy to
*(A cold shower helped **REJUVENATE** the doctor after his long workday.)*

RELEGATE [REL uh gayt]
- assign
*(Unless they demonstrated a special individual talent, the newest members of the choir were **RELEGATED** to singing backup.)*

RELENTLESS [ri LENT lis]
- unyielding
*(The private investigator was **RELENTLESS** in his pursuit of the truth.)*

RELINQUISH [ri LING kwish]
- surrender
*(Despite a court order, the reporter refused to **RELINQUISH** the information told to her in strictest confidence.)*

REMINISCE [rem uh NIS]
- remember the past ("think back")
*(At the high school reunion, friends **REMINISCED** about old times.)*

REMISS [ri MIS]
- negligent/careless
*(For being **REMISS** in his duties, the security guard was given a one-week suspension.)*

REMONSTRATE [ri MAHN strayt]
- protest/object
*(The concerned father **REMONSTRATED** with his daughter over her disregard of the prearranged curfew hour.)*

REMORSE [ri MOHRS]
- guilt and regret
*(The older brother felt **REMORSE** for having let his younger sibling take the blame for his own misdeed.)*

REMOTE [ri MOHT]
- secluded
*(The **REMOTE** island had only recently been discovered by explorers.)*

REMUNERATE [ri MYOO nuh rayt]
- compensate/reward
*(The mechanic was **REMUNERATED** for his travel time en route to and from the location of the stalled car.)*

RENAISSANCE [ren uh SAHNS]
- renewal/rebirth
*(Impressionism triggered an artistic **RENAISSANCE** in the nineteenth century with the likes of Monet, Pissaro and Renoir.)*

RENDEZVOUS [RAHN duh voo; RAHN day voo]
- prearranged meeting
*(The secret lovers arranged a midnight **RENDEZVOUS** at the lake.)*

RENOUNCE [ri NOUNS]
- formally give up
*(The reborn Christian **RENOUNCED** his earlier heretical beliefs.)*

RENOVATE [REN uh vayt]
- remodel and restore
*(Custom designers helped **RENOVATE** the old kitchen by installing new modern appliances.)*

RENOWNED [ri NOUND]
- famous
*(Art galleries display paintings by **RENOWNED** artists, past and present.)*

REPARTEE [ri pahr TEE; ri pahr TAY]
- verbal witticism
*(During dinner, the two scholars bantered and engaged in clever **REPARTEE**.)*

REPAST [ri PAST]
- enjoyable meal
*(At teatime, the British gentleman delighted in a brief but savory **REPAST**.)*

REPENT [ri PENT]
- regret (and make amends for)
*(As he matured, the miscreant **REPENTED** his sordid past.)*

REPERCUSSION [ree pur KUSH un]
- impact/effect
(The sudden shortage of oil had far-reaching economic REPERCUSSIONS.)

REPERTOIRE [REP ur twahr]
- performing inventory
(The musician's REPERTOIRE included songs from the 1970s and 1980s.)

REPINE [ri PIEN]
- complain with dissatisfaction
(As they waited in long lines, motorists REPINED over the ever-increasing inconvenience of purchasing gasoline.)

REPLENISH [ri PLEN ish]
- restore/stock up again on
(Before leaving the underground cave, the spelunkers REPLENISHED their supply of water.)

REPLETE [ri PLEET]
- filled
(The hastily-written manuscript was REPLETE with grammatical errors.)

REPOSE [ri POHZ]
- peaceful relaxation
(With her children visiting the neighbors, the young mother was afforded a few precious moments of rest and REPOSE.)

REPOSITORY [ri PAHZ i tohr ee]
- storage place
(A library is a REPOSITORY for books.)

REPREHENSIBLE [rep ri HEN suh bul]
- shameful
(The school's board of directors voted to dismiss the football coach due to his inexcusably REPREHENSIBLE treatment of his players after a loss to their arch rivals.)

REPRESS [ri PRES]
- hold in/keep under control
(When the prim home-economics teacher slipped on a banana peel, her students were unable to REPRESS their laughter.)

REPRIMAND [REP ruh mand]
- scold formally ("chew out")
(For his inattentiveness during drills, the cadet was REPRIMANDED by the platoon commander.)

REPRISAL [ri PRIE zul]
- retaliation
(The military leader threatened military REPRISALS should his country be invaded over border disputes.)

REPROACH [ri PROHCH]
- criticize
*(The class was **REPROACHED** for their rudeness during the guest speaker's visit.)*

REPROBATE [REP ruh bayt]
- shameless sinner
*(The townspeople shunned the good-for-nothing **REPROBATE**.)*

REPROVE [ri PROOV]
- scold mildly
*(When his wife **REPROVED** him with a sudden and abrupt tug on his shirt, he knew it was time to stop chatting with the waitress.)*

REPUDIATE [ri PYOO dee ayt]
- disavow/reject
*(The proselytized convert **REPUDIATED** all the teachings of his former religion.)*

REPULSIVE [ri PUL siv]
- offensive and disgusting
*(Her boyfriend's **REPULSIVE** behavior in front of her parents made her ashamed that she had invited the boor to dinner in the first place.)*

REPUTABLE [REP yuh tuh bul]
- well-respected
*(When having one's car serviced, it is highly recommended that the job be performed by a **REPUTABLE** mechanic.)*

REPUTED [ri PYOO tid]
- regarded/considered
*(During the acid-rock era of the 1960s, many legendary icons were **REPUTED** to have been heavily into drugs even while performing in concert.)*

REQUISITE [REK wi zit]
- necessary requirement
*(An advanced college degree is a **REQUISITE** for many executive positions.)*

REQUITE [ri KWIET]
- reciprocate/pay back
*(The soldier **REQUITED** the lady's compliment with a polite bow and a kiss on her hand.)*

RESCIND [ri SIND]
- void/cancel
*(When told that his ship was needed to aid in a rescue at sea, the captain immediately **RESCINDED** all shore leaves.)*

RESERVED [ri ZURVD]
- shy and withdrawn
*(Fellow club members found it difficult conversing with the **RESERVED** young man.)*

RESIDUAL [ri ZIJ oo ul]
- leftover
*(The powerful volcanic explosion left a **RESIDUAL** cloud of dust that hovered over most of the island for weeks.)*

RESILIENT [ri ZIL yunt]
- recovering quickly
*(The **RESILIENT** youngster never let a setback deter him from persevering.)*

RESOLUTE [REZ uh loot]
- stubbornly determined
*(The gallant knight was **RESOLUTE** in his quest to locate and rescue the imprisoned princess.)*

RESONANT [REZ uh nunt]
- echoing
*(The baritone had a deep, **RESONANT** voice.)*

RESOURCEFUL [ri SOHRS ful]
- creatively clever
*(The **RESOURCEFUL** hiker fabricated a makeshift tent from leaves and branches.)*

RESPITE [RES pit]
- rest/relief
*(Clouds offered the picnickers a brief **RESPITE** from the intense summer sun.)*

RESPLENDENT [ri SPLEN dunt]
- dazzling
*(The campers were taken aback by the **RESPLENDENT** beauty of the shimmering lake.)*

RESTITUTION [res ti TOO shun]
- compensation/reparation
*(In court, the lad was ordered to make **RESTITUTION** for the broken window by working on weekends for a month.)*

RESTIVE [RES tiv]
- restlessly impatient
*(The colonists grew increasingly **RESTIVE** as they longed for independence from their motherland.)*

RESTIVE [RES tiv]
- stubbornly resistant
*(The **RESTIVE** mule refused to move.)*

RESURRECT [rez uh REKT]
- restore
*(Many feel a critical need to **RESURRECT** the concept of family values.)*

RETALIATE [ri TAL ee ayt]
- strike back (to get even)
*(After having been made the butt of the joke the day before, the student **RETALIATED** by placing gum on the other boy's chair.)*

RETENTIVE [ri TEN tiv]
- able to remember
*(The **RETENTIVE** lad possessed a wealth of historical knowledge.)*

RETICENT [RET i sunt]
- shy and uncommunicative
*(All efforts at coaxing the **RETICENT** boy to participate in the class discussion proved futile.)*

RETIRING [ri TIER ing]
- shy/withdrawn
*(The **RETIRING** lad shunned social gatherings.)*

RETRACT [ri TRAKT]
- withdraw/take back
*(Under threat of a lawsuit, the newspaper **RETRACTED** the allegations made in an earlier article.)*

RETRIBUTION [re truh BYOO shun]
- punishment
*(Seeking **RETRIBUTION** for the murder of his brother, the outlaw hunted down all those involved.)*

RETROGRESSION [re truh GRESH un]
- decline/reversal
*(Many social critics contend that mankind has recently embarked upon a period of moral **RETROGRESSION**.)*

RETROSPECT [RE truh spekt]
- review
*(The television documentary examined the year in **RETROSPECT**.)*

REVEL [REV ul]
- take pleasure and delight
*(When Prohibition was repealed in 1933, citizens **REVELED** in bacchanalian celebration.)*

REVERE [ri VEER]
- worship/respect deeply
*(The impressionable youngster **REVERED** his older brother.)*

REVILE [ri VIEL]
- speak bitterly and abusively of
*(Sportscasters **REVILED** the team owner for unbecoming treatment of his players.)*

REVOKE [ri VOHK]
- withdraw
*(Due to the hurricane's imminent approach, the captain **REVOKED** the sailors' weekend furloughs.)*

RHETORICAL [ri TOHR i kul]
- verbally dramatic
*(Hamlet's "to be or not to be" soliloquy raised several provocative **RHETORICAL** questions regarding man's role in life.)*

RHETORICAL [ri TOHR i kul]
- pretentiously florid
*(The political candidate's **RHETORICAL** speech contained little substance.)*

RIBALD [RIB uld]
- vulgar/indecent
*(Some comedians lack wit and instead resort to **RIBALD** and offensive humor for applause.)*

RIFE [rief]
- widespread
*(Poverty is **RIFE** in many underdeveloped nations.)*

RIFT [rift]
- split
*(Jealousy was the cause of the **RIFT** in the two classmates' friendship.)*

RIGHTEOUS [RIE chus]
- morally good
*(The pious churchgoer was a **RIGHTEOUS** and God-fearing family man.)*

RIGOR [RIG ur]
- difficult challenge/hardship
*(Early pioneers had to endure the **RIGORS** of life in the Old West.)*

RIGOROUS [RIG ur us]
- demanding
*(Every morning, the aerobics instructor put her students through a **RIGOROUS** exercise program.)*

RISIBLE [RIZ uh bul]
- funny
*(Curly Howard's **RISIBLE** clownish manners were greatly responsible for the success of the Three Stooges.)*

RISQUÉ [ri SKAY]
- improper/daringly suggestive
*(The comedian's bawdy and **RISQUÉ** anecdotes were not well-received by the prudish audience.)*

ROBUST [roh BUST; ROH bust]
- strong and healthy
*(The farmer's two sons were **ROBUST** young men.)*

ROSEATE [ROH zee it]
- optimistic/promising
*(Given the grim economic climate, the man's business associates questioned his **ROSEATE** outlook for the coming year.)*

ROTE [roht]
- use of memory and repetition
*(The first year of a foreign language course requires extensive learning by **ROTE**.)*

ROTUND [roh TUND]
- chubby
*(Alfred Hitchcock was a **ROTUND** gentleman who possessed an uncanny flair for mystery and suspense.)*

ROW [rou]
- noisy dispute
*(When a patron accused the bartender of diluting his drink, a **ROW** ensued.)*

RUBICUND [ROO buh kund]
- rosy/reddish
*(The Swedish lass had a **RUBICUND** complexion.)*

RUDDY [RUD ee]
- healthy rosy-red
*(A brisk stroll in the cool mountain air gave the young girl's cheeks a **RUDDY** wholesomeness.)*

RUDIMENTARY [roo duh MEN tuh ree]
- crude
*(The earliest flying machines were **RUDIMENTARY** and highly unpredictable mechanical contraptions.)*

RUE [roo]
- regret
*(As paperwork piled up, the executive **RUED** the day she fired her secretary.)*

RUMINATE [ROO muh nayt]
- meditate
*(During a hiatus from filming, the movie star **RUMINATIED** on the fortuitous events that had led to his selection for the leading role.)*

RURAL [ROOR ul]
- (relating to the) country
*(The recluse savored his **RURAL** existence far from the dense smog-infested city.)*

RUSE [rooz]
- clever/deceptive maneuver
*(Lining up most of the players on the left side of the field was just a **RUSE**; the quarterback's plan was to sprint to the right.)*

RUSTIC [RUS tik]
- rural
*(The movie's opening scene featured the **RUSTIC** beauty of the verdant mountainside.)*

RUSTIC [RUS tik]
- unsophisticated
*(Jed Clampett and his clan were **RUSTIC** hillbilly folks.)*

RUTHLESS [ROOTH lis]
- merciless
*(The Barbary Coast was renowned for its **RUTHLESS** pirates who wreaked havoc in the Mediterranean Sea from the sixteenth through eighteenth centuries.)*

SACCHARINE [SAK uh rin]
- excessively sweet
(Many consider the character Peter Pan too SACCHARINE for their realistic tastes.)

SACRILEGIOUS [SAK ruh lij us]
- disrespectful
(It is generally considered SACRILEGIOUS to curse in the name of God.)

SACROSANCT [SAK roh sangkt]
- sacred and unquestionable
(In times of battle, a commander's orders are SACROSANCT.)

SADISTIC [suh DIS tik]
- cruel
(Ivan the Terrible was a SADISTIC despot and tyrant.)

SAGACIOUS [suh GAY shus]
- shrewd
(A SAGACIOUS investor, the retired schoolteacher anticipated and took full advantage of the economic upturn.)

SALACIOUS [suh LAY shus]
- lustful/obscene
(The sailor's SALACIOUS comment was met with a sharp slap from the barmaid.)

SALIENT [SAY lee unt; SAYL yunt]
- conspicuously noticeable
(Tasmanian devils exhibit SALIENT aggressive traits.)

SALINE [SAY lien; SAY leen]
- salty
(A SALINE solution was used to cleanse the wound.)

SALLOW [SAL oh]
- sickly
(After consuming more than he should have the night before, the young man stumbled out of bed with a SALLOW complexion and bloodshot eyes.)

SALUBRIOUS [suh LOO bree us]
- healthful/healthy
(The troop of hikers relished the SALUBRIOUS mountain air.)

SALUTARY [SAL yuh ter ee]
- beneficial
(The rookie received SALUTARY advice from the coach on improving his baseball swing.)

SANCTIMONIOUS [sangk tuh MOH nee us]
- hypocritically self-righteous
*(The students were not impressed by the politician's **SANCTIMONIOUS** lecture on ethics and morality; they sensed that he himself must have committed skulduggery to have climbed the ladder to political success.)*

SANCTION [SANGK shun]
- authorize and endorse
*(The school's student council committee **SANCTIONED** the fund-raising dance.)*

SANGFROID [sahn FRWAH]
- composure
*(The defendant handled the grueling cross-examination with amazing **SANGFROID**.)*

SANGUINARY [SANG gwuh ner ee]
- bloody
*(The **SANGUINARY** conflict involved two violent rival gangs.)*

SANGUINE [SANG gwin]
- optimistic
*(As latest statistics pointed to a recovery, more economists openly voiced a more **SANGUINE** outlook on the future.)*

SANGUINE [SANG gwin]
- red/ruddy
*(The fair-haired, freckled-faced boy had a **SANGUINE** complexion.)*

SAPID [SAP id]
- savory
*(The international buffet featured a wide variety of **SAPID** exotic delicacies.)*

SAPIENT [SAY pee unt]
- wise
*(A panel of the university's most **SAPIENT** scholars discussed avenues for academic improvement at the institution.)*

SARDONIC [sahr DAHN ik]
- cynically sarcastic
*(The businessman attended the funeral of his lifelong nemesis with **SARDONIC** delight.)*

SATE [sayt]
- satisfy fully
*(The large feast **SATED** the animal's hunger.)*

SATIATE [SAY shee ayt]
- satisfy to excess
*(The congressman's two-hour confession **SATIATED** the reporter's appetite for all the sordid details.)*

SATURATE [SACH uh rayt]
- soak/fill completely
(Three days of constant rainfall SATURATED the earth.)

SATURNINE [SAT ur nien]
- gloomy and depressed
(His SATURNINE silence made everyone around him uneasy.)

SAVOIR FAIRE [sav wahr FAYR]
- social grace and polish
(Even in trying times, the diplomat's SAVOIR FAIRE helped encourage détente.)

SAVORY [SAY vur ee]
- flavorful/tasty
(The ambrosial delicacy was prepared with SAVORY herbs and spices.)

SCARIFY [SKAR uh fie]
- scratch
(During times of drought, farmers must SCARIFY the dry soil to enable water moisture to permeate it.)

SCATHING [SKAY thing]
- bitterly severe
(The newspaper editorial section featured a SCATHING rebuke of the mayor's handling of the bus strike.)

SCHEME [skeem]
- plot
(In the cartoon, the mad scientist SCHEMED to blow up the world.)

SCHISM [SIZ um; SKIZ um]
- division
(Differing political views created a SCHISM within the family.)

SCOUNDREL [SKOUN drul]
- villain
(Robin Hood was regarded by rich townsfolk as an insidious SCOUNDREL and despicable rogue.)

SCOURGE [skurj]
- plague/source of distress
(Jealousy is a SCOURGE that afflicts all people, rich and poor.)

SCRUPULOUS [SKROO pyuh lus]
- morally conscientious
(The SCRUPULOUS and irreproachable politician could not be bribed by powerful special-interest groups.)

SCRUPULOUS [SKROO pyuh lus]
- painstaking
(With SCRUPULOUS accuracy, the forensic artist recreated the face of an ancient hominid using only a skull as reference.)

SCRUTINIZE [SKROOT n iez]
- examine closely and carefully
*(All parties **SCRUTINIZED** the literary contract for accuracy and appropriate changes before signing.)*

SCURRILOUS [SKUR uh lus]
- coarse and offensive ("foul-mouthed")
*(Jean Lafitte was a **SCURRILOUS** pirate.)*

SECEDE [si SEED]
- withdraw
*(Several Southern states threatened to **SECEDE** from the Union over the issue of emancipation of slaves.)*

SECLUDE [si KLOOD]
- isolate
*(Henry David Thoreau **SECLUDED** himself for weeks in his cabin near Walden Pond.)*

SECULAR [SEK yuh lur]
- nonreligious
*(Although religiously affiliated, the radio station played exclusively **SECULAR** music.)*

SEDATE [si DAYT]
- calm and undisturbed
*(Throughout the rough flight, passengers remained surprisingly **SEDATE**.)*

SEDENTARY [SED n ter ee]
- inactive
*(With all the modern conveniences today, people live a much more **SEDENTARY** existence than they did in times past.)*

SEDITIOUS [si DISH us]
- mutinous/rebellious
*(The British considered the colonists' incident referred to as the Boston Tea Party a willful and **SEDITIOUS** act of treason.)*

SEDULOUS [SEJ uh lus]
- conscientiously/persistently hardworking
*(The **SEDULOUS** student attended every optional lecture that was offered.)*

SEEDY [SEE dee]
- shabby/run-down
*(Corruption infiltrated the **SEEDY** side of the town.)*

SEEMLY [SEEM lee]
- proper/suitable
*(The children's **SEEMLY** behavior during the guest speaker's presentation did not go unnoticed by their proud teacher.)*

SELF-EFFACING [self i FAY sing]
- modest/reserved
*(Although he was the star high school quarterback, few would have guessed so by his **SELF-EFFACING** and mild-mannered personality.)*

SEMINAL [SEM uh nul]
- original/fundamental
*(Albert Einstein's **SEMINAL** ideas were the basis for much of today's scientific understanding of time and space.)*

SENESCENCE [se NES uns]
- aging
*(Sooner or later, every person must deal with one's own **SENESCENCE**.)*

SENTENTIOUS [sen TEN shus]
- moralizing
*(A **SENTENTIOUS** phrase such as "crime does not pay" presents a terse, though somewhat hackneyed, bit of useful advice.)*

SENTIENT [SEN shunt]
- aware/perceptive
*(Animals are **SENTIENT** creatures, unlike many lower forms of life.)*

SENTIMENTAL [sen tuh MEN tul]
- tenderly emotional
*(The **SENTIMENTAL** ballad brought tears to many listeners' eyes.)*

SEQUENTIAL [si KWEN shul]
- consecutive/successive
*(In the Civil War account, the historic battles were listed in **SEQUENTIAL** order.)*

SERAPHIC [si RAF ik]
- angelic
*(Smitten with love, the teenager obsessed over the girl whose **SERAPHIC** radiance he could only have envisioned in the most sublime of dreams.)*

SERENDIPITOUS [ser un DIP i tus]
- fortunate
*(Christopher Columbus' journey for a passage to the East led to a **SERENDIPITOUS** discovery.)*

SERENE [suh REEN]
- tranquil
*(The realistic painting captured the **SERENE** beauty of a lake in springtime.)*

SERRATED [SER ay tid]
- jagged/saw-toothed
*(A steak knife often has a **SERRATED** edge.)*

SERVILE [SUR vul; SUR viel]
- submissive/obedient
(Surrounded by her SERVILE retinue, the movie starlet doted on her new-found fame and attention.)

SERVILE [SUR vul; SUR viel]
- menial/degrading
(Unable to find work elsewhere, the single mother was forced to accept a SERVILE job as family maid.)

SHEEPISH [SHEE pish]
- submissive
(The SHEEPISH group followed the leader without argument.)

SHEEPISH [SHEE pish]
- embarrassed
(When his mother caught him stealing cookies from the cookie jar, the young lad flashed a SHEEPISH grin.)

SHIBBOLETH [SHIB uh lith]
- slogan ("pet phrase")
("Feeling groovy" and "life's a gas" were oft-used SHIBBOLETHS during the late 1960s.)

SHIFTLESS [SHIFT lis]
- lazy and unproductive
(The frustrated farmer ordered his SHIFTLESS son to go out and help feed the livestock.)

SHIRK [shurk]
- avoid
(A father should not SHIRK his responsibility to the family by neglecting to provide them with food on the table.)

SHODDY [SHAHD ee]
- inferior
(The diamond bracelet's multiple defects reflected SHODDY workmanship.)

SHOPWORN [SHAHP wohrn]
- overused
(The book's theme of two lovers committing suicide was SHOPWORN and offered nothing that hadn't been written a hundred times before.)

SHORTCOMING [SHOHRT kum ing]
- personal deficiency
(Laziness was the man's most noticeable SHORTCOMING.)

SHREWD [shrood]
- clever and perceptive
(The frugal bookkeeper was a SHREWD and judicious investor.)

SHUN [shun]
- deliberately avoid
(Once she had achieved fame, the fickle starlet SHUNNED her hometown friends.)

SIMILITUDE [si MIL i tood; si MIL i tyood]
- comparative likeness/similarity
*(Scientific researchers noted a **SIMILITUDE** of patterns employed by mice when placed randomly in the maze.)*

SIMULATE [SIM yuh layt]
- imitate
*(A space launch was **SIMULATED** to better prepare the astronauts for the real thing.)*

SINISTER [SIN i stur]
- evil
*(In the spy novel, the mad scientist hatched a **SINISTER** plot to destroy the world.)*

SISYPHEAN [sis uh FEE un]
- endlessly laborious
*(One must recognize and applaud the **SISYPHEAN** effort required of a single parent to raise a family of seven boys.)*

SKEW [skyoo]
- distort
*(The unusually poor test scores from a handful of students **SKEWED** the overall statistical results.)*

SKITTISH [SKIT ish]
- jittery/jumpy
*(When a snake crossed its path, the **SKITTISH** horse bolted.)*

SLANDER [SLAN dur]
- defame
*(The young movie star felt that she had been **SLANDERED** by the interviewer's careless accusations.)*

SLIPSHOD [SLIP shahd]
- carelessly sloppy
*(The makeshift hut was constructed in a **SLIPSHOD** manner.)*

SLOTH [slahth]
- laziness
*(The intense summer heat was blamed for the general **SLOTH** at the factory that afternoon.)*

SLOVENLY [SLUV un lee]
- messy
*(The man's **SLOVENLY** desk reflected his slovenly lifestyle.)*

SMUG [smug]
- conceitedly self-satisfied
*(The high school quarterback's **SMUG** attitude led many to regard him as arrogant, aloof and antisocial.)*

SOBRIQUET [SOH bruh kay; SOH bruh ket]
- nickname
*("The King" is a **SOBRIQUET** for Elvis Presley, the king of rock n' roll.)*

SOJOURN [SOH jurn; soh JURN]
- lodge
(The global travelers SOJOURNED for a couple of days in the Greek tavern.)

SOLACE [SAHL is]
- comfort
(Telephoning a close friend helped her find SOLACE from the intense loneliness.)

SOLEMN [SAHL um]
- serious
(Her sister made a SOLEMN vow not to tell anyone their secret.)

SOLICITOUS [suh LIS i tus]
- anxiously concerned
(Some of the Boy Scout mothers were SOLICITOUS about their sons' safety during the overnight hike.)

SOLUBLE [SAHL yuh bul]
- dissolvable
(Sugar is SOLUBLE in water.)

SOLUBLE [SAHL yuh bul]
- solvable
(Despite the precariousness of their financial dilemma, it was nevertheless a SOLUBLE situation.)

SOMBER [SAHM bur]
- gloomy
(The sporting event turned decidedly SOMBER when it was announced that one of the players had been involved in an automobile accident en route to the affair.)

SOMNOLENT [SAHM nuh lunt]
- drowsy
(Because some medications can produce a SOMNOLENT reaction, one must be careful not to take such drugs before driving.)

SONOROUS [suh NOHR us; SAHN ur us]
- resonant
(When struck, a gong produces a **SONOROUS** sound.)

SOPHOMORIC [sahf uh MOHR ik]
- conceitedly overconfident but poorly knowledgeable
(Although the student professed to know as much about law as did his teacher, his SOPHOMORIC explanation of the legal case proved to all that he was but a novice.)

SOPORIFIC [sahp uh RIF ik]
- causing sleep
(The SOPORIFIC speech lulled several students to doze off.)

SORDID [SOHR did]
- filthy/disgusting
(Oftentimes, those residing in inner-city ghettos must contend with SORDID living conditions.)

SOVEREIGN [SAHV rin; SAHV ur in]
- independent/self-governing
*(In the nineteenth century, Hawaii was a **SOVEREIGN** nation.)*

SOVEREIGN [SAHV rin; SAHV ur in]
- supreme
*(In prehistoric times, the pterosaur reigned **SOVEREIGN** in the skies.)*

SPARSE [spahrs]
- scattered ("spaced out")
*(Greenland has a **SPARSE** population.)*

SPARTAN [SPAHR tn]
- strict and self-disciplined
*(To maintain peak physical conditioning, the **SPARTAN** athlete followed a rigorous daily schedule.)*

SPECIOUS [SPEE shus]
- fallacious (though superficially plausible)
*(Although delivered forcefully and with great conviction, the argument, when examined more closely, revealed factual flaws and **SPECIOUS** reasoning.)*

SPENDTHRIFT [SPEND thrift]
- wasteful
*(The **SPENDTHRIFT** shopper went on lavish and costly binges.)*

SPITEFUL [SPIET ful]
- intentionally mean/hateful
*(In a **SPITEFUL** display of anger for not being given the first piece of cake, the boy threw his sister's serving into the garbage can.)*

SPLENETIC [spli NET ik]
- irritable and bad-tempered
*(During a **SPLENETIC** outburst, the frustrated man kicked the family dog.)*

SPONTANEOUS [spahn TAY nee us]
- natural/unrehearsed
*(Because children are generally **SPONTANEOUS** and socially extroverted, they make friends easily and quickly with one another.)*

SPORADIC [spoh RAD ik]
- infrequent and irregular
*(Only a few **SPORADIC** outbreaks of malaria occurred throughout the country after counteractive measures were taken.)*

SPORTIVE [SPOHR tiv]
- playful
*(After a few drinks, the stodgy group soon became jovial and **SPORTIVE**.)*

SPRAWLING [SPRAW ling]
- widespread
*(In thirteenth century China, Kublai Khan ruled a **SPRAWLING** empire.)*

SPRIGHTLY [SPRIET lee]
- cheerful and lively
*(Each morning, the **SPRIGHTLY** old man would greet his neighbors as he jogged around the block.)*

SPRY [sprie]
- spirited/lively
*(For an octogenarian, the woman was particularly **SPRY**.)*

SPURIOUS [SPYOOR ee us]
- fraudulently false
*(Authorities threatened to take legal action if the company continued to advertise what amounted to patently **SPURIOUS** claims.)*

SPURN [spurn]
- reject with scorn
*(When **SPURNED** by her boyfriend, the jilted woman sought swift revenge.)*

SQUALID [SKWAHL id]
- filthy
*(Residents in the tenement house were subjected to **SQUALID** living conditions.)*

SQUANDER [SKWAHN dur]
- spend wastefully
*(Within a year, the spendthrift had **SQUANDERED** his entire inheritance.)*

STAID [stayd]
- serious and somber
*(The professor was a very **STAID** woman who found little time for frivolity or tomfoolery.)*

STALWART [STAHL wurt]
- courageous and determined
*(The **STALWART** captain braved the angry sea.)*

STALWART [STAHL wurt]
- sturdy/strong
*(The **STALWART**, rugged man easily lifted the piano onto the truck.)*

STAMINA [STAM uh nuh]
- endurance
*(It takes great **STAMINA** to hike up a steep mountain trail.)*

STANCH [stahnch; stanch]
- stop the flow of
*(A tourniquet helped **STANCH** the loss of blood from the open wound.)*

STAR-CROSSED [STAHR krahst]
- ill-fated
(Romeo and Juliet were STAR-CROSSED lovers.)

STARK [stahrk]
- bare
(Upon entering, incoming inmates first noticed the prison's STARK and forbidding appearance.)

STATELY [STAYT lee]
- impressively elegant/magnificent
(Several heads of state attended the STATELY wedding.)

STATUS QUO [stay tus KWOH; stat us KWOH]
- current/existing situation
(Rather than vote for a policy change, the usually dissenting members of the committee supported the STATUS QUO.)

STAUNCH [stahnch]
- steadfastly loyal
(The political candidate was flanked by her STAUNCH supporters.)

STEADFAST [STED fast]
- determined and unwavering
(The eager lad had a STEADFAST desire to one day play quarterback on the high school football team.)

STEALTHY [STEL thee]
- quiet and sneaky
(A lion approaches in a STEALTHY manner to catch its prey off guard.)

STENTORIAN [sten TOHR ee un]
- very loud/strong
(The seasoned thespian had a STENTORIAN voice that could be heard clearly throughout the large auditorium.)

STERN [sturn]
- strict/uncompromising
(The gymnastics coach was a STERN and demanding taskmaster.)

STIFLE [STIE ful]
- suppress
(Rigid dictates STIFLE individual creativity.)

STIPULATE [STIP yuh layt]
- specify (as a requirement)
(Prior to any signing of a cease fire, a clause was agreed upon that STIPULATED the release of all political prisoners.)

STODGY [STAHJ ee]
- dull/boring
(The STODGY movie dragged on without end.)

STODGY [STAHJ ee]
- thick/lumpy
*(The **STODGY** potatoes were difficult to digest.)*

STOIC [STOH ik]
- not showing emotion
*(Her **STOIC** demeanor in the face of such tragedy was instrumental in sparing her children traumatic grief.)*

STOLID [STAHL id]
- unexcitable/spiritless
*(The drama teacher had absolutely no luck inspiring the **STOLID** teenager to convey his feelings in a theatrically expressive manner.)*

STOPGAP [STAHP gap]
- temporary
*(Taking fewer showers was only a **STOPGAP** measure to relieve the water shortage; an effective long-term solution was really needed.)*

STOUT [stout]
- bulky/fat
*(John Candy was a **STOUT** but genuinely lovable comedian.)*

STOUT [stout]
- fearless and determined
*(The **STOUT** sailor braved the open seas to search for the missing crewmember.)*

STRAITLACED [STRAYT layst]
- rigidly proper
*(Attending parties did not conform to his **STRAITLACED** upbringing.)*

STRATAGEM [STRAT uh jum]
- scheme (involving deception)
*(The police devised a **STRATAGEM** in which the suspect would unknowingly be caught red-handed.)*

STRIATED [STRIE ay tid]
- streaked
*(A rainbow consists of **STRIATED** bands of light.)*

STRIDENT [STRIED nt]
- loud and harsh
*(Several students covered their ears during the **STRIDENT** wail of the alarm bell.)*

STRIFE [strief]
- conflict/turmoil
*(Bitter civil **STRIFE** broke out in the ravaged war-torn countryside.)*

STRINGENT [STRIN junt]
- strict
*(The exclusive college maintained **STRINGENT** minimal entrance requirements.)*

STULTIFY [STUL tuh fie]
- hinder and frustrate
*(By branding UFOs a figment of overactive imaginations, the teacher **STULTIFIED** the children's curiosity to learn more about extraterrestrial life.)*

STUPEFY [STOO puh fie]
- stun
*(The assassination of President Kennedy in 1963 **STUPEFIED** the nation.)*

STYGIAN [STIJ ee un; STIJ un]
- infernal
*(After their capture, the prisoners were led into the **STYGIAN** darkness of the forbidding dungeon.)*

SUAVE [swahv]
- charmingly elegant
*(All the ladies at the ball were smitten by the **SUAVE** young man.)*

SUBJUGATE [SUB juh gayt]
- conquer and dominate
*(Under the rule of Kublai Kahn, the Mongols **SUBJUGATED** the Chinese people and eventually ruled the land for ninety years.)*

SUBMISSIVE [sub MIS iv]
- obedient
*(A dog is **SUBMISSIVE** to its master.)*

SUB ROSA [sub ROH zuh]
- secretly/in strictest privacy
*(The FBI meeting with the drug informant was held **SUB ROSA**.)*

SUBSERVIENT [sub SUR vee unt]
- submissive
*(Butlers are trained to act in a **SUBSERVIENT** manner to their employers.)*

SUBSERVIENT [sub SUR vee unt]
- subordinate
*(Reaching one's financial goals should always be **SUBSERVIENT** to attaining a measurable quality of happiness in one's life.)*

SUBSIDE [sub SIED]
- diminish
*(Once the doctor administered the antidote, the pain and swelling quickly **SUBSIDED**.)*

SUBSIDIZE [SUB si diez]
- assist financially
*(A partial scholarship **SUBSIDIZED** the student's college tuition.)*

SUBSTANTIAL [sub STAN shul]
- sizable/significant
*(Much to his surprise, his paycheck reflected a **SUBSTANTIAL** and unexpected raise.)*

SUBSTANTIATE [sub STAN shee ayt]
- verify
*(More concrete evidence was needed to **SUBSTANTIATE** the employees' claims of unsafe working conditions.)*

SUBTERFUGE [sub tur FYOOJ]
- deceptive scheming
*(Huckleberry Finn employed crafty **SUBTERFUGE** to enlist the services of friends to paint his fence.)*

SUBTERRANEAN [sub tuh RAY nee un]
- underground
*(A safety inspection revealed the presence of **SUBTERRANEAN** termites.)*

SUBTLE [SUT l]
- faint/delicate
*(A **SUBTLE** garlic taste added zest to the otherwise bland meal.)*

SUBTLE [SUT l]
- skillfully indirect
*(His wife's **SUBTLE** reminder of the late hour convinced him that it was time to leave the party.)*

SUBVERT [sub VURT]
- undermine/corrupt
*(Introducing a young teenager to the world of illicit activities will **SUBVERT** his moral fiber.)*

SUCCINCT [suk SINGKT]
- clear and concise
*(The political candidate provided **SUCCINCT** responses to the interviewer's pointed questions.)*

SUCCOR [SUK ur]
- aid
*(Nurses arrived on the scene to give **SUCCOR** to the injured.)*

SUCCULENT [SUK yuh lunt]
- juicy
*(The restaurant's prime rib steak was **SUCCULENT** and flavorful.)*

SUCCUMB [suh KUM]
- yield/submit
*(Despite her best efforts to control her weight, she **SUCCUMBED** to temptation by eating an extra piece of pie.)*

SUFFRAGE [SUF rij]
- right to vote
*(Susan B. Anthony was an early champion of women's **SUFFRAGE**.)*

SUFFUSE [suh FYOOZ]
- spread throughout
*(When the shudders were opened, light **SUFFUSED** the room.)*

SULLEN [SUL un]
- gloomy and grouchy
*(The elderly recluse was a habitually **SULLEN** person.)*

SULLY [SUL ee]
- tarnish
*(A minor scandal **SULLIED** the physicist's brilliant reputation.)*

SULTRY [SUL tree]
- very hot and humid
*(The **SULTRY** afternoon left everyone languid and lethargic.)*

SUMMARILY [suh MER uh lee]
- promptly/swiftly
*(Once found guilty, the seditious prisoners were **SUMMARILY** executed.)*

SUMPTUOUS [SUMP choo us]
- luxuriously lavish
*(At the luau, guests were treated to a **SUMPTUOUS** banquet.)*

SUPERCILIOUS [soo pur SIL ee us]
- arrogantly self-important
*(His overnight success turned the once-modest boy into a **SUPERCILIOUS** and condescending braggadocio.)*

SUPEREROGATORY [soo pur uh RAHG uh tohr ee]
- nonessential
*(To impress his employer, the ambitious lad completed several **SUPEREROGATORY** tasks.)*

SUPERFICIAL [soo pur FISH ul]
- shallow/on the surface
*(Fortunately for the soldier, the wound was only **SUPERFICIAL** and not life-threatening.)*

SUPERFLUOUS [soo PUR floo us]
- more than necessary
*(In poetry, success can only be achieved when all **SUPERFLUOUS** words are omitted.)*

SUPERLATIVE [suh PUR luh tiv; soo PUR luh tiv]
- superior
*(Critics hailed the musical for its **SUPERLATIVE** choreography.)*

SUPERNAL [soo PURN l]
- heavenly
*(The fair maiden's **SUPERNAL** beauty mesmerized the love-struck sailor.)*

SUPERNUMERARY [soo pur NOO muh rer ee]
- extra
*(During the busy holiday season, **SUPERNUMERARY** parking lot attendants were called in to work.)*

SUPERSEDE [soo pur SEED]
- replace
(The captain's order SUPERSEDED all those made earlier by his subordinates.)

SUPPLANT [suh PLANT]
- replace
(Unfortunately, more and more people in the workplace are finding themselves SUPPLANTED by computers and other technological devices.)

SUPPLIANT [SUP lee unt]
- begging
(The SUPPLIANT heretic sought forgiveness for his religious infidelity.)

SUPPLICATE [SUP luh kayt]
- beg/pray humbly
(The council chief SUPPLICATED the gods to provide the tribe with much-needed rain.)

SUPPRESS [suh PRES]
- restrain/control ("bottle up")
(Rather than cause a scene at the restaurant, the irate customer SUPPRESSED his anger.)

SUPPRESS [suh PRES]
- crush ("put down")
(The National Guard was called in to SUPPRESS the civil riot.)

SURFEIT [SUR fit]
- overabundance/excess
(The king's banquet featured a SURFEIT of imported delicacies and the choicest of wines.)

SURLY [SUR lee]
- rude/unfriendly
(Neighborhood children avoided the SURLY homeless man who resided in the park.)

SURMOUNT [sur MOUNT]
- overcome
(With perseverance and dedication, a person can SURMOUNT any obstacle.)

SURREALISTIC [suh ree uh LIS tik]
- bizarre and unrealistic
(The art produced by Salvador Dali was often hypnotically SURREALISTIC.)

SURREPTITIOUS [sur up TISH us]
- sneaky and clandestine
(The young boy gained a SURREPTITIOUS view of his older brother together with the sibling's girlfriend.)

SURROGATE [SUR uh gayt; SUR uh git]
- substitute
(On weekend campouts, the scout leader became a SURROGATE father to twelve boys.)

SUSCEPTIBLE [suh SEP tuh bul]
- sensitive/not resistant
(An open wound is **SUSCEPTIBLE** to infection.)

SUSTENANCE [SUS tuh nuns]
- nourishment
(A hearty meal provides much-needed SUSTENANCE to a hungry lad.)

SWARTHY [SWOHR thee; SWOHR thee]
- dark-skinned
(Othello was a man of SWARTHY complexion.)

SYBARITIC [sib uh RIT ik]
- self-indulging/pleasure-seeking
(The wealthy playboy indulged in SYBARITIC grandeur befitting a sultan.)

SYCOPHANT [SIK uh funt]
- servile flatterer ("parasite")
(The powerful and domineering emperor was attended to by his retinue of SYCOPHANTS, each seeking special favor with the nations' ruler.)

SYLVAN [SIL vun]
- wooded/forest-like
(The poet yearned to escape the urban madness and return to the SYLVAN rusticity of country life.)

SYMMETRY [SIM i tree]
- balanced proportions
(The sixteenth-century galleon was refurbished with careful attention paid to preserve the original design's SYMMETRY.)

SYNCHRONOUS [SING kruh nus]
- simultaneously timed
(The team performed a SYNCHRONOUS swimming exercise.)

SYNTHETIC [sin THET ik]
- artificial
(Latex is a coating produced from SYNTHETIC rubber.)

TACIT [TAS it]
- understood (though not openly stated)
(A TACIT agreement was made between the two dorm mates not to play the radio loud while the other was studying.)

TACITURN [TAS i turn]
- untalkative
(The teacher found it very difficult to persuade the TACITURN boy to discuss his thoughts openly in class discussions.)

TACTFUL [TAKT ful]
- sensitive and socially considerate
(To avoid a needless argument, the TACTUL gentleman reassured his wife that she looked strikingly attractive in her polka-dot dress.)

TALISMAN [TAL is mun; TAL iz mun]
- magical/good-luck charm
(Tribal members believed that the witchdoctor's TALISMAN could ward off evil spirits.)

TANGIBLE [TAN juh bul]
- touchable/solid and real
(Money is a TANGIBLE commodity; love is not.)

TANTALIZE [TAN tuh liez]
- tempt teasingly
(The prankish lad TANTALIZED the neighbor's dog by placing a tasty bone too high for the canine to reach.)

TANTAMOUNT [TAN tuh mount]
- equivalent
(His crime of sending documents to the enemy was TANTAMOUNT to treason.)

TAUNT [tahnt]
- jeer at mockingly/insultingly
(The discourteous crowd TAUNTED the novice comedian with hisses and boos.)

TAUT [taht]
- stretched tight
(As the high-wire act began their performance, circus personnel ensured that the cable remained TAUT.)

TAUT [taht]
- emotionally tense
(After two nights without sleep, his nerves were TAUT and his patience low.)

TAUTOLOGICAL [taht uh LAHJ i kul]
- repetitious
(The political speech proved more TAUTOLOGICAL than substantive.)

TAWDRY [TAH dree]
- cheap and showy
(The TAWDRY dress gave others the mistaken impression that she was a prostitute.)

TEDIOUS [TEE dee us]
- lengthy and tiresome
(Grading papers can be a TEDIOUS task.)

TELLTALE [TEL tayl]
- revealing
(Asking his brother for a loan was a TELLTALE sign that he had resumed his gambling ways.)

TEMERITY [tuh MER i tee]
- reckless boldness
*(The young cadet had the **TEMERITY** to challenge the word of his superior officer.)*

TEMPER [TEM pur]
- moderate/soften
*(After a moment of deliberation, the congressman **TEMPERED** his words of condemnation against those who had voted to kill his proposal.)*

TEMPER [TEM pur]
- strengthen
*(The Samurai sword was forged from **TEMPERED** steel.)*

TEMPERATE [TEM pur it; TEM prit]
- mild/pleasant
*(The island was popular for its **TEMPERATE** climatic conditions.)*

TEMPEST [TEM pist]
- violent storm
*(The ship found itself in the midst of an unwelcome **TEMPEST**.)*

TEMPORAL [TEM pur ul]
- temporary
*(Man's **TEMPORAL** stay on Earth pales in comparison to the longevity of the dinosaur.)*

TEMPORAL [TEM pur ul]
- earthly and day-to-day
*(Carpe diem poetry concerns itself with man's **TEMPORAL** pleasures.)*

TEMPORIZE [TEM puh riez]
- delay/stall
*(The lead negotiator **TEMPORIZED** while the hostage-taker's mother was summoned to the scene.)*

TENACIOUS [tuh NAY shus]
- persistently determined
*(An animal's **TENACIOUS** will to survive is a necessity in the wild.)*

TENEBROUS [TEN uh brus]
- dark and gloomy
*(Political dissidents were confined in makeshift cells deep within the walls of the **TENEBROUS** catacomb.)*

TENET [TEN it]
- belief
*(The Anabaptists' distinctive **TENET** was their preference for adult rather than infant baptism.)*

TENTATIVE [TEN tuh tiv]
- hesitant and unsure
*(When traversing the frozen lake, the group proceeded in a deliberate and **TENTATIVE** manner.)*

TENTATIVE [TEN tuh tiv]
- not final
*(Reporters announced that a **TENTATIVE** settlement had been reached between the union and corporate management.)*

TENUOUS [TEN yoo us]
- slender and weak
*(Only a single **TENUOUS** rope kept the damaged scaffold from plummeting to the ground.)*

TEPID [TEP id]
- halfhearted/unenthusiastic
*(She displayed only a **TEPID** interest in attending the class reunion.)*

TERRESTRIAL [tuh RES tree ul]
- earthly/on land
*(Although turtles may live in the water or on land, the tortoise is strictly a **TERRESTRIAL** animal.)*

TERSE [turs]
- effectively concise
*(With less than a minute remaining, the test administrator issued a **TERSE** reminder for students to conclude their essays.)*

TESTY [TES tee]
- irritably impatient
*(Before his first cup of coffee in the morning, he tended to be **TESTY** and unsociable.)*

THERAPEUTIC [ther uh PYOO tik]
- curative/healing
*(Health spas are frequented for their **THERAPEUTIC** value.)*

THESPIAN [THES pee un]
- actor/actress
*(John Carradine was a renowned twentieth-century **THESPIAN**.)*

THRIFTY [THRIF tee]
- economical/stingy
*(A **THRIFTY** shopper is a smart shopper.)*

THRIVE [thriev]
- flourish/prosper
*(Ice cream businesses **THRIVE** during hot summer months.)*

THWART [thwahrt]
- foil/prevent
*(Locked windows **THWARTED** the burglar's efforts to enter the house.)*

TIMBRE [TIM bur; TAM bur]
- tone
*(The operatic baritone had a deep and orotund **TIMBRE**.)*

TIMOROUS [TIM ur us]
- fearfully shy and afraid
*(The **TIMOROUS** accountant feared asking his boss for a day off.)*

TINTINNABULATION [tin ti nab yuh LAY shun]
- ringing/jingling of bells
*(As Christmas Day dawned, the children awoke to the **TINTINNABULATION** of Santa's sleigh flying overhead.)*

TIRADE [TIE rayd; tie RAYD]
- lengthy criticism/denunciation
*(In the locker room after the game, the head coach delivered a bitter **TIRADE** to the team for displaying unsportsmanlike conduct on the field.)*

TITANIC [tie TAN ik]
- huge and mighty
*(Some dinosaurs were **TITANIC** creatures.)*

TOADY [TOH dee]
- servile flatterer
*(The boss's **TOADY** always told him what he wanted to hear.)*

TOCSIN [TAHK sin]
- alarm
*(The **TOCSIN** sent the citizens running for shelter.)*

TORPID [TOHR pid]
- sluggish
*(His mind became **TORPID** from lack of stimulating mental exercise.)*

TORRID [TOHR id]
- sizzling
*(The **TORRID** desert sands made travel on foot unbearable to all but the local natives.)*

TOUT [tout]
- praise highly/publicly
*(The brokerage firm **TOUTED** the success of its investment fund.)*

TOXIC [TAHK sik]
- poisonous
*(**TOXIC** fumes released by the overturned truck forced the evacuation of nearby residents.)*

TRADUCE [truh DOOS]
- slander and shame
*(The pop star was so **TRADUCED** by unfounded rumors that she was afraid to be seen in public.)*

TRANQUIL [TRANG kwil]
- calm
*(The **TRANQIL** waters were inviting to young and old alike.)*

TRANSCEND [tran SEND]
- exceed
*(Philosophers often engage in highly theoretical discussions that **TRANSCEND** the boundaries of most people's understanding.)*

TRANSIENT [TRAN shunt; TRAN zhunt]
- brief/quickly passing
*(Many of William Shakespeare's sonnets describe the **TRANSIENT** nature of youth.)*

TRANSITORY [TRAN si tohr ee; TRAN zi tohr ee]
- short-lived/brief
*(Bell-bottom pants were just another of the **TRANSITORY** fads of the 1960s.)*

TRANSMOGRIFY [trans MAHG ruh fie; tranz MAHG ruh fie]
- change in form/appearance
*(In the science fiction movie, the alien creature **TRANSMOGRIFIED** from a dog into a three-headed serpent.)*

TRANSMUTE [trans MYOOT; tranz MYOOT]
- transform
*(At one time, people believed that alchemists could **TRANSMUTE** lead into gold.)*

TRANSPIRE [tran SPIER]
- occur
*(In the haunted house, ghostly events **TRANSPIRED** during the visitors' overnight stay.)*

TRAVAIL [truh VAYL; TRAV ayl]
- burdensome/hard work
*(Plantation life for slaves consisted of endless toil and **TRAVAIL**.)*

TRAVAIL [truh VAYL; TRAV ayl]
- suffering
*(In his novels, Ernest Hemingway wrote about the **TRAVAILS** of war.)*

TRAVERSE [truh VURS; TRA vurs]
- cross
*(Signs warned visitors not to **TRAVERSE** the stream during the rainy season.)*

TRAVESTY [TRAV is tee]
- shameful mockery
*(Protesters called the one-sided trial a **TRAVESTY** of justice.)*

TREACHEROUS [TRECH ur us]
- deceptively hazardous
*(Over the years, the **TREACHEROUS** path claimed several victims.)*

TREACHEROUS [TRECH ur us]
- disloyal
*(The **TREACHEROUS** recreant was banished from the village.)*

TREMULOUS [TREM yuh lus]
- trembling
*(The old man's **TREMULOUS** hands proved a hindrance in holding a glass of water or eating from a bowl of soup.)*

TREMULOUS [TREM yuh lus]
- fearfully timid
*(The **TREMULOUS** tot hid underneath his mother's skirt.)*

TRENCHANT [TREN chunt]
- keenly/acutely perceptive
*(John Locke's essays present a **TRENCHANT** analysis of the proper role of government in society.)*

TREPIDATION [trep i DAY shun]
- fearful uneasiness
*(When goaded to jump off the highest diving board, the diminutive lad felt extreme **TREPIDATION**.)*

TRIBULATION [trib yuh LAY shun]
- extreme distress/suffering
*(Many have experienced firsthand the trials and **TRIBULATIONS** of a bitterly contested divorce.)*

TRITE [triet]
- overused and unoriginal
*(Critics did not review the play favorably, citing its **TRITE** plot and shallow characterizations.)*

TRIUMPHAL [trie UM ful]
- victorious
*(After the race, the winning horse ran a **TRIUMPHAL** lap around the track to the delight of cheering spectators.)*

TRIVIAL [TRIV ee ul]
- relatively unimportant
*(Students complained that the history examination placed too much emphasis on **TRIVIAL** dates and events.)*

TRUCKLE [TRUK ul]
- yield submissively
*(Rather than assert his own independence, the toady always **TRUCKLED** to his superiors.)*

TRUCULENT [TRUK yuh lunt]
- aggressively belligerent
*(Almost everyone has at one time or another had an encounter with the **TRUCULENT** school bully.)*

TRUNCATE [TRUNG kayt]
- shorten (by cutting)
*(To prevent its fruit from falling on the roof, several branches of the tall mango tree were **TRUNCATED**.)*

TUMID [TOO mid]
- abnormally swollen
*(A **TUMID** stomach is often a sign of severe malnutrition.)*

TUMULTUOUS [too MUL choo us]
- turbulent
(The World War II years were a TUMULTUOUS period in world history.)

TURBID [TUR bid]
- muddy/murky
(After the dam burst, the TURBID waters churned as they rampaged in a violent torrent through the valley below.)

TURGID [TUR jid]
- swollen
(The TURGID flesh wound required immediate medical attention.)

TURGID [TUR jid]
- pompously showy
(The cub reporter's TURGID discourse did not impress the veteran journalist.)

TURMOIL [TUR moil]
- chaos and confusion
(When gun shots rang out, TURMOIL erupted in the auditorium.)

TYRO [TIE roh]
- novice
(The musical TYRO was relegated to third-string in the school band.)

UBIQUITOUS [yoo BIK wi tus]
- existing everywhere
(No matter which island they are visiting, tourists are treated to the UBIQUITOUS aloha spirit of Hawaii.)

ULTERIOR [ul TEER ee ur]
- concealed/unstated
(Knowing her brother only too well, she suspected an ULTERIOR motive behind his guise of complaisant geniality.)

ULTIMATUM [ul tuh MAY tum; ul tuh MAH tum]
- final demand
(The terrorists issued one last ULTIMATUM before threatening to shoot the hostages.)

ULULATION [yoo yuh LAY shun; ul yuh LAY shun]
- wailing
(In the tiny village ravaged by war, one could hear the ULULATION of grieving widows.)

UMBRAGE [UM brij]
- personal offense/resentment
(The young lady took UMBRAGE at the unfounded remarks levied against her boyfriend.)

UNABASHED [un uh BASHT]
- without fear or shame
(The rebel faction echoed their UNABASHED support of the military uprising.)

UNABRIDGED [un uh BRIJD]
- complete/comprehensive
(For a definition of an esoteric or arcane word, one needs to consult an UNABRIDGED dictionary.)

UNASSUMING [un uh SOO ming]
- modest
(Off stage, the pop singer was an ingratiatingly UNASSUMING gentleman.)

UNBRIDLED [un BRIED uld]
- unrestrained
(The audience succumbed to UNBRIDLED laughter during the hilarious skit.)

UNCANNY [un KAN ee]
- amazingly extraordinary
(Because of their UNCANNY sense of smell, beagles are often used at airports to sniff out contraband.)

UNCANNY [un KAN ee]
- uncomfortably strange
(During the séance, an UNCANNY stillness filled the air.)

UNCONSCIONABLE [un KAHN shuh nuh bul]
- outrageous/inexcusable
(Selling defective merchandise to the elderly is an UNCONSCIONABLE and despicable practice.)

UNCOUTH [un KOOTH]
- crude
(Her parents were shocked by her boyfriend's UNCOUTH behavior.)

UNCTUOUS [UNGK choo us]
- artificially/insincerely ingratiating
(The unscrupulous opportunist exhibited UNCTUOUS servility in order to gain a foothold in the elderly man's vast empire.)

UNDAUNTED [un DAHN tid]
- courageously determined
(Although faced with seemingly insurmountable obstacles, the early pioneers remained UNDAUNTED in their pursuit for westward expansion.)

UNDERPIN [un dur PIN]
- strengthen/support
(Statistical evidence helped to UNDERPIN her argument.)

UNDERSCORE [un dur SKOHR]
- emphasize
(The construction supervisor UNDERSCORED the need to complete the project on time.)

UNEQUIVOCAL [un i KWIV uh kul]
- definite/unmistakable
(Man's journey to the moon in 1969 proved to be an UNEQUIVOCAL success.)

UNEXPURGATED [un EK spur gay tid]
- uncensored
*(All the sordid details were included in the **UNEXPRUGATED** account of the acrimonious divorce.)*

UNFLAPPABLE [un FLAP uh bul]
- composed/unruffled
*(Even the most trying of times, the mother of eight young boys always remained patient and **UNFLAPPABLE**.)*

UNGAINLY [un GAYN lee]
- awkward/clumsy
*(A duck walks in an **UNGAINLY** manner.)*

UNILATERAL [yoo nuh LAT ur ul]
- one-sided
*(A **UNILATERAL** decision to escalate military preparedness was frowned upon by the country's allies.)*

UNIMPEACHABLE [un im PEE chuh bul]
- totally honest/faultless
*(The woman's **UNIMPEACHABLE** qualifications made her a prime candidate for the executive position.)*

UNINHIBITED [un in HIB i tid]
- candid and unrestrained
*(When asked what she thought of the party, her **UNINHIBITED** response offended the host.)*

UNMITIGATED [un MIT uh gay tid]
- absolute
*(On the witness stand, the defendant claimed that the testimony made against him was a collection of **UNMITIGATED** lies.)*

UNOBTRUSIVE [un ub TROO siv]
- modest
*(When not in the wrestling ring, the burly man was a surprisingly **UNOBTRUSIVE** and affable gentleman.)*

UNOBTRUSIVE [un ub TROO siv]
- inconspicuous
*(Few realized that the **UNOBTRUSIVE** white building had an indoor swimming pool.)*

UNRULY [un ROO lee]
- rowdy and unmanageable
*(Upset by the referee's questionable call, the **UNRULY** crowd began to pour onto the field in angry protest.)*

UNSCRUPULOUS [un SKROO pyuh lus]
- devious and unprincipled
*(The **UNSCRUPULOUS** businessman tricked his partner into signing over a majority stake in the lucrative enterprise.)*

UNSPEAKABLE [un SPEE kuh bul]
- shocking/horrible
(Many Nazi leaders were charged with committing UNSPEAKABLE crimes against humanity.)

UNSUNG [un SUNG]
- unacknowledged
(Many UNSUNG heroes gave their lives during World War II.)

UNTENABLE [un TEN uh bul]
- unsound/fallacious
(Many consider arguments defending the existence of extraterrestrial life to be irrational and UNTENABLE.)

UNTIMELY [un TIEM lee]
- premature
(The actor's UNTIMELY death took the entire film industry by surprise.)

UNTIMELY [un TIEM lee]
- unfortunate
(Having a flat tire while rushing to the airport was most UNTIMELY.)

UNWIELDY [un WEEL dee]
- unmanageably bulky
(The sledgehammer was much too UNWIELDY for the diminutive youngster to swing.)

UPBRAID [up BRAYD]
- scold/criticize
(The young worker was UPBRAIDED for dawdling.)

UPROARIOUS [up ROHR ee us]
- loud and disorderly
(After the Super Bowl game, the victorious city celebrated in UPROARIOUS fashion.)

UPROARIOUS [up ROHR ee us]
- very funny
(The Broadway musical comedy was an UPROARIOUS success.)

UPSHOT [UP shaht]
- outcome/result
(Few could ever have imagined what the UPSHOT of the fortuitous meeting would be.)

UPSTANDING [up STAN ding]
- honorable
(The lawyer was lauded as an UPSTANDING citizen who fought sedulously for the rights of those oppressed.)

UPSTART [UP stahrt]
- rapid social climber
(The veteran workers felt intimidated by the brash UPSTART employee's novel ideas.)

URBAN [UR bun]
- (relating to the) city
*(The planning committee began an ambitious undertaking for **URBAN** expansion and development.)*

URBANE [ur BAYN]
- suave and elegant
*(All the ladies at the ball were enchanted by the **URBANE** and sophisticated young gentleman.)*

USURP [yoo SURP]
- seize (without legal right)
*(In the midst of the civil uprising, the duke **USURPED** the throne and declared himself the new ruler.)*

UTILITARIAN [yoo til i TAYR ee un]
- practical/useful
*(The **UTILITARIAN** work of art actually served as a timepiece.)*

UXORIOUS [uk SOHR ee us; ug ZOHR ee us]
- submissive (to one's wife)
*(The **UXORIOUS** husband catered to his domineering wife's every whim.)*

VACILLATE [VAS uh layt]
- waver/fluctuate
*(When his star player fouled out of the game, the coach **VACILLATED** on his selection of a replacement.)*

VACUOUS [VAK yoo us]
- empty/vacant ("blank")
*(The hypnotized man gazed into the audience with a **VACUOUS** stare.)*

VAGARY [VAY guh ree; vuh GAYR ee]
- erratic/unpredictable action
*(Residents in the Texas Panhandle must contend with the **VAGARIES** of Mother Nature.)*

VAIN [vayn]
- conceited and self-absorbed
*(Bodybuilders are often characterized as **VAIN** egoists.)*

VAIN [vayn]
- unsuccessful
*(Surfing the internet for over an hour proved a **VAIN** attempt to contact his long-lost sister.)*

VALIANT [VAL yunt]
- courageous and determined
*(Despite her ultimate failure, the plucky lass nonetheless made a **VALIANT** attempt to climb to the top of the tree.)*

VALID [VAL id]
- convincingly logical
*(Though her parents rejected her request to host a weekend party, they nevertheless granted that the young girl had presented **VALID** arguments in her own behalf.)*

VALID [VAL id]
- legally acceptable
(A driver's license is VALID in all fifty states.)

VALIDATE [VAL i dayt]
- confirm/authenticate
(The doctor's medical diagnosis VALIDATED her initial fears.)

VALOR [VAL ur]
- heroic bravery
(Audie Murphy was highly decorated for displaying VALOR on the battlefield during World War II.)

VANGUARD [VAN gahrd]
- forefront
(Nirvana was at the VANGUARD of the 1990s grunge music movement.)

VANQUISH [VANG kwish]
- defeat/conquer
(The thirteenth-century Mongols VANQUISHED their enemies as they extended their rule across the Asian continent.)

VAPID [VAP id]
- dull and uninteresting
(Fellow employees were weary of the dolt's VAPID jokes and vain attempts at clever repartee.)

VARIEGATED [VER ee uh gay tid; VER ee gay tid]
- multicolored/varied
(The quilt was a VARIEGATED patchwork of colorful fabrics.)

VAST [vast]
- extensive
(Early settlers marveled at the VAST wilderness of the Old West.)

VAUNT [vahnt]
- boast about
(The rich lad VAUNTED his family's wealth.)

VEHEMENT [VEE uh munt]
- passionate
(Several committee members expressed their VEHEMENT opposition to the controversial proposal.)

VENAL [VEEN l]
- corrupt/able to be bribed
(Opponents of the administration claimed that the government had become rife with VENAL public officials.)

VENDETTA [ven DET uh]
- lengthy/bitter feud
(For generations the Hatfields and McCoys perpetuated a rancorous VENDETTA, until they one day finally reconciled their differences.)

VENERABLE [VEN ur uh bul]
- greatly respected
*(Many regard the **VENERABLE** William Shakespeare as the greatest playwright of all time.)*

VENERATE [VEN uh rayt]
- honor and respect deeply
*(In Indian tribes, the elder council members are **VENERATED** by their juniors.)*

VENIAL [VEE nee ul; VEEN yul]
- forgivable
*(Everyone has **VENIAL** faults; that's what makes us human.)*

VENOMOUS [VEN uh mus]
- poisonous
*(Black widow spiders are highly **VENOMOUS**.)*

VENOMOUS [VEN uh mus]
- malicious
*(His political rival launched a **VENOMOUS** verbal attack against him predicated on groundless innuendo.)*

VERACIOUS [vuh RAY shus]
- truthful and accurate
*(The veteran reporter provided a **VERACIOUS** and dispassionate account of the protesters' clash with police.)*

VERBATIM [vur BAY tim]
- word for word/exactly
*(When asked what the captain had instructed him to do, the first mate repeated the order **VERBATIM**.)*

VERBOSE [vur BOHS]
- excessively wordy
*(Rather than explain the concept briefly and to the point, the spokesman delivered a **VERBOSE** oration that rambled on for fifteen minutes.)*

VERDANT [VUR dunt]
- lush/green with vegetation
*(The **VERDANT** meadows inspired the artist to compose a paean to country living.)*

VERDANT [VUR dunt]
- inexperienced
*(The **VERDANT** sailor was unprepared to battle the unusually rough seas.)*

VERIFY [VER uh fie]
- prove to be true
*(Due to communication failure, meteorologists were unable to **VERIFY** that the powerful hurricane had indeed struck the capital city of the remote island.)*

VERISIMILITUDE [ver i si MIL i tood; ver i si MIL i tyood]
- realism
*(Although only fictional, the adventures of Sherlock Holmes are portrayed with such **VERISIMILITUDE** that one actually feels as though the detective lived and solved all those mysteries.)*

VERITABLE [VER i tuh bul]
- actual
*(The primeval forest was a **VERITABLE** paradise.)*

VERNAL [VUR nl]
- spring
*(Many couples wed in the **VERNAL** months.)*

VERNAL [VUR nl]
- youthful
*(The elderly pair recaptured the **VERNAL** pleasures of a picnic in the park.)*

VERSATILE [VUR suh til; VUR suh tiel]
- multipurpose
*(A Boy Scout pocket knife is a **VERSATILE** gadget.)*

VERSATILE [VUR suh til; VUR suh tiel]
- multitalented
*(The **VERSATILE** musician was proficient in five different instruments.)*

VERTIGO [VUR tuh goh]
- dizziness
*(Because she suffered from **VERTIGO**, she avoided high places.)*

VERVE [vurv]
- enthusiastic vitality
*(The soprano sang the aria with such **VERVE** that the audience was enraptured.)*

VEX [veks]
- annoy/irritate
*(The homeowner's indecision where to place the furniture **VEXED** the moving crew.)*

VEXATIOUS [vek SAY shus]
- annoyingly bothersome
*(A good night's sleep can be an elusive goal when in the company of a **VEXATIOUS** mosquito.)*

VIABLE [VIE uh bul]
- practical
*(Because he lacked upper-level management experience, the young man was not a **VIABLE** candidate for the executive position.)*

VIABLE [VIE uh bul]
- workable
*(Many feel that during times of spiraling gasoline prices, riding the bus is a **VIABLE** option to driving the car to work.)*

VERISIMILITUDE [ver i si MIL i tood; ver i si MIL i tyood]
 - realism
*(Although only fictional, the adventures of Sherlock Holmes are portrayed with such **VERISIMILITUDE** that one actually feels as though the detective lived and solved all those mysteries.)*

VERITABLE [VER i tuh bul]
 - actual
*(The primeval forest was a **VERITABLE** paradise.)*

VERNAL [VUR nl]
 - spring
*(Many couples wed in the **VERNAL** months.)*

VERNAL [VUR nl]
 - youthful
*(The elderly pair recaptured the **VERNAL** pleasures of a picnic in the park.)*

VERSATILE [VUR suh til; VUR suh tiel]
 - multipurpose
*(A Boy Scout pocket knife is a **VERSATILE** gadget.)*

VERSATILE [VUR suh til; VUR suh tiel]
 - multitalented
*(The **VERSATILE** musician was proficient in five different instruments.)*

VERTIGO [VUR tuh goh]
 - dizziness
*(Because she suffered from **VERTIGO**, she avoided high places.)*

VERVE [vurv]
 - enthusiastic vitality
*(The soprano sang the aria with such **VERVE** that the audience was enraptured.)*

VEX [veks]
 - annoy/irritate
*(The homeowner's indecision where to place the furniture **VEXED** the moving crew.)*

VEXATIOUS [vek SAY shus]
 - annoyingly bothersome
*(A good night's sleep can be an elusive goal when in the company of a **VEXATIOUS** mosquito.)*

VIABLE [VIE uh bul]
 - practical
*(Because he lacked upper-level management experience, the young man was not a **VIABLE** candidate for the executive position.)*

VIABLE [VIE uh bul]
 - workable
*(Many feel that during times of spiraling gasoline prices, riding the bus is a **VIABLE** option to driving the car to work.)*

VIRTUAL [VUR choo ul]
- comparatively equivalent
*(The slow sales season proved a **VIRTUAL** disaster for the smaller stores in the shopping mall.)*

VIRTUOUS [VUR choo us]
- morally honorable
*(The heroic firefighter was eulogized as a **VIRTUOUS** husband and devoted father.)*

VIRULENT [VIR uh lunt; VIR yuh lunt]
- extremely poisonous/harmful
*(Disease-control specialists were flown in to try to contain the outbreak of the **VIRULENT** strain of bacteria.)*

VISAGE [VIZ ij]
- countenance/appearance
*(The ghost town projected a bleak **VISAGE** to passersby.)*

VIS-À-VIS [vee zuh VEE]
- as compared with
*(Sales **VIS-À-VIS** expenses were not satisfactory to the board of directors.)*

VIS-À-VIS [vee zuh VEE]
- face-to-face
*(After conversing with his assistant over the telephone for nearly an hour, the head coach decided that the matter needed to be further discussed **VIS-À-VIS**.)*

VISCERAL [VIS ur ul]
- instinctive ("gut-feeling")
*(Gritting his teeth and clenching his fist was a **VISCERAL** reaction to seeing the innocent young lad mercilessly beaten by his father.)*

VITAL [VIET ul]
- basic and essential
*(A sense of humor is **VITAL** for surviving trying times.)*

VITALITY [vie TAL i tee]
- enthusiastic energy
*(Puppies bubble with **VITALITY**.)*

VITIATE [VISH ee ayt]
- corrupt
*(The consumer interest organization itself became **VITIATED** by special interest groups.)*

VITIATE [VISH ee ayt]
- invalidate
*(In its ruling, the court determined that the fraudulent manner in which the negotiations were conducted **VITIATED** all resulting contracts.)*

VITRIOLIC [vi tree AH lik; vi tree AHL ik]
- scathingly critical
*(The editorial was a **VITRIOLIC** condemnation of recent attempts to build hotels along the beach.)*

VITUPERATE [vie TOO pur ayt; vie TYOO pur ayt]
- criticize/condemn harshly
*(The guest speaker **VITUPERATED** from the podium the inexcusable tactics employed by large corporations to force smaller companies into bankruptcy.)*

VIVACIOUS [vie VAY shus; vi VAY shus]
- lively and cheerful
*(The six-year-old was a **VIVACIOUS** and sprightly tyke.)*

VIVIFY [viv uh fie]
- enliven
*(The jocose student **VIVIFIED** the biology class with his verbal witticisms.)*

VOCIFERATE [voh SIF uh rayt]
- shout
*(At a meeting, several inmates **VOCIFERATED** their displeasure regarding overcrowding in the penitentiary.)*

VOCIFEROUS [voh SIF ur us]
- loud and vocal
*(A **VOCIFEROUS** group of demonstrators marched along the picket line.)*

VOLATILE [VAHL uh tl]
- explosively unstable
*(Any hostage situation is tense and unpredictably **VOLATILE**.)*

VOLITION [voh LISH un]
- free will/conscious choice
*(Attending the poetry reading was of each student's own **VOLITION**.)*

VOLUBLE [VAHL yuh bul]
- fluent and garrulous
*(The **VOLUBLE** teenager loved to chat with friends at the mall.)*

VOLUMINOUS [vuh LOO muh nus]
- extensive/sizable
*(The biographer sifted through a **VOLUMINOUS** collection of letters and faxes in preparation for his book.)*

VORACIOUS [voh RAY shus; vuh RAY shus]
- intense and unsatisfiable
*(A wolf has a **VORACIOUS** appetite.)*

VULNERABLE [VUL nur uh bul]
- susceptible
*(An injured animal is **VULNERABLE** to attack by predators.)*

WAGGISH [WAG ish]
- playfully mischievous/prankish
*(Unlike his somber older brother, the younger boy reveled in practical jokes and other **WAGGISH** diversions.)*

WAN [wahn]
- sickly pale
*(After the lengthy illness, she looked thin and **WAN**.)*

WANE [wayn]
- decrease/decline
*(As the minutes passed, the young man's interest in the political discussion **WANED**.)*

WARRANT [WOHR unt]
- justify
*(Others felt the lad's mistake did not **WARRANT** such a severe scolding.)*

WARY [WAYR ee]
- cautiously watchful
*(It is wise to be **WARY** of claims that appear too good to be true.)*

WASTREL [WAY strul]
- spendthrift
*(The **WASTREL** quickly spent his weekly allowance on frivolous novelties.)*

WAX [waks]
- increase in size/brightness
*(The boy's eyes **WAXED** as he excitedly entered the fragrantly inviting candy store.)*

WAYWARD [WAY wurd]
- unmanageably rebellious
*(Addressing a group of underachieving adolescents, the self-made millionaire alluded to his own **WAYWARD** youth.)*

WAYWARD [WAY wurd]
- unpredictable/inconsistent
*(A tornado's **WAYWARD** path makes it especially dangerous.)*

WHEEDLE [HWEED l]
- coax
*(After much persistence, the teenager managed to **WHEEDLE** her parents into letting her attend the overnight party.)*

WHET [hwet]
- arouse/excite
*(The smell of freshly baked ham **WHETTED** the children's appetite.)*

WHIMSICAL [HWIM zi kul]
- highly imaginative
*(At the evening cookout, the boys and girls listened intently as the storyteller narrated a **WHIMSICAL** tale of a friendly dragon.)*

WHIMSICAL [WHIM zi kul]
- impulsive and unpredictable
*(The **WHIMSICAL** couple surprised everyone by taking an unannounced weekend jaunt to the West Indies.)*

WHIMSY [HWIM zee]
- odd/fanciful notion
*(Because teenagers are often given to **WHIMSIES** about their indestructibility, many engage in activities that are reckless and potentially hazardous.)*

WILLFUL [WIL ful]
- intentional
*(Littering public streets is looked down upon as **WILLFUL** disregard of the law.)*

WILLFUL [WIL ful]
- stubbornly unruly/uncompromising
*(The **WILLFUL** lad refused to stop teasing his sister.)*

WILY [WIE lee]
- cleverly crafty
*(The fox is a **WILY** creature known for its ability to evade capture.)*

WINSOME [WIN sum]
- charming
*(The youngster was a **WINSOME** and delightful lass.)*

WISTFUL [WIST ful]
- sadly wishful and yearning
*(The retired athlete cast a **WISTFUL** look from the stadium stands, remembering the days when he had been revered as the star of his high school football team.)*

WITLESS [WIT lis]
- stupid
*(The **WITLESS** dolt couldn't even follow simple directions.)*

WIZENED [WIZ und]
- shriveled
*(In a cabin nestled deep in the woods, the children encountered a **WIZENED** old hag.)*

WOEBEGONE [WOH bi gahn]
- wretched/sorrowful
*(Soldiers could not help but be moved by the **WOEBEGONE** faces of the young war orphans.)*

WOEFUL [WOH ful]
- tragic and sorrowful
(Tristan and Isolde is a WOEFUL tale of a doomed love affair.)

WONT [wahnt]
- accustomed
(During cold winter evenings, he was WONT to smoke his pipe and read a book near the warm fireplace.)

WRAITH [rayth]
- apparition/ghost
(Legend told that the WRAITH would manifest itself in the guise of a headless Indian seeking revenge on those who betrayed him.)

WRATH [rath]
- vengeful anger
(It is ill advised for any man to incur his wife's WRATH.)

WRETCHED [RECH id]
- miserable/pitiable
(The poor man rued his WRETCHED life of inescapable poverty.)

WRY [rie]
- cleverly sarcastic
(The comedian's WRY wit was not well received by everyone in the audience, many of whom felt the barbs too personal.)

WRY [rie]
- twisted
(A WRY grin appeared on the face of the frustrated blackjack player as the dealer unveiled yet another game-winning hand of 21.)

ZANY [ZAY nee]
- clownish/silly
(Generations have enjoyed the ZANY antics of the Three Stooges.)

ZEAL [zeel]
- passionate enthusiasm
(The young children awaited Christmas morning with anticipatory ZEAL.)

ZENITH [ZEE nith]
- peak
(British literature reached its ZENITH during the Renaissance.)

ZEPHYR [ZEF ur]
- gentle breeze
(A ZEPHYR wafted through the peaceful island paradise.)

ZEST [zest]
- hearty enjoyment
(The old man had a ZEST for life that never waned.)

The *SAT & College Dictionary Workbook* is a companion guide to the *SAT & College Dictionary,* using each of the words in a multiple-choice-format sentence completion. Twenty questions comprise each quiz, and answers are listed at the back of the book.

Of particular note are two unique elements that enhance the concept of "unit mastery":
1) Each sentence is identical to that which appears in the *SAT & College Dictionary,* ensuring that a student who masters the contents of the dictionary itself will master these quizzes.
2) All three word-choices within each sentence appear in the *SAT & College Dictionary.* Therefore, mastery can be gained not only for the answer-word but for all three choices listed.

Students love to succeed, and these quizzes are designed to reward the industrious student with well-deserved success.

This special book contains those "power words" that every ambitious student needs...to excel beyond the modicum of mediocrity toward new heights hitherto unimagined! Let your sights behold a new horizon—let the words guide you there!

The power is in your hands...

The Dream-Come True Textbook for Classroom Teachers

Prior to national release of this text, the author—also an instructor—tested the program on his students, helping them build vocabulary skills necessary to improve college essay-writing and significantly raise scores on college entrance-examinations such as the SAT and ACT. The results have been astounding, but more importantly have been results AFTER students have journeyed to college. Many have kept their books and have continued to use them throughout their college years. In many cases, students have found that once they learned most of the words in the text, they enjoyed reviewing the quizzes to be sure they knew the definitions of all three choices.

This is a mastery-program, which means that once a student is able to master the contents of this book, the student will probably know every word he or she will encounter in college and beyond. This is not the first step in the series; it is the *entire step!* It is not a book that one is expected to master in a week, a month, or even a year. Instead, it is a book that will provide years of valuable reference assistance and a lifetime of vocabulary-building.

SAT & College Dictionary Workbook Quiz 1

[On a separate sheet of paper, write down the letter of the word that best fits in the blank to create a complete and meaningful sentence.]

1. Once the soccer star turned forty, his future prospects quickly began to _____.
   A. ebb
   B. hinder
   C. avert

2. Botanists were baffled as to the classification of the _____ species of plant newly discovered on the remote island.
   A. wretched
   B. exotic
   C. chary

3. In the horrific short story, the victim was _____ within the cement walls of the dark dungeon.
   A. immured
   B. congregated
   C. allayed

4. Construction of the office building was held in _____ until the weather improved.
   A. perdition
   B. abeyance
   C. duplicity

5. The governor delivered a _____ in behalf of the elderly woman's many years of dedicated service to the community.
   A. contumely
   B. sobriquet
   C. panegyric

6. All the women at the ball were enchanted by the _____ gentleman.
   A. debonair
   B. meager
   C. savory

7. The young __ accompanied the elder opera star to stage performances and social engagements.
   A. protégé
   B. demagogue
   C. scoundrel

8. The clouds _____ as the day turned sunny.
   A. mollified
   B. stultified
   C. dissipated

9. When fire broke out in the theater, the audience became _____.
   A. frantic
   B. pestilent
   C. bumptious

10. In his later years, the petty thief became _____ for his misguided life of crime.
    A. sheepish
    B. penitent
    C. fervent

11. People in third-world countries often live in _____ poverty.
    A. abject
    B. fractious
    C. prepossessing

12. A selected parable helped _____ the class to the moral righteousness of being true to oneself.
    A. assuage
    B. edify
    C. inter

13. During Christmastime, delivery of packages is _____ to ensure customer satisfaction.
    A. blandished
    B. expedited
    C. propagated

14. Employers are always eager to hire _____ individuals.
    A. swarthy
    B. prosaic
    C. industrious

15. Hamlet's "to be or not to be" soliloquy raised several provocative _____ questions regarding man's role in life.
    A. inextricable
    B. rhetorical
    C. verbose

16. Only a single _____ rope kept the damaged scaffold from plummeting to the ground.
    A. meager
    B. limber
    C. tenuous

17. Everyone on the team _____ the day the list of those cut from the squad would be posted.
    A. asseverated
    B. dreaded
    C. vilified

18. The new military leader had to contend with a cabal of _____ soldiers.
    A. dispassionate
    B. scrupulous
    C. insurgent

19. The _____ of modern computers was a noisy, bulky contraption.
    A. kith
    B. prototype
    C. exponent

20. Asking his brother for a loan was a ___ sign that he had resumed his gambling ways.
    A. telltale
    B. chronic
    C. pell-mell

(For Quiz Answers, see Answer Section at the end of the book)

SAT & College Dictionary Workbook Quiz 2

[On a separate sheet of paper, write down the letter of the word that best fits in the blank to create a complete and meaningful sentence.]

1. Fans _____ in their team's thrilling come-from-behind victory.
   A. denigrated
   B. exulted
   C. underscored

2. The elusive mouse employed an effective _____ to confuse the attacking hawk.
   A. artifice
   B. malediction
   C. retribution

3. Although turtles may live in the water or on land, the tortoise is strictly a _____ animal.
   A. dogged
   B. terrestrial
   C. rural

4. The smell of freshly baked ham _____ the children's appetite.
   A. whetted
   B. complemented
   C. disported

5. The _____ of the legal community includes extensive use of Latin.
   A. lexicon
   B. populace
   C. rapport

6. As the political conversation grew more heated, the initially casual discussion turned into a _____ debate.
   A. deteriorated
   B. sonorous
   C. protracted

7. During a _____ outburst, the frustrated man kicked the family dog.
   A. disconsolate
   B. lavish
   C. splenetic

8. Patrons of the bar _____ the man's alibi regarding his whereabouts during the period of the crime.
   A. rued
   B. corroborated
   C. infuriated

9. The Medal of Honor was _____ upon the valiant soldier.
   A. touted
   B. bestowed
   C. expended

10. Rather than prolong the argument, the husband _____ to the wishes of his distaff mate.
    A. acceded
    B. imputed
    C. peculated

11. Schoolmates were _____ about the lad's claim to having appeared in a nationally-televised commercial.
    A. dubious
    B. prolix
    C. indefeasible

12. The blue whale is the _____ of the seas.
    A. leviathan
    B. demagogue
    C. catalyst

13. The _____ passenger ordered the least expensive entrée on the ship's restaurant menu.
    A. penurious
    B. frivolous
    C. authoritarian

14. After his favorite hockey team was eliminated in the playoffs, the man was in a particularly _____ mood.
    A. taut
    B. dour
    C. parochial

15. A funeral is not an appropriate setting for _____.
    A. cupidity
    B. levity
    C. forbearance

16. In the science fiction movie, the alien creature _____ from a dog into a three-headed serpent.
    A. diverged
    B. transmogrified
    C. fabricated

17. The unparalleled success of her latest novel placed the author at the _____ of her acclaimed literary career.
    A. conglomerate
    B. acme
    C. plight

18. Due to a sudden upsurge in sales, the company _____ its estimated quarterly profits.
    A. imbued
    B. amended
    C. traduced

19. As a newly-inducted American citizen, he was asked to _____ allegiance to any hostile government or regime.
    A. condone
    B. forswear
    C. transmute

20. As a result of falling from the ladder, the librarian's forearm was _____.
    A. shopworn
    B. livid
    C. raucous

(For Quiz Answers, see Answer Section at the end of the book)

SAT & College Dictionary Workbook Quiz 3

[On a separate sheet of paper, write down the letter of the word that best fits in the blank to create a complete and meaningful sentence.]

1. The _____ hawk swooped down and seized the fleeing mouse.
   A. demure
   B. hackneyed
   C. rapacious

2. Critics decried the novel as a _____ reconstitution of situational schlock.
   A. hackneyed
   B. nimble
   C. poignant

3. After two nights without sleep, his nerves were _____ and his patience low.
   A. docile
   B. nauseous
   C. taut

4. Soothing words by the scoutmaster _____ the children's fear of spending the night outdoors.
   A. eulogized
   B. allayed
   C. sanctioned

5. Although faced with seemingly insurmountable obstacles, the early pioneers remained _____ in their pursuit for westward expansion.
   A. undaunted
   B. inviolate
   C. fearsome

6. To gird for battle, the village _____ its military might.
   A. fortified
   B. suppressed
   C. abridged

7. Adolph Hilter ruled Germany in an _____ manner.
   A. opulent
   B. unimpeachable
   C. autocratic

8. Sherpas are acclimated to the _____ mountain air of Tibet.
   A. intricate
   B. rarefied
   C. voluminous

9. Robin Hood was regarded by rich townsfolk as an insidious _____ and despicable rogue.
   A. protégé
   B. toady
   C. scoundrel

10. After several stormy hours, the heavy winds _____.
    A. fulminated
    B. abated
    C. postulated

11. Winning the class spelling bee _____ the youngster with renewed self-confidence.
    A. whetted
    B. imbued
    C. alleged

12. The tropical island featured a veritable _____ of fruits and vegetables.
    A. cornucopia
    B. anathema
    C. row

13. The _____ boy believed even the most outlandish of stories.
    A. acquisitive
    B. nimble
    C. gullible

14. The teacher's scathing rebuke _____ the innocent boy.
    A. rankled
    B. concatenated
    C. desiccated

15. The rising tide _____ all the footprints on the shoreline.
    A. effaced
    B. balked
    C. replenished

16. The _____ flesh wound required immediate medical attention.
    A. turgid
    B. peripheral
    C. serrated

17. The consumer interest organization itself became _____ by special interest groups.
    A. vitiated
    B. discomfited
    C. transmogrified

18. The television show's panelists were renowned for their _____ viewpoints on most political issues.
    A. vigorous
    B. dissonant
    C. pernicious

19. To help the house sell more quickly, the bedrooms were _____ with new carpeting and drapes.
    A. refurbished
    B. delineated
    C. actuated

20. The alphabet is _____ of twenty-six letters.
    A. comprised
    B. garnered
    C. transpired

(For Quiz Answers, see Answer Section at the end of the book)

SAT & College Dictionary Workbook Quiz 4

[On a separate sheet of paper, write down the letter of the word that best fits in the blank to create a complete and meaningful sentence.]

1. The buxom blonde _____ the love-stricken guard into abandoning his sentry post.
   A. cajoled
   B. lowered
   C. stultified

2. An early and violent storm _____ an unusually hostile winter.
   A. reiterated
   B. presaged
   C. limned

3. Her nervous breakdown was _____ by job-related stress.
   A. endorsed
   B. succumbed
   C. induced

4. Despite the precariousness of their financial dilemma, it was nevertheless a _____ situation.
   A. soluble
   B. futile
   C. restive

5. Ice cream businesses _____ during hot summer months.
   A. vivify
   B. thrive
   C. protrude

6. The thunderstruck father _____ his anger and disappointment when told that his daughter had eloped by offering a toast to the couple's happiness.
   A. seceded
   B. dissembled
   C. fabricated

7. Deserting one's friend in his hour of need is a _____ and selfish act of insensitivity and cowardice.
   A. peerless
   B. despicable
   C. belligerent

8. In her speech, the pacifist candidate _____ military restraint.
   A. languished
   B. rescinded
   C. advocated

9. The frustrated farmer ordered his _____ son to go out and help feed the livestock.
   A. shiftless
   B. infatuated
   C. eclectic

10. The World War II years were a _____ period in world history.
    A. malicious
    B. tumultuous
    C. seditious

11. An _____ decision was made as to which supplies to throw out of the imperiled airplane.
    A. insouciant
    B. unwieldy
    C. arbitrary

12. In her later years, the opera star led a reclusive and _____ existence far from the spotlight of adulation.
    A. treacherous
    B. astute
    C. desolate

13. The _____ teenager enlivened any party.
    A. fail-safe
    B. jaunty
    C. star-crossed

14. The petty thief _____ the purse that had been left on the table.
    A. escalated
    B. purloined
    C. depleted

15. Adding grandmother's piquant sauce to the _____ stew gave it a zesty flavor.
    A. insipid
    B. brash
    C. pensive

16. The fair maiden's _____ beauty mesmerized the love-struck sailor.
    A. supernal
    B. flaccid
    C. iridescent

17. The decision regarding which cereal to buy was left to the _____ of her two children.
    A. discretion
    B. onset
    C. genesis

18. The _____ mathematical word problem challenged even the brightest of students.
    A. sanguine
    B. intrinsic
    C. convoluted

19. The _____ employee caused more problems than he was worth.
    A. feckless
    B. winsome
    C. bereft

20. There was extensive press coverage when the Concorde made its _____ flight.
    A. conspicuous
    B. inaugural
    C. heretical

(For Quiz Answers, see Answer Section at the end of the book)

SAT & College Dictionary Workbook Quiz 5

[On a separate sheet of paper, write down the letter of the word that best fits in the blank to create a complete and meaningful sentence.]

1. When the dictator seized power, his first mission was to _____ all opposing political factions.
   A. absolve
   B. stipulate
   C. extirpate

2. Prior to any signing of a cease fire, a clause was agreed upon that _____ the release of all political prisoners.
   A. connoted
   B. stipulated
   C. prophesied

3. In the spring, the island _____ with lush vegetation.
   A. extolled
   B. burgeoned
   C. personified

4. The invading army _____ the captured city, driving off in fancy cars filled with gold and silver.
   A. despoiled
   B. saturated
   C. augmented

5. The ___ metal could be bent to fit wherever an electrical conductor was needed.
   A. pliable
   B. credible
   C. molten

6. Albert Einstein's _____ ideas were the basis for much of today's scientific understanding of time and space.
   A. seminal
   B. candid
   C. irrevocable

7. A _____ of labor leaders met to determine whether a strike was necessary.
   A. stratagem
   B. coalition
   C. façade

8. The elderly gentleman _____ himself with poise and dignity.
   A. comported
   B. imbued
   C. liberated

9. The powerful movie director's toadies _____ over him in hope that they might be in his next movie.
   A. calumniated
   B. fawned
   C. lowered

10. The musicians' benefit concert reflected an _____ desire to raise money to assist the world's impoverished children.
    A. endemic
    B. iniquitous
    C. ardent

11. There was much ___ about which child would sit in the front seat during the weekend excursion.
    A. mélange
    B. whimsy
    C. ado

12. The _____ dress gave others the mistaken impression that she was a prostitute.
    A. innocuous
    B. tawdry
    C. petty

13. A _____ investigation into the cause of the fire pointed to electrical failure.
    A. preliminary
    B. subterranean
    C. disparate

14. Unwilling to accept defeat, search rescuers persevered through ___ weather conditions.
    A. adverse
    B. irreconcilable
    C. reputable

15. From his irrepressibly _____ imagination, Ray Bradbury wrote extensively in the science fiction genre.
    A. cantankerous
    B. brusque
    C. fecund

16. The strikingly attractive baroness was a woman of _____ taste in fashion.
    A. apathetic
    B. punitive
    C. impeccable

17. The _____ child graduated from high school at age fourteen.
    A. vitriolic
    B. precocious
    C. credible

18. Jed Clampett and his clan were _____ hillbilly folks.
    A. rustic
    B. suave
    C. inanimate

19. The diminutive lad was _____ when it came to jumping off the highest diving board.
    A. apprehensive
    B. guileful
    C. lugubrious

20. While playing cards, the women engaged in pleasant _____.
    A. discourse
    B. penury
    C. niceties

(For Quiz Answers, see Answer Section at the end of the book)

SAT & College Dictionary Workbook Quiz 6

[On a separate sheet of paper, write down the letter of the word that best fits in the blank to create a complete and meaningful sentence.]

1. The children's _____ behavior during the guest speaker's presentation did not go unnoticed by their proud teacher.
   A. inclement
   B. seemly
   C. reprehensible

2. Introducing a young teenager to the world of illicit activities will _____ his moral fiber.
   A. berate
   B. subvert
   C. censure

3. Although four councilmen favored the proposal, a majority _____.
   A. dissented
   B. recapitulated
   C. glowered

4. To maximize space conservation, mobile homes have _____ kitchens.
   A. explicit
   B. compact
   C. portly

5. The national anthem of the United States is a _____ celebrating the country's independence.
   A. paean
   B. boon
   C. catalyst

6. When Prohibition was repealed in 1933, citizens _____ in bacchanalian celebration.
   A. reveled
   B. eulogized
   C. flagged

7. Gritting his teeth and clenching his fist was a _____ reaction to seeing the innocent young lad mercilessly beaten by his father.
   A. visceral
   B. problematic
   C. clarion

8. The desperate farmers prayed for _____ from the year-long drought.
   A. deliverance
   B. adulation
   C. euphoria

9. Anarchy and lawlessness have run _____ in some inner-city neighborhoods.
   A. chronic
   B. infinite
   C. rampant

10. When gun shots rang out, _____ erupted in the auditorium.
    A. precipitation
    B. equipoise
    C. turmoil

11. Several heads of state attended the _____ wedding.
    A. waggish
    B. lugubrious
    C. stately

12. When the prisoners greeted him warmly, the warden sensed intuitively that something was _____.
    A. gainful
    B. amiss
    C. rarefied

13. The young scholar was _____ with Shakespeare's earliest writings.
    A. conversant
    B. prevalent
    C. incarnate

14. After the smaller army _____, a meeting was held to officially turn over the contested land.
    A. prognosticated
    B. incriminated
    C. capitulated

15. Sportscasters _____ the team owner for unbecoming treatment of his players.
    A. effaced
    B. buttressed
    C. reviled

16. The man's _____ demeanor when recounting the events leading up to his employer's mysterious disappearance raised police suspicions of possible complicity.
    A. nonchalant
    B. disconsolate
    C. surrogate

17. An _____ interlaced network of cables and wires connected the communication system.
    A. erratic
    B. adroit
    C. intricate

18. In the nineteenth century, Hawaii was a _____ nation.
    A. lambent
    B. sovereign
    C. picaresque

19. The _____ baseball coach often became embroiled in verbal fisticuffs.
    A. choleric
    B. punctilious
    C. impassive

20. Technical legal jargon is hardly _____ to the lay person.
    A. stodgy
    B. comprehensible
    C. pedagogic

(For Quiz Answers, see Answer Section at the end of the book)

SAT & College Dictionary Workbook Quiz 7

[On a separate sheet of paper, write down the letter of the word that best fits in the blank to create a complete and meaningful sentence.]

1. The preacher's radical and heretical doctrine ____ tenets that rejected traditional values and orthodox beliefs.
   A. excoriated
   B. promulgated
   C. supplanted

2. Because sponges are ____ to water, they are an excellent means to clean up liquid spills quickly and efficiently.
   A. deleterious
   B. permeable
   C. cohesive

3. The wretched inhabitants of the barren wasteland lived in ____ poverty and despair.
   A. profligate
   B. straitlaced
   C. abysmal

4. The poor man rued his ____ life of inescapable poverty.
   A. archaic
   B. wretched
   C. invincible

5. Before stepping aboard the bus, the lady had a ____ that she would soon meet a long-lost friend.
   A. malediction
   B. sobriquet
   C. presentiment

6. In the United States, schooling is ____ for all minors.
   A. impromptu
   B. obligatory
   C. temporal

7. The ____ and irreproachable politician could not be bribed by powerful special-interest groups.
   A. infamous
   B. scrupulous
   C. rambunctious

8. The socialist government was accused of being run by ____ officials.
   A. robust
   B. mandatory
   C. corrupt

9. The prestidigitator ____ the audience with his stunning feats of sleight-of-hand magic.
   A. harassed
   B. enthralled
   C. assailed

10. The clown entered the children's party wearing a ____ robe.
    A. diverse
    B. resilient
    C. motley

11. Many of William Shakespeare's sonnets describe the ____ nature of youth.
    A. commensurate
    B. nostalgic
    C. transient

12. The lioness ____ the male's sexual advances.
    A. belied
    B. debunked
    C. rebuffed

13. The plesiosaur was a ____ creature of the Mesozoic era that grew as long as forty feet.
    A. craven
    B. stentorian
    C. pelagic

14. The politician's corrupt lifestyle developed from ____ ambitions, far from his initial dream of serving the public in a professional and scrupulous manner.
    A. plenary
    B. spendthrift
    C. mercenary

15. A psychologist was called in to determine the root of the young man's ____ sexual behavior.
    A. aberrant
    B. penurious
    C. recumbent

16. The life of the reclusive actress was a paradoxical ____ that baffled even her most ardent fans.
    A. pariah
    B. chagrin
    C. enigma

17. As teens, the group developed an ____ bond of trust that never waned through the passing of time.
    A. egregious
    B. inviolable
    C. urbane

18. William Wordsworth wrote at length on the chaste ____ of his youth.
    A. pandemonium
    B. ken
    C. viridity

19. The meaning of the cryptic cave writing was ____ and subject to interpretation.
    A. ecumenical
    B. ambiguous
    C. multifarious

20. Giant waves generated by the storm severely ____ the island's shoreline.
    A. eroded
    B. protruded
    C. aborted

(For Quiz Answers, see Answer Section at the end of the book)

SAT & College Dictionary Workbook Quiz 8

[On a separate sheet of paper, write down the letter of the word that best fits in the blank to create a complete and meaningful sentence.]

1. Paint is a highly _____ material that should not be stored in containers exposed to extreme heat.
   A. aberrant
   B. combustible
   C. metaphorical

2. Jonathan Swift was a writer known for his _____ wit and irony.
   A. disingenuous
   B. lambent
   C. imminent

3. During World War II, _____ crimes were perpetrated against unsuspecting Jews.
   A. clichéd
   B. didactic
   C. heinous

4. In the spy novel, the mad scientist hatched a _____ plot to destroy the world.
   A. sinister
   B. perilous
   C. dispassionate

5. After the lengthy illness, she looked thin and _____.
   A. wan
   B. intense
   C. elated

6. Gold has a high _____ value and fetches hundreds of dollars per ounce.
   A. intrinsic
   B. emollient
   C. vis-à-vis

7. The adventurous collegians shared a bicycle _____ through South America.
   A. renaissance
   B. interloper
   C. odyssey

8. Having offended his sister with his callous comment, the youngster sought to _____ her with a sincere apology.
   A. rankle
   B. conciliate
   C. exude

9. The ranch was _____ by a wooden picket fence.
   A. emulated
   B. peculated
   C. circumscribed

10. The _____ old man did not endear himself to children.
    A. cantankerous
    B. ineffectual
    C. uproarious

11. Truth is _____.
    A. vacuous
    B. immutable
    C. contemporary

12. Few believed the weightlifter's _____ claim that he was being considered for the upcoming Olympic games.
    A. flatulent
    B. authoritarian
    C. painstaking

13. The actor's _____ estate included a professional tennis court and two Olympic-sized swimming pools.
    A. subterranean
    B. doctrinaire
    C. opulent

14. Even during times of political instability, the military leader's army maintained unwavering _____ to the regime.
    A. tribulation
    B. fidelity
    C. animosity

15. The _____ lad refused to stop teasing his sister.
    A. intolerant
    B. puritanical
    C. willful

16. The _____ insult provoked a row that required the intervention of the police to quell.
    A. gratuitous
    B. pending
    C. adventitious

17. In his own defense, the lad was _____ that he did not leave his sister unattended.
    A. factious
    B. adamant
    C. truculent

18. The unusual painting _____ cheerful reds with lugubrious shades of blue.
    A. juxtaposed
    B. allayed
    C. decried

19. The distraught parents _____ over the disappearance of their daughter.
    A. anguished
    B. gibed
    C. rankled

20. An _____ analysis of the problem clarified many of the reporters' lingering questions.
    A. abrupt
    B. officious
    C. incisive

SAT & College Dictionary Workbook Quiz 9
[On a separate sheet of paper, write down the letter of the word that best fits in the blank to create a complete and meaningful sentence.]

1. Informed that a bear had been spotted in the vicinity, the campers spent the evening in mute _____.
   A. artifice
   B. disquietude
   C. viridity

2. The actor's _____ responses reflected his disinterest in being interviewed.
   A. conversant
   B. laconic
   C. porous

3. At many stores, shoppers are monitored by cameras, though most don't have the slightest _____ that they are being observed.
   A. inkling
   B. delusion
   C. abeyance

4. The young lady took _____ at the unfounded remarks levied against her boyfriend.
   A. ire
   B. animadversion
   C. umbrage

5. The mother _____ the young girl for not paying attention.
   A. expiated
   B. chided
   C. procured

6. Eden was an _____ paradise.
   A. elegiac
   B. ominous
   C. inviolate

7. In his melodramatic way, the movie star expressed his heartfelt sympathy with _____ hyperbole.
   A. ecumenical
   B. histrionic
   C. meteoric

8. Many Nazi leaders were charged with committing _____ crimes against humanity.
   A. unspeakable
   B. jaundiced
   C. flamboyant

9. *Lord of the Rings* is a _____ tale of wizards and dragons.
   A. bedraggled
   B. meek
   C. fanciful

10. The _____ desert sands made travel on foot unbearable to all but the local natives.
    A. elysian
    B. bootless
    C. torrid

11. Audie Murphy, the most decorated soldier of World War II, was the _____ of bravery.
    A. epitome
    B. arbiter
    C. refuge

12. The soldier _____ the lady's compliment with a polite bow and a kiss on her hand.
    A. foiled
    B. compensated
    C. requited

13. To _____ for a lifetime of sexual promiscuity, the contrite man vowed to embark upon a life of marital fidelity.
    A. exalt
    B. prognosticate
    C. atone

14. A cold shower _____ the fatigued jogger.
    A. abated
    B. galvanized
    C. invigorated

15. Students complained that the history examination placed too much emphasis on _____ dates and events.
    A. insurgent
    B. sapient
    C. trivial

16. The congressman's two-hour confession _____ the reporter's appetite for all the sordid details.
    A. consoled
    B. recompensed
    C. satiated

17. The defendant's _____ appeal for clemency drew compassion from the judge.
    A. austere
    B. earnest
    C. shoddy

18. Neighborhood children avoided the _____ homeless man who resided in the park.
    A. surly
    B. hale
    C. genial

19. Greenland has a _____ population.
    A. sparse
    B. pensive
    C. venial

20. During the long-standing feud between the Hatfields and McCoys, uttering the other family's name was _____.
    A. insuperable
    B. salient
    C. anathema

(For Quiz Answers, see Answer Section at the end of the book)

SAT & College Dictionary Workbook Quiz 10

[On a separate sheet of paper, write down the letter of the word that best fits in the blank to create a complete and meaningful sentence.]

1. An _____ poem was read to commemorate the anniversary of the tragic event.
   A. elegiac
   B. ambivalent
   C. unabashed

2. The diamond bracelet's multiple defects reflected _____ workmanship.
   A. industrious
   B. tenacious
   C. shoddy

3. The champion wrestler was a _____ and imposing figure.
   A. hulking
   B. jejune
   C. shiftless

4. Several boys _____ for the attention of the new girl in school.
   A. espied
   B. defied
   C. vied

5. Townsfolk _____ the efforts of the new police commissioner to reduce crime in the city.
   A. lauded
   B. shirked
   C. emulated

6. During the recession, the retail store found itself _____ with mounting debts.
   A. nonplussed
   B. vexed
   C. encumbered

7. Furious at the unwarranted forays by the neighboring country, the leader _____ the previously-established peace settlement.
   A. abrogated
   B. recapitulated
   C. descried

8. Curly Howard's _____ clownish manners were greatly responsible for the success of the Three Stooges.
   A. risible
   B. indolent
   C. trite

9. The _____ political analyst helped explain the historical significance of the referendum.
   A. philistine
   B. addled
   C. erudite

10. The shortstop's outstanding defensive capabilities _____ for his mediocre batting average.
    A. compensated
    B. replenished
    C. flourished

11. Nurses arrived on the scene to give _____ to the injured.
    A. succor
    B. refuge
    C. bliss

12. For a definition of an esoteric or arcane word, one needs to consult an _____ dictionary.
    A. occult
    B. unabridged
    C. instrumental

13. The condemned prisoner issued an _____ plea for mercy.
    A. impassioned
    B. amorous
    C. extenuating

14. Yearbooks often _____ the past twelve months' most memorable moments.
    A. distort
    B. validate
    C. encapsulate

15. Both nations were _____ to compromise over the contested land.
    A. amenable
    B. effusive
    C. sportive

16. The art produced by Salvador Dali was often hypnotically _____.
    A. hypocritical
    B. effusive
    C. surrealistic

17. Far from the extravagance and variety of her sister's Hollywood lifestyle, the schoolteacher led an uneventful and _____ existence.
    A. deleterious
    B. scurrilous
    C. quotidian

18. Though obviously embellished, the fisherman's tale was nevertheless somewhat _____.
    A. proficient
    B. feasible
    C. intricate

19. The discourteous crowd _____ the novice comedian with hisses and boos.
    A. taunted
    B. beseeched
    C. slandered

20. The demagogue's _____ so affected his followers that he had them tightly at his beck and call.
    A. charisma
    B. machination
    C. physiognomy

(For Quiz Answers, see Answer Section at the end of the book)

SAT & College Dictionary Workbook Quiz 11

[On a separate sheet of paper, write down the letter of the word that best fits in the blank to create a complete and meaningful sentence.]

1. The newspaper editorial section featured a _____ rebuke of the mayor's handling of the bus strike.
   A. rhetorical
   B. tepid
   C. scathing

2. As the high-wire act began their performance, circus personnel ensured that the cable remained _____.
   A. circuitous
   B. taut
   C. resolute

3. After the Super Bowl game, the victorious city celebrated in _____ fashion.
   A. glib
   B. uproarious
   C. complacent

4. Ralph Nader has long been a vocal _____ for environmental responsibility.
   A. proponent
   B. apostate
   C. mountebank

5. A good juggler must be _____.
   A. dulcet
   B. saturnine
   C. ambidextrous

6. As the press eagerly looked on, the two wrestlers attacked one another with scathing _____.
   A. invective
   B. whimsy
   C. restitution

7. Romeo and Juliet were _____ lovers.
   A. star-crossed
   B. passé
   C. risqué

8. Playboys enjoy a _____, carefree lifestyle.
   A. hedonistic
   B. sedentary
   C. consequential

9. The ship found itself in the midst of an unwelcome _____.
   A. din
   B. contagion
   C. tempest

10. Everyone wished the newlyweds a long life of _____ bliss.
    A. reclusive
    B. connubial
    C. ephemeral

11. A _____ investor, the retired schoolteacher anticipated and took full advantage of the economic upturn.
    A. sagacious
    B. wayward
    C. rash

12. The impressionable adolescent was bedazzled by the _____ of the bikini-clad babes on the beach.
    A. gluttony
    B. esprit de corps
    C. pulchritude

13. The waggish lad annoyed the substitute teacher with his _____ remarks.
    A. facetious
    B. wretched
    C. inveterate

14. For being _____ in his duties, the security guard was given a one-week suspension.
    A. remiss
    B. deliberate
    C. spontaneous

15. David Blaine's seemingly magical powers _____ bystanders.
    A. dumbfounded
    B. tempered
    C. attenuated

16. Several Southern states threatened to _____ from the Union over the issue of emancipation of slaves.
    A. digress
    B. rebut
    C. secede

17. Over the years, the _____ path claimed several victims.
    A. diverse
    B. modest
    C. treacherous

18. Dark clouds added to the _____ mood of the day.
    A. remote
    B. melancholy
    C. derogatory

19. The drill instructor was known for _____ the young cadets to the brink of tears.
    A. browbeating
    B. impeding
    C. purveying

20. The _____ waiter spilled the wine as he poured it into the glass.
    A. sheepish
    B. maladroit
    C. diffuse

(For Quiz Answers, see Answer Section at the end of the book)

SAT & College Dictionary Workbook Quiz 12

[On a separate sheet of paper, write down the letter of the word that best fits in the blank to create a complete and meaningful sentence.]

1. The _____ ballad brought tears to many listeners' eyes.
   A. pied
   B. sentimental
   C. innate

2. While the guards were asleep, the prisoners embarked upon the _____ task of burrowing an underground escape tunnel by hand.
   A. desultory
   B. herculean
   C. redolent

3. His _____ silence made everyone around him uneasy.
   A. listless
   B. saturnine
   C. venomous

4. Rock stars are often the objects of teenage _____.
   A. hauteur
   B. adulation
   C. reprisals

5. Glass is _____ to water.
   A. amiss
   B. impermeable
   C. mimetic

6. The troop of hikers relished the _____ mountain air.
   A. inebriated
   B. residual
   C. salubrious

7. Salve can be applied as an _____ cream for sunburns.
   A. arid
   B. innocuous
   C. emollient

8. The _____ speech sought to raise community involvement in crime prevention.
   A. subtle
   B. commensurate
   C. hortatory

9. Unable to find work elsewhere, the single mother was forced to accept a _____ job as family maid.
   A. fickle
   B. judicious
   C. servile

10. Despite her ultimate failure, the plucky lass nonetheless made a _____ attempt to climb to the top of the tree.
    A. potent
    B. valiant
    C. solicitous

11. Youth is an _____ yet unforgettable period in one's life.
    A. unabridged
    B. ephemeral
    C. opprobrious

12. His _____ ways led him from fortune to financial ruin.
    A. triumphal
    B. innovative
    C. profligate

13. The frugal bookkeeper was a _____ and judicious investor.
    A. brawny
    B. jocose
    C. shrewd

14. The sum of the integers from 1 to 5, _____, equals 15.
    A. sub rosa
    B. inclusive
    C. verbatim

15. The graceful ballerina radiated an _____ beauty that both enchanted and mesmerized.
    A. ethereal
    B. onerous
    C. archaic

16. Weeks of overwork and stress had left the newspaper editor appearing pale and _____.
    A. palatable
    B. deprecatory
    C. gaunt

17. The stolid lad had a _____ toward laziness.
    A. proclivity
    B. detriment
    C. repartee

18. _____ disregard of the rules was grounds for immediate expulsion from the club.
    A. Apprehensive
    B. Flagrant
    C. Succinct

19. In Indian tribes, the elder council members are _____ by their juniors.
    A. burgeoned
    B. venerated
    C. fathomed

20. The family was under the matriarch's _____ rule.
    A. innocuous
    B. authoritarian
    C. requisite

(For Quiz Answers, see Answer Section at the end of the book)

SAT & College Dictionary Workbook Quiz 13

[On a separate sheet of paper, write down the letter of the word that best fits in the blank to create a complete and meaningful sentence.]

1. The popular new student was _____ and highly personable.
   A. stolid
   B. extroverted
   C. cathartic

2. New evidence _____ to the case was introduced prior to closing summation.
   A. capacious
   B. germane
   C. pertinacious

3. It was _____ that the millionaire was stricken with a common cold.
   A. calamitous
   B. ghastly
   C. ironic

4. Residents protested the construction of a shopping mall on what was regarded as _____ ground.
   A. abstinent
   B. hallowed
   C. renowned

5. Investigators were unable to immediately _____ the cause of the fire.
   A. ascertain
   B. forgo
   C. stifle

6. The plan to build a corridor across the two buildings was both _____ and affordable.
   A. sanguine
   B. waggish
   C. feasible

7. Family reunions are usually _____ and memorable events.
   A. restive
   B. voracious
   C. festive

8. The desert heat _____ the land and forced its inhabitants underground.
   A. dilated
   B. acclimated
   C. parched

9. *The Adventures of Huckleberry Finn* is a _____ novel chronicling a young man's escapades as he travels down the Mississippi River.
   A. frantic
   B. picaresque
   C. contumacious

10. Despite a court order to return to work, the _____ strikers refused to yield an inch until all their demands were met.
    A. intransigent
    B. skittish
    C. repulsive

11. Living beneath the train tracks _____ the dwellers to noise.
    A. accrued
    B. rehabilitated
    C. habituated

12. Benjamin Franklin was himself the victim of an unusual newspaper _____: an article, which, in short, claimed that he was dead.
    A. pandemonium
    B. canard
    C. tirade

13. Cows and other animals drank from the river that _____ through the panoramic countryside.
    A. meandered
    B. converged
    C. desiccated

14. Funds were allocated to _____ the decrepit war memorial.
    A. cache
    B. rehabilitate
    C. validate

15. Many consider filling out tax forms a _____ task.
    A. formidable
    B. mimetic
    C. bombastic

16. Several bars in the area were shut down for promoting illegal and _____ activities within their premises.
    A. flatulent
    B. servile
    C. licentious

17. An executive directive to retreat _____ all previous orders.
    A. countermanded
    B. abnegated
    C. maligned

18. A subpoena is a _____ legal writ to appear in court.
    A. dictatorial
    B. lissome
    C. peremptory

19. As they waited in long lines, motorists _____ over the ever-increasing inconvenience of purchasing gasoline.
    A. repined
    B. gamboled
    C. contravened

20. The picnic turned unpleasant after her _____ husband arrived.
    A. defunct
    B. sacrosanct
    C. querulous

(For Quiz Answers, see Answer Section at the end of the book)

SAT & College Dictionary Workbook Quiz 14

[On a separate sheet of paper, write down the letter of the word that best fits in the blank to create a complete and meaningful sentence.]

1. Becoming an Eagle Scout is a _____ achievement.
   A. virtual
   B. surrealistic
   C. meritorious

2. Traveling through uncharted wilderness tested the gold miners' _____.
   A. chicanery
   B. fortitude
   C. discretion

3. Gregory Peck comported himself with a noble and _____ dignity.
   A. tumid
   B. urban
   C. recherché

4. After accidentally knocking the bowl off the table, the guest offered his _____ apologies.
   A. suave
   B. impromptu
   C. profuse

5. Had the boy who cried "wolf" not been a _____ liar, he may have been saved when the wolf finally did appear.
   A. facetious
   B. resourceful
   C. chronic

6. Summer on the lush island was always greeted with an _____ of vacationers.
   A. aspersion
   B. encomium
   C. influx

7. The powerful movie mogul was surrounded by his _____ toadies.
   A. obsequious
   B. grandiose
   C. impudent

8. Several guards were found to have been _____ in their duties on the evening the prisoner escaped.
   A. derelict
   B. hedonistic
   C. pliant

9. The campers were taken aback by the _____ beauty of the shimmering lake.
   A. livid
   B. inalienable
   C. resplendent

10. His _____ mother-in-law was always giving him unasked-for advice.
    A. wily
    B. bellicose
    C. intrusive

11. The _____ speech attacked both the divine sanctity of the family and the Scriptures which espouse it.
    A. esculent
    B. quizzical
    C. blasphemous

12. The young diplomat handled the delicate negotiation with the _____ of a veteran.
    A. indignation
    B. aplomb
    C. status quo

13. Spencer Tracy _____ many awards over his illustrious acting career.
    A. descried
    B. garnered
    C. piqued

14. Committee members unanimously _____ the proposal to build a new skateboard park.
    A. recollected
    B. conciliated
    C. endorsed

15. The powerful storm inflicted great _____ upon residents of neighboring coastal towns and villages.
    A. repartee
    B. hardship
    C. onus

16. There are many _____ devices which aid in recalling people's names.
    A. mnemonic
    B. tenacious
    C. roseate

17. The cult leader's _____ were a fanatic bunch.
    A. diatribe
    B. infidels
    C. adherents

18. The divisive family feud began as merely a _____ argument.
    A. petty
    B. striated
    C. dolorous

19. Few in the audience could _____ the philosopher's explanation regarding existential morality.
    A. capitulate
    B. fathom
    C. suppress

20. In a regrettably _____ moment of despair, the gambler bet the remainder of his money on the long-shot.
    A. frank
    B. intermittent
    C. rash

(For Quiz Answers, see Answer Section at the end of the book)

SAT & College Dictionary Workbook Quiz 15

[On a separate sheet of paper, write down the letter of the word that best fits in the blank to create a complete and meaningful sentence.]

1. The repentant man _____ his transgressions through volunteer service to the community.
   A. certified
   B. repudiated
   C. expiated

2. At the shopping mall, Santa Claus _____ out candy to each visiting child.
   A. doled
   B. ousted
   C. ceded

3. Because some medications can produce a _____ reaction, one must be careful not to take such drugs before driving.
   A. restive
   B. flagitious
   C. somnolent

4. At birth, the twins were _____ at the hip.
   A. conjoined
   B. annexed
   C. piqued

5. As they neared the end of the search, the treasure hunters _____ at the same location.
   A. schemed
   B. acceded
   C. converged

6. In the lawsuit, the actor claimed that malicious reporting had _____ his good name.
   A. transmogrified
   B. defiled
   C. consecrated

7. Selling his patent to the toy manufacturer was, as it turned out, a fortuitous and highly _____ decision.
   A. becoming
   B. doughty
   C. lucrative

8. Archaeologists continue to find remnants indicating an earlier nascence of _____ man.
   A. immemorial
   B. primordial
   C. mammoth

9. German _____ during World War II forced Jews to flee en masse.
   A. bathos
   B. mélange
   C. pogroms

10. To keep the news article brief but succinct, _____ comments were omitted.
    A. torpid
    B. extraneous
    C. aloof

11. The _____ leader brooked no dissension, dispatching offenders with a swift and merciless public execution.
    A. draconian
    B. venerable
    C. pecuniary

12. Rescuers conducted an _____ all-night search for survivors.
    A. implacable
    B. exhaustive
    C. arbitrary

13. After graduating from college, it is time to seek _____ employment in the workplace.
    A. gainful
    B. eleemosynary
    C. precipitous

14. Land in mountainous regions is usually not _____.
    A. arable
    B. impermeable
    C. shiftless

15. The youngster had a _____ fascination for the macabre.
    A. terse
    B. morbid
    C. complaisant

16. Several unsuspecting victims were _____ into purchasing outdated lottery tickets.
    A. slandered
    B. duped
    C. countermanded

17. To satiate his _____, the king levied an additional tax on his already-overburdened subjects.
    A. cupidity
    B. aversion
    C. lassitude

18. Few were moved or impressed by the candidate's simplistically _____ remedies to the city's complex traffic problems.
    A. furtive
    B. banal
    C. quizzical

19. The proposed two percent raise was deemed an _____ amount by the employees' union.
    A. ornate
    B. unassuming
    C. inconsiderable

20. During the busy holiday season, _____ parking lot attendants were called in to work.
    A. plenary
    B. supernumerary
    C. fractious

(For Quiz Answers, see Answer Section at the end of the book)

SAT & College Dictionary Workbook Quiz 16

[On a separate sheet of paper, write down the letter of the word that best fits in the blank to create a complete and meaningful sentence.]

1. A scout _____ the commander of the nature of terrain that lay ahead.
   A. mobilized
   B. apprised
   C. subjugated

2. His anxious wife _____ him into asking his boss for a long-overdue raise.
   A. acquiesced
   B. espoused
   C. goaded

3. This text endeavors to provide a _____ of words most vital in the college experience.
   A. shortcoming
   B. discourse
   C. lexicon

4. Vanity is one of man's many _____.
   A. foibles
   B. misgivings
   C. qualms

5. Among the eccentric millionaire's _____ was a fascination to wear matching green socks and shoes.
   A. qualms
   B. idiosyncrasies
   C. trepidations

6. The parishioner _____ himself by removing his hat when entering the house of worship.
   A. abased
   B. mitigated
   C. usurped

7. Even though they do not offer ultimate curative value, some medicines are beneficial in helping _____ the painful effects of various diseases.
   A. palliate
   B. encumber
   C. mulct

8. A few _____ words from the wealthy baron expressed his heartfelt gratitude for the retiring butler's many years of devoted service.
   A. somber
   B. felicitous
   C. volatile

9. In his hour of deep despair brought on by a life of desultory purposelessness, the lost soul experienced a personally earthshaking _____ that enlightened him to direct his energies toward helping the nation's homeless children.
   A. verisimilitude
   B. apogee
   C. epiphany

10. The athlete's first acting role turned out to be a _____ and a box-office bomb.
    A. canard
    B. wastrel
    C. fiasco

11. Driving home from work in the rush-hour traffic is one of those _____ problems almost everyone must deal with.
    A. droll
    B. genial
    C. mundane

12. Years of constant grazing and trampling had turned the topsoil _____.
    A. squalid
    B. malleable
    C. effete

13. Once happily married, the estranged couple found their relationship degrading into virulent _____.
    A. equilibrium
    B. vicissitudes
    C. animosity

14. The teenager's _____ display of bravado was intended to impress his girlfriend.
    A. euphonious
    B. servile
    C. ostensible

15. Campers came upon a _____ ghost town once heavily populated by gold miners and their families.
    A. desolate
    B. perilous
    C. transient

16. His attorney _____ the judge to consider the mitigating circumstances surrounding the case.
    A. circumvented
    B. duped
    C. implored

17. Rather than attempt to deal with and resolve the more serious matter, the committee seemed resolved to dwell on _____.
    A. innuendo
    B. ennui
    C. minutiae

18. An _____ student of Japanese language and culture, the young man hoped to one day return to the faraway land of the rising sun.
    A. assiduous
    B. unbridled
    C. extensive

19. A _____ of state funds forced a cutback of transportation services.
    A. diversity
    B. paucity
    C. fruition

20. To prevent child-tampering, many medicines are housed in _____ unbreakable bottles.
    A. rife
    B. fail-safe
    C. diurnal

(For Quiz Answers, see Answer Section at the end of the book)

SAT & College Dictionary Workbook Quiz 17

[On a separate sheet of paper, write down the letter of the word that best fits in the blank to create a complete and meaningful sentence.]

1. The birth of a child is a _____ event.
   A. feeble
   B. recondite
   C. beatific

2. The _____ praise bestowed upon the despotic ruler by his lowly subjects did not sway him to compassion or mercy.
   A. fulsome
   B. illusory
   C. desolate

3. After taking the medicine, she felt _____ and was unable to continue her brisk daily activities.
   A. feral
   B. tedious
   C. lethargic

4. Years of living in the Alaskan wilderness _____ the explorer to the biting cold.
   A. rejuvenated
   B. inured
   C. accoutered

5. Serving in the military is _____ in many countries.
   A. refractory
   B. ambulatory
   C. compulsory

6. The psychiatrist determined that the youngster's violent nightmares manifested the child's _____ hostility toward his stepfather.
   A. flippant
   B. latent
   C. sentimental

7. A recurring _____ in the novel was man's search for self-identity.
   A. motif
   B. consensus
   C. timbre

8. Drunk drivers exhibit a _____ disregard for human life.
   A. blatant
   B. motley
   C. seemly

9. On weekends, the _____ lake attracted scores of tourists and picnickers alike.
   A. lavish
   B. vernal
   C. placid

10. The stone sculpture reflected the _____ of a master craftsman.
    A. wraith
    B. angst
    C. finesse

11. In his later years, Orson Wells was a _____ and imposing figure.
    A. portly
    B. covert
    C. fatuous

12. Fans were shocked at the young singer's untimely _____.
    A. demise
    B. fracas
    C. subterfuge

13. The feared mobster wore a _____ scar on his face.
    A. prominent
    B. ruthless
    C. venal

14. At the wedding banquet, the coordinator _____ the lights in a colorful, eye-catching sequence.
    A. imbued
    B. arrayed
    C. purveyed

15. The impressionable youngster _____ his older brother.
    A. dissembled
    B. revered
    C. encapsulated

16. Alcohol can be _____ to one's memory as well as one's health.
    A. obtrusive
    B. ignoble
    C. deleterious

17. A _____ of fabrics and metal objects comprised the unusual artwork.
    A. coalition
    B. propensity
    C. mélange

18. In a scathing newspaper article, the politician was _____ for having accepted bribes and then denying the veracity of the filmed evidence.
    A. debilitated
    B. implemented
    C. lambasted

19. The coppersmith _____ the coins to a bright luster.
    A. lambasted
    B. retracted
    C. burnished

20. Although not coming right out and saying it, the newspaper article nevertheless _____ that the judges of the beauty contest had been bribed.
    A. dissimulated
    B. insinuated
    C. ensued

(For Quiz Answers, see Answer Section at the end of the book)

SAT & College Dictionary Workbook Quiz 18

[On a separate sheet of paper, write down the letter of the word that best fits in the blank to create a complete and meaningful sentence.]

1. As the meeting degenerated into chaos, hostilities turned to _____ name-calling.
   A. efficacious
   B. nebulous
   C. acrimonious

2. The sensational young quarterback was _____ by fans and fellow players alike.
   A. exalted
   B. honed
   C. abjured

3. His girlfriend's _____ refusal to go to the dance with him left him no other alternative but to go alone.
   A. untenable
   B. emphatic
   C. innovative

4. In some religions, followers must _____ eating meat on occasion.
   A. forgo
   B. acquiesce
   C. repent

5. The vengeful wizard levied a _____ curse on the entire town.
   A. pretentious
   B. fecund
   C. baleful

6. The other players watched with _____ eyes as the freshman was promoted to team captain.
   A. extroverted
   B. bedraggled
   C. jaundiced

7. The brutality of the unprovoked attack _____ the citizens of the tiny community.
   A. exhumed
   B. leavened
   C. appalled

8. Two days after the winning lottery number was announced, the local newspaper _____ the names of the winners.
   A. traduced
   B. disclosed
   C. mollified

9. Outraged community activists _____ the council committee for arbitrarily spending money without first consulting the voters.
   A. objurgated
   B. abdicated
   C. remunerated

10. The _____ waters were inviting to young and old alike.
    A. tranquil
    B. commodious
    C. pastoral

11. The interminable summer vacation had produced in the children a state of lingering _____.
    A. rectitude
    B. ennui
    C. nexus

12. The _____ old curmudgeon chased the group of friendly youngsters out of his front yard.
    A. bilious
    B. gratuitous
    C. primordial

13. A _____ hut made from bamboo and straw served as battalion headquarters.
    A. makeshift
    B. dormant
    C. hallowed

14. The happy-go-lucky lad was a most _____ traveling partner.
    A. hirsute
    B. mercenary
    C. congenial

15. In the cafeteria's dishwashing room, one could hear the _____ of pots, pans and dishes clattering.
    A. penury
    B. din
    C. namesake

16. For safety, supernumerary military supplies were _____ in a nearby cave.
    A. proliferated
    B. cached
    C. indoctrinated

17. To pay his monthly rent, the laid-off pilot was forced to perform _____ tasks for minimum wage.
    A. menial
    B. sovereign
    C. pied

18. Her parents were shocked by her boyfriend's _____ behavior.
    A. itinerant
    B. uncouth
    C. erudite

19. Cars came to an _____ stop as the family of ducks slowly crossed the road.
    A. ingratiating
    B. abrupt
    C. onerous

20. The high school quarterback's _____ attitude led many to regard him as arrogant, aloof and antisocial.
    A. impetuous
    B. garrulous
    C. smug

(For Quiz Answers, see Answer Section at the end of the book)

SAT & College Dictionary Workbook Quiz 19

[On a separate sheet of paper, write down the letter of the word that best fits in the blank to create a complete and meaningful sentence.]

1. She found her _____ in life as a doctor.
   A. ado
   B. niche
   C. gist

2. Soft music is often used to _____ a restless infant.
   A. estrange
   B. stifle
   C. pacify

3. The war veteran asserted that he was _____ when unjustly called a Nazi sympathizer.
   A. immured
   B. defamed
   C. razed

4. The king's banquet featured a _____ of imported delicacies and the choicest of wines.
   A. discord
   B. melee
   C. surfeit

5. Paleontologists have posited a _____ of possible explanations for the extinction of dinosaurs during the Cretaceous period.
   A. coterie
   B. vagary
   C. plethora

6. For his money-saving idea, the clerk received _____ from upper-level management.
   A. furor
   B. probity
   C. approbation

7. In an impulsive and imprudent display of _____, the warrior soldier slapped the captive general in front of his own men.
   A. alacrity
   B. preciosity
   C. hubris

8. The social critic's essay was a _____ against the poor treatment of mentally ill patients in the early twentieth century.
   A. jeremiad
   B. respite
   C. conundrum

9. The aloe vera plant contains an _____ medicinal substance.
   A. emphatic
   B. oleaginous
   C. intermittent

10. The confrontation on the gridiron with his old nemesis seemed like a case of _____.
    A. quid pro quo
    B. adversity
    C. déjà vu

11. Rather than answer to the charges, the suspect _____ as he awaited the arrival of his attorney.
    A. persevered
    B. equivocated
    C. adjured

12. Firing his trustworthy servant to conserve money was a decision he both dreaded and _____.
    A. ostracized
    B. fomented
    C. deplored

13. Other business executives welcomed association with such an august man of moral _____ and social rectitude.
    A. aplomb
    B. probity
    C. valor

14. The lion in *The Wizard of Oz* regarded himself a _____ though pretentiously pompous poltroon.
    A. sisyphean
    B. pusillanimous
    C. contemptuous

15. The couple lay _____ upon the grass, enjoying their precious moments together.
    A. festive
    B. summarily
    C. recumbent

16. In the hospital, _____ patients conversed with bedridden ones.
    A. flagitious
    B. ambulatory
    C. piscatorial

17. The wayward lad had the _____ to blame his parents for his own misdeeds.
    A. multiplicity
    B. absolution
    C. effrontery

18. Before signing on the dotted line, the actor _____ the contract for possible errors or omissions.
    A. desecrated
    B. perused
    C. educed

19. When the storm descended with full fury, the campers sought _____ in a nearby cave.
    A. refuge
    B. stamina
    C. foliage

20. Sports reporters reviled the coach for his _____ verbal assault upon his own young players.
    A. opprobrious
    B. inclusive
    C. tenuous

(For Quiz Answers, see Answer Section at the end of the book)

SAT & College Dictionary Workbook Quiz 20

[On a separate sheet of paper, write down the letter of the word that best fits in the blank to create a complete and meaningful sentence.]

1. At work the _____ dentist could not keep his mind off his pregnant wife, whom he knew might give birth at any moment.
   A. distrait
   B. temporal
   C. instrumental

2. Many people have an _____ to cockroaches.
   A. imbroglio
   B. odyssey
   C. aversion

3. The political candidate's _____ speech contained little substance.
   A. dictatorial
   B. imperative
   C. rhetorical

4. Although she experienced a _____ upbringing, in later years she distanced herself from its tolerance and narrow-mindedness.
   A. puritanical
   B. cumulative
   C. naïve

5. A _____ developed among the ambassadors at the international conference.
   A. comity
   B. hauteur
   C. pleasantry

6. Adult movies oftentimes cater to _____ interests.
   A. prurient
   B. defamatory
   C. saccharine

7. Through her own refined actions and behavior, the dutiful mother hoped to _____ in her children a sense of social propriety.
   A. inculcate
   B. expound
   C. heed

8. Without water, all plants and animals soon _____.
   A. perish
   B. flourish
   C. eradicate

9. The doughty hiker _____ to surmount the sheer cliff.
   A. heeded
   B. assayed
   C. promulgated

10. As paperwork piled up, the executive _____ the day she fired her secretary.
    A. implored
    B. rued
    C. attested

11. The platoon's request for supplies was _____ to their greater need for more manpower.
    A. incumbent
    B. concomitant
    C. nugatory

12. The _____ china was packed in padded boxes for shipping.
    A. obscure
    B. frangible
    C. corporeal

13. The construction supervisor _____ the need to complete the project on time.
    A. reproved
    B. abhorred
    C. underscored

14. Several committee members expressed their _____ opposition to the controversial proposal.
    A. vehement
    B. fretful
    C. impartial

15. The valorous sailor was _____ for his bravery.
    A. reviled
    B. commended
    C. mortified

16. Satellites provide a global _____ in the communication and transmission of ideas.
    A. advent
    B. pall
    C. nexus

17. All plants and animals must _____ to ensure survival.
    A. evade
    B. gainsay
    C. propagate

18. The insulated curmudgeon obstinately maintained his _____ dismissal of technological advances.
    A. genial
    B. discrete
    C. parochial

19. It is ecologically unsound to disturb the _____ in the food chain by causing the extinction of any living species.
    A. viridity
    B. equipoise
    C. schism

20. Sales for the first month reflected an _____ beginning for the fledgling business.
    A. odious
    B. auspicious
    C. unruly

(For Quiz Answers, see Answer Section at the end of the book)

SAT & College Dictionary Workbook Quiz 21

[On a separate sheet of paper, write down the letter of the word that best fits in the blank to create a complete and meaningful sentence.]

1. After an hour of constant marching in the parade, the drummer's energy began to _____.
   A. aver
   B. wont
   C. flag

2. During cold winter evenings, he was _____ to smoke his pipe and read a book near the warm fireplace.
   A. adept
   B. wont
   C. incumbent

3. The boy's eyes _____ as he excitedly entered the fragrantly inviting candy store.
   A. thrived
   B. ebbed
   C. waxed

4. During the acid-rock era of the 1960s, many legendary icons were _____ to have been heavily into drugs even while performing in concert.
   A. reputed
   B. connived
   C. inferred

5. A _____ grin appeared on the face of the frustrated blackjack player as the dealer unveiled yet another game-winning hand of 21.
   A. wry
   B. sanguine
   C. bleak

6. Implementation of the back-up plan was _____ upon the failure of the explosives to detonate as expected.
   A. tantamount
   B. indulgent
   C. contingent

7. A true perfectionist, the man kept his car in _____ condition.
   A. conscientious
   B. veracious
   C. immaculate

8. The untimely death of the President marked a truly _____ day for the nation.
   A. venial
   B. tepid
   C. dolorous

9. Every morning, the aerobics instructor put her students through a _____ exercise program.
   A. coherent
   B. prominent
   C. rigorous

10. His account of how he landed the huge marlin was vividly exciting though equally _____.
    A. brazen
    B. implausible
    C. pungent

11. The lad's _____ antics made his younger sister cry.
    A. brusque
    B. quizzical
    C. trivial

12. The new employee was _____ for his constant tardiness.
    A. berated
    B. fawned
    C. propagated

13. Telephoning a close friend helped her find _____ from the intense loneliness.
    A. bathos
    B. zest
    C. solace

14. The _____ musician was proficient in five different instruments.
    A. inchoate
    B. versatile
    C. multifarious

15. Through _____ from an endless barrage of pointed questions, the suspect eventually confessed.
    A. attrition
    B. predilection
    C. machination

16. The guest speaker _____ from the podium the inexcusable tactics employed by large corporations to force smaller companies into bankruptcy.
    A. vituperated
    B. waned
    C. censored

17. The captain _____ maritime authority by sailing his ship into the restricted harbor.
    A. appalled
    B. contravened
    C. purged

18. The young girl _____ to one day become a famous doctor.
    A. obviated
    B. aspired
    C. evinced

19. The doctor's medical diagnosis _____ her initial fears.
    A. assessed
    B. validated
    C. renovated

20. The boy's _____ behavior at the opera embarrassed his mother.
    A. discreet
    B. staid
    C. juvenile

(For Quiz Answers, see Answer Section at the end of the book)

SAT & College Dictionary Workbook Quiz 22

[On a separate sheet of paper, write down the letter of the word that best fits in the blank to create a complete and meaningful sentence.]

1. For his inattentiveness during drills, the cadet was _____ by the platoon commander.
   A. discomfited
   B. reprimanded
   C. cogitated

2. The veteran reporter provided a _____ and dispassionate account of the protesters' clash with police.
   A. florid
   B. lethargic
   C. veracious

3. Visitors to the island resort participated in a week of _____ revelry.
   A. incorrigible
   B. bacchanalian
   C. motley

4. Vegetation _____ in the rain forest.
   A. flourishes
   B. burnishes
   C. wonts

5. To impress his employer, the ambitious lad completed several _____ tasks.
   A. telltale
   B. extravagant
   C. supererogatory

6. Before his first cup of coffee in the morning, he tended to be _____ and unsociable.
   A. testy
   B. jovial
   C. oblivious

7. The Broadway musical comedy was an _____ success.
   A. expedient
   B. incipient
   C. uproarious

8. No matter which island they are visiting, tourists are treated to the _____ aloha spirit of Hawaii.
   A. inflammatory
   B. ubiquitous
   C. supercilious

9. When informed that she had passed the entrance examination, her relief was _____.
   A. recalcitrant
   B. manifest
   C. insouciant

10. Although frequent in mice, pink-colored eyes are an _____ in humans.
    A. enmity
    B. upstart
    C. anomaly

11. When asked by news reporters if war with the neighboring country was inevitable, the diplomat's _____ response was that only peace is inevitable.
    A. equivocal
    B. aesthetic
    C. spiteful

12. The tribal youths were _____ warriors.
    A. monolithic
    B. gamely
    C. retentive

13. Although in a rush to get to the airport, the _____ man could do no better than encounter red lights at every traffic intersection he reached.
    A. hapless
    B. opportune
    C. circumspect

14. The peaceful villagers were _____ churchgoers.
    A. conjugal
    B. frantic
    C. pious

15. Hotel staff always greeted the guests in a most _____ manner.
    A. ineffable
    B. risqué
    C. cordial

16. The _____ teenager loved to chat with friends at the mall.
    A. spendthrift
    B. voluble
    C. eccentric

17. Border guards _____ the smuggled diamonds.
    A. confiscated
    B. hampered
    C. scarified

18. After the race, the winning horse ran a _____ lap around the track to the delight of cheering spectators.
    A. boorish
    B. triumphal
    C. jovial

19. The committee examined in a _____ manner alternatives to raising money other than by increasing local taxes.
    A. circumspect
    B. factitious
    C. refractory

20. Beverly Hills is an _____ neighborhood.
    A. affluent
    B. otiose
    C. uxorious

(For Quiz Answers, see Answer Section at the end of the book)

SAT & College Dictionary Workbook Quiz 23

[On a separate sheet of paper, write down the letter of the word that best fits in the blank to create a complete and meaningful sentence.]

1. Because children are particularly _____, it is essential to instill in them moral ethics and positive self-esteem.
   A. malleable
   B. shrewd
   C. dynamic

2. Early pioneers were a _____ and determined group.
   A. pompous
   B. rhetorical
   C. hardy

3. Military reinforcements were brought in to repel the anticipated _____ of rebel forces.
   A. inclination
   B. onset
   C. asylum

4. The recluse savored his _____ existence far from the dense smog-infested city.
   A. rural
   B. serendipitous
   C. indefatigable

5. Farmers were grateful for the _____ spring harvest.
   A. exotic
   B. quotidian
   C. bountiful

6. The boy was _____ in his refusal to dance with his sister.
   A. awry
   B. obdurate
   C. dubious

7. Witnesses identified the bearded man as the _____ who committed the robbery.
   A. culprit
   B. toady
   C. leviathan

8. When traversing the frozen lake, the group proceeded in a deliberate and _____ manner.
   A. tentative
   B. brash
   C. objective

9. Penicillin has proven an _____ antidote for bee stings.
   A. efficacious
   B. acerbic
   C. uproarious

10. The lowly subject was _____ about what he uttered while in the presence of the king.
    A. placid
    B. impertinent
    C. chary

11. Many believe that Anna Anderson's claim in 1920 to be the long-lost Princess Anastasia was simply _____.
    A. devoid
    B. preposterous
    C. sacrilegious

12. There was a _____ of three days between contract-negotiations sessions.
    A. hiatus
    B. precipitation
    C. disquietude

13. The teenager's _____ telephone conversation lasted for two hours.
    A. tumid
    B. desultory
    C. makeshift

14. The curmudgeon lived a _____ life in his cabin in the woods.
    A. limpid
    B. reclusive
    C. cantankerous

15. Authorities threatened to take legal action if the company continued to advertise what amounted to patently _____ claims.
    A. spurious
    B. peripatetic
    C. interminable

16. Critics viewed the star's lackluster Shakespearean performance as _____ at best.
    A. sapid
    B. marginal
    C. contrite

17. The farmer's two sons were _____ young men.
    A. virtual
    B. incongruous
    C. robust

18. The elderly recluse was a habitually _____ person.
    A. fanciful
    B. hulking
    C. sullen

19. The various lobbyist groups _____ to form a more potent unit.
    A. coalesced
    B. expunged
    C. tantalized

20. Sliding down the twisted rope _____ his hand.
    A. abated
    B. inculpated
    C. excoriated

(For Quiz Answers, see Answer Section at the end of the book)

SAT & College Dictionary Workbook Quiz 24

[On a separate sheet of paper, write down the letter of the word that best fits in the blank to create a complete and meaningful sentence.]

1. Bringing up her colleague's frequent tardiness _____ an already-strained working relationship.
   A. inculpated
   B. collaborated
   C. exacerbated

2. Low initial customer turnout _____ a shaky future for the retail store.
   A. exhorted
   B. juxtaposed
   C. adumbrated

3. After spraining her ankle, the salesperson walked _____ on it for the remainder of her work shift.
   A. arguably
   B. gingerly
   C. incognito

4. The book report included a _____ of the novel.
   A. harangue
   B. reprisal
   C. précis

5. A magic spell transformed the disheveled Cinderella into a _____ young woman.
   A. mephitic
   B. haggard
   C. comely

6. The hastily-written manuscript was _____ with grammatical errors.
   A. futile
   B. vibrant
   C. replete

7. The two countries were geographical _____.
   A. increments
   B. precursors
   C. antipodes

8. All parties _____ the literary contract for accuracy and appropriate changes before signing.
   A. scrutinized
   B. recollected
   C. extricated

9. Taking fewer showers was only a _____ measure to relieve the water shortage; an effective long-term solution was really needed.
   A. monolithic
   B. prefatory
   C. stopgap

10. Members of the cabal agreed under _____ not to disclose the identity of the faction's headquarters even if threatened by death.
    A. faux pas
    B. covenant
    C. rote

11. After repeated warnings to be quiet, the teacher _____ at the student in a baleful look that promised detention if he didn't cease his chatter that very instant.
    A. venerated
    B. bolstered
    C. glowered

12. Before an airplane ascends, it is _____ that all doors and latches be fully secured.
    A. imperative
    B. superlative
    C. excruciating

13. Adam and Eve resided in an _____ world of purity and innocence.
    A. apropos
    B. elysian
    C. untimely

14. His scheme to get a promotion was, for the most part, _____.
    A. compulsory
    B. sanctimonious
    C. ineffectual

15. The feisty lad was reprimanded for his _____ behavior at the dinner table.
    A. inadvertent
    B. obnoxious
    C. spry

16. The townspeople shunned the good-for-nothing _____.
    A. thespian
    B. reprobate
    C. paragon

17. _____ followers truly believed that alchemists could turn lead into gold.
    A. Credulous
    B. Sapient
    C. Lambent

18. The powerful and domineering emperor was attended to by his retinue of _____, each seeking special favor with the nations' ruler.
    A. sycophants
    B. reprobates
    C. kudos

19. The _____ couple could not even reach a consensus as to where to eat out.
    A. disputatious
    B. sybaritic
    C. vile

20. To make the novel suitable for younger audiences, all objectionable language was _____ and all violent scenes toned down.
    A. expurgated
    B. abridged
    C. waxed

(For Quiz Answers, see Answer Section at the end of the book)

SAT & College Dictionary Workbook Quiz 25

[On a separate sheet of paper, write down the letter of the word that best fits in the blank to create a complete and meaningful sentence.]

1. The _____ gang of hooligans were derided for their acts of thievery and drug-dealing.
   A. garrulous
   B. saturnine
   C. disreputable

2. As a result of their rudeness to the guest speaker, the class of fifth graders was publicly _____ by their teacher.
   A. loathed
   B. castigated
   C. requited

3. A _____ crowd attended the gala celebration.
   A. squalid
   B. diverse
   C. panoramic

4. Before the successful raid by Santa Anna's men, the Alamo was considered an _____ fortress.
   A. impregnable
   B. omniscient
   C. unruly

5. After a week on the island, the castaways had _____ their food supplies.
   A. depleted
   B. harried
   C. procrastinated

6. The girl's poor test scores were _____ with her brilliant academic potential.
   A. incongruous
   B. unilateral
   C. amiss

7. Before being shaped into necklaces, the gold was _____ into one long strand.
   A. attenuated
   B. habituated
   C. relegated

8. All efforts at coaxing the _____ boy to participate in the class discussion proved futile.
   A. reticent
   B. ineffable
   C. fey

9. In the Civil War account, the historic battles were listed in _____ order.
   A. insightful
   B. multifaceted
   C. sequential

10. There are an _____ number of stars in the universe.
    A. exhaustive
    B. infinite
    C. auxiliary

11. Plans to visit faraway planets are still in their _____ stages.
    A. embryonic
    B. urbane
    C. lachrymose

12. After years of hard work and resolute frugality, the couple's dream of buying their own home came to _____.
    A. deliverance
    B. fruition
    C. similitude

13. Praising the current leader in a show of loyalty _____ the corporal's true desire to become the next commander.
    A. thwarted
    B. dissimulated
    C. misconstrued

14. An assortment of recollections was _____ to produce a moving tribute during the eulogy.
    A. resurrected
    B. concatenated
    C. perpetrated

15. Local inns _____ food and lodging at reasonable overnight rates to weary travelers.
    A. consolidate
    B. delegate
    C. purvey

16. The television documentary examined the year in _____.
    A. equilibrium
    B. perdition
    C. retrospect

17. Representing those living in the family shelter, the spokesman _____ against the state government for turning a deaf ear on the homeless.
    A. defamed
    B. inveighed
    C. conjectured

18. The lead negotiator _____ while the hostage-taker's mother was summoned to the scene.
    A. conjectured
    B. reminisced
    C. temporized

19. As a result of spotty attendance, the club member was _____ from secretary to assistant treasurer.
    A. ostracized
    B. sojourned
    C. demoted

20. War is a matter of _____ concern to all involved.
    A. inimical
    B. grave
    C. potent

(For Quiz Answers, see Answer Section at the end of the book)

SAT & College Dictionary Workbook Quiz 26

[On a separate sheet of paper, write down the letter of the word that best fits in the blank to create a complete and meaningful sentence.]

1. A father should not _____ his responsibility to the family by neglecting to provide them with food on the table.
   A. aver
   B. shirk
   C. belie

2. Relevant facts were _____ to further bolster the thesis of the argument.
   A. adduced
   B. foundered
   C. retracted

3. The young girl marveled at the _____ threads of the spider's web.
   A. gossamer
   B. infinitesimal
   C. euphuistic

4. His _____ religious and political views alienated him from mainstream society.
   A. iconoclastic
   B. temperate
   C. chaste

5. In court, the lad was ordered to make _____ for the broken window by working on weekends for a month.
   A. restitution
   B. parity
   C. ado

6. After a lengthy survey of the picnic area, the young man finally _____ his girlfriend sitting on a park bench.
   A. reproached
   B. assayed
   C. descried

7. The unexpectedly cold weather proved a _____ to businesses specializing in sales of winter clothes.
   A. hiatus
   B. repository
   C. boon

8. The intense summer heat was blamed for the general _____ at the factory that afternoon.
   A. sloth
   B. latitude
   C. panache

9. The groundhog is an early _____ of the coming of spring.
   A. harbinger
   B. regimen
   C. apocalypse

10. _____ apricots are a delicious snack food.
    A. Patronized
    B. Desiccated
    C. Audacious

11. The determined teen _____ her mother to let her drive home.
    A. importuned
    B. meted
    C. coalesced

12. The _____ pace of the championship basketball game kept the audience on its feet.
    A. addled
    B. frenetic
    C. philanthropic

13. Life on the moon is fraught with _____ difficulties and complexities.
    A. multifarious
    B. celestial
    C. dormant

14. Featured in the tribal ceremony was an _____ voodoo ritual.
    A. exorbitant
    B. officious
    C. arcane

15. An arbitrator was called upon to resolve the _____ dispute between management and the employees' union.
    A. clandestine
    B. slipshod
    C. factious

16. Class reunions usually lend themselves to much festive conversation, owing largely to the shared _____ of experiences of those who make up the guest list.
    A. propinquity
    B. contumely
    C. apex

17. The businessman attended the funeral of his lifelong nemesis with _____ delight.
    A. sardonic
    B. indignant
    C. ambivalent

18. When supply equals demand, there is economic _____.
    A. equilibrium
    B. verve
    C. plight

19. _____ over the disappearance of her child, the woman had to be sedated by medical personnel.
    A. Timorous
    B. Distraught
    C. Insolent

20. In the spy novel, the mad scientist hatched a _____ scheme to rule the world.
    A. sparse
    B. pithy
    C. diabolic

(For Quiz Answers, see Answer Section at the end of the book)

SAT & College Dictionary Workbook Quiz 27

[On a separate sheet of paper, write down the letter of the word that best fits in the blank to create a complete and meaningful sentence.]

1. The _____ pirate was decried for his dastardly deeds.
   A. gullible
   B. infamous
   C. parsimonious

2. The country boy's _____ manners were somewhat embarrassing to his sophisticated friends.
   A. gauche
   B. bountiful
   C. mephitic

3. Scientists offered a _____ and credible explanation for the unusual celestial sightings.
   A. cordial
   B. lucid
   C. stoic

4. Mosquitoes proved to be a major _____ during the outdoor event.
   A. repast
   B. adherent
   C. menace

5. Rags _____ the drainage pipe, causing the basement to flood.
   A. dissipated
   B. occluded
   C. acclimated

6. Henry David Thoreau _____ modern conveniences and instead chose to live simply in his cottage by Walden Pond.
   A. importuned
   B. engendered
   C. abnegated

7. After she had appeared in the national television commercial, all her classmates _____ her.
   A. lionized
   B. absolved
   C. culled

8. His wife's _____ reminder of the late hour convinced him that it was time to leave the party.
   A. subtle
   B. blithe
   C. pristine

9. The _____ horse could not be successfully domesticated.
   A. contumelious
   B. fractious
   C. illicit

10. Iago conceived an _____ plot to make Othello believe his wife was cheating on him.
    A. opulent
    B. amicable
    C. insidious

11. An entire string section was added to _____ the dramatic musical piece.
    A. upbraid
    B. embellish
    C. castigate

12. Flesh and bones comprise our _____ being.
    A. ruddy
    B. corporeal
    C. impervious

13. Desperate, the lost sailors _____ the gods to show them the way to safety from the storm.
    A. adjured
    B. exorcised
    C. procured

14. The television audience has become so _____ from all the violence shown that, when an actual murder is reported on the news, few are shocked.
    A. jaded
    B. bumptious
    C. pliable

15. The wealthy family was greatly respected for their _____ to those less fortunate.
    A. forbearance
    B. acumen
    C. largess

16. At the international convention, the foreign ambassador was granted _____ discretion.
    A. plenipotentiary
    B. vital
    C. dissolute

17. The Dalai Lama is a _____ and august religious figure.
    A. cumbersome
    B. redoubtable
    C. permeable

18. The punishment _____ out befit the gravity of the crime.
    A. eradicated
    B. convened
    C. meted

19. A magazine _____ of Bob Hope featured the television icon with a Pinocchio-sized nose.
    A. lexicon
    B. wraith
    C. caricature

20. The _____ tale of tragedy left not a dry eye in the audience.
    A. lachrymose
    B. self-effacing
    C. despicable

(For Quiz Answers, see Answer Section at the end of the book)

SAT & College Dictionary Workbook Quiz 28

[On a separate sheet of paper, write down the letter of the word that best fits in the blank to create a complete and meaningful sentence.]

1. The young author had _____ about signing the exclusive contract without the presence of his literary agent.
   A. prerogatives
   B. misgivings
   C. constraints

2. The guest committed a most embarrassing _____ when he addressed the short-haired hostess as "Mr. Smith."
   A. faux pas
   B. quagmire
   C. bon mot

3. His _____ remarks regarding political ethics surprised his worldly associates.
   A. complaisant
   B. jejune
   C. stately

4. The Rockefeller family have long been renowned for their _____ deeds.
   A. definitive
   B. anthropomorphic
   C. philanthropic

5. It is only fitting and proper to treat animals in a _____ manner.
   A. malevolent
   B. humane
   C. substantial

6. A holy man was summoned to _____ the parcel of land where the ancient bones were unearthed.
   A. stanch
   B. consecrate
   C. underpin

7. Unless they demonstrated a special individual talent, the newest members of the choir were _____ to singing backup.
   A. dispelled
   B. encumbered
   C. relegated

8. Because children are generally _____ and socially extroverted, they make friends easily and quickly with one another.
   A. spontaneous
   B. jaundiced
   C. querulous

9. One must recognize and applaud the _____ effort required of a single parent to raise a family of seven boys.
   A. chthonian
   B. sisyphean
   C. imperative

10. A local veterinarian was summoned when the zoo's lions began exhibiting _____ behavior.
    A. abject
    B. erratic
    C. profound

11. Even after witnessing firsthand the maltreatment of street children, government officials remained _____ toward helping them.
    A. outlandish
    B. apathetic
    C. irrefutable

12. The young Republican subscribed to generally _____ political ideology.
    A. subservient
    B. orthodox
    C. ineluctable

13. Discovering that he had forgotten his friend's birthday, the chagrined colleague immediately sent an apologetic _____ birthday card.
    A. jejune
    B. belated
    C. prefatory

14. After the disheartening loss, the bus ride home assumed a _____ atmosphere for the entire soccer team.
    A. humane
    B. mercenary
    C. funereal

15. Several students were _____ in the graffiti incident.
    A. goaded
    B. inculpated
    C. remonstrated

16. Constant reminders from his mother had little effect in persuading the _____ tyke to remain in his playpen.
    A. witless
    B. taciturn
    C. intractable

17. As latest statistics pointed to a recovery, more economists openly voiced a more _____ outlook on the future.
    A. toxic
    B. elusive
    C. sanguine

18. Many scientists have _____ the existence of higher life forms on other planets.
    A. rectified
    B. controverted
    C. indicted

19. In some societies, _____ acts of adultery are punishable by death.
    A. flagitious
    B. woeful
    C. artless

20. To the lovestruck teenage boy, the blonde-haired beauty was the embodiment of an angel as she passed by in her radiant _____.
    A. effulgence
    B. rancor
    C. trepidation

(For Quiz Answers, see Answer Section at the end of the book)

SAT & College Dictionary Workbook Quiz 29

[On a separate sheet of paper, write down the letter of the word that best fits in the blank to create a complete and meaningful sentence.]

1. Children who _____ themselves of chocolates soon realize that too much of a good thing is not always healthy or pleasant.
   A. regale
   B. expend
   C. cloy

2. Man's understanding of life after death remains as _____ today as it was a thousand years ago.
   A. surreptitious
   B. nebulous
   C. virtuous

3. The eminent scientist was able to provide a _____ explanation for the highly extraordinary phenomenon.
   A. draconian
   B. commodious
   C. perspicuous

4. Despite troubling economic signs, the chairman remained _____ about the future.
   A. diligent
   B. optimistic
   C. abstinent

5. The _____ beggar had not taken a shower in months.
   A. bedraggled
   B. prodigious
   C. grueling

6. Upon entering the king's court, the knight made an _____ to the mighty leader.
   A. abeyance
   B. inclination
   C. obeisance

7. The _____ preacher took his message far and wide throughout the land.
   A. hedonistic
   B. peripatetic
   C. agrarian

8. Samuel Clemens wrote under the _____ "Mark Twain."
   A. nemesis
   B. pseudonym
   C. talisman

9. His weak stomach condition necessitated a _____ diet.
   A. feckless
   B. saline
   C. bland

10. The tardy lad hoped the school principal would find his excuse to be _____.
    A. palatable
    B. dubious
    C. comely

11. The introductory math course ran the _____ from basic arithmetic to advanced algebra.
    A. onset
    B. rift
    C. gamut

12. Being overruled by his aide in front of the other national leaders left the President in high _____.
    A. solace
    B. dudgeon
    C. artifice

13. The _____ remark sought to cast aspersions on the winning candidate's probity.
    A. shoddy
    B. malevolent
    C. disinterested

14. Many people charge that government contracts are often awarded _____ rather than through a fair merit-based system.
    A. rote
    B. quid pro quo
    C. incognito

15. Upon conclusion of the unproductive meeting, the ambassador gave the customary _____ bow and then exited the room.
    A. implicit
    B. beneficial
    C. perfunctory

16. Upon hearing of a plot to murder the royal family, the king _____ the throne and fled the country.
    A. obfuscated
    B. fomented
    C. abdicated

17. According to Old Testament belief, Adam and Eve were our earliest _____.
    A. progenitors
    B. disciples
    C. vanguards

18. In most cowboy movies, the good and bad guys are clearly _____.
    A. revered
    B. manumitted
    C. delineated

19. When asked what she thought of the party, her _____ response offended the host.
    A. uninhibited
    B. morbid
    C. sportive

20. All the ladies at the ball were enchanted by the _____ and sophisticated young gentleman.
    A. Spartan
    B. urbane
    C. inveterate

(For Quiz Answers, see Answer Section at the end of the book)

SAT & College Dictionary Workbook Quiz 30

[On a separate sheet of paper, write down the letter of the word that best fits in the blank to create a complete and meaningful sentence.]

1. It seemed obvious to all that the _____ beggar's request for a financial handout was a mere ruse to support his dependency on alcohol.
   A. vain
   B. moot
   C. disingenuous

2. The couple adhered to a carefully planned budget as a _____ safeguard against future financial uncertainties.
   A. stark
   B. provident
   C. willful

3. Vince Lombardi had an _____ career as head football coach for the Green Bay Packers.
   A. eloquent
   B. illustrious
   C. unctuous

4. The _____ and financially-successful speaker motivated audiences wherever he traveled.
   A. dynamic
   B. sheepish
   C. autonomous

5. The island was popular for its _____ climatic conditions.
   A. languid
   B. temperate
   C. cogent

6. Crying can be a _____ way to relieve the stress of grief.
   A. gainful
   B. cathartic
   C. pecuniary

7. In *Paradise Lost*, John Milton described the _____ world of Satan.
   A. eleemosynary
   B. chthonian
   C. plebeian

8. The boss's _____ always told him what he wanted to hear.
   A. culprit
   B. miscreant
   C. toady

9. The ambitious lad completed his chores with _____.
   A. fruition
   B. alacrity
   C. pleasantry

10. A _____ light shone down upon the tiny village.
    A. magniloquent
    B. celestial
    C. profuse

11. An ingenious scheme was _____ to trick the enemy soldiers into believing they were outnumbered.
    A. concocted
    B. quelled
    C. spurned

12. When the truth became known, the boy's _____ lies did not go unpunished.
    A. fearsome
    B. brazen
    C. perceptive

13. In preparation for battle, the soldiers were _____ with protective gear.
    A. instilled
    B. accoutered
    C. purloined

14. The _____ mountain goat pranced from ledge to ledge with apparent ease.
    A. incisive
    B. agile
    C. pedantic

15. Whether man can survive on planets in distant galaxies is _____ because it may be impossible to ever travel that far.
    A. dogmatic
    B. churlish
    C. moot

16. Jellyfish are _____ sea creatures.
    A. draconian
    B. amorphous
    C. nauseous

17. Applause erupted at the completion of the gymnast's _____ performance.
    A. effete
    B. consummate
    C. precipitous

18. The _____ boor could not relate with his worldly associates.
    A. invaluable
    B. artless
    C. sacrosanct

19. Local newspapers feasted over the _____ love affair between the movie star and his younger cousin.
    A. inane
    B. valid
    C. notorious

20. Based on recent sales results, the company was able to _____ a profitable third quarter.
    A. covet
    B. discern
    C. prognosticate

(For Quiz Answers, see Answer Section at the end of the book)

SAT & College Dictionary Workbook Quiz 31

[On a separate sheet of paper, write down the letter of the word that best fits in the blank to create a complete and meaningful sentence.]

1. Many social critics contend that mankind has recently embarked upon a period of moral _____.
   A. purgatory
   B. retrogression
   C. adversity

2. Medical research has led us closer to _____ dreaded diseases such as polio and small pox.
   A. advocating
   B. propounding
   C. eradicating

3. The alternative learning center was established as an _____ extension of the local high school.
   A. autonomous
   B. omniscient
   C. emblematic

4. Prosecuting and defense attorneys are _____ in the courtroom.
   A. mendicants
   B. quislings
   C. adversaries

5. The folk singer's poetically lyrical tunes _____ to a bygone era.
   A. imprecated
   B. skewed
   C. alluded

6. Prior to the sudden and violent eruption, the volcano had been _____ for many years.
   A. vindictive
   B. dormant
   C. temperate

7. Ham _____ a breakfast with eggs.
   A. exhorts
   B. complements
   C. garners

8. Six inches of _____ fell over a twelve-hour period.
   A. havoc
   B. inclination
   C. precipitation

9. The _____ student always submitted his homework on time.
   A. unabashed
   B. rapacious
   C. diligent

10. The alienated boy was filled with a deep-rooted _____ toward his stepfather.
    A. demeanor
    B. propensity
    C. rancor

11. Having a flat tire while rushing to the airport was most _____.
    A. heinous
    B. untimely
    C. plausible

12. It is not good policy for a reporter to _____ the truth to make his article more sensational.
    A. tout
    B. distort
    C. pacify

13. During dinner, the two scholars bantered and engaged in clever _____.
    A. enmity
    B. repartee
    C. déjà vu

14. The newspaper article endeavored to present a _____ explanation for the unusual disappearance of ships in the Bermuda Triangle.
    A. skittish
    B. homologous
    C. credible

15. _____ from his speech, the guest of honor recalled an amusing incident that had occurred earlier in the day.
    A. Meddling
    B. Abnegating
    C. Digressing

16. Throughout his long life, the _____ octogenarian refrained from excessive imbibing or carousing.
    A. extenuating
    B. obsolescent
    C. abstemious

17. The suspect issued a _____ denial of any involvement in the crime.
    A. categorical
    B. reprehensible
    C. garrulous

18. Due to enhanced security at the airport, passengers were forced to endure frustratingly _____ delays.
    A. embryonic
    B. interminable
    C. laconic

19. "Feeling groovy" and "life's a gas" were oft-used _____ during the late 1960s.
    A. lexicons
    B. panegyrics
    C. shibboleths

20. The controversial scientific theory was _____ upon the belief that life may exist in other dimensions.
    A. glowered
    B. foundered
    C. predicated

(For Quiz Answers, see Answer Section at the end of the book)

SAT & College Dictionary Workbook Quiz 32
[On a separate sheet of paper, write down the letter of the word that best fits in the blank to create a complete and meaningful sentence.]

1. In her lectures, the renowned community leader _____ school and national pride.
   A. amended
   B. lamented
   C. espoused

2. The backbone of American society is the _____ family unit.
   A. incipient
   B. cohesive
   C. recalcitrant

3. Few realized that the _____ white building had an indoor swimming pool.
   A. unobtrusive
   B. presumptuous
   C. fastidious

4. The stew was a _____ of savory meats and vegetables.
   A. potpourri
   B. sangfroid
   C. repertoire

5. Guided by the prophet's _____, the voyagers braved the seas in search of the New World.
   A. genesis
   B. pogrom
   C. apocalypse

6. Money is a _____ commodity; love is not.
   A. tangible
   B. reserved
   C. prudent

7. All the ladies at the ball were smitten by the _____ young man.
   A. feral
   B. motley
   C. suave

8. Exploiting children to perform adult tasks is an _____ way to save money.
   A. expedient
   B. ominous
   C. apathetic

9. The lecturer's _____ and digressive explanation led many to forget what his original point was.
   A. feasible
   B. distraught
   C. prolix

10. The underhanded politician _____ his rival by spreading groundless rumors.
    A. calumniated
    B. induced
    C. whetted

11. The _____, rugged man easily lifted the piano onto the truck.
    A. stalwart
    B. rife
    C. virulent

12. An injured animal is _____ to attack by predators.
    A. inadvertent
    B. vulnerable
    C. loath

13. It is generally considered _____ to curse in the name of God.
    A. sacrilegious
    B. inflammable
    C. uncanny

14. _____ by the tempting island lifestyle, the vacationer found it difficult to return to his mundane routine as husband and father.
    A. Incensed
    B. Debauched
    C. Secluded

15. Based on _____ data, surveyors felt the road needed to be expanded to accommodate the increased traffic flow.
    A. primordial
    B. untimely
    C. empirical

16. The _____ couple surprised everyone by taking an unannounced weekend jaunt to the West Indies.
    A. inconsiderate
    B. exotic
    C. whimsical

17. The _____ fashion outfit sported buttons on the side to allow an undisturbed full frontal figure.
    A. odoriferous
    B. expendable
    C. chic

18. The policeman _____ the heedless pedestrian for jaywalking.
    A. goaded
    B. admonished
    C. revoked

19. Her boyfriend's _____ behavior in front of her parents made her ashamed that she had invited the boor to dinner in the first place.
    A. conscientious
    B. repulsive
    C. loath

20. A migraine headache can cause _____ pain.
    A. excruciating
    B. wary
    C. perfunctory

(For Quiz Answers, see Answer Section at the end of the book)

SAT & College Dictionary Workbook Quiz 33

[On a separate sheet of paper, write down the letter of the word that best fits in the blank to create a complete and meaningful sentence.]

1. Despite his anger toward the clumsy waiter, he maintained his composure and handled the matter with _____.
   A. constraint
   B. presentiment
   C. altercation

2. Susan B. Anthony was an early champion of women's _____.
   A. suffrage
   B. quid pro quo
   C. double entendre

3. The 1863 Emancipation Proclamation _____ those enslaved in the rebellious southern United States.
   A. forestalled
   B. divulged
   C. manumitted

4. The lad's _____ behavior was not appreciated by his peers in school.
   A. disinterested
   B. sagacious
   C. arrogant

5. Hindu monks lead an _____ life.
   A. evanescent
   B. ascetic
   C. unequivocal

6. The highly successful businesswoman _____ those who were too lazy to work for a living.
   A. venerated
   B. nonplussed
   C. disdained

7. Sales _____ expenses were not satisfactory to the board of directors.
   A. impending
   B. vis-à-vis
   C. askance

8. In the midst of his busy workweek in the city, the executive longed for those _____ weekends spent at his country estate.
   A. agile
   B. hidebound
   C. idyllic

9. The elderly lady had a kindly _____.
   A. equanimity
   B. vanguard
   C. mien

10. Animals are _____ creatures, unlike many lower forms of life.
    A. sentient
    B. vain
    C. extant

11. The military leader threatened military _____ should his country be invaded over border disputes.
    A. precursors
    B. increments
    C. reprisals

12. Caring for the elderly is oftentimes an _____ task.
    A. unscrupulous
    B. austere
    C. onerous

13. During the turbulent stock market era of the late 1920s and early 1930s, economic _____ turned millionaires into paupers almost overnight.
    A. élan
    B. vicissitudes
    C. acme

14. His overnight success turned the once-modest boy into a _____ and condescending braggadocio.
    A. pious
    B. supercilious
    C. fortuitous

15. During the séance, an _____ stillness filled the air.
    A. ironic
    B. optimistic
    C. uncanny

16. Failing the bar examination left the young man _____ of all hope of ever becoming a lawyer.
    A. inept
    B. bereft
    C. steadfast

17. The rebel leader was _____ by the government as a traitor and spineless coward.
    A. vilified
    B. deified
    C. eulogized

18. Native groups accused the government of _____ their rightful lands.
    A. censuring
    B. appropriating
    C. resurrecting

19. Dark clouds signaled an _____ storm.
    A. amorphous
    B. ungainly
    C. impending

20. The senator's _____ remarks were met with swift retaliation from his detractors.
    A. autonomous
    B. inflammatory
    C. hospitable

(For Quiz Answers, see Answer Section at the end of the book)

SAT & College Dictionary Workbook Quiz 34

[On a separate sheet of paper, write down the letter of the word that best fits in the blank to create a complete and meaningful sentence.]

1. Stealing the sacred talisman led to _____ consequences for the avaricious explorer.
   A. dire
   B. meek
   C. spontaneous

2. Mother's reassuring words _____ her child's fears.
   A. defied
   B. quelled
   C. atoned

3. An opposing faction _____ to oust the senator from his leadership position.
   A. refurbished
   B. enervated
   C. connived

4. Movie stars often travel _____ to avoid being hounded by fans.
   A. summarily
   B. uninhibited
   C. incognito

5. A _____ decision to escalate military preparedness was frowned upon by the country's allies.
   A. populous
   B. unilateral
   C. smug

6. When a snake crossed its path, the _____ horse bolted.
   A. skittish
   B. hedonistic
   C. intrepid

7. Attending the poetry reading was of each student's own _____.
   A. volition
   B. advent
   C. status quo

8. Hostile fans levied a barrage of _____ insults against the referee for his questionable call.
   A. contumelious
   B. quotidian
   C. tacit

9. Many members of the jury would be forever _____ by the guilty verdict they hastily handed down.
   A. controverted
   B. fulminated
   C. harried

10. _____ bulky computers are rapidly being replaced by more efficient compact models.
    A. Abysmal
    B. Inaugural
    C. Obsolescent

11. Emily Post has long been regarded an _____ of social etiquette.
    A. equipoise
    B. arbiter
    C. impunity

12. The movie documented the _____ of the hapless nineteenth century coal miners.
    A. plight
    B. countenance
    C. duress

13. The international buffet featured a wide variety of _____ exotic delicacies.
    A. vast
    B. sapid
    C. temporal

14. The _____ sailor braved the open seas to search for the missing crewmember.
    A. comely
    B. stout
    C. lavish

15. To help streamline costs, business operations were _____ into one main headquarters.
    A. equivocated
    B. rectified
    C. consolidated

16. Tabloid reporters often _____ from a speech only those words that can be construed in a controversial manner.
    A. cull
    B. raze
    C. harry

17. Rather than explain the concept briefly and to the point, the spokesman delivered a _____ oration that rambled on for fifteen minutes.
    A. froward
    B. verbose
    C. phlegmatic

18. The _____ boy refused to take off his cap during dinner.
    A. pious
    B. insolent
    C. circumspect

19. An _____ witty aphorism leavened the tension of the precarious predicament.
    A. execrable
    B. obtrusive
    C. apposite

20. _____ is a must when caring for little tykes.
    A. Solace
    B. Chicanery
    C. Forbearance

(For Quiz Answers, see Answer Section at the end of the book)

SAT & College Dictionary Workbook Quiz 35

[On a separate sheet of paper, write down the letter of the word that best fits in the blank to create a complete and meaningful sentence.]

1. She was in a _____ as to whom to ask to the senior prom.
   A. plethora
   B. fiasco
   C. quandary

2. Accused of _____, the slacker was warned to take his job more seriously if he wanted to keep it.
   A. eluding
   B. malingering
   C. diverting

3. Whales have a _____ appetite.
   A. famished
   B. prodigious
   C. savory

4. To _____ the tragic shortage of food in the war-torn village, canned goods and bags of rice were donated.
   A. forsake
   B. regale
   C. ameliorate

5. The Bubonic Plague was a _____ disease that ravaged Europe in the fourteenth century.
   A. devious
   B. pestilent
   C. contemptible

6. Differing political views created a _____ within the family.
   A. penchant
   B. schism
   C. timbre

7. The quilt was a _____ patchwork of colorful fabrics.
   A. variegated
   B. flagrant
   C. portly

8. The patient experienced an _____ pain in his side.
   A. obsequious
   B. unctuous
   C. acute

9. Success in business demands _____ and follow-through.
   A. attrition
   B. retrospect
   C. initiative

10. The _____ nation aggressively threatened its peaceful neighbors.
    A. hackneyed
    B. scurrilous
    C. belligerent

11. The military junta hatched a _____ scheme to seize government power.
    A. sententious
    B. Machiavellian
    C. grotesque

12. The queen's _____ temperament left her subjects uncertain as to what she might demand next.
    A. mercurial
    B. convivial
    C. vehement

13. After having been made the butt of the joke the day before, the student _____ by placing gum on the other boy's chair.
    A. complied
    B. retaliated
    C. deplored

14. A tow truck was brought in to remove the _____ vehicles parked on the street.
    A. toxic
    B. derelict
    C. licentious

15. A _____ shopper is a smart shopper.
    A. thrifty
    B. miserly
    C. slovenly

16. The 1963 assassination of President John F. Kennedy was a globally _____ event.
    A. licentious
    B. calamitous
    C. torpid

17. On weekend campouts, the scout leader became a _____ father to twelve boys.
    A. formidable
    B. surrogate
    C. genteel

18. From his wife's gruff tone of voice, he _____ that she was not in a pleasant mood.
    A. averted
    B. inferred
    C. elucidated

19. Neighbors enjoyed the _____ block-party.
    A. intransigent
    B. convivial
    C. repulsive

20. The top two teams' star quarterbacks were friends during the off-season but _____ on the gridiron.
    A. tyros
    B. recreants
    C. foes

(For Quiz Answers, see Answer Section at the end of the book)

SAT & College Dictionary Workbook Quiz 36

[On a separate sheet of paper, write down the letter of the word that best fits in the blank to create a complete and meaningful sentence.]

1. Throughout his political and personal life, Jimmy Carter was known as an _____ for human rights.
   A. upstart
   B. enigma
   C. apologist

2. Abraham Lincoln possessed a strikingly august _____.
   A. physiognomy
   B. esprit de corps
   C. anathema

3. In the celestial light, her face radiated an _____ loveliness.
   A. exorbitant
   B. ineffable
   C. autocratic

4. The book's theme of two lovers committing suicide was _____ and offered nothing that hadn't been written a hundred times before.
   A. shopworn
   B. provincial
   C. inevitable

5. At one time, people believed that alchemists could _____ lead into gold.
   A. bolster
   B. dissect
   C. transmute

6. The old man's _____ hands proved a hindrance in holding a glass of water or eating from a bowl of soup.
   A. meticulous
   B. tremulous
   C. nimble

7. To pinpoint possible contradictions, analysts _____ the President's speech on foreign affairs.
   A. dissected
   B. jeered
   C. propagated

8. Sloths are _____ mammals.
   A. exiguous
   B. arboreal
   C. nugatory

9. As they entered the dense jungle, the explorers encountered a band of _____ natives.
   A. atypical
   B. hostile
   C. nebulous

10. The widespread apartment blaze left several families homeless and _____.
    A. paltry
    B. inconsiderable
    C. destitute

11. The legal dispute was resolved in a _____ and impartial manner.
    A. judicious
    B. seminal
    C. disaffected

12. The grandfather clock featured _____ hands.
    A. serendipitous
    B. vernal
    C. luminous

13. The young king was vested with _____ powers.
    A. cumbersome
    B. unflappable
    C. plenary

14. Researchers unearthed an _____ language when they discovered the cave drawings.
    A. archaic
    B. indomitable
    C. unspeakable

15. The _____ ballerina dazzled the audience with her physical dexterity.
    A. lithe
    B. presumptuous
    C. festive

16. Through generous donations, the philanthropic family _____ the performing arts in their community.
    A. espoused
    B. gibed
    C. patronized

17. At the bargaining table, the union representative _____ the employees' demands.
    A. reiterated
    B. imbued
    C. discerned

18. The newly-elected councilman was a _____ to the world of politics.
    A. protégé
    B. neophyte
    C. charlatan

19. A spokesman for the embittered opposition launched a lengthy _____ against the government for increasing taxes to purportedly whitewash years of rampant spending.
    A. penchant
    B. diatribe
    C. melee

20. Whenever she recounted the birth of her child, she would become _____ and melancholy.
    A. remiss
    B. mawkish
    C. ductile

(For Quiz Answers, see Answer Section at the end of the book)

SAT & College Dictionary Workbook Quiz 37

[On a separate sheet of paper, write down the letter of the word that best fits in the blank to create a complete and meaningful sentence.]

1. Although his older sister enjoyed the poignant love story, he found the slow-paced movie too _____ for his taste.
   A. bland
   B. hapless
   C. obstinate

2. Unless they want to receive a single lump-sum payment, lottery winners are paid in annual _____ over a period of a lifetime.
   A. covenants
   B. increments
   C. accolades

3. Two constant days of torrential rain _____ the low-lying village.
   A. inundated
   B. circumscribed
   C. parched

4. Louise L'Amour was a _____ writer of the Old West novels.
   A. belligerent
   B. prolific
   C. vicarious

5. A tornado's _____ path makes it especially dangerous.
   A. blasphemous
   B. wayward
   C. pallid

6. At the battle of Little Bighorn, the Sioux Indians _____ the broken promises by the white man by brutally defeating General Custer and the men of the 7th Cavalry.
   A. avenged
   B. indoctrinated
   C. objurgated

7. A safety inspection revealed the presence of _____ termites.
   A. beneficial
   B. subterranean
   C. factitious

8. When taking a vacation, it _____ a person to confirm hotel lodgings one final time to avoid unexpected problems.
   A. behooves
   B. embellishes
   C. satiates

9. Television viewers were repulsed by the immodest sheik's _____ display of his wealth.
   A. garish
   B. derisive
   C. rustic

10. Saving money in advance _____ the need to later on assume a high-interest loan to pay for college.
    A. obviates
    B. forsakes
    C. derides

11. Two prisoners escaped as a result of overly _____ guards who erroneously felt they had the cells well secured.
    A. strident
    B. pragmatic
    C. complacent

12. Henry Kissinger was revered for his _____ political and diplomatic insight.
    A. wizened
    B. perspicacious
    C. metaphorical

13. Henry David Thoreau _____ himself for weeks in his cabin near Walden Pond.
    A. secluded
    B. interred
    C. hampered

14. In 1863, Abraham Lincoln issued a decree _____ all slaves.
    A. emancipating
    B. usurping
    C. censoring

15. In a _____ display of anger for not being given the first piece of cake, the boy threw his sister's serving into the garbage can.
    A. maladroit
    B. spiteful
    C. laconic

16. In an effort to achieve _____, many businesses have raised women's salaries faster than those of their male counterparts.
    A. duplicity
    B. parity
    C. equanimity

17. The professor was a very _____ woman who found little time for frivolity or tomfoolery.
    A. perverse
    B. staid
    C. whimsical

18. During the violent civil uprising, fleeing families sought _____ in neighboring villages.
    A. ken
    B. asylum
    C. privation

19. The hikers unexpectedly came across a _____ hut in the middle of nowhere.
    A. ramshackle
    B. haggard
    C. paltry

20. To impress the girls at school, the self-absorbed _____ drove up in his father's fancy sports car.
    A. culprit
    B. poseur
    C. menace

(For Quiz Answers, see Answer Section at the end of the book)

SAT & College Dictionary Workbook Quiz 38

[On a separate sheet of paper, write down the letter of the word that best fits in the blank to create a complete and meaningful sentence.]

1. The congresswoman was _____ to support a cost-cutting proposal that would adversely affect employment in her home state.
   A. incredulous
   B. disgruntled
   C. loath

2. Signs cautioned against proceeding further along the _____ trail.
   A. precocious
   B. hazardous
   C. molten

3. While on his diet, he made it a point to _____ dairy products.
   A. squander
   B. eschew
   C. actuate

4. The lengthy illness greatly _____ the elderly patient.
   A. subsidized
   B. imprecated
   C. debilitated

5. With less than a minute remaining, the test administrator issued a _____ reminder for students to conclude their essays.
   A. salutary
   B. mordant
   C. terse

6. The youngster completed the challenging task with amazing _____.
   A. celerity
   B. indignation
   C. plenitude

7. To _____ the embarrassing mishap, the airline management offered a free round trip for each passenger whose luggage had been stolen at the unattended baggage claim station.
   A. rectify
   B. deify
   C. conciliate

8. Speeches by the political _____ stirred up the passion of revolt in his young and malleable audience.
   A. demagogue
   B. reprobate
   C. sycophant

9. Money is _____; human life is not.
   A. redolent
   B. expendable
   C. objective

10. His parents would not _____ any foul language spoken in the house.
    A. retaliate
    B. condone
    C. appropriate

11. In his latest attempt at twisted humor, the satirist featured _____ cartoon characters with multiple eyes and no feet.
    A. grotesque
    B. aesthetic
    C. impoverished

12. Madame Pele is an _____ representation of the Hawaiian volcano goddess.
    A. anthropomorphic
    B. empirical
    C. ulterior

13. Her blind date turned out to be an _____ bore.
    A. insufferable
    B. eminent
    C. affable

14. In poetry, success can only be achieved when all _____ words are omitted.
    A. concomitant
    B. superfluous
    C. wary

15. Because she suffered from _____, she avoided high places.
    A. misgivings
    B. anxiety
    C. vertigo

16. Out of _____ to the elder statesman's senior position, the junior senator allowed the more experienced one to present his views first.
    A. deference
    B. stamina
    C. animadversion

17. Practicing daily helped the young prodigy _____ his piano skills.
    A. peruse
    B. hone
    C. subsidize

18. Having climbed the first thousand feet, the hikers readied themselves for the _____ ascent of the steepest part of the mountain.
    A. arduous
    B. laconic
    C. sapid

19. Their new house sported a red brick _____ with blue and white trim.
    A. apex
    B. façade
    C. caricature

20. The youngster could not grasp the _____ of the adult conversation.
    A. gist
    B. outset
    C. forte

(For Quiz Answers, see Answer Section at the end of the book)

SAT & College Dictionary Workbook Quiz 39

[On a separate sheet of paper, write down the letter of the word that best fits in the blank to create a complete and meaningful sentence.]

1. Copernicus met with much resistance from the _____ society of his day when he proposed that the Earth revolved around the Sun.
    A. sprawling
    B. polychromatic
    C. dogmatic

2. Many people acknowledge crime as an unwelcome _____ of society's emphasis on financial success.
    A. harbinger
    B. inquietude
    C. parameter

3. Over a dozen _____ scientists attended the international symposium.
    A. arrogant
    B. eminent
    C. vigilant

4. Napoleon led his troops with an _____ certainty few dared challenge.
    A. indolent
    B. unconscionable
    C. authoritative

5. Several students covered their ears during the _____ wail of the alarm bell.
    A. luminous
    B. wayward
    C. strident

6. Any hostage situation is tense and unpredictably _____.
    A. uncouth
    B. aghast
    C. volatile

7. Grading papers can be a _____ task.
    A. contentious
    B. dire
    C. tedious

8. The two drinking buddies were asked to leave the establishment after they initiated a barroom _____.
    A. conundrum
    B. mien
    C. fracas

9. Reluctantly, the lone holdout _____ to the majority opinion.
    A. feigned
    B. derided
    C. assented

10. Critics had little good to say about the _____ and shopworn boy-meets-girl situation comedy.
    A. peremptory
    B. superlative
    C. insipid

11. Many young fans _____ their favorite rock stars by dressing and talking in similar fashion.
    A. rebuff
    B. emulate
    C. mulct

12. The movie's opening scene featured the _____ beauty of the verdant mountainside.
    A. indigent
    B. vehement
    C. rustic

13. Few could ever have imagined what the _____ of the fortuitous meeting would be.
    A. upshot
    B. kith
    C. hyperbole

14. The _____ man had difficult purchasing well-fitting clothes.
    A. risible
    B. imperious
    C. corpulent

15. When told that his ship was needed to aid in a rescue at sea, the captain immediately _____ all shore leaves.
    A. rescinded
    B. dissipated
    C. bestowed

16. Constant bickering fostered _____ amongst the committee members.
    A. acumen
    B. savoir faire
    C. discord

17. With perseverance and dedication, a person can _____ any obstacle.
    A. beseech
    B. surmount
    C. defy

18. When scolded by his teacher, the _____ lad defended his misguided behavior.
    A. unequivocal
    B. explicit
    C. impudent

19. Nothing could be done to stop the lava flow from its _____ path headed directly towards the center of town.
    A. inexorable
    B. stolid
    C. truculent

20. After years of stress dealing with city slickers, the doctor relocated to a more idyllic location where he found solace amongst the _____ country folk.
    A. ingenuous
    B. pellucid
    C. apocryphal

(For Quiz Answers, see Answer Section at the end of the book)

SAT & College Dictionary Workbook Quiz 40

[On a separate sheet of paper, write down the letter of the word that best fits in the blank to create a complete and meaningful sentence.]

1. The wealthy businessman _____ to speak a few moments to the group of youngsters.
   A. mobilized
   B. refuted
   C. condescended

2. The scoundrel's flattery was merely a _____ to gain the gullible woman's confidence and the keys to her house.
   A. constraint
   B. ploy
   C. vendetta

3. Unexpectedly heavy turnout at the polls signaled a _____ call for political change.
   A. clarion
   B. gossamer
   C. marginal

4. The vivacious emcee had an ingratiatingly _____ personality.
   A. prepossessing
   B. succulent
   C. inimical

5. The trio _____ to smuggle diamonds through customs.
   A. colluded
   B. eschewed
   C. predicated

6. As the minutes passed, the young man's interest in the political discussion _____.
   A. defamed
   B. waned
   C. satiated

7. The sailor's _____ comment was met with a sharp slap from the barmaid.
   A. indifferent
   B. salacious
   C. empirical

8. After the infamous attack upon Pearl Harbor took place, President Franklin Roosevelt made a _____ decision to declare war on Japan.
   A. momentous
   B. supernumerary
   C. histrionic

9. The peasants were destined to forever tread upon the _____ of the animals they followed.
   A. ordure
   B. succor
   C. aggregate

10. The inmate viewed the time spent behind bars as his personal _____.
    A. anxiety
    B. purgatory
    C. volition

11. The powerful nation suffered an _____ defeat at the hands of their tiny neighbor to the south.
    A. aureate
    B. ignominious
    C. emblematic

12. Nostradamus made several _____ predictions in the sixteenth century that have come eerily true four hundred years later.
    A. empyreal
    B. insipid
    C. ominous

13. The sudden shortage of oil had far-reaching economic _____.
    A. longevity
    B. repercussions
    C. inquietude

14. The kissing bandit _____ the authorities by leaving behind no clues.
    A. ameliorated
    B. renounced
    C. confounded

15. Many feel that during times of spiraling gasoline prices, riding the bus is a _____ option to driving the car to work.
    A. seemly
    B. viable
    C. euphemistic

16. Calling the sensationalized farce a "self-fulfilling prophecy" epitomized the critic's _____ wit.
    A. docile
    B. winsome
    C. mordant

17. A _____ animal often has little chance of survival in the wild.
    A. puny
    B. glacial
    C. viable

18. The malcontent _____ his brother's executive position.
    A. coveted
    B. ascertained
    C. subjugated

19. An _____ resolution brought closure to the month-long divorce proceedings.
    A. amicable
    B. inordinate
    C. objectionable

20. Automatic suspension from school was meted out for any _____ involving cheating.
    A. infraction
    B. aversion
    C. debacle

(For Quiz Answers, see Answer Section at the end of the book)

SAT & College Dictionary Workbook Quiz 41

[On a separate sheet of paper, write down the letter of the word that best fits in the blank to create a complete and meaningful sentence.]

1. "Haste makes waste" is a _____ epigram.
   A. pithy
   B. defunct
   C. gruff

2. A bulldozer was brought in to raze the _____ building.
   A. stalwart
   B. decrepit
   C. putrefied

3. The _____ lad possessed a wealth of historical knowledge.
   A. listless
   B. impecunious
   C. retentive

4. The school's board of directors voted to dismiss the football coach due to his inexcusably _____ treatment of his players after a loss to their arch rivals.
   A. compulsive
   B. zany
   C. reprehensible

5. The _____ businessman tricked his partner into signing over a majority stake in the lucrative enterprise.
   A. fail-safe
   B. headstrong
   C. unscrupulous

6. Hiding in a drainage ditch, the crafty fox _____ the hungry dogs.
   A. simulated
   B. avenged
   C. eluded

7. Having lost their luggage, the travelers found themselves in a most uncomfortable and troubling _____.
   A. savoir faire
   B. predicament
   C. effigy

8. Due to mismanagement, the state found itself enmeshed in an inextricable financial _____.
   A. accord
   B. exigency
   C. ramification

9. At the birthday party, a professional clown _____ the young children.
   A. procrastinated
   B. simulated
   C. diverted

10. People in religiously-sensitive small towns tend to be _____ in their beliefs.
    A. diffident
    B. hidebound
    C. pandemic

11. Independent individuals generally have a stronger _____ toward cats than dogs.
    A. inclination
    B. pathos
    C. attrition

12. It is not polite to cast _____ on another's character.
    A. aspersions
    B. vagaries
    C. plaudits

13. His occupation was that of an _____ salesman.
    A. overt
    B. effete
    C. itinerant

14. Turning professional _____ a golfer from participating in amateur tournaments.
    A. precludes
    B. disabuses
    C. forgoes

15. Announcing his wedding plans during a gala family reunion proved most _____.
    A. fulsome
    B. splenetic
    C. apropos

16. For generations the Hatfields and McCoys perpetuated a rancorous _____, until they one day finally reconciled their differences.
    A. rendezvous
    B. kin
    C. vendetta

17. The coach's career reached its _____ as the team found itself without a single victory.
    A. zenith
    B. girth
    C. nadir

18. The _____ woman comported herself with an aristocratic air.
    A. genteel
    B. brazen
    C. risible

19. By exacting strict penalties for tiny infractions, the king found yet more ways to _____ his subjects of their gold.
    A. devastate
    B. mulct
    C. impute

20. As a result of his _____, the young boy soon found himself noticeably overweight.
    A. viridity
    B. gluttony
    C. asperity

(For Quiz Answers, see Answer Section at the end of the book)

SAT & College Dictionary Workbook Quiz 42

[On a separate sheet of paper, write down the letter of the word that best fits in the blank to create a complete and meaningful sentence.]

1. The _____ of the craftsman's work often determines the value of the end product.
   A. nicety
   B. temerity
   C. effigy

2. Four large bedrooms and a _____ living area helped the house sell quickly when placed on the real estate market.
   A. commodious
   B. populous
   C. fortuitous

3. The two _____ comedy acts played in different parts of the arena.
   A. gauche
   B. concurrent
   C. momentous

4. From her earliest childhood, she was an _____ and devoted tennis fan.
   A. indisposed
   B. avid
   C. uncouth

5. Sugar is _____ in water.
   A. dilatory
   B. acute
   C. soluble

6. At the evening cookout, the boys and girls listened intently as the storyteller narrated a _____ tale of a friendly dragon.
   A. sordid
   B. whimsical
   C. consequential

7. When asked whether she wanted to go to the movies or stay home, the girl shrugged her shoulders in an _____ manner.
   A. agile
   B. obsequious
   C. indifferent

8. During the violent earthquake, only the most well-constructed buildings remained _____.
   A. intact
   B. stolid
   C. conspicuous

9. Years of feuding festered an _____ between the two families.
   A. animus
   B. idiosyncrasy
   C. obeisance

10. After the presentation, one enthusiastic lad _____ his deep interest in the subject by heading directly for the library to undertake additional research.
    A. evinced
    B. waned
    C. colluded

11. The young man wore a most _____ suit and tie to church.
    A. becoming
    B. ephemeral
    C. salacious

12. Many citizens of third-world nations live under _____ and life-threatening conditions.
    A. eccentric
    B. impoverished
    C. languid

13. The helpless boat was sucked into the merciless _____.
    A. maelstrom
    B. conflagration
    C. surfeit

14. The sixteenth-century galleon was refurbished with careful attention paid to preserve the original design's _____.
    A. minutiae
    B. alliance
    C. symmetry

15. Chivalrous knights from near and far sought the hand of the beautiful and _____ princess.
    A. chaste
    B. impecunious
    C. pliant

16. After he was fired, the _____ man spread malicious rumors regarding his former employer.
    A. blithe
    B. scrupulous
    C. vindictive

17. People in their nineties are usually rather _____.
    A. concupiscent
    B. idyllic
    C. frail

18. The lad's _____ attempts to persuade his folks to let him attend the carnival left him angry and frustrated.
    A. rampant
    B. bootless
    C. inconsiderate

19. Relations between the two neighboring countries began to deteriorate after two months of _____ peace negotiations.
    A. sanctimonious
    B. feckless
    C. artful

20. Although the ski resort offered a challenging slope for experienced skiers, it also had a more modest one for _____.
    A. adversaries
    B. novices
    C. poseurs

(For Quiz Answers, see Answer Section at the end of the book)

SAT & College Dictionary Workbook Quiz 43

[On a separate sheet of paper, write down the letter of the word that best fits in the blank to create a complete and meaningful sentence.]

1. Philosophers often engage in highly theoretical discussions that _____ the boundaries of most people's understanding.
   A. commend
   B. transcend
   C. dispel

2. Left unchecked, rabbits will _____ at a remarkable rate.
   A. proliferate
   B. vociferate
   C. expostulate

3. To be more easily spotted in the crowd, the girl wore _____ colors.
   A. rarefied
   B. conspicuous
   C. specious

4. Fed up with his frenetic and unfulfilling lifestyle, the stockbroker resigned his executive position to pursue a more personally pleasing _____ existence.
   A. contiguous
   B. expeditious
   C. pastoral

5. A life spiraling out of control was leading the lost soul on a path doomed to _____.
   A. perdition
   B. senescence
   C. deference

6. In the tiny village ravaged by war, one could hear the _____ of grieving widows.
   A. inkling
   B. ululation
   C. tintinnabulation

7. The man's humble and unobtrusive _____ endeared him to strangers.
   A. animosity
   B. vitality
   C. demeanor

8. The professor's _____ expression left little doubt that he was not the sociable type.
   A. incongruous
   B. pliable
   C. dour

9. Once the letter was typed up, the secretary gave it a _____ review for any obvious errors.
   A. lethargic
   B. cursory
   C. rash

10. Though no word was uttered, there was an _____ agreement between the leaders of the rival gangs to ease hostilities and seek a peaceful coexistence.
    A. implicit
    B. august
    C. unimpeachable

11. Sunlight passed through the tiny _____ in the wall.
    A. invective
    B. talisman
    C. aperture

12. The overbearing upstart exhibited an egotistical _____ that rankled his peers.
    A. nonpareil
    B. hauteur
    C. malaise

13. An _____ investment is prerequisite for any business startup.
    A. affluent
    B. initial
    C. exemplary

14. The controversial talk-show host was _____ with boos and hisses during his appearance at the political rally.
    A. fortified
    B. quashed
    C. assailed

15. Princess Diana was regarded as a _____ of grace and beauty.
    A. neophyte
    B. paragon
    C. façade

16. The gifted young performer possessed an _____ spirit that destined him to eventual stardom.
    A. indomitable
    B. obsequious
    C. elegiac

17. The avid young reader had a _____ for mystery novels.
    A. predilection
    B. niche
    C. gluttony

18. Susan B. Anthony was an early _____ of social change.
    A. wastrel
    B. exponent
    C. quisling

19. The _____ man vowed never again to drive after having consumed alcohol.
    A. petty
    B. inexorable
    C. contrite

20. Hitchhiking across the country, the _____ group ranged in ages from fourteen to forty-five.
    A. germane
    B. motley
    C. ductile

(For Quiz Answers, see Answer Section at the end of the book)

SAT & College Dictionary Workbook Quiz 44

[On a separate sheet of paper, write down the letter of the word that best fits in the blank to create a complete and meaningful sentence.]

1. Coal miners must endure _____ working conditions deep underground.
   A. arbitrary
   B. diurnal
   C. infernal

2. Most universities offer students a _____ of undergraduate courses from which to choose.
   A. diversity
   B. niche
   C. tenet

3. It is _____ for a smoker to tell others that smoking is bad for one's health.
   A. ambiguous
   B. inexplicable
   C. hypocritical

4. Upon seeing the spectral vision, Scrooge _____ with fright.
   A. scarified
   B. blanched
   C. protracted

5. _____ and kin were invited to the reunion celebration.
   A. Kith
   B. Charlatan
   C. Progenitors

6. The teacher found it very difficult to persuade the _____ boy to discuss his thoughts openly in class discussions.
   A. taciturn
   B. staunch
   C. gregarious

7. Moving the _____ old cabinet proved quite a challenge.
   A. rustic
   B. cumbersome
   C. moribund

8. The exotic plant was _____ to the small chain of tropical islands.
   A. urban
   B. endemic
   C. reclusive

9. Large imitation pearls adorned the _____ dress.
   A. demure
   B. gaudy
   C. raucous

10. It is an ignominious act to _____ one's friends in their hour of need.
    A. capitulate
    B. forsake
    C. expropriate

11. His former Republican constituents branded the senator an _____ for switching political parties.
    A. apostate
    B. epiphany
    C. upshot

12. New and irrefutable evidence in the case clearly _____ the two lead suspects.
    A. corroborated
    B. extirpated
    C. incriminated

13. A devoted legion of fans _____ the rock star.
    A. deified
    B. advocated
    C. polarized

14. The mouse was unable to find its way through the _____ maze.
    A. desolate
    B. impassive
    C. labyrinthine

15. Much to his _____, the aspiring basketball player was cut from the varsity squad.
    A. proclivity
    B. fidelity
    C. chagrin

16. Despite her best efforts to control her weight, she _____ to temptation by eating an extra piece of pie.
    A. complied
    B. deferred
    C. succumbed

17. The thirteenth-century Mongols _____ their enemies as they extended their rule across the Asian continent.
    A. dissented
    B. vanquished
    C. comprised

18. It soon became clear that any attempt to persuade her parents to let her borrow the car would be _____.
    A. hostile
    B. oppressive
    C. futile

19. Without his glasses, he could not _____ whether the flight number was 65 or 85.
    A. mitigate
    B. refute
    C. discern

20. Having missed the scheduled appointment due to car trouble, the college applicant felt obliged to write a _____ letter to the admissions counselor.
    A. hidebound
    B. triumphal
    C. deprecatory

(For Quiz Answers, see Answer Section at the end of the book)

SAT & College Dictionary Workbook Quiz 45

[On a separate sheet of paper, write down the letter of the word that best fits in the blank to create a complete and meaningful sentence.]

1. In the spring, the orchard was alive with the trees' ripe fruit and lush _____.
   A. milieu
   B. purview
   C. foliage

2. The gubernatorial candidate threatened to sue the newspaper for _____ his character in a disparaging editorial.
   A. impugning
   B. expurgating
   C. condoning

3. The philanderer found himself caught in an _____ web of lies.
   A. unobtrusive
   B. abysmal
   C. inextricable

4. The joyous parents experienced the _____ of watching their child take her first steps.
   A. incursion
   B. schism
   C. bliss

5. The accused spy endured the unremitting _____ from those who had earlier trusted him.
   A. obloquy
   B. aegis
   C. consternation

6. The hypnotized man gazed into the audience with a _____ stare.
   A. vacuous
   B. dissonant
   C. visceral

7. Jealousy is a _____ that afflicts all people, rich and poor.
   A. scourge
   B. panacea
   C. hardship

8. The religious cleric had a _____ notion that in his lifetime he would witness a world devoid of human conflict.
   A. dire
   B. ravenous
   C. chimerical

9. The doctor issued a favorable _____ regarding the patient's recovery.
   A. visage
   B. prognosis
   C. epitome

10. Bell-bottom pants were just another of the _____ fads of the 1960s.
    A. transitory
    B. bountiful
    C. jocose

11. Residents of the peaceful village _____ the violent acts perpetrated by their belligerent neighboring tribes.
    A. redoubled
    B. inculcated
    C. abhorred

12. The political speech proved more _____ than substantive.
    A. tautological
    B. integral
    C. puissant

13. Visual aids proved an _____ supplement to the lecturer's discussion.
    A. odious
    B. assiduous
    C. expedient

14. The marine biologist possessed _____ knowledge of whales and dolphins.
    A. extensive
    B. adamant
    C. mammoth

15. The _____ duck scurried about, frantically searching for her two missing ducklings.
    A. picaresque
    B. captious
    C. fretful

16. At the lavish buffet, guests were treated to a highly _____ and ambrosial feast.
    A. corpulent
    B. variegated
    C. palatable

17. Listening to the _____ words of a Shakespearean sonnet is an ethereal delight.
    A. clandestine
    B. mellifluous
    C. plenipotentiary

18. At a meeting, several inmates _____ their displeasure regarding overcrowding in the penitentiary.
    A. vociferated
    B. bickered
    C. correlated

19. The castle ghost was said to _____ itself in the guise of a restless knight.
    A. manifest
    B. relinquish
    C. proscribe

20. Military reinforcements were brought in to _____ the peasant uprising.
    A. quash
    B. curtail
    C. dispense

(For Quiz Answers, see Answer Section at the end of the book)

SAT & College Dictionary Workbook Quiz 46

[On a separate sheet of paper, write down the letter of the word that best fits in the blank to create a complete and meaningful sentence.]

1. In a cabin nestled deep in the woods, the children encountered a _____ old hag.
   A. resplendent
   B. wizened
   C. pernicious

2. After the military coup, a _____ government was established.
   A. provisional
   B. vulnerable
   C. fundamental

3. With _____ determination, she completed the arduous task in only one day.
   A. ingenuous
   B. dogged
   C. posthumous

4. The _____ youngster talked back to the principal.
   A. quiescent
   B. brash
   C. impeccable

5. In the famous Al Capp cartoon, Brutus was Popeye's _____ foe.
   A. redoubtable
   B. feeble
   C. indisposed

6. Art galleries display paintings by _____ artists, past and present.
   A. renowned
   B. comprehensive
   C. polychromatic

7. Two years of high school mathematics are usually _____ for enrolling in a chemistry class.
   A. ubiquitous
   B. emphatic
   C. prerequisite

8. The suspect _____ through the back door just as the authorities arrived at his house.
   A. subverted
   B. leavened
   C. decamped

9. John Carradine was a renowned twentieth-century _____.
   A. juggernaut
   B. mountebank
   C. thespian

10. The drama teacher had absolutely no luck inspiring the _____ teenager to convey his feelings in a theatrically expressive manner.
    A. testy
    B. latent
    C. stolid

11. An _____ judge of character, the captain knew to whom to delegate crucial responsibilities.
    A. astute
    B. enterprising
    C. obligatory

12. The _____ youngster didn't realize it was impolite to call the teacher by her first name.
    A. lithe
    B. sallow
    C. callow

13. The village's population was decimated by the virulent _____.
    A. ambience
    B. surfeit
    C. contagion

14. The investment _____ interest at the rate of 5% per annum.
    A. eventuated
    B. sated
    C. accrued

15. The colonists grew increasingly _____ as they longed for independence from their motherland.
    A. lithe
    B. restive
    C. indomitable

16. After being turned down for a promotion he had counted on for months, the man became _____.
    A. inviolable
    B. disconsolate
    C. oppressive

17. The Sahara Desert is home to numerous _____ tribes.
    A. incessant
    B. transitory
    C. nomadic

18. The young girl embroidered the dress with the _____ precision of a master seamstress.
    A. deft
    B. ornate
    C. adverse

19. Signs warned visitors not to _____ the stream during the rainy season.
    A. traverse
    B. sojourn
    C. cede

20. Before the public screening of the movie, a few _____ comments were made praising the efforts of the film crew.
    A. sultry
    B. embryonic
    C. prefatory

(For Quiz Answers, see Answer Section at the end of the book)

SAT & College Dictionary Workbook Quiz 47

[On a separate sheet of paper, write down the letter of the word that best fits in the blank to create a complete and meaningful sentence.]

1. The _____ man would not admit to his obvious error in judgment.
   A. obstinate
   B. inalienable
   C. malleable

2. The constant noise of the jackhammers soon became _____ to nearby tenants.
   A. intolerable
   B. scathing
   C. remiss

3. After the suspects jumped into the getaway car, a high-speed chase _____.
   A. beguiled
   B. instilled
   C. ensued

4. Fidel Castro enjoyed _____ control over Cuba during his long reign as President.
   A. dictatorial
   B. tremulous
   C. ancillary

5. Comedian Danny Kaye had a pleasant _____ with children of all ages.
   A. rapport
   B. propinquity
   C. hiatus

6. Christopher Columbus' journey for a passage to the East led to a _____ discovery.
   A. prerequisite
   B. serendipitous
   C. robust

7. With rifle in hand, the cattle rancher confronted the _____.
   A. interloper
   B. parameter
   C. apologist

8. To help strengthen one's cardiovascular system, a _____ of rigorous daily exercise is often recommended.
   A. physiognomy
   B. tirade
   C. regimen

9. The _____ lad could not be trusted.
   A. doughty
   B. mendacious
   C. soluble

10. Diversifying their selection helped the candy company _____ its sagging sales.
    A. jeer
    B. repress
    C. bolster

11. The persistent defense attorney _____ at every point raised by the prosecutor during the trial.
    A. caviled
    B. gamboled
    C. proffered

12. A bout of the flu left the news reporter appearing _____ and sickly.
    A. congenial
    B. pallid
    C. sultry

13. After the eruption, _____ lava flowed down the side of the volcano.
    A. terrestrial
    B. venomous
    C. molten

14. Surrounded by wolves, the campers found themselves in a _____ predicament.
    A. precarious
    B. sagacious
    C. becoming

15. Having slept poorly the night before, the man was unusually _____ throughout the day.
    A. adept
    B. peevish
    C. undaunted

16. Eyewitness accounts _____ the existence of a large alligator in the nearby lake.
    A. appended
    B. induced
    C. confirmed

17. The _____ couple complained about everything the waiter did.
    A. fractious
    B. iconoclastic
    C. mnemonic

18. The suspect was held under _____ until the police arrived.
    A. aplomb
    B. similitude
    C. duress

19. The comedian's bawdy and _____ anecdotes were not well-received by the prudish audience.
    A. implicit
    B. risqué
    C. sedate

20. The _____ of the bulky package was forty-eight inches.
    A. outset
    B. dearth
    C. girth

(For Quiz Answers, see Answer Section at the end of the book)

SAT & College Dictionary Workbook Quiz 48

[On a separate sheet of paper, write down the letter of the word that best fits in the blank to create a complete and meaningful sentence.]

1. The bearded man projected a kindly _____.
   A. legerdemain
   B. countenance
   C. ruse

2. Whenever he did not get things his way, the _____ lad would throw a temper tantrum.
   A. devious
   B. petulant
   C. amorous

3. The team performed a _____ swimming exercise.
   A. synchronous
   B. grandiose
   C. practicable

4. A second job is always a viable option to _____ the family's income.
   A. augment
   B. underscore
   C. expurgate

5. To leaven the tense atmosphere, the diplomat interjected a _____ anecdote.
   A. redoubtable
   B. tangible
   C. jocular

6. Approaching fire trucks _____ the skittish zoo animals.
   A. lamented
   B. repleted
   C. agitated

7. Others felt the lad's mistake did not _____ such a severe scolding.
   A. verify
   B. compel
   C. warrant

8. From the promontory, the hikers viewed the _____ drop to the ocean below.
   A. precipitous
   B. herculean
   C. irreproachable

9. An _____ plan was conceived to capture the escaped convicts.
   A. orotund
   B. artful
   C. equitable

10. Spring is heralded by the _____ sprouting of flowers.
    A. blithe
    B. incipient
    C. odoriferous

11. The weekly series' increasingly _____ plots presaged the show's imminent cancellation.
    A. placid
    B. jaded
    C. felicitous

12. The date of the championship game remained _____ until transportation could be secured.
    A. pending
    B. intact
    C. awry

13. Prior to having his breakfast, her husband was particularly _____.
    A. plaintive
    B. sylvan
    C. churlish

14. A _____ party was brought in to help negotiate a fair and equitable compromise.
    A. disinterested
    B. munificent
    C. quizzical

15. The _____ trust was renowned for its support of academic arts through scholarships and grants.
    A. comprehensible
    B. stygian
    C. eleemosynary

16. The man found himself in a most peculiar and upsetting _____ when he realized he had taken home one child that was not his own.
    A. purgatory
    B. coterie
    C. imbroglio

17. The _____ meadows inspired the artist to compose a paean to country living.
    A. exiguous
    B. infernal
    C. verdant

18. The acrobat performed the daring feat with dazzling _____ and amazing ease.
    A. éclat
    B. approbation
    C. panacea

19. Due to an _____ flaw in the escape plan, the entire venture was not practicable.
    A. execrable
    B. auxiliary
    C. inherent

20. In his reply to constituents, the beleaguered councilman laced his comments with _____ praise for the integrity of his accuser, who herself was the target of similar allegations.
    A. ironic
    B. patent
    C. capricious

(For Quiz Answers, see Answer Section at the end of the book)

SAT & College Dictionary Workbook Quiz 49

[On a separate sheet of paper, write down the letter of the word that best fits in the blank to create a complete and meaningful sentence.]

1. Most scientists lend no _____ to tales of alien abduction.
   A. angst
   B. credence
   C. rigor

2. Riding his skateboard in the office was one of the eccentric executive's many _____.
   A. quirks
   B. peregrinations
   C. guises

3. Jurors had difficulty _____ the witnesses' vastly differing accounts of the incident.
   A. correlating
   B. obfuscating
   C. arraying

4. Throughout his illustrious career, Rudolf Nureyev performed ballet with unparalleled artistry and _____.
   A. sloth
   B. integrity
   C. panache

5. The _____ youngster made friends with everyone he met.
   A. opportune
   B. sanguinary
   C. affable

6. The randy sailor _____ what the hostess meant when told that it was getting late.
   A. confounded
   B. misconstrued
   C. engendered

7. Protesters called the one-sided trial a _____ of justice.
   A. metamorphosis
   B. travesty
   C. pariah

8. Completion of the _____ construction project was not expected for at least two more years.
   A. forbidding
   B. mammoth
   C. comprehensible

9. The _____ David slew the giant Goliath.
   A. hardy
   B. morbid
   C. nomadic

10. The hairy animal was _____, though it did resemble a bear in its gait.
    A. hortatory
    B. nondescript
    C. boorish

11. The captain issued a _____ for all crewmen to return immediately to the ship.
    A. jeremiad
    B. directive
    C. pantheon

12. Locked out of his car, the puzzled man was unable to _____ where he had last placed his keys.
    A. delegate
    B. exonerate
    C. recollect

13. Spectators marveled at the _____ athletes performing in the acrobatics competition.
    A. limber
    B. surly
    C. florid

14. The traitor was accused of _____ with the enemy.
    A. consorting
    B. ascertaining
    C. wheedling

15. After conversing with his assistant over the telephone for nearly an hour, the head coach decided that the matter needed to be further discussed _____.
    A. quid pro quo
    B. carte blanche
    C. vis-à-vis

16. The _____ feast was fit for a king.
    A. ambrosial
    B. exhaustive
    C. obstreperous

17. His crime of sending documents to the enemy was _____ to treason.
    A. divisive
    B. paramount
    C. tantamount

18. While everyone else at the party was having fun, the snubbed lad sat alone _____ and dejected.
    A. glum
    B. infatuated
    C. abominable

19. When asked by his wife for his _____ opinion, he admitted that the dress did not look good on her.
    A. indisposed
    B. sadistic
    C. candid

20. Inner-city slums are a magnet for those whose lives are enslaved in _____.
    A. éclat
    B. affinity
    C. penury

(For Quiz Answers, see Answer Section at the end of the book)

SAT & College Dictionary Workbook Quiz 50

[On a separate sheet of paper, write down the letter of the word that best fits in the blank to create a complete and meaningful sentence.]

1. All the guests at the party were charmed by the host's _____ young daughter.
   A. funereal
   B. supercilious
   C. amiable

2. Clouds offered the picnickers a brief _____ from the intense summer sun.
   A. levity
   B. respite
   C. strife

3. The _____ trial of the international spies brought worldwide attention.
   A. plebeian
   B. treacherous
   C. infamous

4. Unfortunately, many Viet Nam veterans found themselves treated as _____ upon their return to civilian life.
   A. pariahs
   B. despots
   C. refugees

5. The week-long _____ caused total ruination of the region's harvest.
   A. tocsin
   B. deluge
   C. philippic

6. John Locke's essays present a _____ analysis of the proper role of government in society.
   A. trenchant
   B. meek
   C. prolix

7. Upon entering, incoming inmates first noticed the prison's _____ and forbidding appearance.
   A. jocund
   B. stark
   C. perilous

8. The unpopular ruler was hanged in _____, but the police removed the dummy before the leader arrived.
   A. apocalypse
   B. effigy
   C. symmetry

9. _____ circumstances moved the jury to find the defendant guilty of the lesser charge.
   A. Alienable
   B. Extenuating
   C. Magniloquent

10. Declaring war lies within the _____ of the President.
    A. purview
    B. foray
    C. exodus

11. Junior employees were _____ by senior staff into participating in the financially risky investment.
    A. forestalled
    B. lambasted
    C. coerced

12. The gymnastics coach was a _____ and demanding taskmaster.
    A. cohesive
    B. lucid
    C. stern

13. Bad weather _____ construction of the bridge.
    A. provoked
    B. impeded
    C. confuted

14. The _____ lass skipped gleefully home.
    A. blithe
    B. hallowed
    C. ribald

15. Othello was a man of _____ complexion.
    A. disheveled
    B. swarthy
    C. impassioned

16. The fox is a _____ creature known for its ability to evade capture.
    A. wily
    B. pusillanimous
    C. culpable

17. Amazingly, the two childhood friends met twenty years later in a _____ meeting at Waikiki Beach.
    A. meteoric
    B. salacious
    C. fortuitous

18. Sociably _____, the affable starlet soon became the center of attraction at the ball.
    A. straitlaced
    B. capricious
    C. garrulous

19. Anticipating the bravado typical of her former suitors, the woman was pleasantly surprised by the young man's _____ humility.
    A. jejune
    B. prosaic
    C. artless

20. The irate husband _____ his words of anger so as to not regret them later.
    A. minced
    B. remonstrated
    C. divulged

(For Quiz Answers, see Answer Section at the end of the book)

SAT & College Dictionary Workbook Quiz 51

[On a separate sheet of paper, write down the letter of the word that best fits in the blank to create a complete and meaningful sentence.]

1. The recipient of the actor-of-the-year award accepted the honor with grace and _____.
   A. affectation
   B. suffrage
   C. humility

2. Many environmentalists _____ man's insensitivity toward protection of the rain forest.
   A. ruminate
   B. glean
   C. decry

3. His friends were _____ when told he had braved forty-foot seas in his tiny sailboat.
   A. incredulous
   B. haughty
   C. perspicuous

4. To create a more vivid picture of the loveliness of the tropical island, the author wrote in poetic _____.
   A. valor
   B. hyperbole
   C. affinity

5. When _____ by her boyfriend, the jilted woman sought swift revenge.
   A. condescended
   B. spurned
   C. dissented

6. True to his pledge of religious adherence, the man remained sexually _____ until after he was wed.
   A. abstinent
   B. sedulous
   C. inviolable

7. With her _____ wiles, the vixen had the sailors baying at her every whim.
   A. rigorous
   B. coy
   C. submissive

8. The _____ twig could not be easily snapped.
   A. upstanding
   B. tangible
   C. pliant

9. Marathon negotiations _____ a new and lasting peace agreement between the neighboring countries.
   A. attenuated
   B. effectuated
   C. ruminated

10. Meteorologists _____ to explain the unusual atmospheric conditions.
    A. endeavored
    B. augured
    C. purloined

11. In past centuries, those afflicted with leprosy were shunned and _____.
    A. controverted
    B. ostracized
    C. surmounted

12. On the eve of the play's debut, the cast members felt a high level of _____.
    A. anxiety
    B. hardship
    C. sangfroid

13. Hostage negotiations _____ as a result of mutual distrust.
    A. concatenated
    B. foundered
    C. bickered

14. A chronic kleptomaniac, he had an _____ compulsion to steal.
    A. artful
    B. obsessive
    C. esoteric

15. Three days of constant rainfall _____ the earth.
    A. saturated
    B. incapacitated
    C. decimated

16. Carpe diem poetry concerns itself with man's _____ pleasures.
    A. doctrinaire
    B. temporal
    C. mobile

17. The terrorists issued one last _____ before threatening to shoot the hostages.
    A. ultimatum
    B. initiative
    C. ordure

18. Many schizophrenics suffer from _____ of grandeur.
    A. subterfuge
    B. kudos
    C. delusions

19. With her children visiting the neighbors, the young mother was afforded a few precious moments of rest and _____.
    A. repose
    B. demise
    C. sloth

20. In the problem-solving approach, one must first establish through _____ the most appropriate steps to take to achieve the desired result.
    A. ratiocination
    B. presentiment
    C. discretion

(For Quiz Answers, see Answer Section at the end of the book)

SAT & College Dictionary Workbook Quiz 52

[On a separate sheet of paper, write down the letter of the word that best fits in the blank to create a complete and meaningful sentence.]

1. The highly controversial issue _____ the community.
   A. culminated
   B. polarized
   C. exculpated

2. Residents complained bitterly about the _____ odor coming from the nearby sewage-treatment plant.
   A. arable
   B. noisome
   C. diabolic

3. The helpless and _____ fawn clung to its mother.
   A. fearsome
   B. parochial
   C. intense

4. The brouhaha after the football game was an _____ display of poor sportsmanship.
   A. ethereal
   B. overt
   C. indefeasible

5. When his star player fouled out of the game, the coach _____ on his selection of a replacement.
   A. distended
   B. expostulated
   C. vacillated

6. Time _____ old grudges.
   A. forswears
   B. attenuates
   C. scarifies

7. By branding UFOs a figment of overactive imaginations, the teacher _____ the children's curiosity to learn more about extraterrestrial life.
   A. belied
   B. dismayed
   C. stultified

8. In many countries, _____ treatment of the poor is evidenced by a general lack of government-supported welfare programs.
   A. iniquitous
   B. punitive
   C. astute

9. Because the essay contained such muddled and _____ ideas, the instructor could not give it a passing grade.
   A. convoluted
   B. manifest
   C. intrepid

10. The vain socialite _____ her gold rings and fancy jewelry at the gala event.
    A. cajoled
    B. flaunted
    C. blanched

11. Eyewitness testimony _____ the defendant's account of the incident.
    A. belied
    B. excoriated
    C. occluded

12. The _____ gained notoriety for his dastardly acts of desecration.
    A. prodigy
    B. thespian
    C. miscreant

13. The Southern California earthquake wreaked _____ for millions of residents in 1994.
    A. havoc
    B. asylum
    C. menace

14. An _____ odor emitted by the geyser burned the tourists' eyes.
    A. iridescent
    B. acrid
    C. ungainly

15. Some of the Boy Scout mothers were _____ about their sons' safety during the overnight hike.
    A. disaffected
    B. solicitous
    C. lachrymose

16. Addressing a group of underachieving adolescents, the self-made millionaire alluded to his own _____ youth.
    A. wayward
    B. inflammatory
    C. emaciated

17. Audie Murphy was highly decorated for displaying _____ on the battlefield during World War II.
    A. zest
    B. jeopardy
    C. valor

18. At the literary seminar, the doctoral candidate presented a _____ analysis of the psychological workings of the Renaissance man.
    A. diabolic
    B. recondite
    C. frugal

19. She was habitually _____ in sending out her Christmas cards.
    A. dilatory
    B. mellifluous
    C. spry

20. It is better to _____ one's problems than try to run from them.
    A. confront
    B. reign
    C. succumb

(For Quiz Answers, see Answer Section at the end of the book)

SAT & College Dictionary Workbook Quiz 53

[On a separate sheet of paper, write down the letter of the word that best fits in the blank to create a complete and meaningful sentence.]

1. The general community takes a _____ view of so-called psychics.
   A. jaundiced
   B. fallacious
   C. clichéd

2. Through an unexpected _____, the once-mischievous child became a socially responsible and highly respected teenager.
   A. metamorphosis
   B. aspersion
   C. retrospect

3. The young actor resented being _____ by the more seasoned veterans.
   A. patronized
   B. deplored
   C. convened

4. Residents fled the town and its _____ economy for greener pastures and brighter employment opportunities.
   A. moribund
   B. devoid
   C. arable

5. The _____ mule refused to move.
   A. compulsory
   B. malicious
   C. restive

6. When visited by her grandmother, the lass exhibited behavior _____ of a young princess.
   A. histrionic
   B. becoming
   C. reputed

7. Unfortunately, more and more people in the workplace are finding themselves _____ by computers and other technological devices.
   A. supplanted
   B. confuted
   C. dumbfounded

8. Few believed the old coot's _____ claims of heroism during the war.
   A. bombastic
   B. incontrovertible
   C. querulous

9. Julius Caesar was a greatly revered and feared _____ ruler.
   A. omnipotent
   B. esoteric
   C. insufferable

10. The _____ news reporter would not leave the movie star's dressing room without first getting an interview.
    A. pertinacious
    B. notorious
    C. depraved

11. Champagne is an _____ beverage.
    A. inanimate
    B. officious
    C. effervescent

12. A juggler must possess coordination and _____.
    A. multiplicity
    B. dexterity
    C. travesty

13. Nietzsche's _____ philosophy questioned contemporary religion and morality.
    A. esoteric
    B. amicable
    C. phlegmatic

14. In his sermon, the preacher admonished the licentious sinner, urging him to _____ his wanton lifestyle.
    A. concur
    B. subvert
    C. forsake

15. The whisper of gossip _____ his curiosity.
    A. piqued
    B. alleviated
    C. enthralled

16. _____ rain showers were forecast for the weekend.
    A. Intermittent
    B. Arid
    C. Sprawling

17. The _____ lad would not admit he was wrong even in the face of irrefutable evidence.
    A. notorious
    B. intrinsic
    C. headstrong

18. It is nearly impossible for an _____ gambler to change his risk-taking ways.
    A. inveterate
    B. adept
    C. efficacious

19. The arguable call by the referee caused a _____ throughout the soccer stadium.
    A. levity
    B. ramification
    C. brouhaha

20. The kindness displayed by the veteran actress was just an _____; she was actually bitterly envious of the young upstart.
    A. affectation
    B. enigma
    C. obeisance

(For Quiz Answers, see Answer Section at the end of the book)

SAT & College Dictionary Workbook Quiz 54

[On a separate sheet of paper, write down the letter of the word that best fits in the blank to create a complete and meaningful sentence.]

1. Some dinosaurs were _____ creatures.
   A. jocular
   B. titanic
   C. sardonic

2. Scientists have _____ that life beings from distant worlds may well share some resemblance to earthlings.
   A. postulated
   B. countenanced
   C. exalted

3. Unexpected and _____ problems hindered timely completion of the massive construction project.
   A. provisional
   B. insuperable
   C. sequential

4. Much to his surprise, his paycheck reflected a _____ and unexpected raise.
   A. fallacious
   B. substantial
   C. herculean

5. Residents in the Texas Panhandle must contend with the _____ of Mother Nature.
   A. parameters
   B. vagaries
   C. homage

6. The six-year-old was a _____ and sprightly tyke.
   A. preposterous
   B. vivacious
   C. bilious

7. Poverty is _____ in many underdeveloped nations.
   A. somber
   B. rife
   C. impoverished

8. Her _____ husband restricted her from seeing old friends.
   A. domineering
   B. inflammable
   C. sprightly

9. Animal lovers expressed their _____ over the barbaric means employed to rid the community of the unwanted stray dogs.
   A. panache
   B. indignation
   C. élan

10. Rather than vote for a policy change, the usually dissenting members of the committee supported the _____.
    A. status quo
    B. propriety
    C. aggregate

11. Littering public streets is looked down upon as _____ disregard of the law.
    A. self-effacing
    B. willful
    C. ineffectual

12. Mutual interest in hip-hop music _____ a camaraderie between the two former rivals.
    A. bestowed
    B. engendered
    C. parched

13. The professor's ill-chosen words _____ an argument.
    A. deferred
    B. provoked
    C. curtailed

14. The teacher laughingly pondered the _____ suggestion that she let her students exchange clothes as part of their foreign "exchange" program.
    A. turgid
    B. jocose
    C. plaintive

15. Lining up most of the players on the left side of the field was just a _____; the quarterback's plan was to sprint to the right.
    A. shibboleth
    B. ruse
    C. prognosis

16. The young writer's agent recommended that her characterizations be less _____ and instead more succinctly delineated.
    A. tremulous
    B. diffuse
    C. perfidious

17. Restaurant food is prepared under strictly _____ conditions.
    A. hygienic
    B. righteous
    C. affluent

18. Custom designers helped _____ the old kitchen by installing new modern appliances.
    A. culminate
    B. appropriate
    C. renovate

19. Friends and fellow associates poured forth _____ at the beloved foreman's retirement party.
    A. encomiums
    B. anathemas
    C. vicissitudes

20. One should always heed the _____ "buyer beware" when purchasing a used car "as is."
    A. scourge
    B. fracas
    C. caveat

(For Quiz Answers, see Answer Section at the end of the book)

SAT & College Dictionary Workbook Quiz 55

[On a separate sheet of paper, write down the letter of the word that best fits in the blank to create a complete and meaningful sentence.]

1. To avoid any erosion of investor confidence, the chairman _____ the company's growth-oriented goals for the coming year with a series of carefully-constructed charts.
   A. abjured
   B. elucidated
   C. skewed

2. A plaque honored the _____ contribution made to help build the neighborhood child-care center.
   A. munificent
   B. remote
   C. superficial

3. Besides being fined for having committed the crime, the culprit was also ordered to pay _____ damages.
   A. eternal
   B. deprecatory
   C. punitive

4. The primeval forest was a _____ paradise.
   A. veritable
   B. preternatural
   C. blatant

5. The majority voted to _____ the current club president.
   A. oust
   B. deplete
   C. estrange

6. The radio news reporter provided a _____ minute-by-minute account of the highly-publicized execution.
   A. verdant
   B. dispassionate
   C. patent

7. When the true culprit of the crime confessed, the innocent suspect was at last _____.
   A. apprised
   B. exonerated
   C. tempered

8. Amish people live an _____ life, forgoing many modern conveniences.
   A. austere
   B. omnipotent
   C. impending

9. The island chain suffered a _____ outbreak of malaria.
   A. pandemic
   B. contentious
   C. venerable

10. Audie Murphy was decorated for his _____ valor on the battlefield.
    A. peerless
    B. verdant
    C. dissolute

11. The admissions counselor was a _____ judge of an applicant's personal commitment.
    A. condign
    B. jejune
    C. percipient

12. The local chapter of the Chamber of Commerce _____ to address the latest downturn in business sales.
    A. convened
    B. abjured
    C. incited

13. When the shutters were opened, light _____ the room.
    A. rebuked
    B. suffused
    C. distorted

14. The _____ bodybuilder was the envy of all the girls at the beach.
    A. brawny
    B. penurious
    C. halcyon

15. In today's age of technology, even the most advanced computers will soon become _____.
    A. contingent
    B. euphonious
    C. outmoded

16. Visitors stood _____ at the sight of the devastation.
    A. aghast
    B. hirsute
    C. nondescript

17. The leftover meal _____ in the garbage can.
    A. putrefied
    B. disparaged
    C. perished

18. The teacher _____ in a threateningly implicit manner when the class would not settle down.
    A. lowered
    B. digressed
    C. infuriated

19. To protect the town from approaching floodwaters, the National Guard was _____.
    A. suppressed
    B. facilitated
    C. mobilized

20. After spending a week adrift on the ocean, the rescued survivors appeared _____ and emotionally drained.
    A. meticulous
    B. haggard
    C. abstruse

(For Quiz Answers, see Answer Section at the end of the book)

SAT & College Dictionary Workbook Quiz 56

[On a separate sheet of paper, write down the letter of the word that best fits in the blank to create a complete and meaningful sentence.]

1. Life, liberty and the pursuit of happiness are every American's _____ rights.
   A. chthonian
   B. inalienable
   C. sylvan

2. For their daily discussion, the professor _____ to the class the possibility that life may exist in other dimensions.
   A. estranged
   B. propounded
   C. dispersed

3. Legend told that the _____ would manifest itself in the guise of a headless Indian seeking revenge on those who betrayed him.
   A. gist
   B. leviathan
   C. wraith

4. Years of quarreling _____ the Hatfields and the McCoys.
   A. alienated
   B. galvanized
   C. reciprocated

5. Impressionism triggered an artistic _____ in the nineteenth century with the likes of Monet, Pissarro and Renoir.
   A. malaise
   B. charisma
   C. renaissance

6. Unhappy with the game's outcome, the _____ crowd threw bottles onto the field.
   A. serene
   B. raucous
   C. convivial

7. Severe rainstorms _____ the rescuers' efforts to reach the stranded hikers.
   A. conjoined
   B. regressed
   C. hindered

8. The authenticity of the newly-discovered Rembrandt painting was highly _____.
   A. refulgent
   B. dubious
   C. variegated

9. After receiving her payout, the lottery winner immediately began to spend money in an unwise and _____ manner.
   A. ambidextrous
   B. wry
   C. extravagant

10. A _____ concrete slab covered the fallout shelter.
    A. tenebrous
    B. monolithic
    C. supererogatory

11. The heated argument was replete with derisive taunts and unabashed _____.
    A. repose
    B. contumely
    C. potpourri

12. During the daring aerial acrobatics act, the feeling of suspense in the audience was _____.
    A. soluble
    B. corporeal
    C. palpable

13. The city council _____ the likelihood of balancing the budget without having to raise local taxes.
    A. dreaded
    B. assessed
    C. induced

14. Passengers always appreciate a _____ flight attendant.
    A. complaisant
    B. meretricious
    C. rhetorical

15. The committee _____ the treasurer for having squandered much of their investment capital on worthless stocks.
    A. censured
    B. arrogated
    C. intimidated

16. Rigid dictates _____ individual creativity.
    A. stifle
    B. confirm
    C. elicit

17. The helpless ship _____ amid the jagged rocks.
    A. foundered
    B. subverted
    C. contravened

18. Spiritual leaders of the agrarian tribe performed a ritual dance in honor of their _____ deity in hope they would receive deliverance from the interminable drought.
    A. recherché
    B. omniscient
    C. doleful

19. Hiding inside a garbage can, the refugee managed to _____ capture by his pursuers.
    A. evade
    B. amend
    C. mince

20. The _____ child constantly interrupted his mother.
    A. baleful
    B. prodigious
    C. impertinent

(For Quiz Answers, see Answer Section at the end of the book)

SAT & College Dictionary Workbook Quiz 57

[On a separate sheet of paper, write down the letter of the word that best fits in the blank to create a complete and meaningful sentence.]

1. Rain showers _____ the outdoor festivities.
   A. scrutinized
   B. assimilated
   C. curtailed

2. Many children _____ taking a bath.
   A. loathe
   B. encroach
   C. defile

3. A crew of workers repaired the downed telephone cable in an _____ manner.
   A. obnoxious
   B. abject
   C. expeditious

4. Man's _____ stay on Earth pales in comparison to the longevity of the dinosaur.
   A. temporal
   B. chronological
   C. mnemonic

5. Sooner or later, every person must deal with one's own _____.
   A. ultimatum
   B. senescence
   C. bedlam

6. The inexperienced teller was publicly _____ for leaving the bank safe open.
   A. rebuked
   B. disconcerted
   C. commended

7. A large nail _____ from the wall where the painting once hung.
   A. protruded
   B. eroded
   C. diverged

8. New Year's Eve is a convivial and _____ occasion.
   A. felicitous
   B. solicitous
   C. meritorious

9. The community came together to offer _____ assistance in rebuilding those homes that had been destroyed in the fire.
   A. reputable
   B. amenable
   C. gratuitous

10. During the annual meeting of stockholders, corporate executives were deluged by _____ complaints from disgruntled investors.
    A. roseate
    B. copious
    C. indurate

11. The upstanding citizen was _____ by unfounded rumors that he was actually a former Nazi.
    A. maligned
    B. exulted
    C. shunned

12. The dutiful clerk had been with the small private company since its _____.
    A. demise
    B. inception
    C. approbation

13. When not in the wrestling ring, the burly man was a surprisingly _____ and affable gentleman.
    A. stodgy
    B. iniquitous
    C. unobtrusive

14. Opponents of the administration claimed that the government had become rife with _____ public officials.
    A. feral
    B. venal
    C. ironic

15. He refused to lend any additional money to his _____ brother, knowing that the money would likely be gambled away at the racetrack.
    A. impecunious
    B. assiduous
    C. omnipotent

16. In most areas, snow in spring is highly _____.
    A. magnanimous
    B. atypical
    C. synthetic

17. Tourists are likely to encounter _____ on the streets of India.
    A. proponents
    B. foes
    C. mendicants

18. The issue regarding man's evolution has often been the _____ of heated and protracted debate.
    A. genesis
    B. pall
    C. causerie

19. Faced with such _____ evidence against him, the suspect had no other choice but to plead guilty and place himself at the mercy of the court.
    A. puerile
    B. incontrovertible
    C. cognizant

20. Drug dealers are _____ to all who value the welfare of children.
    A. anathema
    B. integral
    C. unassuming

(For Quiz Answers, see Answer Section at the end of the book)

SAT & College Dictionary Workbook Quiz 58

[On a separate sheet of paper, write down the letter of the word that best fits in the blank to create a complete and meaningful sentence.]

1. The actor's _____ speech at the awards ceremony was agonizingly painful to endure.
    A. unobtrusive
    B. discursive
    C. subtle

2. The government _____ a portion of the contested land back to the native inhabitants.
    A. honed
    B. ceded
    C. seceded

3. After lengthy negotiations, the two rival parties reached a mutual peace _____.
    A. accord
    B. franchise
    C. propriety

4. His mind became _____ from lack of stimulating mental exercise.
    A. inordinate
    B. torpid
    C. pessimistic

5. Only the hardiest of explorers could endure the arctic region's _____ climate.
    A. chronic
    B. glacial
    C. indifferent

6. The government _____ all property purchased from the proceeds of the felon's illegal activities.
    A. ousted
    B. expropriated
    C. wheedled

7. The movie director would not _____ tardiness by any member of his crew.
    A. intervene
    B. palliate
    C. countenance

8. Over time, an _____ developed among the recruits.
    A. esprit de corps
    B. obeisance
    C. apotheosis

9. The veteran prestidigitator was a master of _____.
    A. legerdemain
    B. caricature
    C. paradox

10. Automobiles are _____ today even in many of the most remote regions of the world.
    A. replete
    B. domineering
    C. prevalent

11. Courses in mathematics were the student's _____ throughout high school.
    A. zenith
    B. retrogression
    C. forte

12. Corroborating evidence _____ to the veracity of the witness's account.
    A. manifested
    B. predicated
    C. attested

13. After debating the issue for weeks without resolution, it was agreed upon that a more _____ approach was needed to help end the strike.
    A. celebrated
    B. grueling
    C. pragmatic

14. Bitter civil _____ broke out in the ravaged war-torn countryside.
    A. strife
    B. dilemma
    C. havoc

15. The _____ bottle-throwing crowd bore the onus fo the umpires' decision to halt the little-league baseball game.
    A. insightful
    B. obstreperous
    C. banal

16. The threadbare plot was _____ of novelty or originality.
    A. nonchalant
    B. unexpurgated
    C. devoid

17. Man has long been in awe of Mother Nature's _____ powers.
    A. halcyon
    B. inscrutable
    C. optimistic

18. Impurities in gold _____ its value.
    A. debase
    B. relegate
    C. impugn

19. The cause of the mysterious illness _____ the medical community.
    A. converged
    B. perplexed
    C. exacerbated

20. The young man's _____ remark impressed his teacher.
    A. coy
    B. profound
    C. grotesque

(For Quiz Answers, see Answer Section at the end of the book)

SAT & College Dictionary Workbook Quiz 59

[On a separate sheet of paper, write down the letter of the word that best fits in the blank to create a complete and meaningful sentence.]

1. An advanced college degree is a _____ for many executive positions.
    A. consensus
    B. requisite
    C. predicament

2. To avoid a needless argument, the _____ gentleman reassured his wife that she looked strikingly attractive in her polka-dot dress.
    A. forlorn
    B. tactful
    C. germane

3. The veteran writer was _____ of the young upstart, regarding him as merely a talentless opportunist.
    A. apprehensive
    B. indulgent
    C. contemptuous

4. When swimming at an unfamiliar beach, it is wise to always _____ the lifeguard's advice.
    A. circumvent
    B. heed
    C. blandish

5. The lad's _____ glances at his neighbor's test did not go unnoticed by the teacher.
    A. mobile
    B. furtive
    C. oppressive

6. On the bus, the stranger's _____ stare left the young woman feeling fearfully uneasy.
    A. woebegone
    B. inimical
    C. aureate

7. In its final century, the Roman civilization had grown _____ through political malfeasance and corruption.
    A. moot
    B. effete
    C. verbatim

8. After the long and bumpy boat ride, many passengers felt _____.
    A. nauseous
    B. sanguine
    C. reticent

9. Seeking _____ for the murder of his brother, the outlaw hunted down all those involved.
    A. retribution
    B. déjà vu
    C. empathy

10. Fishing had long been the doctor's weekend _____.
    A. nicety
    B. tempest
    C. diversion

11. Neighbors marveled at the _____ growth of an apple tree in the middle of the otherwise barren plot of land.
    A. invidious
    B. adventitious
    C. seditious

12. The tribal rain dance has been performed since time _____.
    A. immemorial
    B. didactic
    C. puritanical

13. The _____ husband catered to his domineering wife's every whim.
    A. staunch
    B. uxorious
    C. vociferous

14. The homeowner's indecision where to place the furniture _____ the moving crew.
    A. tantalized
    B. vexed
    C. enticed

15. Preaching to his _____, the priest cautioned against succumbing to the temptations of evil.
    A. disciples
    B. animus
    C. minutiae

16. The plot to kidnap the queen was abruptly _____ when it was learned that the king had prepared defensively for such an eventuality.
    A. propitiated
    B. aborted
    C. exculpated

17. Staying out later than permitted kindled her parents' _____.
    A. prowess
    B. amity
    C. ire

18. Because of the instructor's reputation for giving _____ lectures, students avoided registering for his class.
    A. jejune
    B. stark
    C. chic

19. The antique store specialized in _____ objects d'art.
    A. clarion
    B. recherché
    C. verdant

20. One who serves in the public interest ought to be a person of irreproachable honor and _____.
    A. dexterity
    B. rectitude
    C. travail

(For Quiz Answers, see Answer Section at the end of the book)

SAT & College Dictionary Workbook Quiz 60

[On a separate sheet of paper, write down the letter of the word that best fits in the blank to create a complete and meaningful sentence.]

1. A duck walks in an _____ manner.
   A. ungainly
   B. intermittent
   C. obnoxious

2. Early settlers marveled at the _____ wilderness of the Old West.
   A. nefarious
   B. vast
   C. prolific

3. A distinct _____ separates vertebrates from invertebrates.
   A. peregrination
   B. ululation
   C. dichotomy

4. A _____ vapor arose from the sewer.
   A. contemptuous
   B. mephitic
   C. venomous

5. His international success earned the musician _____ in his home town.
   A. charisma
   B. kudos
   C. altercations

6. The lugubrious ambience was _____ somewhat with a humorous though inspiring anecdote.
   A. excoriated
   B. debauched
   C. leavened

7. Rumors of a sales tax increase _____ an angry outcry from the community.
   A. lionized
   B. elicited
   C. traversed

8. Guests displayed _____ conduct during the formal celebrity dinner.
   A. spartan
   B. ingenuous
   C. decorous

9. When oil supplies became abnormally low, wholesale prices quickly _____.
   A. escalated
   B. abrogated
   C. retaliated

10. Cavemen were _____ creatures.
    A. hirsute
    B. decrepit
    C. punctilious

11. Rather than employ a more _____ approach, the vocational school preferred on-the-job training.
    A. deprecatory
    B. pedagogic
    C. frugal

12. The political candidate was flanked by her _____ supporters.
    A. vis-à-vis
    B. staunch
    C. makeshift

13. Prices in the fancy store were unaffordably _____.
    A. unilateral
    B. arcane
    C. exorbitant

14. Weeks of diligent negotiation _____ in a lasting peace treaty.
    A. suffused
    B. assayed
    C. eventuated

15. A school reunion affords adults the opportunity to be once again in the _____ company of childhood friends.
    A. jocund
    B. sporadic
    C. diligent

16. Any oil embargo usually carries with it serious worldwide _____.
    A. parameters
    B. ramifications
    C. infractions

17. Because children are very _____, they are oftentimes the target of unscrupulous adults seeking to enlist their services.
    A. virtuous
    B. pliable
    C. beatific

18. His lavish and _____ spending habits quickly depleted the family's savings.
    A. prodigal
    B. doleful
    C. miserly

19. For aiding the enemy government in time of war, the mercenary was branded a _____.
    A. poseur
    B. quisling
    C. denizen

20. The older brother felt _____ for having let his younger sibling take the blame for his own misdeed.
    A. euphoria
    B. discord
    C. remorse

(For Quiz Answers, see Answer Section at the end of the book)

SAT & College Dictionary Workbook Quiz 61

[On a separate sheet of paper, write down the letter of the word that best fits in the blank to create a complete and meaningful sentence.]

1. The earliest flying machines were _____ and highly unpredictable mechanical contraptions.
   A. rudimentary
   B. versatile
   C. infallible

2. A _____ phrase such as "crime does not pay" presents a terse, though somewhat hackneyed, bit of useful advice.
   A. thrifty
   B. vital
   C. sententious

3. Tasmanian devils are _____ and highly territorial marsupials.
   A. pugnacious
   B. debonair
   C. vapid

4. A funeral is a _____ affair.
   A. venal
   B. doleful
   C. therapeutic

5. _____ liquids should be stored in a cool, dry place.
   A. Inflammable
   B. Pelagic
   C. Auspicious

6. The beloved senator was a man of utmost moral _____.
   A. éclat
   B. vitality
   C. integrity

7. When introduced, the guests exchanged _____.
   A. pleasantries
   B. covenants
   C. rapport

8. The couple _____ over where to dine.
   A. quibbled
   B. deigned
   C. insinuated

9. In some prisons, inmates are granted occasional _____ visits.
   A. fey
   B. conjugal
   C. refulgent

10. An open wound is _____ to infection.
    A. disingenuous
    B. endemic
    C. susceptible

11. Despite a valiant effort to remain solvent, it soon became clear to all that the company's demise was _____.
    A. star-crossed
    B. veritable
    C. inevitable

12. A bigot is _____ of those expressing conflicting opinions or beliefs.
    A. vigilant
    B. intolerant
    C. woeful

13. Through the power of concentration, some people can walk barefoot over glass and remain _____ to the pain.
    A. impervious
    B. relentless
    C. pretentious

14. Continuous rain _____ the workers' efforts to complete the roof repairs.
    A. effaced
    B. abhorred
    C. hampered

15. The librarian was visibly disturbed by the _____ amount of chatter around her.
    A. sporadic
    B. inordinate
    C. profound

16. To sound more educated, the young woman spoke with an air of _____.
    A. celerity
    B. preciosity
    C. impunity

17. The baritone had a deep, _____ voice.
    A. disparate
    B. incumbent
    C. resonant

18. Three city blocks were devastated by the awesome _____.
    A. recreant
    B. conflagration
    C. apotheosis

19. Attending parties did not conform to his _____ upbringing.
    A. jocular
    B. uproarious
    C. straitlaced

20. The mechanic was _____ for his travel time en route to and from the location of the stalled car.
    A. countermanded
    B. remunerated
    C. inculcated

(For Quiz Answers, see Answer Section at the end of the book)

SAT & College Dictionary Workbook Quiz 62

[On a separate sheet of paper, write down the letter of the word that best fits in the blank to create a complete and meaningful sentence.]

1. Disenchanted by the slow progress of the meeting, the board member excused himself under the _____ of suddenly having a headache.
   A. strife
   B. impetus
   C. pretense

2. In her moments of deep reflection, the aging cinematic star _____ to those glorious days when legions of fans followed her every move.
   A. regressed
   B. deterred
   C. subsided

3. As enemy troops approached, the battalion commander _____ his men to hold their ground.
   A. exhorted
   B. ameliorated
   C. warranted

4. The television exposé sought to _____ magicians' claims that a table can be made to magically rise off the floor.
   A. induce
   B. debunk
   C. meander

5. Despite numerous pleas from his advisers, the wealthy and powerful king remained _____ to the plight of his impoverished subjects.
   A. indifferent
   B. spurious
   C. ambiguous

6. After years of obscurity, the innovative producer won the _____ of the movie world with her award-winning documentary.
   A. credence
   B. plaudits
   C. alliance

7. His _____ commentary had no relevance to the discussion and merely made an already-protracted meeting even lengthier.
   A. covert
   B. dulcet
   C. otiose

8. The thief had no _____ about stealing the lady's purse.
   A. delusions
   B. qualms
   C. predilections

9. Critics did not review the play favorably, citing its _____ plot and shallow characterizations.
   A. trite
   B. momentous
   C. inscrutable

10. The insubordinate sailor _____ the captain's orders.
    A. agitated
    B. traversed
    C. defied

11. Much debate has taken place regarding the _____ differences between the sexes.
    A. formidable
    B. concerted
    C. putative

12. The defendant handled the grueling cross-examination with amazing _____.
    A. sangfroid
    B. remorse
    C. pulchritude

13. Rather than take her job seriously, the _____ receptionist polished her nails while chatting on the phone to her equally flighty friends.
    A. frivolous
    B. bucolic
    C. mendacious

14. The _____ mother-in-law constantly meddled in the young couple's affairs.
    A. officious
    B. insurgent
    C. disheveled

15. Sports figures are often mistakenly revered as _____ of society.
    A. havens
    B. antipodes
    C. paradigms

16. Silas Marner was a _____ person who loved to count his gold.
    A. miserly
    B. suppliant
    C. discursive

17. Close friends cautioned the young man that his allegiance to the subversive organization would prove a _____ influence on his political career.
    A. miniscule
    B. tautological
    C. baneful

18. For an octogenarian, the woman was particularly _____.
    A. insatiable
    B. pestilent
    C. spry

19. The two brothers' offices were in close _____ to one another.
    A. latitude
    B. proximity
    C. umbrage

20. Over the years, the _____ of rainfall turned the once-thriving savanna into a barren wasteland.
    A. suffrage
    B. dearth
    C. menace

(For Quiz Answers, see Answer Section at the end of the book)

SAT & College Dictionary Workbook Quiz 63

[On a separate sheet of paper, write down the letter of the word that best fits in the blank to create a complete and meaningful sentence.]

1. New evidence _____ previously held theories regarding the whereabouts of the lost civilization.
   A. deterred
   B. refuted
   C. sullied

2. Although religiously affiliated, the radio station played exclusively _____ music.
   A. righteous
   B. secular
   C. irreconcilable

3. Criminals are seen by many as a _____ to society.
   A. menace
   B. diversion
   C. prototype

4. Elves were known to be _____ creatures.
   A. sordid
   B. fey
   C. wizened

5. The collapse of the major firm cast a _____ on the entire industry.
   A. brouhaha
   B. deluge
   C. pall

6. Due to the hurricane's imminent approach, the captain _____ the sailors' weekend furloughs.
   A. revoked
   B. countenanced
   C. aborted

7. The couple's verbal _____ intensified as the evening progressed.
   A. double entendre
   B. altercation
   C. rectitude

8. The aloof supervisor would not _____ to converse casually with her underlings.
   A. allude
   B. deign
   C. upbraid

9. Early pioneers had to endure the _____ of life in the Old West.
   A. compunctions
   B. rigors
   C. dichotomy

10. Police charged a _____ former employee with two counts of arson.
    A. disgruntled
    B. paramount
    C. valiant

11. The large feast _____ the animal's hunger.
    A. marred
    B. sated
    C. deteriorated

12. The _____ dolt couldn't even follow simple directions.
    A. witless
    B. authoritative
    C. reticent

13. Stealing from his own parents was a most _____ act.
    A. ignoble
    B. arbitrary
    C. morose

14. Summer vacation is a time of _____ for youngsters.
    A. mirth
    B. chagrin
    C. temerity

15. To expand his already vast empire, the king _____ the territory that lay to the south.
    A. ensued
    B. annexed
    C. precluded

16. As he cruised in his Corvette playing his radio at full volume, the _____ playboy scoured the streets for attractive single girls.
    A. penitent
    B. facetious
    C. insouciant

17. Through an _____ error, the esteemed professor was excluded from the list of invited guests.
    A. inadvertent
    B. abject
    C. unexpurgated

18. A powerful business _____ was formed from several smaller companies.
    A. conglomerate
    B. prototype
    C. mendicant

19. Her sister made a _____ vow not to tell anyone their secret.
    A. solemn
    B. chary
    C. variegated

20. The elderly pair recaptured the _____ pleasures of a picnic in the park.
    A. penurious
    B. stodgy
    C. vernal

(For Quiz Answers, see Answer Section at the end of the book)

SAT & College Dictionary Workbook Quiz 64

[On a separate sheet of paper, write down the letter of the word that best fits in the blank to create a complete and meaningful sentence.]

1. Many in the courtroom were taken aback by the defendant's _____ apology to his victim.
   A. synchronous
   B. effusive
   C. acrimonious

2. The young lad possessed a _____ and charmingly infectious personality.
   A. sullen
   B. hidebound
   C. vibrant

3. Albert Einstein was a _____ twentieth century physicist.
   A. devout
   B. preeminent
   C. sumptuous

4. When the firecracker exploded, the movie theater erupted into _____.
   A. asperity
   B. pandemonium
   C. dexterity

5. Crocodiles have a _____ that can exceed one hundred years.
   A. countenance
   B. longevity
   C. dichotomy

6. Several teachers had to _____ to break up the playground melee.
   A. quibble
   B. intervene
   C. postulate

7. For his health, he made a New Year's resolution to _____ his alcoholic ways.
   A. forswear
   B. thwart
   C. concede

8. Although the committee seemed resolute in their decision, one concerned citizen nevertheless addressed the panel and vehemently _____ against removal of the old banyan tree.
   A. vociferated
   B. abrogated
   C. expostulated

9. When communication with the airliner was lost, ground personnel feared that something serious might have gone _____.
   A. awry
   B. grave
   C. occult

10. The _____ couple bickered over every little issue.
    A. contentious
    B. perspicacious
    C. effervescent

11. The young children awaited Christmas morning with anticipatory _____.
    A. invective
    B. absolution
    C. zeal

12. Because of their _____ sense of smell, beagles are often used at airports to sniff out contraband.
    A. extravagant
    B. uncanny
    C. initial

13. The delivery person was _____ handsomely for his expeditious service.
    A. reprimanded
    B. compensated
    C. stipulated

14. To enhance its own wealth, the truculent tribe conducted periodic _____ on its weaker neighbors.
    A. influxes
    B. forays
    C. qualms

15. Many popular expressions soon fall into _____ and are quickly replaced by more-contemporary ones.
    A. desuetude
    B. turmoil
    C. purview

16. The scoundrel's _____ attempt to convince the old woman to sign over the deed to her house failed when her husband showed up.
    A. guileful
    B. nascent
    C. practicable

17. Veiled intimidation by the police _____ the rock concert fans.
    A. incensed
    B. consecrated
    C. ebbed

18. Much to the _____ of coastline residents, the national meteorological center reported that their towns would likely soon be hit by a powerful tsunami generated by a sizable seismic disturbance.
    A. animus
    B. repercussion
    C. consternation

19. Nostradamus _____ turbulent times during the latter part of the first millennium.
    A. concurred
    B. disseminated
    C. prophesied

20. The farmer was a _____ and God-fearing Christian.
    A. derisive
    B. rambunctious
    C. meek

(For Quiz Answers, see Answer Section at the end of the book)

SAT & College Dictionary Workbook Quiz 65

[On a separate sheet of paper, write down the letter of the word that best fits in the blank to create a complete and meaningful sentence.]

1. The youngster was a _____ and delightful lass.
   A. morose
   B. winsome
   C. petulant

2. The pop star was so _____ by unfounded rumors that she was afraid to be seen in public.
   A. dreaded
   B. confronted
   C. traduced

3. The earliest _____ tools date as far back as the Paleolithic period.
   A. abstruse
   B. orotund
   C. extant

4. A special council meeting was _____ to address the sudden increase in neighborhood crime.
   A. flaunted
   B. convened
   C. replenished

5. While the customer was not looking, the _____ salesman raised the price on the sale item.
   A. peripatetic
   B. devious
   C. autocratic

6. The lad's stubbornly _____ nature manifested itself in his proclivity to do what his parents asked him not to do.
   A. deprecatory
   B. uncanny
   C. perverse

7. Many feel that Tiger Woods is _____ the most exciting golfer on the professional circuit today.
   A. sardonically
   B. arguably
   C. immutably

8. His _____ refusal to help his wife clean the dishes incurred her wrath.
   A. credulous
   B. brusque
   C. inchoate

9. It often takes many hard-fought and laborious years of touring before an artist receives his due recognition and _____ from the music world.
   A. obloquy
   B. ploys
   C. accolades

10. To preserve their low crime rate in the tiny town, the _____ residents kept close watch on uninvited guests.
    A. vigilant
    B. sovereign
    C. complaisant

11. The young boy gained a _____ view of his older brother together with the sibling's girlfriend.
    A. surreptitious
    B. vigorous
    C. frenetic

12. Romeo pledged his _____ love for Juliet.
    A. artful
    B. versatile
    C. eternal

13. Winning the coveted world championship title marked the _____ of the chess master's brilliant career.
    A. apex
    B. inclination
    C. rift

14. Rumors are often the result of _____ gossip.
    A. sentient
    B. diaphanous
    C. malicious

15. The _____ boy had no intention of working during the summer vacation months, choosing instead to idle away the time in restful repose.
    A. bemused
    B. resonant
    C. indolent

16. Only in their _____ stage, the contract talks had much remaining to be resolved.
    A. supernal
    B. versatile
    C. nascent

17. Her _____ boyfriend declined the offer to attend an opera.
    A. corrupt
    B. philistine
    C. baleful

18. After months in concentration camps, many of the _____ prisoners were at the brink of starvation.
    A. arrant
    B. unsung
    C. emaciated

19. In his grand murals, artist Wyland _____ his underwater scenes with deeply penetrating blues and greens.
    A. connoted
    B. imbued
    C. presaged

20. The young worker was _____ for dawdling.
    A. upbraided
    B. compensated
    C. abstained

(For Quiz Answers, see Answer Section at the end of the book)

SAT & College Dictionary Workbook Quiz 66

[On a separate sheet of paper, write down the letter of the word that best fits in the blank to create a complete and meaningful sentence.]

1. The unusually poor test scores from a handful of students _____ the overall statistical results.
   A. concocted
   B. admonished
   C. skewed

2. The remote island enjoyed a _____ year-round climate.
   A. multifaceted
   B. lithe
   C. genial

3. In comedies, the expression "going to bed" is often intended as a _____.
   A. paragon
   B. vendetta
   C. double entendre

4. In the light, a soap bubble displays an _____ glow.
   A. iridescent
   B. arable
   C. emollient

5. The _____ whelp defied the teacher's demands by continuing to play his radio in class.
   A. inebriated
   B. ponderous
   C. contumacious

6. Due to communication failure, meteorologists were unable to _____ that the powerful hurricane had indeed struck the capital city of the remote island.
   A. sanction
   B. verify
   C. essay

7. An animal may _____ death to ward off an attack from a belligerent adversary.
   A. proliferate
   B. blanch
   C. feign

8. After their capture, the prisoners were led into the _____ darkness of the forbidding dungeon.
   A. felicitous
   B. stygian
   C. empyreal

9. Words of motherly comfort helped _____ the child's fear of getting a haircut.
   A. malinger
   B. warrant
   C. dispel

10. In his novels, Ernest Hemingway wrote about the _____ of war.
    A. braggadocio
    B. idiosyncrasy
    C. travails

11. When the apartment window was opened, the _____ sounds of the bustling city below suffused the room.
    A. sentimental
    B. bland
    C. raucous

12. The villain's smile _____ his evil intent.
    A. impeded
    B. sullied
    C. belied

13. Rumors often stem from _____ speculation.
    A. belated
    B. omniscient
    C. fallacious

14. _____ to strangers in need, the kindly woman offered them free meals and overnight lodging.
    A. Hospitable
    B. Stringent
    C. Auspicious

15. Last-minute negotiations helped _____ a crippling strike.
    A. avert
    B. forsake
    C. putrefy

16. The lad's _____ hair style attracted stares from other students.
    A. concupiscent
    B. outlandish
    C. acute

17. The lowly servant earned a _____ salary.
    A. slipshod
    B. droll
    C. meager

18. Jane Goodall's research on the habits of primates is a _____ and caring glimpse into the behavior of man's closest relatives.
    A. froward
    B. perceptive
    C. tranquil

19. British literature reached its _____ during the Renaissance.
    A. zenith
    B. exponent
    C. accord

20. The _____ movie dragged on without end.
    A. miniscule
    B. introverted
    C. stodgy

SAT & College Dictionary Workbook Quiz 67

[On a separate sheet of paper, write down the letter of the word that best fits in the blank to create a complete and meaningful sentence.]

1. The young lady was so _____ that when asked to stay overnight, she thought it was to help tidy up the house.
   A. naïve
   B. sullen
   C. preposterous

2. The _____ gown was made from silk and lace.
   A. diaphanous
   B. peripheral
   C. transitory

3. An expert was brought in to _____ the authenticity of the dubious painting.
   A. immure
   B. certify
   C. prevaricate

4. After spending two days in the cave without food, the boys were _____.
   A. pedantic
   B. famished
   C. concomitant

5. The powerful watchdog flashed its _____ teeth at the would-be trespasser.
   A. forbidding
   B. illustrious
   C. perspicuous

6. In Japan, it is _____ upon a visitor to remove his shoes before entering the house.
   A. subservient
   B. recumbent
   C. incumbent

7. A _____ of stock analysts gathered every Friday to discuss the week's business events.
   A. coterie
   B. potpourri
   C. maelstrom

8. The esoterically _____ dissertation was a struggle to follow.
   A. vain
   B. ponderous
   C. ebullient

9. Lakes offer visitors a pleasingly _____ vista.
   A. insatiable
   B. aesthetic
   C. petulant

10. The man's _____ desk reflected his slovenly lifestyle.
    A. inept
    B. slovenly
    C. meticulous

11. Lemmings are _____ rodents.
    A. migratory
    B. connubial
    C. euphemistic

12. To the Greeks, Aphrodite was the _____ of beauty.
    A. homage
    B. apotheosis
    C. surrogate

13. The Anabaptists' distinctive _____ was their preference for adult rather than infant baptism.
    A. kin
    B. dudgeon
    C. tenet

14. Oftentimes, those residing in inner-city ghettos must contend with _____ living conditions.
    A. sordid
    B. fanciful
    C. baneful

15. When his mother caught him stealing cookies from the cookie jar, the young lad flashed a _____ grin.
    A. hapless
    B. sheepish
    C. plaintive

16. Ivan the Terrible was a _____ despot and tyrant.
    A. valiant
    B. destitute
    C. sadistic

17. Psychologists have long been intrigued by the _____ personality of those afflicted by schizophrenia.
    A. dauntless
    B. substantial
    C. protean

18. The _____ society, with members in over forty different countries worldwide, strived to promote international religious harmony.
    A. ecumenical
    B. introverted
    C. celestial

19. As a result of his _____ manner when around strangers, he acquired the reputation of a snob.
    A. aloof
    B. fetid
    C. resilient

20. The _____ conflict involved two violent rival gangs.
    A. concerted
    B. sanguinary
    C. taut

(For Quiz Answers, see Answer Section at the end of the book)

SAT & College Dictionary Workbook Quiz 68

[On a separate sheet of paper, write down the letter of the word that best fits in the blank to create a complete and meaningful sentence.]

1. Brushing one's teeth is an _____ part of oral hygiene.
   A. ebullient
   B. integral
   C. auxiliary

2. The _____ man could not muster enough courage to ask his boss for a raise.
   A. meek
   B. smug
   C. depraved

3. The headwaiter was _____ when it came to setting the dinner table; every fork and spoon had to be correctly positioned.
   A. punctilious
   B. glib
   C. ignominious

4. The principal did not appreciate the lad's _____ commentary.
   A. cacophonous
   B. flippant
   C. hygienic

5. The operatic baritone had a deep and orotund _____.
   A. timbre
   B. hubris
   C. din

6. Lettering on the street signs was _____ due to the dense fog.
   A. askance
   B. specious
   C. obscure

7. To accommodate the newspaper's space restrictions, the reporter was asked to _____ his lengthy account of the events.
   A. laud
   B. rebut
   C. abridge

8. Mules are known for their _____ stubbornness.
   A. derogatory
   B. innate
   C. audacious

9. Each morning, the _____ old man would greet his neighbors as he jogged around the block.
   A. juvenile
   B. sprightly
   C. irascible

10. Fellow employees were weary of the dolt's _____ jokes and vain attempts at clever repartee.
    A. jocose
    B. polemic
    C. vapid

11. After being continually _____ by his wife to buy her the expensive dress in the showroom window, he relented and presented it to her as an anniversary gift.
    A. effectuated
    B. intervened
    C. harassed

12. _____ lawsuits waste taxpayer money.
    A. Cathartic
    B. Frivolous
    C. Authoritative

13. A regimen of daily exercise is highly _____ for young and old alike.
    A. indifferent
    B. beneficial
    C. obsessive

14. The passing of the legendary icon left the musical world with a _____ sense of loss.
    A. profound
    B. humane
    C. deliberate

15. Jack the Ripper is thought to have _____ numerous gruesome murders in the 1880's.
    A. perpetrated
    B. corroborated
    C. endorsed

16. Bar owners must also bear the _____ when an intoxicated customer is later involved in an automobile accident.
    A. affectation
    B. empathy
    C. onus

17. The _____ lad wouldn't stop talking long enough to let anyone else speak.
    A. convoluted
    B. bacchanalian
    C. loquacious

18. The nation _____ the passing of the former leader.
    A. debunked
    B. assented
    C. lamented

19. With tornadoes in the vicinity, residents spent the evening in restless _____.
    A. cupidity
    B. desuetude
    C. inquietude

20. New members of the fraternity were _____ in the club's codes and practices.
    A. assessed
    B. indoctrinated
    C. coalesced

(For Quiz Answers, see Answer Section at the end of the book)

SAT & College Dictionary Workbook Quiz 69
[On a separate sheet of paper, write down the letter of the word that best fits in the blank to create a complete and meaningful sentence.]

1. Many religious leaders have been ostracized for their _____ ideologies.
   A. choleric
   B. dispassionate
   C. heretical

2. A _____ quarrel led to the band's breakup.
   A. divisive
   B. retentive
   C. tentative

3. The first mate was given _____ on all decisions concerning the upcoming transoceanic race.
   A. carte blanche
   B. bedlam
   C. savoir faire

4. The private investigator was _____ in his pursuit of the truth.
   A. relentless
   B. consequential
   C. puerile

5. The brokerage firm _____ the success of its investment fund.
   A. touted
   B. disparaged
   C. loathed

6. The veteran workers felt intimidated by the brash _____ employee's novel ideas.
   A. ignoble
   B. suppliant
   C. upstart

7. The cruel _____ summarily executed those who defied his authority.
   A. apostate
   B. despot
   C. zephyr

8. A space launch was _____ to better prepare the astronauts for the real thing.
   A. contrived
   B. evoked
   C. simulated

9. In a _____ display of wealth, the poseur flaunted her diamond ring with the hope no one would recognize it as merely inferior zirconium.
   A. residual
   B. meretricious
   C. copious

10. The court jester _____ the king with his zany antics.
    A. browbeat
    B. regaled
    C. elucidated

11. With the threat of war looming near, the tiny nation urgently needed to expand its _____ army.
    A. zany
    B. uncanny
    C. exiguous

12. Latest economic signs _____ well for continued business growth in the retail sector.
    A. maligned
    B. augured
    C. vituperated

13. A _____ and caustic vapor emanated from the geyser.
    A. crass
    B. vexatious
    C. potent

14. Offering to pay for the broken window helped _____ the irate shop owner.
    A. enthrall
    B. placate
    C. demean

15. Upon hearing cries from miners down below, rescuers _____ their efforts to clear the debris and pull the men to safety.
    A. liberated
    B. disported
    C. redoubled

16. The defendant was fully _____ of the seriousness of the crime he was charged with.
    A. apposite
    B. portentous
    C. cognizant

17. The unusual compound was an _____ of rare gemstones.
    A. imbroglio
    B. ennui
    C. aggregate

18. When asked whether she wanted to go to the mall or the movies, the young girl gave an _____ shrug.
    A. excruciating
    B. oblivious
    C. ambivalent

19. For dropping the potentially game-winning touchdown pass, the player was the target of _____ commentary by the press.
    A. derisive
    B. taciturn
    C. moribund

20. Landing on the moon was one of man's most _____ achievements.
    A. inevitable
    B. scrupulous
    C. celebrated

(For Quiz Answers, see Answer Section at the end of the book)

SAT & College Dictionary Workbook Quiz 70

[On a separate sheet of paper, write down the letter of the word that best fits in the blank to create a complete and meaningful sentence.]

1. Because she was a ____ worker, her services were in particularly high demand.
   A. fundamental
   B. limpid
   C. conscientious

2. In his leisure moments, the cruise-line passenger ____ around the deck.
   A. perambulated
   B. comported
   C. distended

3. The jocose student ____ the biology class with his verbal witticisms.
   A. perplexed
   B. detested
   C. vivified

4. International commerce carries with it complex and ____ problems.
   A. ghastly
   B. preoccupied
   C. multifaceted

5. The actor portrayed Romeo with such passion and ____ that all the women in the audience wished they were his Juliet.
   A. élan
   B. comity
   C. tocsin

6. On the witness stand, the defendant claimed that the testimony made against him was a collection of ____ lies.
   A. stern
   B. unmitigated
   C. palatable

7. The will granted ____ property rights to the heirs.
   A. expeditious
   B. secular
   C. alienable

8. The exclusive college maintained ____ minimal entrance requirements.
   A. outmoded
   B. stringent
   C. profuse

9. When asked to contribute fifty dollars to the holiday fund, the secretary initially ____ but then reluctantly consented.
   A. balked
   B. litigated
   C. desecrated

10. Visitors proceeded in a ____ manner down the rickety staircase.
    A. bellicose
    B. deliberate
    C. retiring

11. The movie's dialogue included many instances of ____ language.
    A. impregnable
    B. objectionable
    C. loquacious

12. Residents of the isolated village held a deep-seated ____ toward strangers.
    A. paucity
    B. antipathy
    C. integrity

13. The demagogue's ____ oratory ignited the prejudices of his misguided flock.
    A. orotund
    B. herculean
    C. convoluted

14. In an interview prior to the arrival of the home team, the visiting coach callously ____ their talent and leadership.
    A. inveigled
    B. scrutinized
    C. denigrated

15. The ____ afternoon left everyone languid and lethargic.
    A. destitute
    B. sultry
    C. bilious

16. The Abominable Snowman has earned its name due to the reportedly ____ odor it emits.
    A. abominable
    B. judicious
    C. protean

17. The ____ cur would even rob his own family to support his drug habit.
    A. petulant
    B. contemptible
    C. desolate

18. The haunted house produced an ____ in those who ventured within.
    A. impetus
    B. upshot
    C. angst

19. The Salk vaccine has proven ____ in helping reduce the incidence of paralytic poliomyelitis.
    A. plausible
    B. menial
    C. instrumental

20. The court ____ the janitor from the charge of petty theft when another man confessed to the crime.
    A. implored
    B. exculpated
    C. cajoled

(For Quiz Answers, see Answer Section at the end of the book)

SAT & College Dictionary Workbook Quiz 71

[On a separate sheet of paper, write down the letter of the word that best fits in the blank to create a complete and meaningful sentence.]

1. The auditorium was filled with the harp's _____ mellifluence.
   A. sisyphean
   B. artless
   C. dulcet

2. The love Judas Iscariot initially showed for Jesus was just a _____.
   A. dilemma
   B. pretense
   C. scourge

3. Given the grim economic climate, the man's business associates questioned his _____ outlook for the coming year.
   A. roseate
   B. glum
   C. frail

4. "The King" is a _____ for Elvis Presley, the king of rock n' roll.
   A. sobriquet
   B. bon mot
   C. namesake

5. The police devised a _____ in which the suspect would unknowingly be caught red-handed.
   A. stratagem
   B. fiasco
   C. directive

6. Animals from far and wide _____ at the watering hole.
   A. propounded
   B. congregated
   C. appended

7. Both _____ and entertaining, the lesson inspired students to become more politically involved.
   A. trite
   B. didactic
   C. intolerable

8. In retrospect, it was a _____ decision not to have invested in the fledgling company.
   A. fickle
   B. vile
   C. prudent

9. In a free society, liberty is an _____ human right.
   A. acquisitive
   B. unsung
   C. indefeasible

10. During the month-long garbage strike, a _____ odor permeated the city streets.
    A. fetid
    B. wistful
    C. ribald

11. The distraught parent _____ his son for coming home after midnight.
    A. placated
    B. chastised
    C. extolled

12. After much persistence, the teenager managed to _____ her parents into letting her attend the overnight party.
    A. irk
    B. vex
    C. wheedle

13. The Hall of Fame is baseball's _____, an homage to the sport's best.
    A. cornucopia
    B. pantheon
    C. aperture

14. Setting his neighbors' house ablaze while they slept was an _____ act of cowardly revenge.
    A. odious
    B. interminable
    C. arrogant

15. Medical personnel were flown in to the remote jungle to attempt to eradicate the _____ strain of malaria.
    A. inexorable
    B. autochthonous
    C. quixotic

16. The _____ man treated his underlings as servants and his peers as rabble.
    A. meritorious
    B. extroverted
    C. pompous

17. Many immigrants to America were _____ fleeing intolerable conditions in their homeland.
    A. poltroons
    B. refugees
    C. arbiters

18. More concrete evidence was needed to _____ the employees' claims of unsafe working conditions.
    A. fathom
    B. embellish
    C. substantiate

19. An _____ array of musical pieces was played during the evening concert.
    A. amorphous
    B. eclectic
    C. obstreperous

20. The mayor's unfavorable decision to support a ban on fireworks prompted hundreds of _____ telephone calls to his office.
    A. timorous
    B. deprecatory
    C. homologous

(For Quiz Answers, see Answer Section at the end of the book)

SAT & College Dictionary Workbook Quiz 72

[On a separate sheet of paper, write down the letter of the word that best fits in the blank to create a complete and meaningful sentence.]

1. Once house pets, many dogs in poor neighborhoods have become _____ and dangerous.
   A. feral
   B. retiring
   C. voluble

2. At the conclusion of the news broadcast, the day's top stories were _____.
   A. recapitulated
   B. disavowed
   C. confirmed

3. A _____ fog slowed the flow of traffic on the freeway.
   A. swarthy
   B. regal
   C. dense

4. During the televised interview, the _____ politician pledged sweeping changes in administrative policy, though few seriously expected him to deliver on any of his promises.
   A. glib
   B. piscatorial
   C. rigorous

5. Puppies bubble with _____.
   A. bliss
   B. credence
   C. vitality

6. No one else on the panel concurred with the _____ comment that politics is responsible for all the ills in the world today.
   A. choleric
   B. perfidious
   C. inane

7. After realizing that he was driving down a dead end street, the shamefaced man _____ that he should have followed his wife's directions.
   A. refuted
   B. arrogated
   C. conceded

8. Jealousy was the cause of the _____ in the two classmates' friendship.
   A. pretense
   B. obloquy
   C. rift

9. In the movie *Citizen Kane*, the _____ mogul sought to run his own daily newspaper.
   A. acquisitive
   B. derelict
   C. portentous

10. "Downsizing staff" is a _____ equivalent to "firing employees."
    A. vernal
    B. raucous
    C. euphemistic

11. An amended budget policy was _____ shortly after the new governor assumed office.
    A. edified
    B. burgeoned
    C. implemented

12. The student looked _____ to see what answers the person seated next to him had selected.
    A. askance
    B. garishly
    C. sallowly

13. The entire town was _____ over the home team's glorious championship victory.
    A. discursive
    B. ignominious
    C. jubilant

14. Facial features were _____ in the surrealistic painting, producing a macabre effect.
    A. proscribed
    B. gleaned
    C. distorted

15. The powerful volcanic explosion left a _____ cloud of dust that hovered over most of the island for weeks.
    A. fleeting
    B. combustible
    C. residual

16. A confession by the bankteller _____ the clerk of the crime of embezzlement.
    A. absolved
    B. exacerbated
    C. placated

17. Many couples wed in the _____ months.
    A. molten
    B. vernal
    C. esculent

18. The _____ lad could not be depended upon to complete any serious task.
    A. capricious
    B. flaccid
    C. prominent

19. The biographer sifted through a _____ collection of letters and faxes in preparation for his book.
    A. puny
    B. sapid
    C. voluminous

20. The headstrong child _____ his parents' wishes to be home by eight o'clock.
    A. rued
    B. flouted
    C. dissuaded

(For Quiz Answers, see Answer Section at the end of the book)

SAT & College Dictionary Workbook Quiz 73

[On a separate sheet of paper, write down the letter of the word that best fits in the blank to create a complete and meaningful sentence.]

1. Comedian Steven Wright's offbeat perspective adds to his _____ sense of humor.
    A. testy
    B. indelible
    C. droll

2. The panelist's _____ argument could not be readily refuted.
    A. cogent
    B. arcane
    C. stalwart

3. The arrest of a prominent political protester _____ a civil riot.
    A. incited
    B. denigrated
    C. vaunted

4. The king's palace retained a _____ splendor reminiscent of the Renaissance.
    A. regal
    B. preliminary
    C. shopworn

5. In underdeveloped countries, sewers are often the _____ for homeless children.
    A. pogrom
    B. requisite
    C. haven

6. Air is a _____ component for the survival of all living matter.
    A. beatific
    B. fundamental
    C. lucrative

7. The man's wife became _____ at the inference that she alone was responsible for the family's financial woes.
    A. indignant
    B. deliberate
    C. profligate

8. During Mardi Gras, police are needed to monitor the _____ crowds.
    A. rambunctious
    B. pungent
    C. exquisite

9. The _____ group followed the leader without argument.
    A. sheepish
    B. inherent
    C. frenetic

10. The latest computer models feature _____ data storage coupled with easy access to immediate retrieval.
    A. virulent
    B. capacious
    C. mawkish

11. Dictators have been known to loot their nations' treasuries with _____.
    A. duress
    B. impunity
    C. alacrity

12. The neighborhood gang of ruffians endeavored to _____ the citizens with veiled threats of retaliation should their illicit activities be reported to the authorities.
    A. emancipate
    B. fawn
    C. intimidate

13. Pollyanna was an _____ lass with irrepressible optimism.
    A. ambrosial
    B. ebullient
    C. indurate

14. Trout could be seen traveling in schools across the _____ stream.
    A. soluble
    B. hardy
    C. limpid

15. The defendant vocally _____ his noninvolvement in the crime.
    A. induced
    B. presaged
    C. asseverated

16. The _____ workers sought union representation.
    A. disaffected
    B. turgid
    C. genteel

17. The _____ tale involved voodoo dolls and ritual human sacrifice.
    A. macabre
    B. serene
    C. pedagogic

18. Many people have a _____ for chocolates.
    A. compunction
    B. quandary
    C. penchant

19. The suspect adamantly _____ the allegations levied against him.
    A. avowed
    B. shunned
    C. refuted

20. The callous judge dismissed the attorney's _____ plea for leniency for her client.
    A. somnolent
    B. fervent
    C. witless

(For Quiz Answers, see Answer Section at the end of the book)

SAT & College Dictionary Workbook Quiz 74

[On a separate sheet of paper, write down the letter of the word that best fits in the blank to create a complete and meaningful sentence.]

1. The captain _____ the dilemma before formulating a plan of escape from the sinking ship.
   A. apprised
   B. cogitated
   C. litigated

2. The makeshift hut was _____ from palm leaves and bamboo.
   A. appropriated
   B. tempered
   C. fabricated

3. The scurrilously sinister scoundrel employed devilish _____ to assume complete control of the wealthy woman's vast fortune.
   A. quirks
   B. premonitions
   C. machinations

4. The sharp-edged ceramic dish _____ the surface of the new desk.
   A. marred
   B. subsided
   C. chided

5. Wheelchair ramps help _____ access into and out of buildings.
   A. transpire
   B. facilitate
   C. patronize

6. Shakespeare's great tragedies exude a universal _____.
   A. aegis
   B. pathos
   C. ululation

7. Social and political corruption led to the ancient Roman civilization's _____.
   A. travail
   B. demise
   C. amity

8. The homeowner attempted to _____ state law by building the extension without proper permits.
   A. forswear
   B. circumvent
   C. refurbish

9. The rich lad _____ his family's wealth.
   A. saturated
   B. confiscated
   C. vaunted

10. A person of shrewd business _____, the woman knew not to sell her share in the fledgling but promising company.
    A. adulation
    B. foresight
    C. milieu

11. It required an effort not to doze off during the lecturer's _____ discourse on evolution.
    A. prosaic
    B. deft
    C. exemplary

12. After fleeing the war-ravaged country, the former insurgent _____ all allegiance to the rebel faction.
    A. entreated
    B. abjured
    C. propagated

13. For many days after the volcano erupted, a _____ of soot hung over the town, blocking out the sun.
    A. shibboleth
    B. pall
    C. foliage

14. Eating an artichoke for the first time, the little tyke had a _____ look on his face.
    A. bemused
    B. gregarious
    C. reserved

15. The law student's _____ remark exposed his ignorance regarding the workings of the judicial system.
    A. bereft
    B. supernumerary
    C. fatuous

16. Many popular hair styles of the past quickly become _____.
    A. gaunt
    B. passé
    C. desolate

17. The provocative presentation _____ a surprising number of questions from the young audience.
    A. substantiated
    B. behooved
    C. educed

18. The concerned father _____ with his daughter over her disregard of the prearranged curfew hour.
    A. aggrandized
    B. remonstrated
    C. delineated

19. She displayed only a _____ interest in attending the class reunion.
    A. tepid
    B. jubilant
    C. pellucid

20. Diamond-cutters ply their craft with _____ precision.
    A. erratic
    B. meticulous
    C. putrid

(For Quiz Answers, see Answer Section at the end of the book)

SAT & College Dictionary Workbook Quiz 75

[On a separate sheet of paper, write down the letter of the word that best fits in the blank to create a complete and meaningful sentence.]

1. Staging *Macbeth* as a comedy is a _____ notion.
   A. ludicrous
   B. divisive
   C. credulous

2. Through cunning _____, Huckleberry Finn persuaded his friends to paint his fence while he sat back and observed.
   A. chicanery
   B. metamorphosis
   C. proclivity

3. Envy and jealousy perpetrate _____ rumors.
   A. derelict
   B. stout
   C. pestilent

4. Jewish prisoners _____ hopelessly in concentration camps during World War II.
   A. disseminated
   B. languished
   C. vanquished

5. In the lawsuit, the litigant accused the reporter of _____ his good name by calling him a crooked politician.
   A. besmirching
   B. perpetrating
   C. superseding

6. The "meaning of life" is a philosophical _____ that has haunted mankind for millennia.
   A. respite
   B. nemesis
   C. conundrum

7. Listeners were enraptured by the _____ sounds produced by the trio of harps.
   A. euphonious
   B. willful
   C. ardent

8. When struck, a gong produces a _____ sound.
   A. sonorous
   B. gossamer
   C. maudlin

9. The lawyer was lauded as an _____ citizen who fought sedulously for the rights of those oppressed.
   A. infamous
   B. upstanding
   C. equable

10. In her half-time _____, the basketball coach emphasized the need for total personal commitment to achieve success both in sports and in life.
    A. panegyric
    B. harangue
    C. apogee

11. The rustic couple's _____ manners met with glacial stares from the elite restaurant patrons.
    A. frail
    B. plebeian
    C. regal

12. A library is a _____ for books.
    A. pinnacle
    B. repository
    C. juggernaut

13. Experts considered the unsigned painting an _____ work uncannily resembling the art of Edouard Manet.
    A. apocryphal
    B. irate
    C. untenable

14. Although he was the star high school quarterback, few would have guessed so by his _____ and mild-mannered personality.
    A. voracious
    B. elite
    C. self-effacing

15. The prosecuting attorney _____ the defense's claim that it was too dark to have identified the attacker.
    A. demurred
    B. rebutted
    C. evinced

16. _____ in several languages, the ambassador was able to negotiate a meeting between the two foreign dignitaries.
    A. Domineering
    B. Proficient
    C. Shrewd

17. The lamb was _____ in the holy fire.
    A. consorted
    B. perished
    C. immolated

18. As he was being transferred to another location, the unruly prisoner _____ against his handlers.
    A. tempered
    B. despised
    C. fulminated

19. A priest was summoned to _____ the demonic spirits that lived in the haunted house.
    A. exorcise
    B. rejuvenate
    C. castigate

20. "To kill two birds with one stone" is a _____ expression that offends nature-loving conservationists.
    A. recherché
    B. clichéd
    C. maladroit

(For Quiz Answers, see Answer Section at the end of the book)

SAT & College Dictionary Workbook Quiz 76

[On a separate sheet of paper, write down the letter of the word that best fits in the blank to create a complete and meaningful sentence.]

1. A dog is _____ to its master.
   A. feeble
   B. submissive
   C. diminutive

2. The court jester made a _____ attempt to soothe the emperor's wrath.
   A. capacious
   B. feeble
   C. protean

3. At his sentencing, the condemned man bellowed forth a series of _____ against those who indirectly contributed to his life of crime.
   A. maledictions
   B. harbingers
   C. shortcomings

4. A _____ rush into the stock market can prove a financially costly mistake.
   A. turbid
   B. precipitous
   C. vivacious

5. The science fair participants were _____ and industrious students.
   A. seraphic
   B. august
   C. earnest

6. Under threat of a lawsuit, the newspaper _____ the allegations made in an earlier article.
   A. flaunted
   B. denounced
   C. retracted

7. The two friends engaged in a pleasant telephone _____.
   A. jeremiad
   B. prognosis
   C. causerie

8. Even the most trying of times, the mother of eight young boys always remained patient and _____.
   A. feckless
   B. painstaking
   C. unflappable

9. A driver's license is _____ in all fifty states.
   A. valid
   B. solemn
   C. prevalent

10. At the testimonial dinner, the guest of honor amused his well-wishers with a litany of _____.
    A. innuendos
    B. bon mots
    C. quagmires

11. Emily Post outlined the _____ within which one must behave to be socially proper.
    A. parameters
    B. travails
    C. celerity

12. The council chief _____ the gods to provide the tribe with much-needed rain.
    A. conjoined
    B. facilitated
    C. supplicated

13. Rather than assert his own independence, the toady always _____ to his superiors.
    A. truckled
    B. complemented
    C. quibbled

14. Residents vehemently _____ that the reported midnight celestial sightings were no hoax.
    A. endeavored
    B. averred
    C. reproved

15. The buxom blonde _____ the rich old romantic into buying her a diamond ring.
    A. defiled
    B. chastised
    C. inveigled

16. A sponge is an elastic and _____ skeletal mass.
    A. culinary
    B. porous
    C. servile

17. Once the doctor administered the antidote, the pain and swelling quickly _____.
    A. persevered
    B. consolidated
    C. subsided

18. Only a few _____ outbreaks of malaria occurred throughout the country after counteractive measures were taken.
    A. condign
    B. sporadic
    C. obstinate

19. The heroic firefighter was eulogized as a _____ husband and devoted father.
    A. secular
    B. virtuous
    C. brawny

20. Latex is a coating produced from _____ rubber.
    A. conjugal
    B. synthetic
    C. insuperable

(For Quiz Answers, see Answer Section at the end of the book)

SAT & College Dictionary Workbook Quiz 77

[On a separate sheet of paper, write down the letter of the word that best fits in the blank to create a complete and meaningful sentence.]

1. To confirm the disputed cause of death, the coroner ordered that the body be _____ and an autopsy performed.
   A. ascribed
   B. subjugated
   C. exhumed

2. The grueling hike up the steep hill _____ the cadets.
   A. enervated
   B. cloyed
   C. vilified

3. The _____ youngster never let a setback deter him from persevering.
   A. resilient
   B. coherent
   C. ludicrous

4. A suggestion was made to take a more _____ look at the traffic problem before instituting any stopgap measures.
   A. implausible
   B. fulsome
   C. comprehensive

5. Desecrating a tomb is an _____ act of disrespect.
   A. amenable
   B. untimely
   C. egregious

6. As a result of human incursion, the population of the Tasmanian wolf was _____ to the point of extinction.
   A. decimated
   B. annexed
   C. inhibited

7. *Tristan and Isolde* is a _____ tale of a doomed love affair.
   A. woeful
   B. roseate
   C. diaphanous

8. The soldiers suggested that a _____ traitor from within their ranks may have led to their capture.
   A. tenebrous
   B. perfidious
   C. cursory

9. A steak knife often has a _____ edge.
   A. serrated
   B. rubicund
   C. disparate

10. Mark Antony delivered an _____ speech to the Roman masses.
    A. aureate
    B. innumerable
    C. oleaginous

11. Because teenagers are often given to _____ about their indestructibility, many engage in activities that are reckless and potentially hazardous.
    A. whimsies
    B. initiatives
    C. chicanery

12. The stewardess maintained her _____ even as the plane tossed and turned in the storm.
    A. parity
    B. vertigo
    C. equanimity

13. At the symposium, the eminent scientist _____ his views regarding the origin of the universe.
    A. expounded
    B. vitiated
    C. acceded

14. The customer became _____ when told the sale item could not be exchanged.
    A. soporific
    B. irate
    C. provincial

15. The restaurant's prime rib steak was _____ and flavorful.
    A. hardy
    B. succulent
    C. famished

16. Statistical evidence helped to _____ her argument.
    A. incriminate
    B. underpin
    C. avenge

17. Many companies that are now _____ were, in their time, industry leaders.
    A. morose
    B. defunct
    C. aloof

18. The secret lovers arranged a midnight _____ at the lake.
    A. rendezvous
    B. demise
    C. odyssey

19. In the locker room after the game, the head coach delivered a bitter _____ to the team for displaying unsportsmanlike conduct on the field.
    A. tirade
    B. diversion
    C. paean

20. The young singing sensation experienced a _____ rise to stardom.
    A. meteoric
    B. putative
    C. factious

(For Quiz Answers, see Answer Section at the end of the book)

SAT & College Dictionary Workbook Quiz 78

[On a separate sheet of paper, write down the letter of the word that best fits in the blank to create a complete and meaningful sentence.]

1. Critics disparaged the comedic play as an _____ descent into mediocrity.
    A. innocuous
    B. emaciated
    C. ulterior

2. A Boy Scout pocket knife is a _____ gadget.
    A. versatile
    B. malleable
    C. gaudy

3. Victory was close at hand when she _____ the opposing debater's primary premise.
    A. subverted
    B. confuted
    C. asseverated

4. Escargot is a popular _____ delicacy.
    A. pertinacious
    B. acrid
    C. esculent

5. During battle, the beetle sought to _____ the rival by turning it on its back.
    A. coerce
    B. disport
    C. incapacitate

6. The promise of riches beyond their wildest dreams _____ the exhausted prospectors to continue in their search for gold.
    A. balked
    B. induced
    C. exorcised

7. The _____ moonglow shone in the window.
    A. lambent
    B. immutable
    C. definitive

8. Rococo furniture is characterized by its highly _____ style.
    A. hospitable
    B. ornate
    C. succulent

9. By confessing, he hoped to _____ himself of the guilt that had haunted him for months.
    A. debase
    B. abase
    C. purge

10. During the Civil War, the _____ Confederates fought against an unending stream of opposition.
    A. dauntless
    B. sedate
    C. bacchanalian

11. Sir Lancelot _____ his love for Guinevere.
    A. repudiated
    B. enervated
    C. avowed

12. The class was _____ for their rudeness during the guest speaker's visit.
    A. reproached
    B. exonerated
    C. condescended

13. Locked windows _____ the burglar's efforts to enter the house.
    A. dismayed
    B. evaded
    C. thwarted

14. The _____ portion of cheese was sufficient to feed the scrawny mouse.
    A. ponderous
    B. minuscule
    C. subtle

15. Some people have an _____ for taking risks while behind the wheel of a car.
    A. infraction
    B. umbrage
    C. affinity

16. The weary woman looked _____ at the hooded man sitting on the other side of the bus.
    A. mawkish
    B. askance
    C. gingerly

17. The senator's moral integrity was _____.
    A. irreproachable
    B. bucolic
    C. eclectic

18. The Galapagos tortoise is the island's _____.
    A. disciple
    B. namesake
    C. inception

19. Despite its action and suspense, the movie lacked a _____ story-line.
    A. cryptic
    B. steadfast
    C. plausible

20. Many feel that the current tax structure is unfairly _____ to those most in need of tax relief.
    A. banal
    B. oppressive
    C. contemptible

(For Quiz Answers, see Answer Section at the end of the book)

SAT & College Dictionary Workbook Quiz 79

[On a separate sheet of paper, write down the letter of the word that best fits in the blank to create a complete and meaningful sentence.]

1. Thousands of people lost their life's savings during the 1929 stock market _____.
   A. martinet
   B. retribution
   C. debacle

2. Before having had his morning cup of coffee, the man was particularly _____.
   A. irascible
   B. sentient
   C. pious

3. The realistic painting captured the _____ beauty of a lake in springtime.
   A. innumerable
   B. convoluted
   C. serene

4. Selling defective merchandise to the elderly is an _____ and despicable practice.
   A. unconscionable
   B. irrevocable
   C. equivocal

5. Christopher Columbus _____ the queen into giving him additional sailors for his voyage in search of a new world.
   A. fabricated
   B. blandished
   C. vindicated

6. Man is but a pawn of the _____ hand of fate.
   A. ineluctable
   B. synchronous
   C. tremulous

7. The constant strain of deadlines took its toll on the overworked reporter, who suffered in later years from chronic _____.
   A. lassitude
   B. avarice
   C. deference

8. Once she had achieved fame, the fickle starlet _____ her hometown friends.
   A. shunned
   B. repented
   C. befriended

9. A _____ odor emanated from the crypt.
   A. saline
   B. dulcet
   C. vile

10. Rather than seek absolution for his crime, the prisoner _____ those responsible for his capture.
    A. buttressed
    B. dumbfounded
    C. imprecated

11. Personal computers marked the _____ of a new age of mobile technology.
    A. advent
    B. gloaming
    C. sustenance

12. The pubescent lad devised a _____ but sophomoric scheme to win the heart of the homecoming queen.
    A. calamitous
    B. pompous
    C. quixotic

13. Critics hailed the musical for its _____ choreography.
    A. fleeting
    B. iconoclastic
    C. superlative

14. The _____ neighbor couldn't keep his nose out of other people's affairs.
    A. bumptious
    B. nonchalant
    C. infallible

15. Uninterested in socializing with peers, the _____ lad preferred instead the desolate comfort of staying home and recording his thoughts in poetry.
    A. eminent
    B. introverted
    C. vivacious

16. The sound of reporters banging on her front door at midnight _____ the poor woman.
    A. nonplussed
    B. bantered
    C. equivocated

17. The van had a _____ coloration, blotches of white and grey contrasting with the original black paint.
    A. pied
    B. concurrent
    C. dissonant

18. Despite a court order, the reporter refused to _____ the information told to her in strictest confidence.
    A. cogitate
    B. relinquish
    C. decry

19. It takes great _____ to hike up a steep mountain trail.
    A. discourse
    B. stamina
    C. zeal

20. Once the miscreant had successfully completed the rehabilitation program, the charge of vandalism was _____ from his criminal record.
    A. vivified
    B. abstained
    C. expunged

(For Quiz Answers, see Answer Section at the end of the book)

SAT & College Dictionary Workbook Quiz 80

[On a separate sheet of paper, write down the letter of the word that best fits in the blank to create a complete and meaningful sentence.]

1. An audit revealed that funds had been _____ from the drama club's treasury.
   A. devastated
   B. adduced
   C. peculated

2. The mother's reassuring words helped _____ her young daughter's fears of riding the roller coaster.
   A. expedite
   B. stupefy
   C. assuage

3. The lion _____ supreme in the jungle.
   A. incites
   B. vies
   C. reigns

4. Fellow club members found it difficult conversing with the _____ young man.
   A. malevolent
   B. reserved
   C. deft

5. After a moment of deliberation, the congressman _____ his words of condemnation against those who had voted to kill his proposal.
   A. coerced
   B. demoted
   C. tempered

6. The Loch Ness monster has long been reported to be an actual surviving _____ of the deep.
   A. denizen
   B. motif
   C. sycophant

7. The cub reporter's _____ discourse did not impress the veteran journalist.
   A. innate
   B. turgid
   C. valid

8. Riding a bicycle can be a _____ and healthful exercise.
   A. tranquil
   B. vigorous
   C. deleterious

9. It is a person's _____ to say what he or she believes.
   A. prerogative
   B. inkling
   C. mien

10. Close friends _____ the couple in their hour of grief.
    A. revered
    B. consoled
    C. anguished

11. In the company of her minions, the beauty queen displayed a _____ air of superiority.
    A. haughty
    B. migratory
    C. defamatory

12. The Statue of Liberty _____ individual liberty and freedom.
    A. personifies
    B. correlates
    C. forswears

13. Not even the earthquake's aftershocks could _____ the rescuers' efforts to locate survivors.
    A. meddle
    B. exult
    C. deter

14. The Barbary Coast was renowned for its _____ pirates who wreaked havoc in the Mediterranean Sea from the sixteenth through eighteenth centuries.
    A. whimsical
    B. ruthless
    C. provident

15. For added clarity, a glossary was _____ to the textbook.
    A. repined
    B. appended
    C. expropriated

16. A _____ agreement was made between the two dorm mates not to play the radio loud while the other was studying.
    A. palpable
    B. furtive
    C. tacit

17. The woman's _____ qualifications made her a prime candidate for the executive position.
    A. sanguinary
    B. intrepid
    C. unimpeachable

18. The awkward lad was _____ by his friends for his performance on the dance floor.
    A. bantered
    B. pacified
    C. expunged

19. When asked what the captain had instructed him to do, the first mate repeated the order _____.
    A. verbatim
    B. incognito
    C. straitlaced

20. A rock is an _____ object.
    A. inanimate
    B. ascetic
    C. obdurate

(For Quiz Answers, see Answer Section at the end of the book)

SAT & College Dictionary Workbook Quiz 81

[On a separate sheet of paper, write down the letter of the word that best fits in the blank to create a complete and meaningful sentence.]

1. Aluminum is a _____ metallic element often used as an electrical or thermal conductor.
   A. sophomoric
   B. palpable
   C. ductile

2. The _____ waft of chocolate chip cookies attracted passersby to enter the store.
   A. redolent
   B. wayward
   C. chimerical

3. Thick wooden beams helped _____ the sagging ceiling.
   A. buttress
   B. instigate
   C. obviate

4. Neighboring kingdoms feared the powerful emperor, whose armies staged periodic _____ in search of new slaves.
   A. incursions
   B. paradigms
   C. coalitions

5. Unfounded rumors and _____ can besmirch a person's good name.
   A. ratiocination
   B. directives
   C. innuendos

6. Reaching one's financial goals should always be _____ to attaining a measurable quality of happiness in one's life.
   A. feasible
   B. subservient
   C. guileful

7. A _____ stomach is often a sign of severe malnutrition.
   A. tumid
   B. rotund
   C. peevish

8. A lion approaches in a _____ manner to catch its prey off guard.
   A. stealthy
   B. candid
   C. migratory

9. It took three people to carry the _____ package.
   A. ponderous
   B. cumulative
   C. inconsiderate

10. The Arab leader's mansion boasted _____ halls lined with precious objects d'art.
    A. grandiose
    B. infamous
    C. eternal

11. A noisy, bulky contraption was the _____ of today's modern computer.
    A. pretense
    B. archetype
    C. haven

12. The evangelist _____ the virtues of chastity and abstinence.
    A. extolled
    B. appropriated
    C. traduced

13. The _____ neighbor invited himself over for dinner.
    A. presumptuous
    B. stringent
    C. frivolous

14. After a few drinks, the stodgy group soon became jovial and _____.
    A. livid
    B. insipid
    C. sportive

15. The _____ recreant was banished from the village.
    A. treacherous
    B. jaunty
    C. precocious

16. Disease-control specialists were flown in to try to contain the outbreak of the _____ strain of bacteria.
    A. inaugural
    B. susceptible
    C. virulent

17. A _____ wafted through the peaceful island paradise.
    A. précis
    B. zephyr
    C. nadir

18. The ambrosial delicacy was prepared with _____ herbs and spices.
    A. savory
    B. incarnate
    C. effervescent

19. The spilled chemicals quickly _____ throughout the lake.
    A. personified
    B. dispersed
    C. foundered

20. Only recently have citizens in lesser-developed nations been extended the _____.
    A. franchise
    B. nexus
    C. gloaming

(For Quiz Answers, see Answer Section at the end of the book)

SAT & College Dictionary Workbook Quiz 82

[On a separate sheet of paper, write down the letter of the word that best fits in the blank to create a complete and meaningful sentence.]

1. The proud lady refused to _____ herself by scrubbing the kitchen floor.
   A. requite
   B. demean
   C. consort

2. Even though he considered himself only a social drinker, his _____ ways eventually led him to seeking help from Alcoholics Anonymous.
   A. intemperate
   B. culinary
   C. percipient

3. Beagles possess an _____ sense of smell.
   A. acute
   B. expedient
   C. ostentatious

4. The proselytized convert _____ all the teachings of his former religion.
   A. repudiated
   B. disclosed
   C. conceded

5. The misdirected lad had no _____ about taking money out of the store's cash register for his personal use.
   A. compunctions
   B. retrogressions
   C. antipodes

6. Once made, he knew his decision to resign as head basketball coach would be _____.
   A. novel
   B. irrevocable
   C. posthumous

7. Huckleberry Finn employed crafty _____ to enlist the services of friends to paint his fence.
   A. subterfuge
   B. conflagration
   C. effulgence

8. The _____ tot hid underneath his mother's skirt.
   A. irate
   B. bombastic
   C. tremulous

9. Off stage, the pop singer was an ingratiatingly _____ gentleman.
   A. intolerable
   B. obsessive
   C. unassuming

10. Julius Caesar was an _____ and much-feared Roman emperor.
    A. arbitrary
    B. earnest
    C. orthodox

11. The crowd caught a _____ glimpse of the glamorous singer as she drove by in her motorcade.
    A. fleeting
    B. chic
    C. maudlin

12. The entire family, including in-laws, were _____ Christians.
    A. devout
    B. peremptory
    C. torrid

13. Prior to working out the details, the prisoners drafted an _____ plan of escape.
    A. inchoate
    B. apposite
    C. obligatory

14. The musician's _____ included songs from the 1970s and 1980s.
    A. archetype
    B. motif
    C. repertoire

15. The _____ captain braved the angry sea.
    A. intemperate
    B. peremptory
    C. stalwart

16. A _____ garlic taste added zest to the otherwise bland meal.
    A. fearsome
    B. gamely
    C. subtle

17. Three authors _____ on a book chronicling the events leading up to the Civil War.
    A. perused
    B. essayed
    C. collaborated

18. A hearty meal provides much-needed _____ to a hungry lad.
    A. sustenance
    B. bravado
    C. fortitude

19. The _____ accountant feared asking his boss for a day off.
    A. jocund
    B. timorous
    C. stalwart

20. The ambassador _____ the king to reconsider his decision to declare war.
    A. evoked
    B. repined
    C. beseeched

(For Quiz Answers, see Answer Section at the end of the book)

SAT & College Dictionary Workbook Quiz 83

[On a separate sheet of paper, write down the letter of the word that best fits in the blank to create a complete and meaningful sentence.]

1. Lions are _____ creatures who predominate on the savanna.
   A. permeable
   B. immaculate
   C. formidable

2. The intense heat made everyone in the classroom rather _____.
   A. rancid
   B. avid
   C. listless

3. The economic analyst presented a _____ outlook for summer retail sales.
   A. pessimistic
   B. frivolous
   C. cordial

4. Pirates were known as a _____ lot who sought one ship after another to plunder.
   A. livid
   B. rapacious
   C. graphic

5. The sonnets of William Shakespeare were the epitome of _____ Elizabethan verse.
   A. arduous
   B. woebegone
   C. euphuistic

6. When the football team won the championship game, there was _____ that evening in the streets.
   A. fortitude
   B. tintinnabulation
   C. bedlam

7. Wallabies are _____ to Australia.
   A. contemporary
   B. indigenous
   C. alienable

8. The Salk Vaccine was a _____ of significant twentieth century medical advancements against dreaded diseases.
   A. respite
   B. tenet
   C. precursor

9. With all the modern conveniences today, people live a much more _____ existence than they did in times past.
   A. sedentary
   B. indigenous
   C. provisional

10. The candidate was an _____ and eloquent speaker.
    A. adroit
    B. equable
    C. opprobrious

11. A newly-installed alarm system _____ the attempted break-in.
    A. infringed
    B. foiled
    C. coveted

12. Visible signs of an impending hurricane _____ the tiny community into preparedness.
    A. eschewed
    B. spurned
    C. galvanized

13. Fatigue _____ the hiker to rest awhile.
    A. secluded
    B. endeavored
    C. compelled

14. The captain's urgent announcement to securely fasten seat belts _____ the nervous passengers.
    A. taunted
    B. dismayed
    C. quashed

15. Jean Lafitte was a _____ pirate.
    A. diffuse
    B. scurrilous
    C. magnanimous

16. A partial scholarship _____ the student's college tuition.
    A. subsidized
    B. berated
    C. debased

17. Children could pet the _____ horse without fear of being bitten or attacked.
    A. solemn
    B. inherent
    C. docile

18. The proud community heaped _____ praise on their local hero.
    A. fickle
    B. lavish
    C. hardy

19. A rainbow consists of _____ bands of light.
    A. itinerant
    B. striated
    C. percipient

20. Selling its unprofitable subsidiary allowed the firm to _____ bankruptcy.
    A. rehabilitate
    B. adduce
    C. forestall

(For Quiz Answers, see Answer Section at the end of the book)

SAT & College Dictionary Workbook Quiz 84

[On a separate sheet of paper, write down the letter of the word that best fits in the blank to create a complete and meaningful sentence.]

1. To better inform the council of their various options, an _____ historian was brought in to illustrate similar instances in the past.
   A. authoritative
   B. indignant
   C. obdurate

2. It is impolite and disrespectful to _____ on another's chosen privacy.
   A. aspire
   B. infringe
   C. reign

3. The President addressed the _____ in his annual nationwide speech.
   A. regimen
   B. franchise
   C. populace

4. Butlers are trained to act in a _____ manner to their employers.
   A. subservient
   B. feckless
   C. mandatory

5. Knowing her brother only too well, she suspected an _____ motive behind his guise of complaisant geniality.
   A. infinite
   B. objectionable
   C. ulterior

6. Elders delight in the _____ satisfaction of watching their grandchildren play.
   A. vicarious
   B. stoic
   C. intransigent

7. Generations have enjoyed the _____ antics of the Three Stooges.
   A. initial
   B. zany
   C. abstemious

8. The students were not impressed by the politician's _____ lecture on ethics and morality; they sensed that he himself must have committed skullduggery to have climbed the ladder to political success.
   A. cognizant
   B. sanctimonious
   C. incisive

9. The _____ dancer graced the stage with her ballerina-like steps.
   A. vicarious
   B. dilatory
   C. nimble

10. The chemical compound consisted of three _____ elements.
    A. undaunted
    B. gaudy
    C. discrete

11. The boys good-naturedly engaged one another in a round of _____ banter.
    A. atypical
    B. tactful
    C. innocuous

12. Wholesale annihilation reached its _____ during World War II when two atomic bombs were dropped on unsuspecting cities.
    A. ultimatum
    B. apogee
    C. exodus

13. The grand jury _____ six men in connection with the string of recent bank robberies.
    A. alleged
    B. indicted
    C. litigated

14. In order to meet his monthly rent obligations, the man sought _____ assistance from his local church.
    A. pecuniary
    B. heinous
    C. conscientious

15. Unexpectedly strong sales in their first week presaged a _____ future for the young business.
    A. dour
    B. vociferous
    C. propitious

16. Beachgoers flocked to bask in the noonday sun's _____ rays.
    A. desultory
    B. melancholy
    C. refulgent

17. Reporters announced that a _____ settlement had been reached between the union and corporate management.
    A. lucid
    B. tentative
    C. poignant

18. Everyone has _____ faults; that's what makes us human.
    A. disputatious
    B. sententious
    C. venial

19. The slow sales season proved a _____ disaster for the smaller stores in the shopping mall.
    A. virtual
    B. sordid
    C. putrid

20. Renoir's impressionist artworks reflect _____ detail.
    A. disputatious
    B. painstaking
    C. tacit

(For Quiz Answers, see Answer Section at the end of the book)

SAT & College Dictionary Workbook Quiz 85

[On a separate sheet of paper, write down the letter of the word that best fits in the blank to create a complete and meaningful sentence.]

1. In any classroom, the safety of the students should be of _____ concern to the teacher.
    A. titanic
    B. paramount
    C. contiguous

2. The mendacious lad's mother knew that his claim of never having filched cookies from the cookie jar was a _____ falsehood.
    A. patent
    B. fallow
    C. callow

3. Bats are nocturnal creatures; humans are generally _____ ones.
    A. vapid
    B. intractable
    C. diurnal

4. Judges pride themselves on their _____ analysis of disputes presented before them.
    A. prurient
    B. apathetic
    C. impartial

5. After the war, the tiny nation was _____ from totalitarian rule.
    A. contrived
    B. liberated
    C. decamped

6. The seasoned thespian had a _____ voice that could be heard clearly throughout the large auditorium.
    A. voluble
    B. stentorian
    C. philistine

7. In prehistoric times, the pterosaur reigned _____ in the skies.
    A. jubilant
    B. invaluable
    C. sovereign

8. A brisk stroll in the cool mountain air gave the young girl's cheeks a _____ wholesomeness.
    A. diffident
    B. sanguinary
    C. ruddy

9. The _____ crew was on the verge of mutiny.
    A. crass
    B. dour
    C. recalcitrant

10. The waggish lad's _____ behavior on the bus was met with a swift rebuke by the driver.
    A. decorous
    B. tautological
    C. puerile

11. Lifeboat survivors had to cope with the _____ of being stranded in the open ocean.
    A. exigencies
    B. accolades
    C. quirks

12. The actor's _____ death took the entire film industry by surprise.
    A. untimely
    B. invidious
    C. profound

13. The Navy Seals are an _____ military group.
    A. anthropomorphic
    B. unobtrusive
    C. elite

14. Misplacing the important company report _____ her boss.
    A. assuaged
    B. vituperated
    C. infuriated

15. Laziness was the man's most noticeable _____.
    A. canard
    B. shortcoming
    C. paradox

16. A loud noise outside momentarily _____ the housekeeper's attention from her activities.
    A. temporized
    B. diverted
    C. intimidated

17. Rather than risk the dangers associated with cigarettes, many choose to _____ from smoking altogether.
    A. manumit
    B. abstain
    C. reproach

18. When told by the doctor that she had given birth to healthy twins, the new mother was _____.
    A. contumacious
    B. intransigent
    C. ecstatic

19. The war hero was awarded a _____ medal of honor.
    A. meretricious
    B. categorical
    C. posthumous

20. Rather than seek to resolve the problem with a pragmatic approach, the school administrator adhered to his ineffectual _____ ideologies.
    A. doctrinaire
    B. veracious
    C. noxious

(For Quiz Answers, see Answer Section at the end of the book)

SAT & College Dictionary Workbook Quiz 86
[On a separate sheet of paper, write down the letter of the word that best fits in the blank to create a complete and meaningful sentence.]

1. As he matured, the miscreant _____ his sordid past.
   A. repented
   B. demeaned
   C. superseded

2. The _____ man deserted his battalion while in the midst of combat.
   A. craven
   B. lachrymose
   C. rudimentary

3. The soprano sang the aria with such _____ that the audience was enraptured.
   A. verve
   B. furor
   C. rancor

4. In his anger, the motorist lashed out with a _____ barrage of insults.
   A. headstrong
   B. caustic
   C. sedentary

5. The decision to enter World War II was, for all Americans, a grave and highly _____ action.
   A. consequential
   B. subservient
   C. forlorn

6. Even into his nineties, George Bernard Shaw possessed a _____ mind and trenchant wit.
   A. nimble
   B. durable
   C. resonant

7. The Ebola is a _____ strain of virus.
   A. corpulent
   B. derelict
   C. pernicious

8. When it comes time to study, many tend to _____ and eventually find themselves cramming the night before.
   A. effectuate
   B. procrastinate
   C. detest

9. The rookie received _____ advice from the coach on improving his baseball swing.
   A. salutary
   B. wily
   C. pending

10. The _____ taskmaster demanded that his crew work nonstop until the cargo was unloaded.
    A. abrupt
    B. sprightly
    C. oppressive

11. The _____ stage could be set up within an hour.
    A. superfluous
    B. mobile
    C. comprehensive

12. The gallant knight was _____ in his quest to locate and rescue the imprisoned princess.
    A. loquacious
    B. resolute
    C. eclectic

13. It is wise to be _____ of claims that appear too good to be true.
    A. wary
    B. disingenuous
    C. awry

14. The retired athlete cast a _____ look from the stadium stands, remembering the days when he had been revered as the star of his high school football team.
    A. blatant
    B. malevolent
    C. wistful

15. In the library display window lay the _____ book on the Roman Empire.
    A. acquisitive
    B. treacherous
    C. definitive

16. Many famous and successful people have had to overcome their share of _____ in their earlier years.
    A. largess
    B. adversity
    C. preciosity

17. Results of the experiment _____ with recent research findings.
    A. concurred
    B. truckled
    C. appeased

18. Modern teaching methods were subjected to unrelenting _____ from the conservative educator.
    A. élan
    B. animadversions
    C. prowess

19. The _____ sent the citizens running for shelter.
    A. tocsin
    B. epiphany
    C. paean

20. The tiny nation's _____ climate made it a year-round haven for tourists.
    A. passé
    B. equable
    C. ancillary

(For Quiz Answers, see Answer Section at the end of the book)

SAT & College Dictionary Workbook Quiz 87

[On a separate sheet of paper, write down the letter of the word that best fits in the blank to create a complete and meaningful sentence.]

1. Unlike his cheerful younger brother, the older sibling was _____ and ill-tempered.
   A. dauntless
   B. morose
   C. thrifty

2. The editorial was a _____ condemnation of recent attempts to build hotels along the beach.
   A. loath
   B. dense
   C. vitriolic

3. _____ by the complex problem, the youngster refused to work on it any longer.
   A. Inveigled
   B. Reviled
   C. Addled

4. Bodybuilders are often characterized as _____ egoists.
   A. distraught
   B. woeful
   C. vain

5. Despite his best effort, he could not _____ his friend from entering the dark and forbidding cave.
   A. propitiate
   B. impugn
   C. dissuade

6. Realizing that his _____ contributions would benefit few, if any, the senator left the political arena to pursue a more personally satisfying career in education.
   A. amiable
   B. implicit
   C. picayune

7. The _____ island had only recently been discovered by explorers.
   A. remote
   B. preeminent
   C. illusory

8. Almost everyone has at one time or another had an encounter with the _____ school bully.
   A. exuberant
   B. truculent
   C. penitent

9. Twenty years in prison seemed _____ punishment for the scoundrel's treacherous deeds.
   A. condign
   B. indefatigable
   C. reticent

10. For all his efforts, the waiter was rewarded with only a _____ tip.
    A. paltry
    B. disreputable
    C. tawdry

11. Although he thought the bar hostess really loved him, the young romantic was in fact merely another victim of the temptress's _____.
    A. succor
    B. pathos
    C. duplicity

12. The precocious lad took personal pride in being part of the university's academic _____.
    A. rendezvous
    B. milieu
    C. dudgeon

13. The young movie star felt that she had been _____ by the interviewer's careless accusations.
    A. despoiled
    B. slandered
    C. harassed

14. A _____ meeting was arranged between the two young lovers.
    A. fractious
    B. mercurial
    C. clandestine

15. Already on a tight budget, the father was _____ to raising his son's weekly allowance.
    A. indisposed
    B. elated
    C. amenable

16. The first year of a foreign language course requires extensive learning by _____.
    A. inception
    B. rote
    C. plaudits

17. At the luau, guests were treated to a _____ banquet.
    A. sumptuous
    B. harrowing
    C. ludicrous

18. In the haunted house, ghostly events _____ during the visitors' overnight stay.
    A. transpired
    B. dispensed
    C. congregated

19. His attorney claimed he had confessed under _____ and not of his own volition.
    A. antipathy
    B. duress
    C. probity

20. Upon his death, the king was _____ in an elaborate crypt.
    A. disdained
    B. exhumed
    C. interred

(For Quiz Answers, see Answer Section at the end of the book)

SAT & College Dictionary Workbook Quiz 88

[On a separate sheet of paper, write down the letter of the word that best fits in the blank to create a complete and meaningful sentence.]

1. A _____ effort was made to correct all spelling errors in his report.
   A. conscientious
   B. luminous
   C. spurious

2. A panel of the university's most _____ scholars discussed avenues for academic improvement at the institution.
   A. concise
   B. valid
   C. sapient

3. The website displayed _____ pictures of the fatal car crash.
   A. morbid
   B. querulous
   C. deprecatory

4. A sense of humor is _____ for surviving trying times.
   A. impertinent
   B. vital
   C. ecstatic

5. The _____ young lass caught the fancy of the older boys.
   A. turbid
   B. demure
   C. irascible

6. The two rival city-states became enmeshed in an _____ over border rights.
   A. imbroglio
   B. alliance
   C. exigency

7. The group of youths _____ themselves with a game of miniature golf.
   A. inured
   B. reviled
   C. disported

8. The irate gambler _____ that the dealer was cheating.
   A. flouted
   B. taunted
   C. alleged

9. Under the influence of alcohol, the motorist's words and thoughts were not _____.
   A. coherent
   B. flagrant
   C. pliable

10. Over the years, a deep _____ had developed between the two rival football coaches.
    A. enmity
    B. verve
    C. harangue

11. Recent television ads seeking contributions to help the poor in Third World countries have shown children with stomachs _____ as a result of severe malnutrition.
    A. distended
    B. transcended
    C. incensed

12. The _____ attitude of the townspeople made modernization of the neighborhood an impossibility.
    A. erudite
    B. vindictive
    C. provincial

13. Emphysema can result from the _____ effects of smoking over the period of a lifetime.
    A. seedy
    B. indigenous
    C. cumulative

14. The _____ juggler mesmerized the audience with his gravity-defying act.
    A. bemused
    B. adept
    C. prodigal

15. The only clue the _____ kissing bandit left behind was a purple rose.
    A. elusive
    B. ascetic
    C. mordant

16. The _____ passenger remained unruffled even when the airplane encountered severe turbulence.
    A. caustic
    B. fretful
    C. phlegmatic

17. The revolutionary organization was accused of _____ terroristic ideology.
    A. propagating
    B. emancipating
    C. abdicating

18. The global travelers _____ for a couple of days in the Greek tavern.
    A. dilated
    B. sojourned
    C. assented

19. Black widow spiders are highly _____.
    A. venomous
    B. ravenous
    C. striated

20. A romantically _____ man, the mariner fell in love with every beautiful woman he met.
    A. puny
    B. impetuous
    C. rotund

(For Quiz Answers, see Answer Section at the end of the book)

SAT & College Dictionary Workbook Quiz 89

[On a separate sheet of paper, write down the letter of the word that best fits in the blank to create a complete and meaningful sentence.]

1. People who litter show a _____ disrespect for the land upon which they live.
   A. palatable
   B. blithe
   C. tawdry

2. To _____ the angry crowd that had waited an extra hour for the carnival to open, the manager doled out free passes to ride the Ferris wheel.
   A. surmount
   B. mollify
   C. befriend

3. The old sailor was known for his vain _____.
   A. braggadocio
   B. fidelity
   C. lassitude

4. Children and adults alike were fascinated by the _____ horses featured at the carnival.
   A. diminutive
   B. ambidextrous
   C. modest

5. A minor scandal _____ the physicist's brilliant reputation.
   A. sullied
   B. despised
   C. beguiled

6. In the historical maritime account, the events preceding the collision of the Titanic with the iceberg were detailed in _____ order.
   A. chronological
   B. frangible
   C. restive

7. The boorish man's _____ behavior offended the aristocratic couple.
   A. labyrinthine
   B. terse
   C. crass

8. The newly refurbished hotel boasted a _____ decor.
   A. contemporary
   B. pestilent
   C. stentorian

9. At teatime, the British gentleman delighted in a brief but savory _____.
   A. sustenance
   B. imbroglio
   C. repast

10. It is important that young athletes be _____ of the notion that all professional sports figures are millionaires.
    A. precluded
    B. sated
    C. disabused

11. The _____ diminutive David challenged the mighty Goliath.
    A. doughty
    B. vexatious
    C. incredulous

12. The court's ruling found the captain _____ of negligence in the devastating oil spill.
    A. ruthless
    B. propitious
    C. culpable

13. Many feel a critical need to _____ the concept of family values.
    A. resurrect
    B. concoct
    C. implement

14. Geysers exude a _____ odor.
    A. becoming
    B. pungent
    C. delectable

15. Upset by the referee's questionable call, the _____ crowd began to pour onto the field in angry protest.
    A. jaundiced
    B. unruly
    C. stealthy

16. Abraham Lincoln was a person of _____ countenance.
    A. insipid
    B. provisional
    C. august

17. While in Minnesota, the family visited their _____.
    A. progenitors
    B. scoundrels
    C. kin

18. The FBI meeting with the drug informant was held _____.
    A. pell-mell
    B. nonpareil
    C. sub rosa

19. To prevent its fruit from falling on the roof, several branches of the tall mango tree were _____.
    A. besmirched
    B. dissected
    C. truncated

20. In the 1960s, protest marches served as a _____ for social change.
    A. bon mot
    B. repose
    C. catalyst

(For Quiz Answers, see Answer Section at the end of the book)

SAT & College Dictionary Workbook Quiz 90

[On a separate sheet of paper, write down the letter of the word that best fits in the blank to create a complete and meaningful sentence.]

1. The shooting star produced an _____ vaporous trail that resembled a brilliant but fleeting tail.
   A. arboreal
   B. evanescent
   C. unabridged

2. The team was lambasted by the press for their _____ performance on the field.
   A. wizened
   B. impetuous
   C. execrable

3. Hecklers _____ at and harassed the unwelcome speaker.
   A. gibed
   B. deplored
   C. besmirched

4. In a _____ display of absolution, Pope John Paul blessed the very person who had earlier attempted to assassinate him.
   A. seminal
   B. magnanimous
   C. gruff

5. The young cadet had the _____ to challenge the word of his superior officer.
   A. largess
   B. temerity
   C. consternation

6. The _____ work of art actually served as a timepiece.
   A. utilitarian
   B. enterprising
   C. stopgap

7. In a show of poor sportsmanship, the losing team captain interjected a _____ remark regarding his counterpart's integrity.
   A. pastoral
   B. derogatory
   C. scrupulous

8. Unable to muster enough courage to ask her boyfriend to the dance, the _____ adolescent anxiously awaited a phone call from him instead.
   A. sovereign
   B. adamant
   C. diffident

9. After the team's loss in the playoffs, the press _____ the manager and his staff, calling them "amateurs."
   A. vaunted
   B. feigned
   C. disparaged

10. The teenager's outrageous behavior at the banquet _____ his parents.
    A. temporized
    B. admonished
    C. mortified

11. The oil magnate's wayward son led a _____ life as playboy and debaucher.
    A. dissolute
    B. pandemic
    C. graphic

12. Many so-called psychics and fortune-tellers are mere _____.
    A. apologists
    B. charlatans
    C. refugees

13. Man's journey to the moon in 1969 proved to be an _____ success.
    A. unequivocal
    B. invincible
    C. earnest

14. _____ remarks oftentimes trigger heated confrontations.
    A. Consummate
    B. Puissant
    C. Incendiary

15. _____ by the sweet promise of Hollywood fame and fortune, the young woman packed her suitcase and left her family behind.
    A. Inundated
    B. Transmuted
    C. Beguiled

16. The eminent world traveler was a _____ and enlightening conversationalist.
    A. resolute
    B. jovial
    C. diminutive

17. After consuming more than he should have the night before, the young man stumbled out of bed with a _____ complexion and bloodshot eyes.
    A. tumultuous
    B. sallow
    C. bleak

18. The eager lad had a _____ desire to one day play quarterback on the high school football team.
    A. lucrative
    B. macabre
    C. steadfast

19. Plantation life for slaves consisted of endless toil and _____.
    A. disquietude
    B. travail
    C. prowess

20. Because the new city ordinance _____ existing state law, it was reviewed for possible amending.
    A. contravened
    B. exuded
    C. protruded

(For Quiz Answers, see Answer Section at the end of the book)

SAT & College Dictionary Workbook Quiz 91

[On a separate sheet of paper, write down the letter of the word that best fits in the blank to create a complete and meaningful sentence.]

1. After a tentative pause, the boy _____ climbing the rope.
   A. attested
   B. truncated
   C. essayed

2. Based on past experience, the business analyst _____ that interest rates were bound to rise in the coming months.
   A. alluded
   B. malingered
   C. conjectured

3. The _____ youngster refused to conform to school rules.
   A. autochthonous
   B. ponderous
   C. froward

4. In its true form, cinema verité does not exercise restraint when depicting _____ sex or violence.
   A. acrimonious
   B. graphic
   C. redoubtable

5. In times of trouble at sea, the crew had _____ faith in their captain's judgment and decisions.
   A. captious
   B. implicit
   C. ecstatic

6. Shirley Temple's _____ dimpled smile made her everyone's favorite child actress.
   A. delectable
   B. ingratiating
   C. authoritative

7. Students were offered a wide _____ of topics for their science projects.
   A. foresight
   B. repertoire
   C. latitude

8. Although delivered forcefully and with great conviction, the argument, when examined more closely, revealed factual flaws and _____ reasoning.
   A. rancid
   B. otiose
   C. specious

9. At the high school reunion, friends _____ about old times.
   A. burnished
   B. demurred
   C. reminisced

10. The boys' cross-country jaunt was _____ by their desire for adventure.
    A. actuated
    B. expiated
    C. lauded

11. Riding on a roller coaster can be an _____ and memorable experience.
    A. apocryphal
    B. inextricable
    C. exhilarating

12. A passerby _____ his assistance to help the elderly lady cross the street.
    A. proffered
    B. doled
    C. juxtaposed

13. It is rude to _____ in other people's private affairs.
    A. regress
    B. meddle
    C. collude

14. Chefs prepared a _____ feast for the visiting dignitaries.
    A. lethal
    B. solvent
    C. culinary

15. Surrounded by her _____ retinue, the movie starlet doted on her new-found fame and attention.
    A. inconsequential
    B. servile
    C. recalcitrant

16. The Purple Heart is _____ of wartime injury through valor.
    A. uxorious
    B. askance
    C. emblematic

17. Juliet's charm left an _____ impression in Romeo's heart.
    A. indelible
    B. acrid
    C. unspeakable

18. In the dead of night, the _____ howl of a lone wolf could be heard.
    A. plaintive
    B. frank
    C. imminent

19. After the dam burst, the _____ waters churned as they rampaged in a violent torrent through the valley below.
    A. pelagic
    B. mundane
    C. turbid

20. Unhappy with university policy, the disgruntled professor sought to _____ insurgence within the academic ranks.
    A. foment
    B. infer
    C. renounce

(For Quiz Answers, see Answer Section at the end of the book)

SAT & College Dictionary Workbook Quiz 92

[On a separate sheet of paper, write down the letter of the word that best fits in the blank to create a complete and meaningful sentence.]

1. Villagers avoided inflaming the ever-present temper of their _____ adversaries to the north.
   A. pusillanimous
   B. bellicose
   C. dubious

2. Former players _____ their coach at a testimonial dinner.
   A. purged
   B. eulogized
   C. arrayed

3. A proposal to raise taxes caused widespread _____ throughout the community.
   A. furor
   B. hubris
   C. mirth

4. In her dreams she had a _____ of an airplane crash.
   A. repast
   B. premonition
   C. foresight

5. After a week out of the refrigerator, the butter had turned _____.
   A. pristine
   B. rancid
   C. indelible

6. The fair-haired, freckled-faced boy had a _____ complexion.
   A. sanguine
   B. taciturn
   C. funereal

7. Because he lacked upper-level management experience, the young man was not a _____ candidate for the executive position.
   A. viable
   B. stout
   C. tantamount

8. The unscrupulous opportunist exhibited _____ servility in order to gain a foothold in the elderly man's vast empire.
   A. exquisite
   B. jaded
   C. unctuous

9. The old man had a _____ for life that never waned.
   A. prerogative
   B. zest
   C. fortitude

10. Teenage siblings often _____ over use of the telephone.
    A. encroach
    B. perplex
    C. bicker

11. The young deer _____ in the open field.
    A. gamboled
    B. reminisced
    C. behooved

12. The firm's accounting problems were merely a _____ to more serious financial concerns.
    A. precursor
    B. gamut
    C. foray

13. In many high schools, successful completion of an algebra and geometry course is _____ for graduation.
    A. renowned
    B. consummate
    C. mandatory

14. At an international soccer game, one questionable call by a referee can _____ a serious row in the stands.
    A. instigate
    B. circumscribe
    C. perambulate

15. Scoring his final touchdown at age forty _____ an already stellar football career.
    A. supplicated
    B. culminated
    C. decimated

16. The imaginative lad had a _____ for exaggeration.
    A. volition
    B. propensity
    C. demeanor

17. The _____ shopper went on lavish and costly binges.
    A. spendthrift
    B. marginal
    C. discreet

18. The young actress's _____ smile reflected her uneasiness at the awards ceremony.
    A. frenetic
    B. affected
    C. rustic

19. The assassination of President Kennedy in 1963 _____ the nation.
    A. stupefied
    B. confiscated
    C. disdained

20. The _____ lad shouted wildly when he saw his visiting uncle descending the airplane.
    A. limber
    B. orotund
    C. exuberant

(For Quiz Answers, see Answer Section at the end of the book)

SAT & College Dictionary Workbook Quiz 93

[On a separate sheet of paper, write down the letter of the word that best fits in the blank to create a complete and meaningful sentence.]

1. The _____ man treated the lowly beggar to a hearty meal.
   A. indigent
   B. perverse
   C. benevolent

2. A bird's wings are _____ to a human's arms.
   A. homologous
   B. superfluous
   C. extraneous

3. When asked by his wife where he had been all afternoon, the beach-going shirker _____ by claiming he was helping a friend repair a lawnmower.
   A. prevaricated
   B. espied
   C. schemed

4. Corruption infiltrated the _____ side of the town.
   A. seedy
   B. inane
   C. torrid

5. Throughout the heated debate, the moderator maintained an _____ and objective countenance.
   A. affected
   B. impassive
   C. ostensible

6. The demagogue sought to sway the _____ masses to violence and revolt.
   A. ductile
   B. sonorous
   C. judicious

7. To cover up his misdeed, the boy _____ an alibi that he had gone to the movies that afternoon.
   A. fabricated
   B. caviled
   C. avowed

8. Only his closest friends knew the real reason for the man's _____ behavior.
   A. serrated
   B. ambulatory
   C. eccentric

9. Although only fictional, the adventures of Sherlock Holmes are portrayed with such _____ that one actually feels as though the detective lived and solved all those mysteries.
   A. mirth
   B. humility
   C. verisimilitude

10. Faced with _____ evidence, the defendant changed his plea to "guilty."
    A. sedulous
    B. hypocritical
    C. irrefutable

11. Rather than cause a scene at the restaurant, the irate customer _____ his anger.
    A. suppressed
    B. protracted
    C. augmented

12. The once-turgid plant _____ in the intense summer sun.
    A. bantered
    B. flagged
    C. decamped

13. The rustic cowboy responded to the urban sophisticate's question in a _____ and terse manner.
    A. mellifluous
    B. tenuous
    C. gruff

14. The sledgehammer was much too _____ for the diminutive youngster to swing.
    A. compact
    B. jaunty
    C. unwieldy

15. Gold is a _____ metal highly desirable as jewelry.
    A. rapacious
    B. chimerical
    C. malleable

16. When goaded to jump off the highest diving board, the diminutive lad felt extreme _____.
    A. comity
    B. trepidation
    C. jeopardy

17. The child prodigy had an _____ desire to read.
    A. insatiable
    B. empirical
    C. orthodox

18. From the lengthy bout of depression lingered a chronically enervating _____.
    A. foible
    B. plethora
    C. malaise

19. With the video camera focused directly on him, the emboldened lad was _____ to stick his hand into the lion's cage.
    A. habituated
    B. chastised
    C. enticed

20. The prankish lad _____ the neighbor's dog by placing a tasty bone too high for the canine to reach.
    A. meted
    B. tantalized
    C. duped

(For Quiz Answers, see Answer Section at the end of the book)

SAT & College Dictionary Workbook Quiz 94

[On a separate sheet of paper, write down the letter of the word that best fits in the blank to create a complete and meaningful sentence.]

1. Few cared to socialize with the _____, vulgar lout.
   A. boorish
   B. irreproachable
   C. recherché

2. The _____ setting was ideal for the naturalist painter.
   A. incendiary
   B. saccharine
   C. bucolic

3. The _____ Hawaiian feast was fit for a king.
   A. delectable
   B. ubiquitous
   C. recumbent

4. The nightclub entertainer's _____ quips were well received by the audience.
   A. sub rosa
   B. impromptu
   C. unmitigated

5. Few ever penetrated the _____ sea captain's crusty shell.
   A. putative
   B. indurate
   C. seraphic

6. The renegade was branded an _____ coward.
   A. arrant
   B. unobtrusive
   C. elysian

7. Though her parents rejected her request to host a weekend party, they nevertheless granted that the young girl had presented _____ arguments in her own behalf.
   A. stern
   B. turgid
   C. valid

8. Newly-presented conclusive evidence _____ the wrongly-accused suspect of the serious crime.
   A. distorted
   B. vindicated
   C. indicted

9. In the 1960s, draft dodgers were often _____ as traitors.
   A. stupefied
   B. denounced
   C. invigorated

10. True to his _____ nature, the elderly man left only a meager tip.
    A. frugal
    B. precarious
    C. chronic

11. The verdant fields seemed so majestically serene in the _____.
    A. quagmire
    B. gloaming
    C. nadir

12. The movie intermission offered an _____ moment to purchase popcorn and a soft drink.
    A. opportune
    B. acute
    C. exhilarating

13. Fortunately for the soldier, the wound was only _____ and not life-threatening.
    A. superficial
    B. gratuitous
    C. impervious

14. The _____ man derived pleasure from showing the neighborhood children lewd and suggestive films.
    A. depraved
    B. telltale
    C. heretical

15. Seasoned travelers can quickly _____ themselves to new surroundings.
    A. dissuade
    B. acclimate
    C. inveigh

16. The pious churchgoer was a _____ and God-fearing family man.
    A. righteous
    B. diaphanous
    C. guileful

17. After spending a leisurely week on the exotic island, visitors often sought to _____ the relaxed and carefree lifestyle into their own.
    A. underpin
    B. assimilate
    C. extirpate

18. Fame plays to a _____ crowd, as many a forgotten star will attest.
    A. fickle
    B. connubial
    C. tremulous

19. In his _____, the business mogul was not satisfied until he had driven his competitor to bankruptcy.
    A. guise
    B. ordure
    C. avarice

20. Wolfgang Amadeus Mozart was a musical _____.
    A. miscreant
    B. adherent
    C. prodigy

(For Quiz Answers, see Answer Section at the end of the book)

SAT & College Dictionary Workbook Quiz 95

[On a separate sheet of paper, write down the letter of the word that best fits in the blank to create a complete and meaningful sentence.]

1. A model is a _____ representation of an actual or idealized object.
   A. dogmatic
   B. proficient
   C. mimetic

2. The wealthy playboy indulged in _____ grandeur befitting a sultan.
   A. disgruntled
   B. garish
   C. sybaritic

3. The gallant knight demonstrated his _____ in battle.
   A. debacle
   B. rigor
   C. prowess

4. A _____ solution was used to cleanse the wound.
   A. saline
   B. wan
   C. porous

5. Winning the million-dollar lottery left the housewife in a state of shock and _____.
   A. ratiocination
   B. euphoria
   C. pretense

6. After three days stranded on the deserted island, the shipwreck survivors found themselves in _____ need of food and water.
   A. adventitious
   B. trivial
   C. dire

7. Mountain climbing can be a _____ venture.
   A. perilous
   B. dogged
   C. caustic

8. Unlike his somber older brother, the younger boy reveled in practical jokes and other _____ diversions.
   A. bland
   B. implausible
   C. waggish

9. The candidate inveighed against the _____ comments levied upon him by his opponent.
   A. defamatory
   B. glum
   C. ostensible

10. The comedian's _____ wit was not well received by everyone in the audience, many of whom felt the barbs too personal.
    A. amiable
    B. harrowing
    C. wry

11. The _____ chemical had to be stored in a cool, dry location.
    A. caustic
    B. durable
    C. propitious

12. His _____ boss was constantly nagging him over the most trivial of details.
    A. meretricious
    B. captious
    C. fleet

13. Nothing could dampen the enthusiasm of the _____ tot.
    A. effervescent
    B. motley
    C. rapacious

14. The antique watch reflected _____ detail and workmanship.
    A. agrarian
    B. exquisite
    C. mercurial

15. Old and young alike enjoyed being in the company of the _____ and pleasant young man.
    A. modest
    B. relentless
    C. prolific

16. Yo Yo Ma's _____ solo cello performance drew a standing ovation.
    A. equivocal
    B. peevish
    C. artful

17. Residents in the tenement house were subjected to _____ living conditions.
    A. concurrent
    B. discrete
    C. squalid

18. When the sound system unexpectedly failed, the band was noticeably _____.
    A. disconcerted
    B. quixotic
    C. nondescript

19. Through years of neglect, the condition of the house _____ to such an extent that it was condemned by the State.
    A. deteriorated
    B. assayed
    C. vitiated

20. Mark Antony was an _____ Roman statesman who lived during the reign of Julius Caesar.
    A. eloquent
    B. ambrosial
    C. unmitigated

(For Quiz Answers, see Answer Section at the end of the book)

SAT & College Dictionary Workbook Quiz 96

[On a separate sheet of paper, write down the letter of the word that best fits in the blank to create a complete and meaningful sentence.]

1. All parties felt that the court settlement was both _____ and feasible.
   A. veritable
   B. abstemious
   C. equitable

2. The _____ speech lulled several students to doze off.
   A. irrefutable
   B. eloquent
   C. soporific

3. China is a _____ nation.
   A. populous
   B. gaunt
   C. supererogatory

4. Those within close political circles realized that the old leader's death was _____.
   A. redolent
   B. imminent
   C. untenable

5. A panel was commissioned to _____ the budget's practicability.
   A. assay
   B. disavow
   C. prevaricate

6. Patrons chuckled at the drunkard's _____ display of grief over the spilled drink.
   A. maudlin
   B. sinister
   C. dense

7. It is unwise to come to work appearing slovenly and _____.
   A. verbose
   B. disheveled
   C. utilitarian

8. Army cadets are subjected to a _____ and rigorous training program.
   A. morbid
   B. grueling
   C. cacophonous

9. To _____ his critics, the songwriter altered the tune's offensive lyrics.
   A. appease
   B. divert
   C. provoke

10. Success was the _____ that impelled the ambitious entrepreneur to work both day and night.
    A. anomaly
    B. précis
    C. impetus

11. A _____ erupted among the agitated spectators during the soccer finals.
    A. melee
    B. renaissance
    C. pall

12. The _____ hiker fabricated a makeshift tent from leaves and branches.
    A. resourceful
    B. ineffectual
    C. terrestrial

13. During times of drought, farmers must _____ the dry soil to enable water moisture to permeate it.
    A. flag
    B. scarify
    C. raze

14. The rebel faction echoed their _____ support of the military uprising.
    A. unabashed
    B. ironic
    C. myriad

15. Contaminants in the lake rendered the water no longer _____.
    A. hazardous
    B. potable
    C. toxic

16. Vandals _____ the war memorial plaque by painting a swastika on it.
    A. desecrated
    B. perambulated
    C. assimilated

17. In his waning years, the wealthy and powerful ruler yearned for those _____ days of youth.
    A. acerbic
    B. chronological
    C. halcyon

18. The massive explosion was traced to a single _____ device.
    A. cogent
    B. incendiary
    C. prudent

19. When his wife _____ him with a sudden and abrupt tug on his shirt, he knew it was time to stop chatting with the waitress.
    A. despoiled
    B. assailed
    C. reproved

20. The generous benefactor _____ the homeless lad.
    A. repressed
    B. befriended
    C. inured

(For Quiz Answers, see Answer Section at the end of the book)

SAT & College Dictionary Workbook Quiz 97

[On a separate sheet of paper, write down the letter of the word that best fits in the blank to create a complete and meaningful sentence.]

1. His _____ wit added piquant flavor to his caustic movie reviews.
   A. acerbic
   B. salutary
   C. picayune

2. Although they occasionally traded with neighboring villages, the _____ community was basically self-sufficient.
   A. agrarian
   B. flatulent
   C. nefarious

3. It is natural for teenagers to _____ their independence from parental controls.
   A. assert
   B. encapsulate
   C. reprimand

4. The report was both clear and _____.
   A. fatuous
   B. menial
   C. concise

5. Vast tracts of forest were _____ by the extensive fire.
   A. devastated
   B. piqued
   C. vacillated

6. Relegated to obscurity following the decline of her movie career, the _____ woman lived a reclusive existence bereft of her once-adoring fans.
   A. callow
   B. forlorn
   C. pragmatic

7. The child's _____ chatter nearly drove the babysitter to madness.
   A. surly
   B. fecund
   C. incessant

8. The _____ defense attorney ferreted out and interviewed every witness to the crime.
   A. pugnacious
   B. indefatigable
   C. frangible

9. In its ruling, the court determined that the fraudulent manner in which the negotiations were conducted _____ all resulting contracts.
   A. compensated
   B. vitiated
   C. infringed

10. The governor felt _____ for those whose homes had been destroyed in the hurricane.
    A. empathy
    B. privation
    C. viridity

11. Visitors enjoyed the restful _____ of the serene neighborhood park.
    A. ambience
    B. humility
    C. effulgence

12. Lungs _____ during inhalation.
    A. dilate
    B. meander
    C. truncate

13. Twentieth century flight has afforded man the opportunity to share the _____ realm once exclusively the domain of winged creatures.
    A. empyreal
    B. verdant
    C. parsimonious

14. Poolside bathers _____ at the children's boisterous horseplay.
    A. demurred
    B. irked
    C. truckled

15. Business failures are often _____ to poor management.
    A. circumscribed
    B. educed
    C. imputed

16. By proclaiming himself its president, the bold upstart _____ to himself control of the newly-formed club.
    A. arrogated
    B. comported
    C. reiterated

17. A poor diet can prove _____ to one's health and welfare.
    A. autochthonous
    B. elusive
    C. inimical

18. Tribal members believed that the witchdoctor's _____ could ward off evil spirits.
    A. façade
    B. pseudonym
    C. talisman

19. A good night's sleep can be an elusive goal when in the company of a _____ mosquito.
    A. distrait
    B. spiteful
    C. vexatious

20. The headstrong lad refused to _____ with the school's strict dress code.
    A. gainsay
    B. revel
    C. comply

(For Quiz Answers, see Answer Section at the end of the book)

SAT & College Dictionary Workbook Quiz 98

[On a separate sheet of paper, write down the letter of the word that best fits in the blank to create a complete and meaningful sentence.]

1. The drama ran the gamut from gripping realism to near-comical _____.
   A. senescence
   B. bathos
   C. diversity

2. In the midst of the civil uprising, the duke _____ the throne and declared himself the new ruler.
   A. expounded
   B. asserted
   C. usurped

3. Discovering a _____ for all the world's ills is a fanciful though highly unlikely prospect.
   A. cornucopia
   B. panacea
   C. stratagem

4. Residents of the sleepy town were stunned by the string of _____ murders.
   A. chimerical
   B. mundane
   C. ghastly

5. Having committed several serious crimes, the man was deemed a _____ to society and sentenced to prison.
   A. brouhaha
   B. prodigy
   C. detriment

6. Although the medicine was purported to be a cure for all ailments, the elixir was merely soda water and the seller nothing but a _____.
   A. mountebank
   B. tyro
   C. zephyr

7. Years of bickering _____ the once-happy couple.
   A. estranged
   B. attenuated
   C. inveighed

8. Lack of daily exercise had left him with _____ muscles.
   A. flaccid
   B. baneful
   C. pliable

9. For some _____ reason, the lights in the auditorium suddenly started flickering.
   A. surrealistic
   B. inexplicable
   C. resplendent

10. The beauty queen traversed the catwalk with the _____ elegance of a seraphic sylph.
    A. feasible
    B. lissome
    C. ramshackle

11. During the earthquake, students dashed _____ into the hallways.
    A. pell-mell
    B. askance
    C. carte blanche

12. At the service station, the financially strapped travelers were in a _____ over how to pay for groceries and still have money left for gas.
    A. quagmire
    B. deluge
    C. ploy

13. Although unsigned, the poignant circus painting was _____ to early Pablo Picasso.
    A. elicited
    B. proffered
    C. ascribed

14. Bonuses were rare when working for the _____ shop owner.
    A. parsimonious
    B. gamely
    C. copious

15. _____ and bedridden with the flu, the young secretary was unable to go to work as scheduled.
    A. Bucolic
    B. Redolent
    C. Indisposed

16. City planners came up with an _____ and economical way to reduce downtown traffic congestion.
    A. unbridled
    B. innovative
    C. expendable

17. A cold shower helped _____ the doctor after his long workday.
    A. aspire
    B. rejuvenate
    C. browbeat

18. Faced with mounting debts and economic uncertainty, the company's future looked _____.
    A. haughty
    B. bleak
    C. scathing

19. In thirteenth century China, Kublai Khan ruled a _____ empire.
    A. sprawling
    B. nomadic
    C. preoccupied

20. The landscape artist gloated over the _____ of his grounds.
    A. viridity
    B. girth
    C. finesse

(For Quiz Answers, see Answer Section at the end of the book)

SAT & College Dictionary Workbook Quiz 99

[On a separate sheet of paper, write down the letter of the word that best fits in the blank to create a complete and meaningful sentence.]

1. By _____ his own accomplishments, he gained a reputation both for his expertise and his immodesty.
   A. mortifying
   B. aggrandizing
   C. ruminating

2. Behind on his car payments, the man was in _____ of having the vehicle repossessed.
   A. proximity
   B. duress
   C. jeopardy

3. Those who are heavy smokers sooner or later often find themselves suffering from _____ breathing difficulties.
   A. fastidious
   B. chronic
   C. preeminent

4. The _____ neighbor constantly stuck her nose into the newlyweds' affairs.
   A. affable
   B. incendiary
   C. obtrusive

5. For siding with the enemy when the opposition had temporarily gained the upper hand, the _____ was shunned by his fellow countrymen.
   A. paradigm
   B. novice
   C. recreant

6. When having one's car serviced, it is highly recommended that the job be performed by a _____ mechanic.
   A. macabre
   B. hygienic
   C. reputable

7. The makeshift hut was constructed in a _____ manner.
   A. compact
   B. mnemonic
   C. slipshod

8. When asked if he had authorized the break-in of the Watergate offices, President Nixon initially _____ any involvement in the crime.
   A. satiated
   B. disavowed
   C. minced

9. It is ill advised for any man to incur his wife's _____.
   A. wrath
   B. bravado
   C. zeal

10. The _____ heretic sought forgiveness for his religious infidelity.
    A. congenial
    B. suppliant
    C. hortatory

11. The unpopular candidate was booed and _____ throughout his speech.
    A. extricated
    B. cloyed
    C. jeered

12. The senator's _____ voice obviated the need for a microphone.
    A. euphuistic
    B. splenetic
    C. orotund

13. The defendant responded to the prosecutor's accusations with _____.
    A. longevity
    B. tribulation
    C. asperity

14. As the special event neared, the bride became unusually _____ with the guests' seating arrangements.
    A. convivial
    B. resourceful
    C. preoccupied

15. The _____ building material was both fireproof and water-resistant.
    A. durable
    B. soporific
    C. gauche

16. The _____ child would not do his homework.
    A. deliberate
    B. prodigal
    C. refractory

17. Within a year, the spendthrift had _____ his entire inheritance.
    A. squandered
    B. inundated
    C. connived

18. Once a _____ of the committee was achieved regarding the date for their next meeting, a motion was made to adjourn the session for the afternoon.
    A. maelstrom
    B. populace
    C. consensus

19. Nirvana was at the _____ of the 1990s grunge music movement.
    A. vanguard
    B. turmoil
    C. archetype

20. Only members of the tribe were privy to their _____ rituals.
    A. viable
    B. esoteric
    C. artless

(For Quiz Answers, see Answer Section at the end of the book)

SAT & College Dictionary Workbook Quiz 100

[On a separate sheet of paper, write down the letter of the word that best fits in the blank to create a complete and meaningful sentence.]

1. At the baseball Hall of Fame, fans pay _____ to the best in the sport, past and present.
   A. plenitude
   B. fidelity
   C. homage

2. To maintain peak physical conditioning, the _____ athlete followed a rigorous daily schedule.
   A. munificent
   B. Spartan
   C. arduous

3. Darwin's Theory of Evolution has long been fodder for _____ debate.
   A. culpable
   B. dilatory
   C. polemic

4. The judge sentenced the man to a punishment _____ with the heinous crime.
   A. dynamic
   B. potable
   C. commensurate

5. Before leaving the underground cave, the spelunkers _____ their supply of water.
   A. alleviated
   B. replenished
   C. escalated

6. Under the rule of Kublai Khan, the Mongols _____ the Chinese people and eventually ruled the land for ninety years.
   A. subjugated
   B. relinquished
   C. importuned

7. The _____ lad shunned social gatherings.
   A. flamboyant
   B. retiring
   C. ingratiating

8. An animal's _____ will to survive is a necessity in the wild.
   A. tenacious
   B. prepossessing
   C. insidious

9. Her _____ demeanor in the face of such tragedy was instrumental in sparing her children traumatic grief.
   A. combustible
   B. stoic
   C. intrusive

10. The sporting event turned decidedly _____ when it was announced that one of the players had been involved in an automobile accident en route to the affair.
    A. disaffected
    B. somber
    C. forbidding

11. Even in trying times, the diplomat's _____ helped encourage détente.
    A. lexicon
    B. effrontery
    C. savoir faire

12. The merchant was _____ for the broken vase.
    A. recompensed
    B. accrued
    C. consoled

13. Constant hostile outbursts from the audience _____ the comedian.
    A. suffused
    B. misconstrued
    C. discomfited

14. When she discovered that the controversial issue had been debated and voted upon in her absence, the board member was visibly _____.
    A. enticed
    B. piqued
    C. dissembled

15. The _____ supervisor alienated his staff with his intolerance of and callous disregard for their input.
    A. peremptory
    B. impartial
    C. surreptitious

16. Chills and a fever often signal the _____ of the flu.
    A. onset
    B. contagion
    C. epitome

17. _____ fumes emanating from the geyser caused breathing difficulties for several of the visiting tourists.
    A. Categorical
    B. Inscrutable
    C. Noxious

18. Many consider arguments defending the existence of extraterrestrial life to be irrational and _____.
    A. illustrious
    B. novel
    C. untenable

19. People buy lottery tickets with _____ hopes of becoming millionaires overnight.
    A. illusory
    B. obscure
    C. aghast

20. Movies are reviewed and objectionable scenes _____ before they are allowed to be shown during family programming.
    A. fortified
    B. occluded
    C. censored

(For Quiz Answers, see Answer Section at the end of the book)

SAT & College Dictionary Workbook Quiz 101

[On a separate sheet of paper, write down the letter of the word that best fits in the blank to create a complete and meaningful sentence.]

1. The sea captain possessed a _____ perspicacity of Mother Nature's inscrutable ways.
   A. concise
   B. preternatural
   C. trenchant

2. Before laying the foundation for the new hospital complex, several old and abandoned buildings on the lot had to be _____.
   A. atoned
   B. razed
   C. immolated

3. Although the student professed to know as much about law as did his teacher, his _____ explanation of the legal case proved to all that he was but a novice.
   A. jaded
   B. sophomoric
   C. perspicacious

4. Having _____ their food supplies, the stranded hikers were forced to subsist on insects and berries.
   A. expended
   B. vanquished
   C. accoutered

5. The _____ woman enjoyed hosting informal parties.
   A. inimical
   B. naïve
   C. gregarious

6. Some comedians lack wit and instead resort to _____ and offensive humor for applause.
   A. ribald
   B. vast
   C. immemorial

7. A wolf has a _____ appetite.
   A. voracious
   B. stygian
   C. plenipotentiary

8. The _____ lad defied the school bully.
   A. tactful
   B. explicit
   C. audacious

9. The ghost town projected a bleak _____ to passersby.
   A. visage
   B. onset
   C. influx

10. Kleptomaniacs have a _____ desire to steal things.
    A. malleable
    B. compulsive
    C. redoubtable

11. Early promotions are usually reserved for only the most _____ of employees.
    A. enterprising
    B. dolorous
    C. noisome

12. The starry-eyed schoolgirl became _____ with the new boy in school.
    A. infatuated
    B. submissive
    C. concerted

13. The documentary on mental illness afforded viewers an _____ glimpse into the world of schizophrenia.
    A. insightful
    B. equitable
    C. arrant

14. In the dominant years of ancient Rome, the _____ Roman army conquered Italy and the entire Mediterranean world.
    A. invincible
    B. equivocal
    C. melancholy

15. The _____ pallbearers carried the casket of their beloved friend to the waiting hearse.
    A. infernal
    B. lugubrious
    C. dire

16. The pikake plant emits a pleasantly _____ perfume.
    A. debonair
    B. odoriferous
    C. prurient

17. An _____ clause was added to the author's contract, giving him full television rights.
    A. extant
    B. ancillary
    C. outmoded

18. Once found guilty, the seditious prisoners were _____ executed.
    A. arguably
    B. gingerly
    C. summarily

19. Surfing the internet for over an hour proved a _____ attempt to contact his long-lost sister.
    A. vain
    B. salubrious
    C. magnanimous

20. To defend against the school bully, the group of younger boys formed a protective _____.
    A. gamut
    B. alliance
    C. symmetry

(For Quiz Answers, see Answer Section at the end of the book)

SAT & College Dictionary Workbook Quiz 102

[On a separate sheet of paper, write down the letter of the word that best fits in the blank to create a complete and meaningful sentence.]

1. Unable to ascend the mountain's face, the hikers reached the summit via a _____ route.
   A. circuitous
   B. synthetic
   C. Machiavellian

2. Television censors refused to air the _____ scene.
   A. incontrovertible
   B. rubicund
   C. concupiscent

3. The nation's leader delivered a violent _____ against those foreign powers who had profited from the exportation of drugs to his country.
   A. philippic
   B. causerie
   C. anomaly

4. The sailor's _____ adventure involved an enormous man-eating shark.
   A. arboreal
   B. celestial
   C. piscatorial

5. Upon their arrival, the medical supplies were _____ to eagerly-awaiting doctors.
   A. dispensed
   B. promulgated
   C. instigated

6. At the auction, the art collector _____ several rare Renaissance paintings.
   A. estranged
   B. flouted
   C. procured

7. The British considered the colonists' incident referred to as the Boston Tea Party a willful and _____ act of treason.
   A. enterprising
   B. seditious
   C. upstanding

8. John Candy was a _____ but genuinely lovable comedian.
   A. stout
   B. belated
   C. labyrinthine

9. _____ fumes released by the overturned truck forced the evacuation of nearby residents.
   A. Ethereal
   B. Toxic
   C. Fervent

10. Unable to reach an amenable compromise, both parties chose to _____ the civil matter.
    A. convene
    B. agitate
    C. litigate

11. The conference inspired a _____ of ideas and suggestions.
    A. premonition
    B. multiplicity
    C. visage

12. Through highly-charged accusations, the belligerent protester attempted to _____ the peaceful tenor of the senator's speech.
    A. obfuscate
    B. incapacitate
    C. abase

13. Many regard the _____ William Shakespeare as the greatest playwright of all time.
    A. venerable
    B. idyllic
    C. ubiquitous

14. The heretic was _____ for his inflammatory criticism of the Church.
    A. culled
    B. proscribed
    C. augured

15. Andre the Giant was a _____ wrestler.
    A. herculean
    B. precipitous
    C. rapacious

16. The defense attorney _____ the judge to allow her more time to prepare for trial.
    A. entreated
    B. asserted
    C. rebuked

17. When the prim home-economics teacher slipped on a banana peel, her students were unable to _____ their laughter.
    A. repress
    B. comprise
    C. exhort

18. During a hiatus from filming, the movie star _____ on the fortuitous events that had led to his selection for the leading role.
    A. edified
    B. debilitated
    C. ruminated

19. Liberace was a _____ pianist who entertained the audience with his comic wit and musical genius.
    A. bland
    B. panoramic
    C. flamboyant

20. Because the poetic allusions of John Milton are beyond the _____ of most students, only a handful are truly able to appreciate the metaphorical and allegorical richness of works such as *Paradise Lost*.
    A. propinquity
    B. ken
    C. finesse

(For Quiz Answers, see Answer Section at the end of the book)

SAT & College Dictionary Workbook Quiz 103

[On a separate sheet of paper, write down the letter of the word that best fits in the blank to create a complete and meaningful sentence.]

1. The tribal shaman was believed powerful enough to communicate directly with _____ forces.
   A. intact
   B. virtual
   C. occult

2. No Shakespearean tragedy is more _____ than that of *Romeo and Juliet*.
   A. poignant
   B. lethal
   C. somnolent

3. When asked if he liked the hat his wife had chosen for the occasion, he replied in a _____ manner that offended her.
   A. baleful
   B. pessimistic
   C. frank

4. In times of battle, a commander's orders are _____.
   A. willful
   B. sacrosanct
   C. impermeable

5. Even into her nineties, she remained a _____ and hearty woman.
   A. hale
   B. churlish
   C. polemic

6. Despite the difficulty in lifting the heavy suitcase, the youngster _____ until he managed to get it into the car.
   A. deigned
   B. eventuated
   C. persevered

7. When she turned the gun on her attacker, he gave her a _____ look of disbelief.
   A. quizzical
   B. perceptive
   C. despicable

8. Espionage is often conducted under _____, cloak-and-dagger conditions.
   A. insufferable
   B. ponderous
   C. covert

9. The company's rosy earnings outlook proved somewhat _____ to investors; the stock had already risen in anticipation of the favorable news.
   A. disreputable
   B. inconsequential
   C. apropos

10. To the scientific community, uncorroborated assertions are regarded as having _____ value.
    A. nugatory
    B. esoteric
    C. gratuitous

11. Her _____ display of the borrowed mink stole afforded her little satisfaction, for no one noticed it on her.
    A. pretentious
    B. glacial
    C. celebrated

12. Throughout the rough flight, passengers remained surprisingly _____.
    A. incorrigible
    B. tentative
    C. sedate

13. The _____ potatoes were difficult to digest.
    A. stodgy
    B. pithy
    C. limpid

14. The Samurai sword was forged from _____ steel.
    A. tempered
    B. dispersed
    C. lambent

15. Firemen were called to _____ trapped passengers from the wreckage.
    A. extricate
    B. remunerate
    C. appall

16. The committee voted to _____ its final decision until after both sides had presented their cases.
    A. stanch
    B. rebuff
    C. defer

17. As a show of respect, the runner-up contained her disappointment behind a _____ of happiness and joy for the contest winner.
    A. caveat
    B. travail
    C. façade

18. For conducting allegedly _____ activities, the organization was constantly under police surveillance.
    A. affected
    B. nascent
    C. illicit

19. The _____ parent set few restrictions on her children.
    A. indulgent
    B. elite
    C. compulsive

20. Within the decorative mural, horses were _____ as winged warriors.
    A. contravened
    B. limned
    C. shirked

(For Quiz Answers, see Answer Section at the end of the book)

SAT & College Dictionary Workbook Quiz 104

[On a separate sheet of paper, write down the letter of the word that best fits in the blank to create a complete and meaningful sentence.]

1. When caught, the villain paid dearly for his _____ deeds.
   A. adroit
   B. viable
   C. nefarious

2. While addressing the Vice President, the senator conducted himself with the utmost of _____.
   A. ire
   B. exigency
   C. propriety

3. _____ wolves attacked the injured animal.
   A. Ravenous
   B. Waggish
   C. Blasphemous

4. Alfred Hitchcock was a _____ gentleman who possessed an uncanny flair for mystery and suspense.
   A. sparse
   B. potable
   C. rotund

5. The _____ headwaiter insisted that utensils be set in a specific arrangement.
   A. fastidious
   B. complacent
   C. resplendent

6. Wolves are _____ creatures.
   A. intrusive
   B. vulnerable
   C. feral

7. The judge _____ the juror for having discussed the case with a newspaper reporter.
   A. compelled
   B. excoriated
   C. adumbrated

8. In the cartoon, the mad scientist _____ to blow up the world.
   A. schemed
   B. doled
   C. calumniated

9. The political candidate provided _____ responses to the interviewer's pointed questions.
   A. vis-à-vis
   B. reputed
   C. succinct

10. The Sahara Desert is an _____ region in North Africa.
    A. implacable
    B. overt
    C. arid

11. The poet yearned to escape the urban madness and return to the _____ rusticity of country life.
    A. exuberant
    B. sylvan
    C. inexplicable

12. The musical _____ was relegated to third-string in the school band.
    A. tyro
    B. proponent
    C. interloper

13. The _____ quickly spent his weekly allowance on frivolous novelties.
    A. infidel
    B. wastrel
    C. foe

14. An additional lane was added to help _____ the rush-hour traffic.
    A. alleviate
    B. pique
    C. hinder

15. Faced with mounting medical bills, the couple was faced with the _____ of either selling their stocks at a loss or taking out a third mortgage.
    A. menace
    B. dilemma
    C. travesty

16. Bitterly envious that his classmate was chosen to lead the band, the rancorous lad spawned an _____ rumor to derail the selection.
    A. austere
    B. invidious
    C. earnest

17. In life, every new challenge carries with it _____ opportunities and possibilities.
    A. innumerable
    B. outlandish
    C. decorous

18. Only those closest to the case could decode the _____ message left behind.
    A. intractable
    B. cryptic
    C. latent

19. An autopsy revealed only an _____ amount of arsenic in the blood stream, hardly a lethal dose.
    A. austere
    B. extensive
    C. infinitesimal

20. The heat of the tropics contributed to the predominately _____ local lifestyle.
    A. languid
    B. contrite
    C. decrepit

(For Quiz Answers, see Answer Section at the end of the book)

SAT & College Dictionary Workbook Quiz 105

[On a separate sheet of paper, write down the letter of the word that best fits in the blank to create a complete and meaningful sentence.]

1. The _____ branch swayed resiliently in the breeze.
   A. viable
   B. lithe
   C. ruddy

2. The Joker was Batman's _____.
   A. nemesis
   B. deliverance
   C. pseudonym

3. Beachgoers frolicked in the pounding surf, _____ to the dangers of the accompanying rip current.
   A. hapless
   B. insolent
   C. oblivious

4. The instructor's _____ analysis made the complex scientific theory pleasantly palpable.
   A. tumultuous
   B. pellucid
   C. bereft

5. Critics _____ the negotiator's halfhearted efforts to resolve the bitter dispute.
   A. lowered
   B. quelled
   C. derided

6. The anarchist's highly charged rhetoric _____ an angry response from the conservative crowd.
   A. waxed
   B. evoked
   C. patronized

7. Avaricious salesmen in the fancy boutique rushed to greet each customer with a _____ display of unctuous servility.
   A. factitious
   B. sisyphean
   C. caustic

8. Mountain goats are _____ animals that can leap from ledge to ledge with the greatest of ease.
   A. calamitous
   B. hulking
   C. fleet

9. The junior executive had a most ingratiatingly _____ personality.
   A. ductile
   B. genial
   C. adverse

10. The evil ruler was regarded by many of his subjects as the devil _____.
    A. incarnate
    B. supernal
    C. ostentatious

11. J. K. Rowling reached the _____ of success with her *Harry Potter* novels.
    A. forte
    B. pinnacle
    C. nadir

12. Although a hurricane appears _____ when the eye passes overhead, it is only a matter of minutes before the violent winds resume.
    A. incessant
    B. sinister
    C. quiescent

13. The rustic countryside was a scene _____ of the poet's early childhood.
    A. becoming
    B. redolent
    C. inclusive

14. Smitten with love, the teenager obsessed over the girl whose _____ radiance he could only have envisioned in the most sublime of dreams.
    A. seraphic
    B. titanic
    C. immaculate

15. The preacher _____ the congregation to cease their evil and blasphemous ways and begin a new life of righteousness.
    A. aggrandized
    B. exhorted
    C. revoked

16. Over the years, the basketball announcer _____ valuable tidbits of information from interviews with the sport's top players.
    A. chided
    B. peculated
    C. gleaned

17. The Garden of Eden boasted a _____ of vegetation.
    A. verisimilitude
    B. plenitude
    C. braggadocio

18. _____ sounds filled the auditorium as the orchestral instruments were tuned.
    A. Lissome
    B. Visceral
    C. Cacophonous

19. Children of doctors often have a strong _____ to also enter the medical profession.
    A. paucity
    B. antipathy
    C. inclination

20. The 1929 stock market crash left a large segment of the nation's population _____ and placed the country's economy on the brink of collapse.
    A. picayune
    B. sybaritic
    C. indigent

(For Quiz Answers, see Answer Section at the end of the book)

SAT & College Dictionary Workbook Quiz 106

[On a separate sheet of paper, write down the letter of the word that best fits in the blank to create a complete and meaningful sentence.]

1. William Wordsworth extolled the _____ loveliness of the countryside.
   A. infinitesimal
   B. euphemistic
   C. pristine

2. The car's back tires became stuck in a _____.
   A. predicament
   B. row
   C. quagmire

3. The Swedish lass had a _____ complexion.
   A. grave
   B. rubicund
   C. superficial

4. A tourniquet helped _____ the loss of blood from the open wound.
   A. foil
   B. erode
   C. stanch

5. Having earned the dubious reputation as an _____ gambler, the man found it nearly impossible to secure a loan from anyone.
   A. abstemious
   B. unflappable
   C. incorrigible

6. Despite the other boy's physical superiority, the _____ lightweight stood his ground and refused to let the mighty Goliath push him around.
   A. coy
   B. intrepid
   C. lugubrious

7. The television documentary provided _____ coverage of the historic political rally.
   A. insidious
   B. tentative
   C. objective

8. The _____ student attended every optional lecture that was offered.
   A. impudent
   B. volatile
   C. sedulous

9. For fleeing the battlefield as soon as the fighting began, the young warrior was branded a _____.
   A. poltroon
   B. novice
   C. martinet

10. It is a _____ that banks are least willing to lend money to those who need it the most.
    A. paradox
    B. ruse
    C. faux pas

11. All the sordid details were included in the _____ account of the acrimonious divorce.
    A. extraneous
    B. unexpurgated
    C. flippant

12. Pacifists _____ the use of violence to settle disputes.
    A. thrive
    B. deplore
    C. anguish

13. Many _____ heroes gave their lives during World War II.
    A. illicit
    B. unsung
    C. evanescent

14. To settle the seemingly interminable strike, management _____ to the implacable union's demands.
    A. diverted
    B. palliated
    C. acquiesced

15. In the children's fairy tale, the wolf appeared in the _____ of a sheep.
    A. acme
    B. guise
    C. pinnacle

16. _____ weather forced the cancellation of the annual employee picnic.
    A. Peerless
    B. Inclement
    C. Ramshackle

17. The victorious councilman highlighted the evening with a _____ acceptance speech.
    A. sequential
    B. hale
    C. magniloquent

18. Julius Caesar was a _____ Roman general and statesman.
    A. voluminous
    B. puissant
    C. sophomoric

19. The little rascal's misbehavior was a _____ attempt to anger and frustrate his babysitter.
    A. deliberate
    B. taut
    C. benevolent

20. The National Guard was called in to _____ the civil riot.
    A. confound
    B. suppress
    C. disconcert

(For Quiz Answers, see Answer Section at the end of the book)

SAT & College Dictionary Workbook Quiz 107

[On a separate sheet of paper, write down the letter of the word that best fits in the blank to create a complete and meaningful sentence.]

1. Health spas are frequented for their _____ value.
   A. oleaginous
   B. therapeutic
   C. juvenile

2. Many have experienced firsthand the trials and _____ of a bitterly contested divorce.
   A. boons
   B. detriments
   C. tribulations

3. The audience succumbed to _____ laughter during the hilarious skit.
   A. unbridled
   B. jaded
   C. pugnacious

4. The _____ sailor was unprepared to battle the unusually rough seas.
   A. verdant
   B. inexorable
   C. expedient

5. The stowaway _____ to board and exit the ship without being detected.
   A. contrived
   B. languished
   C. reveled

6. There were many problems from the _____ of the space mission.
   A. outset
   B. consensus
   C. incursion

7. The penitent sinner sought _____ from the Church for his blasphemous and profane past.
   A. remorse
   B. encomium
   C. absolution

8. The _____ young warrior could not shoot his arrow straight.
   A. staid
   B. inept
   C. rudimentary

9. When told she could not park in the reserved stall, the shopper became _____.
   A. livid
   B. sacrilegious
   C. cursory

10. Of all the actresses appearing, she was the _____ in terms of movie experience and career success.
    A. adversary
    B. precursor
    C. nonpareil

11. The English teacher's _____ proclivity for grammatical correctness stifled student creativity in their fictional writing.
    A. acute
    B. futile
    C. pedantic

12. To _____ the powerful ruler, neighboring villages sent gifts and other offerings of peace and subservience.
    A. debauch
    B. propitiate
    C. collaborate

13. When a patron accused the bartender of diluting his drink, a _____ ensued.
    A. row
    B. philippic
    C. foible

14. Scientific researchers noted a _____ of patterns employed by mice when placed randomly in the maze.
    A. desuetude
    B. similitude
    C. pantheon

15. The plane's rough landing was a _____ experience for all aboard.
    A. wry
    B. harrowing
    C. myriad

16. A _____ effort was made by the guests to find the missing ring.
    A. concerted
    B. dissolute
    C. fallow

17. Tasmanian devils exhibit _____ aggressive traits.
    A. wry
    B. impeccable
    C. salient

18. The rainbow is a _____ arc.
    A. mercurial
    B. polychromatic
    C. utilitarian

19. Some people become embarrassingly _____ after imbibing only one or two beers.
    A. inebriated
    B. stealthy
    C. Machiavellian

20. His vibrant personality _____ warmth and charm.
    A. exuded
    B. verified
    C. appeased

(For Quiz Answers, see Answer Section at the end of the book)

SAT & College Dictionary Workbook Quiz 108

[On a separate sheet of paper, write down the letter of the word that best fits in the blank to create a complete and meaningful sentence.]

1. Drugs and alcohol can be a _____ combination.
   A. felicitous
   B. lethal
   C. harrowing

2. Reporters on the scene were repulsed by the _____ smell of decaying flesh.
   A. formidable
   B. putrid
   C. seedy

3. The school's student council committee _____ the fund-raising dance.
   A. renovated
   B. cached
   C. sanctioned

4. The captain's order _____ all those made earlier by his subordinates.
   A. confronted
   B. reciprocated
   C. superseded

5. During the Crusades, _____ were often condemned to die on the gallows.
   A. infidels
   B. neophytes
   C. diatribes

6. Witnessing the effects of alcoholic abuse by his older sibling taught the young man an _____ lesson.
   A. unconscionable
   B. abominable
   C. invaluable

7. Before the family left on their vacation, the house-sitter was given _____ instructions for the care of the plants and goldfish.
   A. explicit
   B. wayward
   C. aberrant

8. The new-car owner proudly paraded his vehicle in an _____ display of vanity and self-delight.
   A. ostentatious
   B. ardent
   C. unwieldy

9. In his _____ moments alone, the young businessman contemplated whether he was truly happy with his career.
   A. stopgap
   B. manifest
   C. pensive

10. Her parents were _____ over the news that the youngster had won the state spelling bee.
    A. convoluted
    B. elated
    C. nostalgic

11. In the children's television program, adult characters played _____ roles.
    A. hazardous
    B. corrupt
    C. peripheral

12. Given the precarious location of the trapped miners, reaching them safely became highly _____.
    A. hostile
    B. impregnable
    C. problematic

13. The elderly woman lived a _____ life subsisting on her paltry retirement allowance.
    A. stout
    B. penurious
    C. devout

14. She smiled at the new boy in the class who, in turn, _____ shyly.
    A. reciprocated
    B. demoted
    C. substantiated

15. In _____ metonymy, the poet referred to the sun as "a beacon of the holy cross."
    A. dour
    B. metaphorical
    C. chaste

16. _____ ideas often precede notable inventions.
    A. Novel
    B. Intemperate
    C. Distrait

17. Political dissidents were confined in makeshift cells deep within the walls of the _____ catacomb.
    A. obsolescent
    B. tenebrous
    C. puritanical

18. In her discussion, the noted physicist delved into an _____ analysis of quantum mechanics.
    A. egregious
    B. abstruse
    C. unscrupulous

19. To build the neighborhood playground, the City Council first needed to _____ necessary funds.
    A. appropriate
    B. invigorate
    C. squander

20. Despite the mediator's best efforts to arrange a compromise, both opposing factions remained _____ and vowed to escalate the conflict.
    A. implacable
    B. circuitous
    C. rampant

(For Quiz Answers, see Answer Section at the end of the book)

SAT & College Dictionary Workbook Quiz 109

[On a separate sheet of paper, write down the letter of the word that best fits in the blank to create a complete and meaningful sentence.]

1. Few animals can match the tiger's _____ as a hunter.
   A. prowess
   B. dearth
   C. wrath

2. Despite pressure from the police, the reporter refused to _____ the source of his confidential information.
   A. inhibit
   B. divulge
   C. recompense

3. The passing of years living abroad _____ him from his hometown companions.
   A. rescinded
   B. estranged
   C. vindicated

4. Many consider the character Peter Pan too _____ for their realistic tastes.
   A. wan
   B. therapeutic
   C. saccharine

5. By taking care of homeless animals, the mother _____ in her children a healthy love and respect for all living things.
   A. denounced
   B. instilled
   C. supplanted

6. The movie star's _____ glance caught the admiring fan off guard.
   A. amorous
   B. mendacious
   C. pernicious

7. _____ land lay adjacent to the active croplands.
   A. Fallow
   B. Noxious
   C. Problematic

8. In the two reports, the committee discovered _____ findings regarding areas in need of improvement.
   A. disparate
   B. vacuous
   C. susceptible

9. The platoon commander was a no-nonsense _____.
   A. poltroon
   B. despot
   C. martinet

10. The invasion of hostile troops resulted in a sudden _____ of the native villagers to safer outlying territories.
    A. exodus
    B. quandary
    C. aperture

11. The stream _____ into two rivulets, each heading in a distinctly different direction.
    A. diverged
    B. insinuated
    C. vied

12. Lack of rainfall may _____ the growth of plants.
    A. inhibit
    B. elude
    C. mar

13. Self-defense was offered as a motive in the hope of _____ the seriousness of the defendant's crime.
    A. prophesying
    B. supplicating
    C. mitigating

14. With _____ accuracy, the forensic artist recreated the face of an ancient hominid using only a skull as reference.
    A. diffuse
    B. preliminary
    C. scrupulous

15. Though untested, the concept seemed both _____ and economically viable.
    A. cryptic
    B. practicable
    C. transient

16. Once the threat had passed, the pusillanimous poseur demonstrated his _____ by claiming he could have stood up to the bully at any time.
    A. purview
    B. wrath
    C. bravado

17. The two veteran rivals _____ one another on and off the football field.
    A. transcended
    B. flagged
    C. despised

18. Fences were constructed to prevent outsiders from _____ on the farmer's land.
    A. lionizing
    B. encroaching
    C. alienating

19. Her business _____ was greatly responsible for her financial success.
    A. effrontery
    B. acumen
    C. pulchritude

20. In his poetry, William Wordsworth provided us with a _____ description of the English countryside.
    A. pallid
    B. bootless
    C. florid

(For Quiz Answers, see Answer Section at the end of the book)

SAT & College Dictionary Workbook Quiz 110

[On a separate sheet of paper, write down the letter of the word that best fits in the blank to create a complete and meaningful sentence.]

1. A _____ group of demonstrators marched along the picket line.
   A. rural
   B. vociferous
   C. strident

2. Common goals fostered an _____ between the former rivals.
   A. exigency
   B. onus
   C. amity

3. The reborn Christian _____ his earlier heretical beliefs.
   A. disabused
   B. renounced
   C. adumbrated

4. Rather than densely concentrated, the atom's molecules were uncharacteristically _____.
   A. diffuse
   B. trenchant
   C. intolerant

5. Information regarding the dangers of nuclear waste was _____ throughout the community.
   A. polarized
   B. immolated
   C. disseminated

6. His political rival launched a _____ verbal attack against him predicated on groundless innuendo.
   A. salient
   B. venomous
   C. fetid

7. Soldiers could not help but be moved by the _____ faces of the young war orphans.
   A. exhilarating
   B. sadistic
   C. woebegone

8. To more quickly finish cleaning the house, a specific task was _____ to each of the children.
   A. vacillated
   B. delegated
   C. objurgated

9. The young artist worked under the _____ of a movie magnate.
   A. aegis
   B. legerdemain
   C. restitution

10. His debilitating illness _____ his daily activities.
    A. expedited
    B. circumscribed
    C. manifested

11. The American flag often _____ patriotism and freedom.
    A. connotes
    B. entreats
    C. redoubles

12. The planning committee began an ambitious undertaking for _____ expansion and development.
    A. urban
    B. incendiary
    C. stately

13. As Christmas Day dawned, the children awoke to the _____ of Santa's sleigh flying overhead.
    A. proximity
    B. repercussion
    C. tintinnabulation

14. Many students _____ final exams week.
    A. vitiate
    B. detest
    C. alienate

15. The _____ lad ate the last piece of cake and left his younger sister with nothing but leftover crumbs.
    A. inconsiderate
    B. perfunctory
    C. subservient

16. Though it hadn't been tested, the escape plan appeared to be _____.
    A. infallible
    B. effete
    C. culpable

17. A backache often produces _____ pain in the lumbar region.
    A. effervescent
    B. intense
    C. avid

18. The baby's incessant crying _____ the babysitter.
    A. caviled
    B. irked
    C. dissimulated

19. The pirate ships were humbled into submission by the queen's naval _____.
    A. hyperbole
    B. juggernaut
    C. caveat

20. When thinking of one's high school days, it is easy to become _____.
    A. vibrant
    B. nostalgic
    C. contumelious

(For Quiz Answers, see Answer Section at the end of the book)

> **QUIZ-EVALUATION**
> (per page/20 words)
>
> **Number Correct**
> + 17 – 20:   *Excellent*   **(A)**
> + 13 – 16:   *Good*   **(B)**
> + 10 – 12:   *Fair*   **(C)**

(note: To maintain maximum randomness of answers, this workbook was created under nonselective computer production. In the book's entirety, no letter answer appears more often than any other, but with random selection any specific quiz may feature an imbalanced number of one letter over the others. This is the true nature of a randomly produced text.)

SAT & College Dictionary Workbook Answers

Quiz 1
1. A. ebb
2. B. exotic
3. A. immured
4. B. abeyance
5. C. panegyric
6. A. debonair
7. A. protégé
8. C. dissipated
9. A. frantic
10. B. penitent
11. A. abject
12. B. edify
13. B. expedited
14. C. industrious
15. B. rhetorical
16. C. tenuous
17. B. dreaded
18. C. insurgent
19. B. prototype
20. A. telltale

Quiz 2
1. B. exulted
2. A. artifice
3. B. terrestrial
4. A. whetted
5. A. lexicon
6. C. protracted
7. C. splenetic
8. B. corroborated
9. B. bestowed
10. A. acceded
11. A. dubious
12. A. leviathan
13. A. penurious
14. B. dour
15. B. levity
16. B. transmogrified
17. B. acme
18. B. amended
19. B. forswear
20. B. livid

Quiz 3
1. C. rapacious
2. A. hackneyed
3. C. taut
4. B. allayed
5. A. undaunted
6. A. fortified
7. C. autocratic
8. B. rarefied
9. C. scoundrel
10. B. abated
11. B. imbued
12. A. cornucopia
13. C. gullible
14. A. rankled
15. A. effaced
16. A. turgid
17. A. vitiated
18. B. dissonant
19. A. refurbished
20. A. comprised

Quiz 4
1. A. cajoled
2. B. presaged
3. C. induced
4. A. soluble
5. B. thrive
6. B. dissembled
7. B. despicable
8. C. advocated
9. A. shiftless
10. B. tumultuous
11. C. arbitrary
12. C. desolate
13. B. jaunty
14. B. purloined
15. A. insipid
16. A. supernal
17. A. discretion
18. C. convoluted
19. A. feckless
20. B. inaugural

Quiz 5
1. C. extirpate
2. B. stipulated
3. B. burgeoned
4. A. despoiled
5. A. pliable
6. A. seminal
7. B. coalition
8. A. comported
9. B. fawned
10. C. ardent
11. C. ado
12. B. tawdry
13. A. preliminary
14. A. adverse
15. C. fecund
16. C. impeccable
17. B. precocious
18. A. rustic
19. A. apprehensive
20. A. discourse

Quiz 6
1. B. seemly
2. B. subvert
3. A. dissented
4. B. compact
5. A. paean
6. A. reveled
7. A. visceral
8. A. deliverance
9. C. rampant
10. C. turmoil
11. C. stately
12. B. amiss
13. A. conversant
14. C. capitulated
15. C. reviled
16. A. nonchalant
17. C. intricate
18. B. sovereign
19. A. choleric
20. B. comprehensible

SAT & College Dictionary Workbook Answers

Quiz 7

1. B. promulgated
2. B. permeable
3. C. abysmal
4. B. wretched
5. C. presentiment
6. B. obligatory
7. B. scrupulous
8. C. corrupt
9. B. enthralled
10. C. motley
11. C. transient
12. C. rebuffed
13. C. pelagic
14. C. mercenary
15. A. aberrant
16. C. enigma
17. B. inviolable
18. C. viridity
19. B. ambiguous
20. A. eroded

Quiz 8

1. B. combustible
2. B. lambent
3. C. heinous
4. A. sinister
5. A. wan
6. A. intrinsic
7. C. odyssey
8. B. conciliate
9. C. circumscribed
10. A. cantankerous
11. B. immutable
12. A. flatulent
13. C. opulent
14. B. fidelity
15. C. willful
16. A. gratuitous
17. B. adamant
18. A. juxtaposed
19. A. anguished
20. C. incisive

Quiz 9

1. B. disquietude
2. B. laconic
3. A. inkling
4. C. umbrage
5. B. chided
6. C. inviolate
7. B. histrionic
8. A. unspeakable
9. C. fanciful
10. C. torrid
11. A. epitome
12. C. requited
13. C. atone
14. C. invigorated
15. C. trivial
16. C. satiated
17. B. earnest
18. A. surly
19. A. sparse
20. C. anathema

Quiz 10

1. A. elegiac
2. C. shoddy
3. A. hulking
4. C. vied
5. A. lauded
6. C. encumbered
7. A. abrogated
8. A. risible
9. C. erudite
10. A. compensated
11. A. succor
12. B. unabridged
13. A. impassioned
14. C. encapsulate
15. A. amenable
16. C. surrealistic
17. C. quotidian
18. B. feasible
19. A. taunted
20. A. charisma

Quiz 11

1. C. scathing
2. B. taut
3. B. uproarious
4. A. proponent
5. C. ambidextrous
6. A. invective
7. A. star-crossed
8. A. hedonistic
9. C. tempest
10. B. connubial
11. A. sagacious
12. C. pulchritude
13. A. facetious
14. A. remiss
15. A. dumbfounded
16. C. secede
17. C. treacherous
18. B. melancholy
19. A. browbeating
20. B. maladroit

Quiz 12

1. B. sentimental
2. B. herculean
3. B. saturnine
4. B. adulation
5. B. impermeable
6. C. salubrious
7. C. emollient
8. C. hortatory
9. C. servile
10. B. valiant
11. B. ephemeral
12. C. profligate
13. C. shrewd
14. B. inclusive
15. A. ethereal
16. C. gaunt
17. A. proclivity
18. B. Flagrant
19. B. venerated
20. B. authoritarian

SAT & College Dictionary Workbook Answers

Quiz 13
1. B. extroverted
2. B. germane
3. C. ironic
4. B. hallowed
5. A. ascertain
6. C. feasible
7. C. festive
8. C. parched
9. B. picaresque
10. A. intransigent
11. C. habituated
12. B. canard
13. A.. meandered
14. B. rehabilitate
15. A. formidable
16. C. licentious
17. A. countermanded
18. C. peremptory
19. A. repined
20. C. querulous

Quiz 14
1. C. meritorious
2. B. fortitude
3. C. recherché
4. C. profuse
5. C. chronic
6. C. influx
7. A. obsequious
8. A. derelict
9. C. resplendent
10. C. intrusive
11. C. blasphemous
12. B. aplomb
13. B. garnered
14. C. endorsed
15. B. hardship
16. A. mnemonic
17. C. adherents
18. A. petty
19. B. fathom
20. C. rash

Quiz 15
1. C. expiated
2. A. doled
3. C. somnolent
4. A. conjoined
5. C. converged
6. B. defiled
7. C. lucrative
8. B. primordial
9. C. pogroms
10. B. extraneous
11. A. draconian
12. B. exhaustive
13. A. gainful
14. A. arable
15. B. morbid
16. B. duped
17. A. cupidity
18. B. banal
19. C. inconsiderable
20. B. supernumerary

Quiz 16
1. B. apprised
2. C. goaded
3. C. lexicon
4. A. foibles
5. B. idiosyncrasies
6. A. abased
7. A. palliate
8. B. felicitous
9. C. epiphany
10. C. fiasco
11. C. mundane
12. C. effete
13. C. animosity
14. C. ostensible
15. A. desolate
16. C. implored
17. C. minutiae
18. A. assiduous
19. B. paucity
20. B. fail-safe

Quiz 17
1. C. beatific
2. A. fulsome
3. C. lethargic
4. B. inured
5. C. compulsory
6. B. latent
7. A. motif
8. A. blatant
9. C. placid
10. C. finesse
11. A. portly
12. A. demise
13. A. prominent
14. B. arrayed
15. B. revered
16. C. deleterious
17. C. mélange
18. C. lambasted
19. C. burnished
20. B. insinuated

Quiz 18
1. C. acrimonious
2. A. exalted
3. B. emphatic
4. A. forgo
5. C. baleful
6. C. jaundiced
7. C. appalled
8. B. disclosed
9. A. objurgated
10. A. tranquil
11. B. ennui
12. A. bilious
13. A. makeshift
14. C. congenial
15. B. din
16. B. cached
17. A. menial
18. B. uncouth
19. B. abrupt
20. C. smug

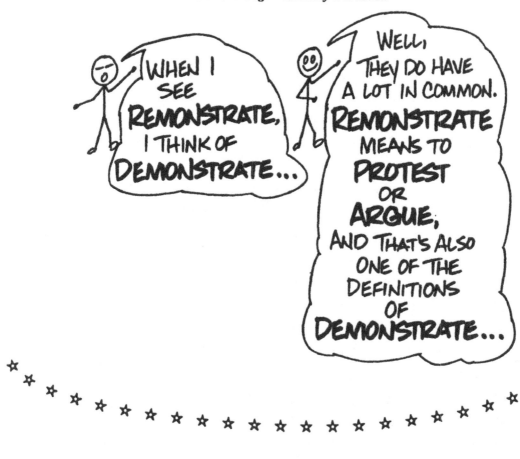

SAT & College Dictionary Workbook Answers

Quiz 19
1. B. niche
2. C. pacify
3. B. defamed
4. C. surfeit
5. C. plethora
6. C. approbation
7. C. hubris
8. A. jeremiad
9. B. oleaginous
10. C. déjà vu
11. B. equivocated
12. C. deplored
13. B. probity
14. B. pusillanimous
15. C. recumbent
16. B. ambulatory
17. C. effrontery
18. B. perused
19. A. refuge
20. A. opprobrious

Quiz 20
1. A. distrait
2. C. aversion
3. C. rhetorical
4. A. puritanical
5. A. comity
6. A. prurient
7. A. inculcate
8. A. perish
9. B. assayed
10. B. rued
11. B. concomitant
12. B. frangible
13. C. underscored
14. A. vehement
15. B. commended
16. C. nexus
17. C. propagate
18. C. parochial
19. B. equipoise
20. B. auspicious

Quiz 21
1. C. flag
2. B. wont
3. C. waxed
4. A. reputed
5. A. wry
6. C. contingent
7. C. immaculate
8. C. dolorous
9. C. rigorous
10. B. implausible
11. B. quizzical
12. A. berated
13. C. solace
14. B. versatile
15. A. attrition
16. A. vituperated
17. B. contravened
18. B. aspired
19. B. validated
20. C. juvenile

Quiz 22
1. B. reprimanded
2. C. veracious
3. B. bacchanalian
4. A. flourishes
5. C. supererogatory
6. A. testy
7. C. uproarious
8. B. ubiquitous
9. B. manifest
10. C. anomaly
11. A. equivocal
12. B. gamely
13. A. hapless
14. C. pious
15. C. cordial
16. B. voluble
17. A. confiscated
18. B. triumphal
19. A. circumspect
20. A. affluent

Quiz 23
1. A. malleable
2. C. hardy
3. B. onset
4. A. rural
5. C. bountiful
6. B. obdurate
7. A. culprit
8. A. tentative
9. A. efficacious
10. C. chary
11. B. preposterous
12. A. hiatus
13. B. desultory
14. B. reclusive
15. A. spurious
16. B. marginal
17. C. robust
18. C. sullen
19. A. coalesced
20. C. excoriated

Quiz 24
1. C. exacerbated
2. C. adumbrated
3. B. gingerly
4. C. précis
5. C. comely
6. C. replete
7. C. antipodes
8. A. scrutinized
9. C. stopgap
10. B. covenant
11. C. glowered
12. A. imperative
13. B. elysian
14. C. ineffectual
15. B. obnoxious
16. B. reprobate
17. A. Credulous
18. A. sycophants
19. A. disputatious
20. A. expurgated

SAT & College Dictionary Workbook Answers

Quiz 25
1. C. disreputable
2. B. castigated
3. B. diverse
4. A. impregnable
5. A. depleted
6. A. incongruous
7. A. attenuated
8. A. reticent
9. C. sequential
10. B. infinite
11. A. embryonic
12. B. fruition
13. B. dissimulated
14. B. concatenated
15. C. purvey
16. C. retrospect
17. B. inveighed
18. C. temporized
19. C. demoted
20. B. grave

Quiz 26
1. B. shirk
2. A. adduced
3. A. gossamer
4. A. iconoclastic
5. A. restitution
6. C. descried
7. C. boon
8. A. sloth
9. A. harbinger
10. B. Desiccated
11. A. importuned
12. B. frenetic
13. A. multifarious
14. C. arcane
15. C. factious
16. A. propinquity
17. A. sardonic
18. A. equilibrium
19. B. Distraught
20. C. diabolic

Quiz 27
1. B. infamous
2. A. gauche
3. B. lucid
4. C. menace
5. B. occluded
6. C. abnegated
7. A. lionized
8. A. subtle
9. B. fractious
10. C. insidious
11. B. embellish
12. B. corporeal
13. A. adjured
14. A. jaded
15. C. largess
16. A. plenipotentiary
17. B. redoubtable
18. C. meted
19. C. caricature
20. A. lachrymose

Quiz 28
1. B. misgivings
2. A. faux pas
3. B. jejune
4. C. philanthropic
5. B. humane
6. B. consecrate
7. C. relegated
8. A. spontaneous
9. B. sisyphean
10. B. erratic
11. B. apathetic
12. B. orthodox
13. B. belated
14. C. funereal
15. B. inculpated
16. C. intractable
17. C. sanguine
18. B. controverted
19. A. flagitious
20. A. effulgence

Quiz 29
1. C. cloy
2. B. nebulous
3. C. perspicuous
4. B. optimistic
5. A. bedraggled
6. C. obeisance
7. B. peripatetic
8. B. pseudonym
9. C. bland
10. A. palatable
11. C. gamut
12. B. dudgeon
13. B. malevolent
14. B. quid pro quo
15. C. perfunctory
16. C. abdicated
17. A. progenitors
18. C. delineated
19. A. uninhibited
20. B. urbane

Quiz 30
1. C. disingenuous
2. B. provident
3. B. illustrious
4. A. dynamic
5. B. temperate
6. B. cathartic
7. B. chthonian
8. C. toady
9. B. alacrity
10. B. celestial
11. A. concocted
12. B. brazen
13. B. accoutered
14. B. agile
15. C. moot
16. B. amorphous
17. B. consummate
18. B. artless
19. C. notorious
20. C. prognosticate

SAT & College Dictionary Workbook Answers

Quiz 31
1. B. retrogression
2. C. eradicating
3. A. autonomous
4. C. adversaries
5. C. alluded
6. B. dormant
7. B. complements
8. C. precipitation
9. C. diligent
10. C. rancor
11. B. untimely
12. B. distort
13. B. repartee
14. C. credible
15. C. Digressing
16. C. abstemious
17. A. categorical
18. B. interminable
19. C. shibboleths
20. C. predicated

Quiz 32
1. C. espoused
2. B. cohesive
3. A. unobtrusive
4. A. potpourri
5. C. apocalypse
6. A. tangible
7. C. suave
8. A. expedient
9. C. prolix
10. A. calumniated
11. A. stalwart
12. B. vulnerable
13. A. sacrilegious
14. B. Debauched
15. C. empirical
16. C. whimsical
17. C. chic
18. B. admonished
19. B. repulsive
20. A. excruciating

Quiz 33
1. A. constraint
2. A. suffrage
3. C. manumitted
4. C. arrogant
5. B. ascetic
6. C. disdained
7. B. vis-á-vis
8. C. idyllic
9. C. mien
10. A. sentient
11. C. reprisals
12. C. onerous
13. B. vicissitudes
14. B. supercilious
15. C. uncanny
16. B. bereft
17. A. vilified
18. B. appropriating
19. C. impending
20. B. inflammatory

Quiz 34
1. A. dire
2. B. quelled
3. C. connived
4. C. incognito
5. B. unilateral
6. A. skittish
7. A. volition
8. A. contumelious
9. C. harried
10. C. Obsolescent
11. B. arbiter
12. A. plight
13. B. sapid
14. B. stout
15. C. consolidated
16. A. cull
17. B. verbose
18. B. insolent
19. C. apposite
20. C. Forbearance

Quiz 35
1. C. quandary
2. B. malingering
3. B. prodigious
4. C. ameliorate
5. B. pestilent
6. B. schism
7. A. variegated
8. C. acute
9. C. initiative
10. C. belligerent
11. B. Machiavellian
12. A. mercurial
13. B. retaliated
14. B. derelict
15. A. thrifty
16. B. calamitous
17. B. surrogate
18. B. inferred
19. B. convivial
20. C. foes

Quiz 36
1. C. apologist
2. A. physiognomy
3. B. ineffable
4. A. shopworn
5. C. transmute
6. B. tremulous
7. A. dissected
8. B. arboreal
9. B. hostile
10. C. destitute
11. A. judicious
12. C. luminous
13. C. plenary
14. A. archaic
15. A. lithe
16. C. patronized
17. A. reiterated
18. B. neophyte
19. B. diatribe
20. B. mawkish

SAT & College Dictionary Workbook Answers

Quiz 37
1. A. bland
2. B. increments
3. A. inundated
4. B. prolific
5. B. wayward
6. A. avenged
7. B. subterranean
8. A. behooves
9. A. garish
10. A. obviates
11. C. complacent
12. B. perspicacious
13. A. secluded
14. A. emancipating
15. B. spiteful
16. B. parity
17. B. staid
18. B. asylum
19. A. ramshackle
20. B. poseur

Quiz 38
1. C. loath
2. B. hazardous
3. B. eschew
4. C. debilitated
5. C. terse
6. A. celerity
7. A. rectify
8. A. demagogue
9. B. expendable
10. B. condone
11. A. grotesque
12. A. anthropomorphic
13. A. insufferable
14. B. superfluous
15. C. vertigo
16. A. deference
17. B. hone
18. A. arduous
19. B. façade
20. A. gist

Quiz 39
1. C. dogmatic
2. C. parameter
3. B. eminent
4. C. authoritative
5. C. strident
6. C. volatile
7. C. tedious
8. C. fracas
9. C. assented
10. C. insipid
11. B. emulate
12. C. rustic
13. A. upshot
14. C. corpulent
15. A. rescinded
16. C. discord
17. B. surmount
18. C. impudent
19. A. inexorable
20. A. ingenuous

Quiz 40
1. C. condescended
2. B. ploy
3. A. clarion
4. A. prepossessing
5. A. colluded
6. B. waned
7. B. salacious
8. A. momentous
9. A. ordure
10. B. purgatory
11. B. ignominious
12. C. ominous
13. B. repercussions
14. C. confounded
15. B. viable
16. C. mordant
17. A. puny
18. A. coveted
19. A. amicable
20. A. infraction

Quiz 41
1. A. pithy
2. B. decrepit
3. C. retentive
4. C. reprehensible
5. C. unscrupulous
6. C. eluded
7. B. predicament
8. B. exigency
9. C. diverted
10. B. hidebound
11. A. inclination
12. A. aspersions
13. C. itinerant
14. A. precludes
15. C. apropos
16. C. vendetta
17. C. nadir
18. A. genteel
19. B. mulct
20. B. gluttony

Quiz 42
1. A. nicety
2. A. commodious
3. B. concurrent
4. B. avid
5. C. soluble
6. B. whimsical
7. C. indifferent
8. A. intact
9. A. animus
10. A. evinced
11. A. becoming
12. B. impoverished
13. A. maelstrom
14. C. symmetry
15. A. chaste
16. C. vindictive
17. C. frail
18. B. bootless
19. B. feckless
20. B. novices

SAT & College Dictionary Workbook Answers

Quiz 43

1. B. transcend
2. A. proliferate
3. B. conspicuous
4. C. pastoral
5. A. perdition
6. B. ululation
7. C. demeanor
8. C. dour
9. B. cursory
10. A. implicit
11. C. aperture
12. B. hauteur
13. B. initial
14. C. assailed
15. B. paragon
16. A. indomitable
17. A. predilection
18. B. exponent
19. C. contrite
20. B. motley

Quiz 44

1. C. infernal
2. A. diversity
3. C. hypocritical
4. B. blanched
5. A. Kith
6. A. taciturn
7. B. cumbersome
8. B. endemic
9. B. gaudy
10. B. forsake
11. A. apostate
12. C. incriminated
13. A. deified
14. C. labyrinthine
15. C. chagrin
16. C. succumbed
17. B. vanquished
18. C. futile
19. C. discern
20. C. deprecatory

Quiz 45

1. C. foliage
2. A. impugning
3. C. inextricable
4. C. bliss
5. A. obloquy
6. A. vacuous
7. A. scourge
8. C. chimerical
9. B. prognosis
10. A. transitory
11. C. abhorred
12. A. tautological
13. C. expedient
14. A. extensive
15. C. fretful
16. C. palatable
17. B. mellifluous
18. A. vociferated
19. A. manifest
20. A. quash

Quiz 46

1. B. wizened
2. A. provisional
3. B. dogged
4. B. brash
5. A. redoubtable
6. A. renowned
7. C. prerequisite
8. C. decamped
9. C. thespian
10. C. stolid
11. A. astute
12. C. callow
13. C. contagion
14. C. accrued
15. B. restive
16. B. disconsolate
17. C. nomadic
18. A. deft
19. A. traverse
20. C. prefatory

Quiz 47

1. A. obstinate
2. A. intolerable
3. C. ensued
4. A. dictatorial
5. A. rapport
6. B. serendipitous
7. A. interloper
8. C. regimen
9. B. mendacious
10. C. bolster
11. A. caviled
12. B. pallid
13. C. molten
14. A. precarious
15. B. peevish
16. C. confirmed
17. A. fractious
18. C. duress
19. B. risqué
20. C. girth

Quiz 48

1. B. countenance
2. B. petulant
3. A. synchronous
4. A. augment
5. C. jocular
6. C. agitated
7. C. warrant
8. A. precipitous
9. B. artful
10. B. incipient
11. B. jaded
12. A. pending
13. C. churlish
14. A. disinterested
15. C. eleemosynary
16. C. imbroglio
17. C. verdant
18. A. éclat
19. C. inherent
20. A. ironic

SAT & College Dictionary Workbook Answers

Quiz 49
1. B. credence
2. A. quirks
3. A. correlating
4. C. panache
5. C. affable
6. B. misconstrued
7. B. travesty
8. B. mammoth
9. A. hardy
10. B. nondescript
11. B. directive
12. C. recollect
13. A. limber
14. A. consorting
15. C. vis-á-vis
16. A. ambrosial
17. C. tantamount
18. A. glum
19. C. candid
20. C. penury

Quiz 50
1. C. amiable
2. B. respite
3. C. infamous
4. A. pariahs
5. B. deluge
6. A. trenchant
7. B. stark
8. B. effigy
9. B. Extenuating
10. A. purview
11. C. coerced
12. C. stern
13. B. impeded
14. A. blithe
15. B. swarthy
16. A. wily
17. C. fortuitous
18. C. garrulous
19. C. artless
20. A. minced

Quiz 51
1. C. humility
2. C. decry
3. A. incredulous
4. B. hyperbole
5. B. spurned
6. A. abstinent
7. B. coy
8. C. pliant
9. B. effectuated
10. A. endeavored
11. B. ostracized
12. A. anxiety
13. B. foundered
14. B. obsessive
15. A. saturated
16. B. temporal
17. A. ultimatum
18. C. delusions
19. A. repose
20. A. ratiocination

Quiz 52
1. B. polarized
2. B. noisome
3. A. fearsome
4. B. overt
5. C. vacillated
6. B. attenuates
7. C. stultified
8. A. iniquitous
9. A. convoluted
10. B. flaunted
11. A. belied
12. C. miscreant
13. A. havoc
14. B. acrid
15. B. solicitous
16. A. wayward
17. C. valor
18. B. recondite
19. A. dilatory
20. A. confront

Quiz 53
1. A. jaundiced
2. A. metamorphosis
3. A. patronized
4. A. moribund
5. C. restive
6. B. becoming
7. A. supplanted
8. A. bombastic
9. A. omnipotent
10. A. pertinacious
11. C. effervescent
12. B. dexterity
13. A. esoteric
14. C. forsake
15. A. piqued
16. A. Intermittent
17. C. headstrong
18. A. inveterate
19. C. brouhaha
20. A. affectation

Quiz 54
1. B. titanic
2. A. postulated
3. B. insuperable
4. B. substantial
5. B. vagaries
6. B. vivacious
7. B. rife
8. A. domineering
9. B. indignation
10. A. status quo
11. B. willful
12. B. engendered
13. B. provoked
14. B. jocose
15. B. ruse
16. B. diffuse
17. A. hygienic
18. C. renovate
19. A. encomiums
20. C. caveat

SAT & College Dictionary Workbook

SAT & College Dictionary Workbook Answers

Quiz 55
1. B. elucidated
2. A. munificent
3. C. punitive
4. A. veritable
5. A. oust
6. B. dispassionate
7. B. exonerated
8. A. austere
9. A. pandemic
10. A. peerless
11. C. percipient
12. A. convened
13. B. suffused
14. A. brawny
15. C. outmoded
16. A. aghast
17. A. putrefied
18. A. lowered
19. C. mobilized
20. B. haggard

Quiz 56
1. B. inalienable
2. B. propounded
3. C. wraith
4. A. alienated
5. C. renaissance
6. B. raucous
7. C. hindered
8. B. dubious
9. C. extravagant
10. B. monolithic
11. B. contumely
12. C. palpable
13. B. assessed
14. A. complaisant
15. A. censured
16. A. stifle
17. A. foundered
18. B. omniscient
19. A. evade
20. C. impertinent

Quiz 57
1. C. curtailed
2. A. loathe
3. C. expeditious
4. A. temporal
5. B. senescence
6. A. rebuked
7. A. protruded
8. A. felicitous
9. C. gratuitous
10. B. copious
11. A. maligned
12. B. inception
13. C. unobtrusive
14. B. venal
15. A. impecunious
16. B. atypical
17. C. mendicants
18. A. genesis
19. B. incontrovertible
20. A. anathema

Quiz 58
1. B. discursive
2. B. ceded
3. A. accord
4. B. torpid
5. B. glacial
6. B. expropriated
7. C. countenance
8. A. esprit de corps
9. A. legerdemain
10. C. prevalent
11. C. forte
12. C. attested
13. C. pragmatic
14. A. strife
15. B. obstreperous
16. C. devoid
17. B. inscrutable
18. A. debase
19. B. perplexed
20. B. profound

Quiz 59
1. B. requisite
2. B. tactful
3. C. contemptuous
4. B. heed
5. B. furtive
6. B. inimical
7. B. effete
8. A. nauseous
9. A. retribution
10. C. diversion
11. B. adventitious
12. A. immemorial
13. B. uxorious
14. B. vexed
15. A. disciples
16. B. aborted
17. C. ire
18. A. jejune
19. B. recherché
20. B. rectitude

Quiz 60
1. A. ungainly
2. B. vast
3. C. dichotomy
4. B. mephitic
5. B. kudos
6. C. leavened
7. B. elicited
8. C. decorous
9. A. escalated
10. A. hirsute
11. B. pedagogic
12. B. staunch
13. C. exorbitant
14. C. eventuated
15. A. jocund
16. B. ramifications
17. B. pliable
18. A. prodigal
19. B. quisling
20. C. remorse

SAT & College Dictionary Workbook Answers

Quiz 61
1. A. rudimentary
2. C. sententious
3. A. pugnacious
4. B. doleful
5. A. Inflammable
6. C. integrity
7. A. pleasantries
8. A. quibbled
9. B. conjugal
10. C. susceptible
11. C. inevitable
12. B. intolerant
13. A. impervious
14. C. hampered
15. B. inordinate
16. B. preciosity
17. C. resonant
18. B. conflagration
19. C. straitlaced
20. B. remunerated

Quiz 62
1. C. pretense
2. A. regressed
3. A. exhorted
4. B. debunk
5. A. indifferent
6. B. plaudits
7. C. otiose
8. B. qualms
9. A. trite
10. C. defied
11. C. putative
12. A. sangfroid
13. A. frivolous
14. A. officious
15. C. paradigms
16. A. miserly
17. C. baneful
18. C. spry
19. B. proximity
20. B. dearth

Quiz 63
1. B. refuted
2. B. secular
3. A. menace
4. B. fey
5. C. pall
6. A. revoked
7. B. altercation
8. B. deign
9. B. rigors
10. A. disgruntled
11. B. sated
12. A. witless
13. A. ignoble
14. A. mirth
15. B. annexed
16. C. insouciant
17. A. inadvertent
18. A. conglomerate
19. A. solemn
20. C. vernal

Quiz 64
1. B. effusive
2. C. vibrant
3. B. preeminent
4. B. pandemonium
5. B. longevity
6. B. intervene
7. A. forswear
8. C. expostulated
9. A. awry
10. A. contentious
11. C. zeal
12. B. uncanny
13. B. compensated
14. B. forays
15. A. desuetude
16. A. guileful
17. A. incensed
18. C. consternation
19. C. prophesied
20. C. meek

Quiz 65
1. B. winsome
2. C. traduced
3. C. extant
4. B. convened
5. B. devious
6. C. perverse
7. B. arguably
8. B. brusque
9. C. accolades
10. A. vigilant
11. A. surreptitious
12. C. eternal
13. A. apex
14. C. malicious
15. C. indolent
16. C. nascent
17. B. philistine
18. C. emaciated
19. B. imbued
20. A. upbraided

Quiz 66
1. C. skewed
2. C. genial
3. C. double entendre
4. A. iridescent
5. C. contumacious
6. B. verify
7. C. feign
8. B. stygian
9. C. dispel
10. C. travails
11. C. raucous
12. C. belied
13. C. fallacious
14. A. Hospitable
15. A. avert
16. B. outlandish
17. C. meager
18. B. perceptive
19. A. zenith
20. C. stodgy

SAT & College Dictionary Workbook Answers

Quiz 67
1. A. naïve
2. A. diaphanous
3. B. certify
4. B. famished
5. A. forbidding
6. C. incumbent
7. A. coterie
8. B. ponderous
9. B. aesthetic
10. B. slovenly
11. A. migratory
12. B. apotheosis
13. C. tenet
14. A. sordid
15. B. sheepish
16. C. sadistic
17. C. protean
18. A. ecumenical
19. A. aloof
20. B. sanguinary

Quiz 68
1. B. integral
2. A. meek
3. A. punctilious
4. B. flippant
5. A. timbre
6. C. obscure
7. C. abridge
8. B. innate
9. B. sprightly
10. C. vapid
11. C. harassed
12. B. Frivolous
13. B. beneficial
14. A. profound
15. A. perpetrated
16. C. onus
17. C. loquacious
18. C. lamented
19. C. inquietude
20. B. indoctrinated

Quiz 69
1. C. heretical
2. A. divisive
3. A. carte blanche
4. A. relentless
5. A. touted
6. C. upstart
7. B. despot
8. C. simulated
9. B. meretricious
10. B. regaled
11. C. exiguous
12. B. augured
13. C. potent
14. B. placate
15. C. redoubled
16. C. cognizant
17. C. aggregate
18. C. ambivalent
19. A. derisive
20. C. celebrated

Quiz 70
1. C. conscientious
2. A. perambulated
3. C. vivified
4. C. multifaceted
5. A. élan
6. B. unmitigated
7. C. alienable
8. B. stringent
9. A. balked
10. B. deliberate
11. B. objectionable
12. B. antipathy
13. A. orotund
14. C. denigrated
15. B. sultry
16. A. abominable
17. B. contemptible
18. C. angst
19. C. instrumental
20. B. exculpated

Quiz 71
1. C. dulcet
2. B. pretense
3. A. roseate
4. A. sobriquet
5. A. stratagem
6. B. congregated
7. B. didactic
8. C. prudent
9. C. indefeasible
10. A. fetid
11. B. chastised
12. C. wheedle
13. B. pantheon
14. A. odious
15. B. autochthonous
16. C. pompous
17. B. refugees
18. C. substantiate
19. B. eclectic
20. B. deprecatory

Quiz 72
1. A. feral
2. A. recapitulated
3. C. dense
4. A. glib
5. C. vitality
6. C. inane
7. C. conceded
8. C. rift
9. A. acquisitive
10. C. euphemistic
11. C. implemented
12. A. askance
13. C. jubilant
14. C. distorted
15. C. residual
16. A. absolved
17. B. vernal
18. A. capricious
19. C. voluminous
20. B. flouted

SAT & College Dictionary Workbook

SAT & College Dictionary Workbook Answers

Quiz 73
1. C. droll
2. A. cogent
3. A. incited
4. A. regal
5. C. haven
6. B. fundamental
7. A. indignant
8. A. rambunctious
9. A. sheepish
10. B. capacious
11. B. impunity
12. C. intimidate
13. B. ebullient
14. C. limpid
15. C. asseverated
16. A. disaffected
17. A. macabre
18. C. penchant
19. C. refuted
20. B. fervent

Quiz 74
1. B. cogitated
2. C. fabricated
3. C. machinations
4. A. marred
5. B. facilitate
6. B. pathos
7. B. demise
8. B. circumvent
9. C. vaunted
10. B. foresight
11. A. prosaic
12. B. abjured
13. B. pall
14. A. bemused
15. C. fatuous
16. B. passé
17. C. educed
18. B. remonstrated
19. A. tepid
20. B. meticulous

Quiz 75
1. A. ludicrous
2. A. chicanery
3. C. pestilent
4. B. languished
5. A. besmirching
6. C. conundrum
7. A. euphonious
8. A. sonorous
9. B. upstanding
10. B. harangue
11. B. plebeian
12. B. repository
13. A. apocryphal
14. C. self-effacing
15. B. rebutted
16. B. Proficient
17. C. immolated
18. C. fulminated
19. A. exorcise
20. B. clichéd

Quiz 76
1. B. submissive
2. B. feeble
3. A. maledictions
4. B. precipitous
5. C. earnest
6. C. retracted
7. C. causerie
8. C. unflappable
9. A. valid
10. B. bon mots
11. A. parameters
12. C. supplicated
13. A. truckled
14. B. averred
15. C. inveigled
16. B. porous
17. C. subsided
18. B. sporadic
19. B. virtuous
20. B. synthetic

Quiz 77
1. C. exhumed
2. A. enervated
3. A. resilient
4. C. comprehensive
5. C. egregious
6. A. decimated
7. A. woeful
8. B. perfidious
9. A. serrated
10. A. aureate
11. A. whimsies
12. C. equanimity
13. A. expounded
14. B. irate
15. B. succulent
16. B. underpin
17. B. defunct
18. A. rendezvous
19. A. tirade
20. A. meteoric

Quiz 78
1. A. innocuous
2. A. versatile
3. B. confuted
4. C. esculent
5. C. incapacitate
6. B. induced
7. A. lambent
8. B. ornate
9. C. purge
10. A. dauntless
11. C. avowed
12. A. reproached
13. C. thwarted
14. B. minuscule
15. C. affinity
16. B. askance
17. A. irreproachable
18. B. namesake
19. C. plausible
20. B. oppressive

SAT & College Dictionary Workbook Answers

Quiz 79
1. C. debacle
2. A. irascible
3. C. serene
4. A. unconscionable
5. B. blandished
6. A. ineluctable
7. A. lassitude
8. A. shunned
9. C. vile
10. C. imprecated
11. A. advent
12. C. quixotic
13. C. superlative
14. A. bumptious
15. B. introverted
16. A. nonplussed
17. A. pied
18. B. relinquish
19. B. stamina
20. C. expunged

Quiz 80
1. C. peculated
2. C. assuage
3. C. reigns
4. B. reserved
5. C. tempered
6. A. denizen
7. B. turgid
8. B. vigorous
9. A. prerogative
10. B. consoled
11. A. haughty
12. A. personifies
13. C. deter
14. B. ruthless
15. B. appended
16. C. tacit
17. C. unimpeachable
18. A. bantered
19. A. verbatim
20. A. inanimate

Quiz 81
1. C. ductile
2. A. redolent
3. A. buttress
4. A. incursions
5. C. innuendos
6. B. subservient
7. A. tumid
8. A. stealthy
9. A. ponderous
10. A. grandiose
11. B. archetype
12. A. extolled
13. A. presumptuous
14. C. sportive
15. A. treacherous
16. C. virulent
17. B. zephyr
18. A. savory
19. B. dispersed
20. A. franchise

Quiz 82
1. B. demean
2. A. intemperate
3. A. acute
4. A. repudiated
5. A. compunctions
6. B. irrevocable
7. A. subterfuge
8. C. tremulous
9. C. unassuming
10. A. arbitrary
11. A. fleeting
12. A. devout
13. A. inchoate
14. C. repertoire
15. C. stalwart
16. C. subtle
17. C. collaborated
18. A. sustenance
19. B. timorous
20. C. beseeched

Quiz 83
1. C. formidable
2. C. listless
3. A. pessimistic
4. B. rapacious
5. C. euphuistic
6. C. bedlam
7. B. indigenous
8. C. precursor
9. A. sedentary
10. A. adroit
11. B. foiled
12. C. galvanized
13. C. compelled
14. B. dismayed
15. B. scurrilous
16. A. subsidized
17. C. docile
18. B. lavish
19. B. striated
20. C. forestall

Quiz 84
1. A. authoritative
2. B. infringe
3. C. populace
4. A. subservient
5. C. ulterior
6. A. vicarious
7. B. zany
8. B. sanctimonious
9. C. nimble
10. C. discrete
11. C. innocuous
12. B. apogee
13. B. indicted
14. A. pecuniary
15. C. propitious
16. C. refulgent
17. B. tentative
18. C. venial
19. A. virtual
20. B. painstaking

SAT & College Dictionary Workbook Answers

Quiz 85
1. B. paramount
2. A. patent
3. C. diurnal
4. C. impartial
5. B. liberated
6. B. stentorian
7. C. sovereign
8. C. ruddy
9. C. recalcitrant
10. C. puerile
11. A. exigencies
12. A. untimely
13. C. elite
14. C. infuriated
15. B. shortcoming
16. B. diverted
17. B. abstain
18. C. ecstatic
19. C. posthumous
20. A. doctrinaire

Quiz 86
1. A. repented
2. A. craven
3. A. verve
4. B. caustic
5. A. consequential
6. A. nimble
7. C. pernicious
8. B. procrastinate
9. A. salutary
10. C. oppressive
11. B. mobile
12. B. resolute
13. A. wary
14. C. wistful
15. C. definitive
16. B. adversity
17. A. concurred
18. B. animadversions
19. A. tocsin
20. B. equable

Quiz 87
1. B. morose
2. C. vitriolic
3. C. Addled
4. C. vain
5. C. dissuade
6. C. picayune
7. A. remote
8. B. truculent
9. A. condign
10. A. paltry
11. C. duplicity
12. B. milieu
13. B. slandered
14. C. clandestine
15. A. indisposed
16. B. rote
17. A. sumptuous
18. A. transpired
19. B. duress
20. C. interred

Quiz 88
1. A. conscientious
2. C. sapient
3. A. morbid
4. B. vital
5. B. demure
6. A. imbroglio
7. C. disported
8. C. alleged
9. A. coherent
10. A. enmity
11. A. distended
12. C. provincial
13. C. cumulative
14. B. adept
15. A. elusive
16. C. phlegmatic
17. A. propagating
18. B. sojourned
19. A. venomous
20. B. impetuous

Quiz 89
1. B. blithe
2. B. mollify
3. A. braggadocio
4. A. diminutive
5. A. sullied
6. A. chronological
7. C. crass
8. A. contemporary
9. C. repast
10. C. disabused
11. A. doughty
12. C. culpable
13. A. resurrect
14. B. pungent
15. B. unruly
16. C. august
17. C. kin
18. C. sub rosa
19. C. truncated
20. C. catalyst

Quiz 90
1. B. evanescent
2. C. execrable
3. A. gibed
4. B. magnanimous
5. B. temerity
6. A. utilitarian
7. B. derogatory
8. C. diffident
9. C. disparaged
10. C. mortified
11. A. dissolute
12. B. charlatans
13. A. unequivocal
14. C. Incendiary
15. C. Beguiled
16. B. jovial
17. B. sallow
18. C. steadfast
19. B. travail
20. A. contravened

SAT & College Dictionary Workbook

SAT & College Dictionary Workbook Answers

Quiz 91
1. C. essayed
2. C. conjectured
3. C. froward
4. B. graphic
5. B. implicit
6. B. ingratiating
7. C. latitude
8. C. specious
9. C. reminisced
10. A. actuated
11. C. exhilarating
12. A. proffered
13. B. meddle
14. C. culinary
15. B. servile
16. C. emblematic
17. A. indelible
18. A. plaintive
19. C. turbid
20. A. foment

Quiz 92
1. B. bellicose
2. B. eulogized
3. A. furor
4. B. premonition
5. B. rancid
6. A. sanguine
7. A. viable
8. C. unctuous
9. B. zest
10. C. bicker
11. A. gamboled
12. A. precursor
13. C. mandatory
14. A. instigate
15. B. culminated
16. B. propensity
17. A. spendthrift
18. B. affected
19. A. stupefied
20. C. exuberant

Quiz 93
1. C. benevolent
2. A. homologous
3. A. prevaricated
4. A. seedy
5. B. impassive
6. A. ductile
7. A. fabricated
8. C. eccentric
9. C. verisimilitude
10. C. irrefutable
11. A. suppressed
12. B. flagged
13. C. gruff
14. C. unwieldy
15. C. malleable
16. B. trepidation
17. A. insatiable
18. C. malaise
19. C. enticed
20. B. tantalized

Quiz 94
1. A. boorish
2. C. bucolic
3. A. delectable
4. B. impromptu
5. B. indurate
6. A. arrant
7. C. valid
8. B. vindicated
9. B. denounced
10. A. frugal
11. B. gloaming
12. A. opportune
13. A. superficial
14. A. depraved
15. B. acclimate
16. A. righteous
17. B. assimilate
18. A. fickle
19. C. avarice
20. C. prodigy

Quiz 95
1. C. mimetic
2. C. sybaritic
3. C. prowess
4. A. saline
5. B. euphoria
6. C. dire
7. A. perilous
8. C. waggish
9. A. defamatory
10. C. wry
11. A. caustic
12. B. captious
13. A. effervescent
14. B. exquisite
15. A. modest
16. C. artful
17. C. squalid
18. A. disconcerted
19. A. deteriorated
20. A. eloquent

Quiz 96
1. C. equitable
2. C. soporific
3. A. populous
4. B. imminent
5. A. assay
6. A. maudlin
7. B. disheveled
8. B. grueling
9. A. appease
10. C. impetus
11. A. melee
12. A. resourceful
13. B. scarify
14. A. unabashed
15. B. potable
16. A. desecrated
17. C. halcyon
18. B. incendiary
19. C. reproved
20. B. befriended

SAT & College Dictionary Workbook Answers

Quiz 97
1. A. acerbic
2. A. agrarian
3. A. assert
4. C. concise
5. A. devastated
6. B. forlorn
7. C. incessant
8. B. indefatigable
9. B. vitiated
10. A. empathy
11. A. ambience
12. A. dilate
13. A. empyreal
14. A. demurred
15. C. imputed
16. A. arrogated
17. C. inimical
18. C. talisman
19. C. vexatious
20. C. comply

Quiz 98
1. B. bathos
2. C. usurped
3. B. panacea
4. C. ghastly
5. C. detriment
6. A. mountebank
7. A. estranged
8. A. flaccid
9. B. inexplicable
10. B. lissome
11. A. pell-mell
12. A. quagmire
13. C. ascribed
14. A. parsimonious
15. C. Indisposed
16. B. innovative
17. B. rejuvenate
18. B. bleak
19. A. sprawling
20. A. viridity

Quiz 99
1. B. aggrandizing
2. C. jeopardy
3. B. chronic
4. C. obtrusive
5. C. recreant
6. C. reputable
7. C. slipshod
8. B. disavowed
9. A. wrath
10. B. suppliant
11. C. jeered
12. C. orotund
13. C. asperity
14. C. preoccupied
15. A. durable
16. C. refractory
17. A. squandered
18. C. consensus
19. A. vanguard
20. B. esoteric

Quiz 100
1. C. homage
2. B. Spartan
3. C. polemic
4. C. commensurate
5. B. replenished
6. A. subjugated
7. B. retiring
8. A. tenacious
9. B. stoic
10. B. somber
11. C. savoir faire
12. A. recompensed
13. C. discomfited
14. B. piqued
15. A. peremptory
16. A. onset
17. C. Noxious
18. C. untenable
19. A. illusory
20. C. censored

Quiz 101
1. B. preternatural
2. B. razed
3. B. sophomoric
4. A. expended
5. C. gregarious
6. A. ribald
7. A. voracious
8. C. audacious
9. A. visage
10. B. compulsive
11. A. enterprising
12. A. infatuated
13. A. insightful
14. A. invincible
15. B. lugubrious
16. B. odoriferous
17. B. ancillary
18. C. summarily
19. A. vain
20. B. alliance

Quiz 102
1. A. circuitous
2. C. concupiscent
3. A. philippic
4. C. piscatorial
5. A. dispensed
6. C. procured
7. B. seditious
8. A. stout
9. B. Toxic
10. C. litigate
11. B. multiplicity
12. A. obfuscate
13. A. venerable
14. B. proscribed
15. A. herculean
16. A. entreated
17. A. repress
18. C. ruminated
19. C. flamboyant
20. B. ken

SAT & College Dictionary Workbook Answers

Quiz 103
1. C. occult
2. A. poignant
3. C. frank
4. B. sacrosanct
5. A. hale
6. C. persevered
7. A. quizzical
8. C. covert
9. B. inconsequential
10. A. nugatory
11. A. pretentious
12. C. sedate
13. A. stodgy
14. A. tempered
15. A. extricate
16. C. defer
17. C. façade
18. C. illicit
19. A. indulgent
20. B. limned

Quiz 104
1. C. nefarious
2. C. propriety
3. A. Ravenous
4. C. rotund
5. A. fastidious
6. C. feral
7. B. excoriated
8. A. schemed
9. C. succinct
10. C. arid
11. B. sylvan
12. A. tyro
13. B. wastrel
14. A. alleviate
15. B. dilemma
16. B. invidious
17. A. innumerable
18. B. cryptic
19. C. infinitesimal
20. A. languid

Quiz 105
1. B. lithe
2. A. nemesis
3. C. oblivious
4. B. pellucid
5. C. derided
6. B. evoked
7. A. factitious
8. C. fleet
9. B. genial
10. A. incarnate
11. B. pinnacle
12. C. quiescent
13. B. redolent
14. A. seraphic
15. B. exhorted
16. C. gleaned
17. B. plenitude
18. C. Cacophonous
19. C. inclination
20. C. indigent

Quiz 106
1. C. pristine
2. C. quagmire
3. B. rubicund
4. C. stanch
5. C. incorrigible
6. B. intrepid
7. C. objective
8. C. sedulous
9. A. poltroon
10. A. paradox
11. B. unexpurgated
12. B. deplore
13. B. unsung
14. C. acquiesced
15. B. guise
16. B. Inclement
17. C. magniloquent
18. B. puissant
19. A. deliberate
20. B. suppress

Quiz 107
1. B. therapeutic
2. C. tribulations
3. A. unbridled
4. A. verdant
5. A. contrived
6. A. outset
7. C. absolution
8. B. inept
9. A. livid
10. C. nonpareil
11. C. pedantic
12. B. propitiate
13. A. row
14. B. similitude
15. B. harrowing
16. A. concerted
17. C. salient
18. B. polychromatic
19. A. inebriated
20. A. exuded

Quiz 108
1. B. lethal
2. B. putrid
3. C. sanctioned
4. C. superseded
5. A. infidels
6. C. invaluable
7. A. explicit
8. A. ostentatious
9. C. pensive
10. B. elated
11. C. peripheral
12. C. problematic
13. B. penurious
14. A. reciprocated
15. B. metaphorical
16. A. Novel
17. B. tenebrous
18. B. abstruse
19. A. appropriate
20. A. implacable

SAT & College Dictionary Workbook

— To remember what **VENIAL** means, I just think of **TRIVIAL**. They both end with –**IAL**!

— Interesting word association.... Of course **VENIAL** more precisely means **FORGIVABLE**, as in a person's sins or trespasses. But as they aren't serious, I guess you could call them **TRIVIAL**. However, don't **TRIVIALIZE** any **VENIAL** faults; they are faults nonetheless!

— By the way is **VENIAL** related to **VENAL**?

— No! **VENAL** means **CORRUPT** as in **VENAL** public figures of a corrupt government.

— So a **VENAL** government does not suffer from **VENIAL** misdeeds?!

— Now you've got it.... they're almost <u>opposite</u>! And that's no <u>trivial</u> distinction!

SAT & College Dictionary Workbook Answers

Quiz 109

1. A. prowess
2. B. divulge
3. B. estranged
4. C. saccharine
5. B. instilled
6. A. amorous
7. A. Fallow
8. A. disparate
9. C. martinet
10. A. exodus
11. A. diverged
12. A. inhibit
13. C. mitigating
14. C. scrupulous
15. B. practicable
16. C. bravado
17. C. despised
18. B. encroaching
19. B. acumen
20. C. florid

Quiz 110

1. B. vociferous
2. C. amity
3. B. renounced
4. A. diffuse
5. C. disseminated
6. B. venomous
7. C. woebegone
8. B. delegated
9. A. aegis
10. B. circumscribed
11. A. connotes
12. A. urban
13. C. tintinnabulation
14. B. detest
15. A. inconsiderate
16. A. infallible
17. B. intense
18. B. irked
19. B. juggernaut
20. B. nostalgic

* *

**If you liked this book,
please share your comments
on AMAZON.com
for others to see**

* *

- Is IMPUNITY related to IMPUGN?
- No, although both are pronounced the same (im-pyūn′). IMPUGN means to ATTACK A PERSON'S CHARACTER through allegations or innuendo, whereas IMPUNITY really means FREEDOM FROM PUNISHMENT. A dictator does things with IMPUNITY....
- And what happens if someone attempts to IMPUGN his character?
- I can assure you that person won't be able to speak with IMPUNITY for long!

SAT & College Dictionary Workbook

Student's Name: _____

Keep Track of Your Scores!

Quiz #	# Correct	Quiz #	# Correct	Quiz #	# Correct

SAT & College Dictionary Workbook

DOES INFLAMMATORY MEAN INFLAMMABLE?

NOT EXACTLY. BOTH WORDS DO HAVE SOMETHING IN COMMON WITH **INFLAME**, BUT **INFLAMMATORY** MEANS TO **AROUSE**, ESPECIALLY **ANGER**.... **INFLAMMABLE**, HOWEVER, MOST OFTEN MEANS **CAPABLE** OF **CATCHING FIRE**.

BUT THEN THEY ARE SIMILAR.... AFTER ALL, EACH ONE CAN **INFLAME** A SITUATION.

WHEN YOU LOOK AT IT LIKE THAT, I GUESS YOU'RE RIGHT!

Made in the USA
Coppell, TX
31 May 2024

32982090R00188